NEW YORK AND THE FIRST WORLD WAR

Ashgate Studies in First World War History

Series Editor

John Bourne
The University of Birmingham, UK

The First World War is a subject of perennial interest to historians and is often regarded as a watershed event, marking the end of the nineteenth century and the beginning of the 'modern' industrial world. The sheer scale of the conflict and massive loss of life means that it is constantly being assessed and reassessed to examine its lasting military, political, sociological, industrial, cultural and economic impact. Reflecting the latest international scholarly research, the Ashgate Studies in First World War History series provides a unique platform for the publication of monographs on all aspects of the Great War. Whilst the main thrust of the series is on the military aspects of the conflict, other related areas (including cultural, political and social) are also addressed. Books published are aimed primarily at a post-graduate academic audience, furthering exciting recent interpretations of the war, whilst still being accessible enough to appeal to a wider audience of educated lay readers.

Also in this series

An Historian in Peace and War
The Diaries of Harold Temperley
Edited by T.G. Otte

'A Student in Arms'
Donald Hankey and Edwardian Society at War
Ross Davies

The Ordeal of Peace: Demobilization and the Urban Experience
in Britain and Germany, 1917–1921
Adam R. Seipp

New York and the First World War

Shaping an American City

ROSS J. WILSON
University of Chichester, UK

Routledge
Taylor & Francis Group

LONDON AND NEW YORK

First published 2014 by Ashgate Publishing

2 Park Square, Milton Park, Abingdon, Oxfordshire OX14 4RN
52 Vanderbilt Avenue, New York, NY 10017

Routledge is an imprint of the Taylor & Francis Group, an informa business

First issued in paperback 2020

British Library Cataloguing in Publication Data
A catalogue record for this book is available from the British Library

The Library of Congress has cataloged the printed edition as follows:
Wilson, Ross J., 1981-
  New York and the First World War : shaping an American city / by Ross J. Wilson.
     pages cm. – (Ashgate studies in First World War history)
  Includes bibliographical references and index.
  ISBN 978-1-4724-1949-1 (hardcover)
1. World War, 1914-1918 – New York (State) – New
York. 2. New York (N.Y.) – History – 20th century. I. Title.

  D570.85.N5N82 2014
  940.3'7471–dc23

                                                                      2014015627

  ISBN 978-1-4724-1949-1 (hbk)
  ISBN 978-0-367-59693-4 (pbk)

Contents

Series Editor's Preface

When the United States of America entered the First World War on the side of the Entente, on 6 April 1917, it did so most self-consciously as an 'Associated Power' not as an 'Ally'. This careful distinction exemplified official American ambivalence about the conflict, which the US government eventually chose to be 'in' but not 'of'. President Wilson had narrowly won a second term in the election of November 1916 on the slogan 'he kept us out of the War', but in important respects the USA had been in the war from the start. Although the path to war was smoothed by the grotesque incompetence of German diplomacy, the lack of political understanding of German strategy, especially the resort to unrestricted submarine warfare, and the collapse of Tsarist autocracy, it was the inter-connectedness of US and Entente economic interests, and the vast fortunes made from the war by American capitalists, that made US belligerency almost inevitable. Nowhere were these links, and the fortunes made from them, more apparent than in the great city of New York. The United States in 1914 was fundamentally white, rural, northern European and Protestant. New York was uncompromisingly urban, Jewish, Catholic, southern European and black, with a burgeoning population of hyphenated-Americans on both sides of the conflict. The very existence of New York challenged established views of what it was to be an American. The outbreak of a great European war was immediately of interest to its citizens, not least in the well-established ethnic presses. The city authorities were aware from the outset that a European war had the potential for inflaming conflict at home and for compromising the nation's studied 'neutrality'. Once the USA joined the conflict the city was faced with a new need to police potential agitators and 'aliens'. When the war was over there was a capacity for further conflict over how the war was to be commemorated and what meaning it was to be given among the city's diverse ethnic groups. In this fascinating and original study Ross Wilson explores the complex and varied ways in which the city and its citizens responded to the First World War and to the emergence on the world stage of the USA as a great power, responses that altered the politics, economics and social identities within the city fundamentally and forever.

John Bourne
Birmingham
June 2014

List of Figures

List of Tables

Acknowledgements

All books are a product of a network of associations, experiences and ideas. Therefore, I would like to extend my deepest thanks to the individuals who have assisted in bringing this book to publication. Acknowledgements are due to the publishing team at Ashgate, who have been supportive throughout a long process which saw this book develop into its current form. My gratitude should be stated to the staff at the New York Public Library, the Brooklyn Library and the Queens Library, who patiently supported me over the years as I developed this project. I would also like to express my thanks towards the staff and students of the University of Chichester, Pace University and the New York Institute of Technology. My special thanks are due to those who have helped me develop my ideas for this work. It is the example of their fine scholarship and teaching which has served as an inspiration to continue my own research. Whilst any faults are entirely my own, any credit should be shared with them. These individuals include Professor Julian Richards, Dr Dominic Perring, Dr Kate Giles, Dr Jonathan Finch, Dr Geoff Cubitt, Dr John Clay, Dr Kalliopi Fouseki, Dr Emma Waterton and Alex Sotheran. I would also like to extend my particular thanks to Dr Laurajane Smith, Professor Richard Bessel and Dr Kevin Walsh for their helpful advice and criticism. Finally, I would like to dedicate this work to my family. Guy, Pippa, Freddie, Arthur, Drew, Ellis, Bryn and Jill, I am indebted to your kindness. The majority of this book was written in the United States, and my thanks are due to my family there: Steve, Cindy, Ian, Lucy and Edwin. To my parents, Margaret and Roger, who always encouraged and enabled my studies, I cannot thank you enough. To Nancy, this book is for you.

Chapter 1

Introduction

The subject of this book is the city of New York during the First World War; a period when the metropolis witnessed vast alterations in its governance, its citizens and its perception within the wider continental United States. The conflict brought the political, demographic and cultural changes that had occurred in the city during the preceding century into greater focus. Foremost amongst these concerns was that of the city's character, its identity and the attitudes of its residents in relation to the rest of the nation. This situation arose because of the particular role New York had played in the transformation of the United States; from a collection of rebellious colonies in the late eighteenth century to an industrialised nation ascending to the coveted status of 'world power' at the beginning of the twentieth century. The city had been foremost in fuelling this great expansion, enabling the dictum of the nation's 'manifest destiny', by serving as the entranceway to millions of migrants seeking to pursue the promise of the revolution: life, liberty and the pursuit of happiness. However, whilst the city had 'made America' through its place as the embarkation point for life in the new world, this role had also come to make America suspicious of the city by the late nineteenth century. A city fuelled by migration, home to ethnic, religious and political diversity, began to be imagined as the antithesis to the image of the nation which had been cultivated through westward expansion. With the settling of the west, the nation of immigrants began to suspect the émigré as lacking in the possession of the singular qualities that made 'an American'.

These concerns were seemingly compounded with the alteration in the patterns of migration in the latter half of the nineteenth century which saw increasing numbers of southern Europeans and eastern European Jewish communities replacing the traditional source of emigrants from northern Europe.[1] The nation's character was assumed to be compromised by this immigration from new parts of the old world.[2] New York became representative of the ills of the United States as its heterogeneous character was assumed to be incompatible with the concept of 'one nation indivisible'. In these circumstances, the city and its citizens were tested in their loyalty to the nation with the outbreak of war in August 1914. The effects of this conflict in Europe were soon experienced in New York. Indeed, due to its pre-eminent position as a financial and trading centre, its role in the conflict was realised far sooner than elsewhere in the United States. As a city

---

[1] E. Bogen, 1987. *Immigration in New York*. New York, NY: Praeger.

[2] A.M. Blake, 1999. *How New York Became American, 1890–1924*. Baltimore, MD. Johns Hopkins University Press, p. 5.

comprised of immigrants from across Europe, the development of the war also placed the city's residents under greater scrutiny. Religious, ethnic and national ties all shaped responses to the war in New York and each represented a potential point of conflict within the metropolis. As different groups within the city pledged their support for opposing sides in the conflagration, both the peace of the city and the neutral status of the United States were perceived to be in peril. Therefore, although the United States Congress only declared war on Germany in April 1917, the city of New York can be assessed to be involved in the struggle from the very outset of the conflict.

It is this history which shall be the focus of assessment within this book – since, from the declarations of war in Europe during August 1914, plans, policies and preventative measures were put in place to ensure the loyalty of the residents of the city and to maintain the appearance of impartiality. These schemes were also born out of pre-war concerns of the 'American' character of the immigrant population of the metropolis. During the war, the city's inhabitants would be encouraged to represent the city authority's ideal of 'one city, one nation, and one loyalty'. With the entry of the nation into the 'European War', the focus of this campaign altered to ensure that New York's immigrant community could steel themselves and represent the nation in a time of war. Once again, the profusion of political and ethnic identities was assumed to suppress the ability of these residents to affirm themselves as '100 per cent American'. Wartime programmes of integration and the demand that residents affirm their loyalty through voluntary initiatives and in some cases physical coercion brought the war directly to the city's inhabitants. After the cessation of hostilities and the return of soldiers from overseas, the wartime experience of the city became a contested object, used by authorities and organisations to maintain the effort of imposing a singular 'national character' onto the diverse citizens of New York. In this manner, we can see the history of New York during the First World War as integral to the wider study of the conflict, as it forms direct links with the issues, concerns and events that created and sustained the maelstrom that engulfed European nation states. The war can also be seen as vital in the development of the city, ensuring its economic and cultural pre-eminent status through the intellectual, industrial and trading links forged through the demands of wartime. However, the war can be regarded as the basis upon which the city's identity was altered, evidenced in the thoughts, habits and ideals of its residents. From a city perceived to be a haven of foreign influence and alien ideas, the First World War made New York into the American metropolis of the twentieth century.

Modernism and the First World War: Europe and the United States

The First World War has come to be regarded as possessing a legacy that shaped the events of the twentieth century, thereby serving as a formative influence on the contemporary world.[3] Indeed, the events of the four years of war are considered to be so defining that an array of significant cultural, political and social shifts have been examined as emanating from the conditions wrought by the conflict. Perhaps the most significant of these effects of the First World War is the supposition that the conflict heralded a new, modern era across the world. In this assessment, the experience of industrialised warfare, the effect of mass death on society and the exposure of traditional values of endeavour and sacrifice as 'the old lie' ensured the birth of a modernist age.[4] The advent of this age is considered to be most suitably expressed through the works of literature, art and sculpture that were produced in the aftermath of the conflict. From the disjointed structure of T.S. Eliot's *The Wasteland*,[5] the broken narrative of James Joyce's *Ulysses*,[6] to the cubism of Pablo Picasso and the surrealism of Salvador Dali, the ruins of the conflict, ideological, material and human, are regarded as the basis of the twentieth century.[7] Such is the legacy of the conflict that the literary scholar Paul Fussell considered the war to have engineered an ironic mode of communication borne out of the horrors witnessed on the battlefields:

> Every war is ironic because every war is worse than expected. Every war constitutes an irony of situation because its means are so melodramatically disproportionate to its presumed ends.[8]

As part of this modernist programme ushered in by the First World War, the expression of new identities, both national and political, are also presumed to be constituted on the battlefields.[9] The imperial possessions of European powers were provided with national narratives through which, for example, concepts of belonging and place within Australia, New Zealand and Canada were developed. In this respect, European hegemony across the globe was challenged and nationalist movements for independency were forged within the crucible of war.

---

[3]   J.M. Winter, G. Parker and M. Harbeck, 2000. Introduction. In J.M Winter, G. Parker and M. Harbeck (eds), *The Great War and the Twentieth Century*. New Haven, CT: Yale University Press, pp. 1–12.

[4]   M. Eksteins, 1989. *Rites of Spring: The Great War and the Birth of the Modern Age*. Boston, MA: Houghton Mifflin.

[5]   T.S. Eliot, 1924. *The Wasteland*. London: Hogarth Press.

[6]   J. Joyce, 1922. *Ulysses*. Paris: Shakespeare and Company.

[7]   V. Sherry, 2003. *The Great War and the Language of Modernism*. Oxford: Oxford University Press; T. Tate, 1998. *Modernism, History and the First World War*, Manchester: Manchester University Press.

[8]   P. Fussell, 1975. *The Great War and Modern Memory*. Oxford: Oxford University Press.

[9]   J.F. Vance, 1997. *Death So Noble: Memory, Meaning, and the First World War*. Vancouver, BC: University of British Columbia Press; A. Thomson, 1994. *Anzac Memories: Living With the Legend*. Oxford: Oxford University Press.

However, this account is one which has been most strongly promoted within European and its dominions' historiography of the war.[10] Across the former combatant states of Europe, the war as a tragic event, fuelling the rise of new modes of expression, is a common thread of interpretation. The ascendancy of this approach has obscured the experience and impact of the war of others apart from European or European colonial subjects.[11] In recent years, this oversight has been addressed with detailed studies of the repercussions of the conflict for individuals from the Indian subcontinent, the African colonies, East Asia, the Caribbean and South America.[12] In this consideration, what was a global war during 1914 to 1918 has now been recognised and studied as such in the present.[13] It is in this broadening of perspectives that we can place the experience of the United States during the war. Whilst the arrival of American material and manpower is regarded as shifting the balance of power in favour of the Entente against their struggle with the Central Powers, the experience of the war for the citizens and the wider nation has been somewhat neglected in comparison to its European counterparts.[14] Too often the nation and its people are regarded from a view askew – as a final, extra scene in the bloody drama that unfolded on the battlefields.[15] This is perhaps due to the late entry of the United States in the war, after the catastrophic losses in the battles of the Somme, Verdun, Passchendaele and Gallipoli, but it also reflects a peculiar absence of the memory of the war across the nation.

Indeed, whereas the remembrance of the war within Europe has generated and continues to generate a great deal of public, scholarly and political debate, the war in American memory appears not to evoke the same level of obsession.[16] This could be explained in the context of the delayed involvement of the United States Army during the war. However, the total number of American deaths from combat and illness during the conflict numbered over 100,000 – more than double the fatalities of the Vietnam War (1955–1975). United States troops also witnessed the full horrors of industrialised warfare in operations, such as that

---

[10]   S. Das, 2011. Introduction. In S. Das (ed.) *Race, Empire and First World War Writing*. Cambridge: Cambridge University Press, pp. 1–32.

[11]   G. Xu, 2011. *Strangers on the Western Front: Chinese Workers in the Great War*. Cambridge: Cambridge University Press.

[12]   D. Omissi, 1999. *Indian Voices of the Great War: Soldiers' Letters, 1914–18*. Basingstoke: Palgrave Macmillan; R. Smith, 2004. *Jamaican Volunteers in the First World War: Race, Masculinity and the Development of National Consciousness*. Manchester: Manchester University Press.

[13]   J. Morrow, 2005. *The Great War: An Imperial History*. London: Routledge.

[14]   J.D. Keene, 2000. *The United States and the First World War*. Harlow: Longman.

[15]   R. Zieger, 2001. *America's Great War: World War I and the American Experience*. Oxford: Rowman and Littlefield; R. Schaffer, 1991. *America in the Great War: The Rise of the War Welfare State*. Oxford: Oxford University Press.

[16]   S. Trout, 2010. *On the Battlefield of Memory: The First World War and American Remembrance, 1919 to 1941*. Tuscaloosa, AL: University of Alabama Press.

at the Battle of the Argonne Forest, during September 1918, which claimed the lives of nearly 26,000.[17] Yet discussions on the impact and the remembrance of the war in the United States have been, until recent years, largely mute. In some respects, perhaps the events of 1914–1918 were reduced in their significance because of the post-war politics of the United States Government. The war was swiftly followed by an unprecedented economic expansion, international isolation, struggles over political representation, the difficult enforcement of the prohibition of alcohol and then the onset of the Great Depression after 1929, when the world's pre-eminent democracy was shaken by events that appeared unsolvable through the established routes of government. In this context, perhaps the First World War pales into comparison against the wider history of the nation. However, such assessments fail to address a key point in historical investigation: to understand the event in context, rather than in the light of retrospective analysis. Set against the backdrop of the wider twentieth century, the First World War might not appear to have shaped the nation, but in terms of those who witnessed the events, the war possessed a transformative agenda, heralding a modern era that dramatically altered the values and ideals of an 'American' identity.

The United States and the First World War

The study of the United States and its participation in the global conflagration of 1914–1918 has been steadily developed in recent years. Whilst the war once was a lacuna of historical analysis in the otherwise rigorous assessment of twentieth-century American history, there now exists a sizeable body of literature that examines the variety of perspectives that the conflict generated across the nation.[18] Traditionally, analyses had calculated the way in which politicians and military staff responded to the development of the war in Europe and altered American policy towards the status of a fully-fledged global power.[19] However, since the 1980s, with altering trends within American historiography, a greater regard for the social and cultural changes that accompanied the conflict has been expressed

---

[17] R. Ferrell, 2007. *America's Deadliest Battle: Meuse-Argonne, 1918.* Lawrence, KA: University Press of Kansas.

[18] R. Schaffer, 1978. *The United States in World War I: A Selected Bibliography.* Santa Barbara, CA: ABC-CLIO; D.R. Woodward, 1985. *America and World War I: A Selected Annotated Bibliography of English-language Sources.* New York, NY: Garland.

[19] R.R. May, 1959. *The World War and American Isolation, 1914–1917.* Cambridge, MA: Harvard University Press; J. Coogan, 1981. *The End of Neutrality: The United States, Britain, and Maritime Rights, 1899–1915.* Ithaca, NY: Cornell University Press; P. Devlin 1975. *Too Proud to Fight: Woodrow Wilson's Neutrality.* Oxford: Oxford University Press; T. Knock, 1992. *To End All Wars: Woodrow Wilson and the Quest for a New World Order.* Princeton, NJ: Princeton University Press.

by historians.[20] Perhaps the forerunner in this field was the work of David Kennedy, *Over Here: The First World War and American Society*.[21] This work provided a detailed assessment of the meanings of the conflict for American society. Kennedy assessed how individuals responded to the changes wrought by war and reacted through cultural and social forms to reshape attitudes and ideas within the United States. In this manner, the study's great strength was to demonstrate the impact of the war on the nation beyond a purely military and political sphere.

This study has been followed by a variety of historical analyses that have sought to place the conflict of 1914–1918 as a central part of twentieth-century American history.[22] For example, Jennifer Keene's seminal work *Doughboys: The Great War and the Remaking of America* follows on the path set by Kennedy in highlighting how the wartime experience of troops in the US Army was influential in the development of social legislation during the post-war period.[23] Whilst these studies have expanded the remit of the historical analysis of the war in the United States, it is notable that research has remained focused on the figure of the soldier.[24] Indeed, the experience of war for the combatant has been used to examine far wider aspects of society in the United States. For example, scholars have used the recruitment, draft and training of troops within the United States to examine issues of gender, citizenship and identity in the context of the changing political and social structures of the nation at the outset of the twentieth century.[25] Within these studies, the soldiers of New York have featured prominently, as representatives of the city's diverse immigrant communities who served in the US Army. Historians have examined the composition of the battalions of New York, volunteers and draftees, to assess how communities

[20]   B. Farwell, 1999. *Over There: The United States in the Great War, 1917–1918.* New York, NY: Norton.

[21]   D. Kennedy, 1980. *Over Here: The First World War and American Society.* Oxford: Oxford University Press.

[22]   J. Whiteclay Chambers, 1992. *The Tyranny of Change: America in the Progressive Era, 1890–1920.* New York, NY: St. Martin's.

[23]   J.D. Keene, 2001. *Doughboys: The Great War and the Remaking of America.* Baltimore, MD: Johns Hopkins University Press.

[24]   J. Eisenhower, 2001. *Yanks: The Epic Story of the American Army in World War I.* New York, NY: The Free Press; M. Grotelueschen, 2006. *The AEF Way of War: The American Army and Combat in World War I.* Cambridge: Cambridge University Press.

[25]   C. Capozzola, 2008. *Uncle Sam Wants You: World War I and the Making of the Modern American Citizen.* Oxford: Oxford University Press; N.G. Ford, 1997. 'Mindful of the Traditions of His Race': Dual Identity and Foreign-born Soldiers in the First World War American Army. *Journal of American Ethnic History*, 16(2): 35–57; N.G. Ford, 2001. *Americans All: Foreign-born Soldiers in World War I.* College Station, TX: Texas A&M University Press; G. Shenk, 2006. *Work or Fight: Race, Gender, and the Draft in World War I.* New York: Palgrave Macmillan; C.M. Sterba, 2003. *Good Americans: Italian and Jewish Immigrants During the First World War.* Oxford: Oxford University Press.

considered their martial role in defending the principles of the nation in relation to their status as émigrés in their adopted homeland.[26]

This work also draws upon the recent prominent studies of the African American experience in the First World War, where the experiences of soldiers from the city have been reassessed in the context of political representation and civil rights in the wider nation.[27] For example, the experiences of members of the 369th Infantry Regiment, recruited from the city's predominantly African American community in Harlem and known as the 'Harlem Hellfighters' are, therefore, viewed within the context of the struggle against the racial politics of the era.[28] This book also assesses the post-war era, following in the same vein as a number of other studies which have examined the influence of veterans' groups within American politics, particularly with regard to the formation of the American Legion, and the development of isolationism or anti-immigration stances.[29] Within this approach, the soldiers of the conflict are viewed as altering the nation through their service and experience. As emblems of the United States, as representatives of the values of the country, the historical issues of immigration, slavery and citizenship are regarded as writ large in the role of America's diverse population in the First World War.[30]

With this emphasis on the significance of the soldier experience in the development of the nation in the twentieth century, it is perhaps unsurprising that scholars are demonstrating the way in which the memory of the war in the United States has been created, maintained, obscured and forgotten.[31] These studies have tackled the peculiar object of the memory of the Great War in the United States. Whilst European-focused scholars have consistently subscribed to the presumption of the remembrance of the war across European nation states fuelled a change in society and culture, the commemoration of the conflict

---

[26] M.J. Hogan, 2007. *The Shamrock Battalion in the Great War*. Columbia, MI: University of Missouri Press; R. Slotkin, 2005. *Lost Battalions: The Great War and the Crisis of American Nationality*. New York, NY: Henry Holt.

[27] A.E. Barbeau and F. Henri, 1996. *The Unknown Soldiers: African-American Troops in World War I*. New York, NY: Da Capo Press.

[28] B. Harris, 2002. *The Hellfighters of Harlem: African-American Soldiers Who Fought for the Right to Fight for Their Country*. New York, NY: Carroll & Graf; P. Nelson, 2009. *A More Unbending Battle: The Harlem Hellfighters' Struggle for Freedom in WWI and Equality at Home*. New York, NY: Basic Civitas.

[29] L. Budreau, 2010. *Bodies of War: World War I and the Politics of Commemoration in America, 1919–1933*. New York, NY: New York University Press, 2010.

[30] J. Alexander, 2004. *Ethnic Pride, American Patriotism: Slovaks and Other New Immigrants in the Interwar Era*. Philadelphia, PA: Temple University Press; C. Williams, 2010. *Torchbearers of Democracy: African American Soldiers in the World War I Era*. Chapel Hill, NC: University of North Carolina Press.

[31] J. Cooper, 2003. The Great War and American Memory. *Virginia Quarterly Review*, 79(1): 70–84.

in the United States appears to be subsumed by the later events of what can be arguably claimed to be the 'American century'. The apparent absence of memory of the First World War in the United States is almost regarded by some European historians to be a national failing – that such a catastrophic event that afflicted the continent could be so blithely forgotten elsewhere. However, this assessment is drawn from the assumption of a singular mode of assessment for such a complex nation.

Indeed, individuals such as John Bodnar and G. Kurt Piehler have stressed the local structures of memory in the American experience of war.[32] For example, in their study of the Massachusetts town of Orange, Glassberg and Moore demonstrate the way in which the conflict profoundly shaped neighbourhood and district politics:

> ... the Orange World War I monument recalls not the militant 100 percent Americanism and ideological purity traditionally associated with veterans' groups but rather a kind of patriotism from the ground up, one that uses the symbolism of stars, flags, and the war dead to address local concerns and diverse but powerful emotions close to home. The statue of the returning soldier connects the sacrifice of war not for the abstract nation-state but rather for the town's real way of life and its children.[33]

What these studies do reveal is the great potential for study of the locality in the history and memory of the war in the United States. This particular approach has perhaps been eclipsed by the overwhelming emphasis placed on the figure of the soldier in the nation's experience of the war.[34] However, in the context of a 'new wave' of First World War studies over the last decade, which has driven the assessment of previously ignored areas of investigation and their military, economic, social or political connections to the conflict, a different mode of analysing the history of the First World War in the United States can emerge.

---

[32]   J. Bodnar, 1992. *Remaking America: Public Memory, Commemoration, and Patriotism in the Twentieth Century*. Princeton, NJ: Princeton University Press; J. Bodnar, 1994. Public Memory in an American City: Commemoration in Cleveland. In J.R Gillis (ed.) *Commemorations: The Politics of National Identity*. Princeton, NJ: Princeton University Press, pp. 74–89; G.K. Piehler, 1994. The War Dead and the Gold Star: American Commemoration of the First World War. In J.R Gillis (ed.) *Commemorations: The Politics of National Identity*. Princeton, NJ: Princeton University Press, pp. 168–218; G.K. Piehler, 1995. *Remembering War: The American Way*. Washington, DC: Smithsonian Institution Press.

[33]   D. Glassberg and J.M. Moore, 1996. Patriotism in Orange: The Memory of World War I in a Massachusetts Town. In J. Bodnar (ed.), *Bonds of Affection: Americans Define their Patriotism*. Princeton, NJ: Princeton University Press, p. 189.

[34]   E. Coffman, 1968. *The War to End All Wars: The American Military Experience in World War I*. Oxford: Oxford University Press; J. Whiteclay Chambers, 1987. *To Raise an Army: The Draft Comes to Modern America*. New York, NY: Free Press.

First World War Studies: Breaking New Ground

The academic study of the war of 1914–1918 has developed substantially in recent years. Whilst the field of enquiry had been traditionally dominated by military history, expressing concern with the formation, training and employment of troops in the field, it now encompasses a variety of approaches and objects of study.[35] In part, this alteration has been the product of the work of historians who demonstrated the way in which alternative accounts of the conflict had been overlooked and neglected.[36] The value of these studies was the manner in which they expertly demonstrated the intricate ways in which the battlefields and the home front were entwined during the course of the war.[37] Such a revision countered the position forwarded within the post-war novels and memoirs of the war, where veterans of the conflict represented troops as separated from a civilian population who were unaware of the horrors of combat.[38] Scholars have rejected this traditional assumption and instead reiterated the place of the war as a multifaceted experience. Rather than examine the effect of the war purely on the nation or on the armed forces, the effect of the war was seen to be borne by specific communities of individuals, trades, political groups, regions and places. The research undertaken within this remit has been termed a 'new wave' of First World War studies that embraces new subject areas, alternative approaches and interdisciplinary agendas.[39] This has given rise to innovative analyses that fuse literary, anthropological and sociological concepts with historical research to develop the way the war is studied and to generate distinctive assessments of the conflict.[40]

It is in this regard that we can consider the examination of the urban environment in the context of the conflict. In a variety of ways, towns and cities were at the forefront of the events of 1914–1918: the wartime target of opposing combatants,

---

[35] P. Purseigle, 2005. Introduction. Warfare and Belligerence: Approaches to the First World War. In P. Purseigle (Ed.) *Warfare and Belligerence: Perspectives in First World War Studies*. Leiden and Boston, MA: Brill, pp. 1–37; P. Purseigle and J. Macleod, 2004. Introduction: Perspectives in First World War Studies. In J. Macleod and P. Purseigle (eds), *Uncovered Fields: Perspectives in First World War Studies*. Leiden and Boston, MA: Brill, pp. 1–23.

[36] J. Winter, 1992. *Sites of Memory, Sites of Mourning: The Great War in European Cultural History*. Cambridge: Cambridge University Press.

[37] H. McCartney, 2005. *The Liverpool Territorials in the First World War*. Cambridge: Cambridge University Press; M. Connelly, 2006. *Steady the Buffs: A Regiment, a Region and the Great War*. Oxford: Oxford University Press.

[38] S. Sassoon, 1932. *Memoirs of a Fox-Hunting Man*. London: Faber and Faber; E. Hemingway. 1929. A *Farewell to Arms*. New York, NY: Charles Scribner's Sons.

[39] R. Wilson, 2011. *Landscapes of the Western Front: Materiality during the Great War*. London: Routledge.

[40] A. Schnapp, 1998. Une archéologie de la Grande Guerre estelle possible? In A. Schnapp (ed.), *14–18: Aujourd'hui, Today, Heute. No. 2, l'archéologie et al Grande Guerre*. Péronne: Historial de la Grande Guerre, pp. 19–27.

the refuge of civilians fleeing the onslaught of war and the concern of authorities in managing their civilian populations. The study of the city in wartime is, therefore, a highly suitable means of understanding the far-reaching effects of the conflict as all aspects of the experience of the war, the privations, opportunities and alterations, are distilled within the metropolis.[41] As such, the study of the wartime metropolis or municipality has gathered increasing interest from scholars who have demonstrated its significance for understanding the processes of the conflict. The key work in this field remains the unsurpassable, two-volume work edited by Jay Winter and Jean-Louis Roberts, *Capital Cities at War: Paris, London, Berlin 1914–1919*.[42] In this account, the nature of the conflict within the city is explored in minute detail, with eminent scholars of the war highlighting how the politics, economics, society and culture of European metropolises were reshaped and, in turn, impacted upon the pursuit of the war. Whether the issues of the recruitment of manpower, the control of political dissidents or the post-war commemoration in the city, the urban experience of the First World War was placed at the centre of concern.

The study was also noticeable for its comparative approach, placing European capital cities together to demonstrate the common elements that tied together the citizens, the structures and the authorities of cities in wartime.[43] This agenda has been developed by further analyses which have also sought to use comparative agendas to interpret how the conflict possessed a transformative effect for urban centres. Funck and Chickering have also made a highly significant contribution to this field in their wider study of wartime cities across the first half of the twentieth century.[44] Within this edited volume, a number of researchers brought to light the significance of the urban experience during the First World War not just as a microcosm of national and international issues but as a specific locale in which the effects of the war were lived by individuals and communities.[45] These studies

---

[41]   See Healy, M. 2004. *Vienna and the Fall of the Habsburg Empire: Total War and Everyday Life in World War I*. Cambridge: Cambridge University Press.

[42]   J.-L. Robert and J.M. Winter, 1997. *Capital Cities at War: Paris, London, Berlin 1914–1919. Volume 1*. Cambridge: Cambridge University Press; J.-L. Robert and J.M. Winter, 2007. *Capital Cities at War: Paris, London, Berlin 1914–1919. Volume 2*. Cambridge: Cambridge University Press.

[43]   F. Walter and R. Hudemann (eds), 1997. *Villes et guerres mondiales au XXe siècle*. Paris and Montreal: L'Harmattan.

[44]   M. Funck and R. Chickering (eds), 2004. *Endangered Cities: Military Power and Urban Societies in the Era of the World Wars*. Leiden and Boston, MA: Brill; S. Goebel and D. Keene (eds), 2011. *Cities into Battlefields: Metropolitan Scenarios, Experiences and Commemorations of Total War*. Farnham: Ashgate.

[45]   B. Majerus, 2004. Controlling Urban Society during World War I: Cooperation between Belgian Authorities and the Forces of Military Occupation. In M. Funck and R. Chickering (eds), *Endangered Cities: Military Power and Urban Societies in the Era of the World Wars*. Leiden and Boston, MA: Brill, pp. 65–80; A. Hofmann, 2004. Reweaving the Urban Fabric: Multiethnicity and Occupation in Lódz, 1914–1918. In M. Funck and R.

have been conducted under the wider interpretation of the issues surrounding the denotation 'total war' for the 1914–1918 conflict.[46] In this respect, the study of the urban experience of the First World War is an extension of the theatre of operations where issues of morale, mobilisation, discipline and material provision are equally applicable to soldier and civilian alike.

As part of the movement towards the study of the city in wartime, scholars have attempted to expand analyses beyond logistics to explore the practices of metropolitan life during the conflict. Perhaps the most clearly practiced example of this approach has been Chickering's study of the German town of Freiberg during the 1914–1918 war.[47] Whilst this study takes as its basis the principle of total war, it also examines the social, cultural and psychological effects of the conflict upon the civilian populace. This study appears to be highly influenced by the embrace of an interdisciplinary agenda within First World War studies as it applies a sensuous geographical reading of the urban landscape to assess how the war was felt by the inhabitants of Freiberg. Similarly, Seipp explores the responses in both Manchester and Munich to the manner in which the conflict shaped the lives of the inhabitants of these major European cities.[48] This detailed work also assesses the impact of the post-war world on the respective cities, demonstrating the similarities faced by citizens as urban authorities sought to manage their populations in the uncertain aftermath of the First World War. The study of the city in wartime has, therefore, became a growing area of concern for both academic and, increasingly, public audiences.[49] Nevertheless, the investigation of the metropolis during the conflict has been restricted to a European agenda; the role of non-European cities in the war has remained unaddressed.

The Study of the Metropolis

The consideration of the urban experience of the First World War outside of the major area of operations in Europe is a new area for the study of the war. In keeping with the recent movements within First World War studies, particularly the expansion of analysis to incorporate other areas that were shaped by the conflict, the study of the wartime city beyond the confines of Europe represents as yet unchartered territory for scholars. This situation may have arisen from the

---

Chickering (eds), *Endangered Cities: Military Power and Urban Societies in the Era of the World Wars*. Leiden and Boston, MA: Brill, pp. 81–94.

[46] R. Chickering and S. Förster (eds), 2000. *Great War, Total War: Combat and Mobilization on the Western Front, 1914–1918*. Cambridge: Cambridge University Press.

[47] R. Chickering, 2007. *The Great War and Urban Life in Germany: Freiburg, 1914–1918*. Cambridge: Cambridge University Press.

[48] A.R. Seipp, 2009. *The Ordeal of Peace: Demobilization and the Urban Experience in Britain and Germany, 1917–1921*. Farnham: Ashgate.

[49] P. Yeates, 2012. *A City in Wartime: Dublin 1914–1918*. Dublin: Gill and Macmillan.

assumption of priority traditionally accorded to the continent from which the war emerged and upon which the majority of individuals lost their lives. This position is undermined by the recognition of the complex set of networks created by the war. Imperial, economic, cultural and political ties ensured that the conflict's impact was felt across the globe, with cities as the hub of these international activities firmly implicated in all aspects of the war.[50] Nevertheless, the study of the urban environment beyond the cities of Europe, whether from neutral or participating nations, does pose certain methodological and theoretical issues. Whereas European cities can be seen to be directly involved in the conflict and studies of these conurbations can be made in direct reference to the events of the war, the assessment of cities beyond that continent must inevitably be completed in a more oblique approach. The war for these cities did not serve as a direct presence on the lives of citizens and the institutions of these municipalities; rather, it served as a means to draw existing issues into focus. Certainly, like their European wartime counterparts, enmeshed in the immediate circumstances of the war, these metropolises saw drastic alterations in the nature of authority, the habits of individuals and the functions of organisations. However, these changes occurred within a framework formed through the conflict, rather in the context of the war itself.

Therefore, the methods and approaches drawn upon to analyse these cities, beyond the traditional assumption of the 'arena of war', require a different mode of assessment. The city at war in these circumstances requires far more attention to the contexts and concerns that shaped the city before the advent of war. Conflict in these cities served to cast existing issues into a new light, accentuating the divides and reiterating points of authority. In this respect, the study of these urban areas can be enhanced through an engagement with the wider field of urban history and cultural geography.[51] From Mumford's classic study of the city's development in connection with human civilisation,[52] urban history has developed a range of agendas and practices which assess the architectural structures, the political formation and the social construction of cities to interpret issues of space, place, power and identity within the modern metropolis.[53] Recent trends within urban studies have particularly emphasised the multitude of ways in which cities are the subject of authority and control, to examine how individuals, groups and communities within the metropolis are governed and in turn acquiesce in or disrupt

---

[50]   B. Albert, 2002. *South America and the First World War: The Impact of the War on Brazil, Argentina, Peru and Chile.* Cambridge: Cambridge University Press.

[51]   M. Ogborn, 1998. *Spaces of Modernity: London's Geographies, 1680–1780.* London and New York: Guilford Press.

[52]   L. Mumford, 1963. *The City in History.* London: Martin Secker and Warburg.

[53]   S.S. Fainstein and S. Campbell (eds), 2011. *Readings in Urban Theory.* Oxford: Wiley-Blackwell.

that governance.[54] Western cities of the late nineteenth century and early twentieth century have been especially noted for their capacity to act in this manner; in a Foucauldian interpretation, urban areas are deemed to serve as 'technologies of the self'.[55] During this era, concerns were expressed that the concept of the city was fundamentally flawed, that the century of unrestrained capitalism and industrialisation had left cities such as London, Manchester, Chicago and New York afflicted with the diseases of material deprivation, acute poverty, social inequalities and political radicalism.

The great pioneering social surveys of the era revealed the failure of cities to support their ever-growing populations.[56] Across a number of nations, reform movements sought to rectify this situation to improve and 'cultivate' the city and its inhabitants. Architectural, political and social initiatives were enacted to ensure the health of the body politic, whilst also enabling a far greater degree of control over the lives, habits and ideals of the populace. From the dystopian visions of reformers, therefore, emerged a utopian ideal of 'curing' the ills of the metropolis through the redesign of the material and psychological environment of the city. Issues of class, identity and governance were negotiated within this context as the urban form was re-imagined as a functional, 'healthy' and unified conglomeration.[57] The advent of the First World War directly shaped these arguments as the conflict encouraged and exacerbated concerns regarding citizenship, nationality and the role of authority. It is on this basis that a study of cities beyond the scope of the war can be made. Separated, perhaps, from the direct repercussions of the battlefields, removed from the way in which the conflict framed the practice of daily life, the level of involvement of the war from these municipalities was no less significant. The war for these cities placed a greater focus on the prevailing concerns of managing and changing the potentially discordant voices, perspectives and experiences that constituted these metropolises.

New York and the First World War

It is under this framework of analysis that the city of New York during the First World War will be examined. The city represents an ideal case by which

---

[54] A. Lees, 1985. *Cities Perceived: Urban Society in European and American Thought, 1820–1940*. Manchester: Manchester University Press.

[55] J. Walkowitz, 1992. *City of Dreadful Delight: Narratives of Sexual Danger in Late Victorian London*. Chicago, IL: University of Chicago Press.

[56] H. Mayhew, 1851. *Life and Labour and the London Poor, Vol. 1*. London: George Woodfall and Son; C. Booth, 1903. *Life and Labour of the People in London: Summary*. London: Macmillan; B.S. Rowntree, 1902. *Poverty: A Study of Town Life*. London: Macmillan; J. Riis, 1890. *How the Other Half Lives*. New York, NY: Charles Scribner's Sons.

[57] E. Howard, 1898. *To-Morrow: A Peaceful Path to Real Reform*. London: Swan Sonnenschein.

to explore the absences in current study and forward agendas for the future. It also provides an opportunity to explore an alternative perspective in the history of the war of 1914–1918 in the United States. Whereas, traditionally, studies have focused on the experiences of soldiers within the US Army, this examination demonstrates the wider potential of the analysis of the war within the nation at a local level, demonstrating the complex nature of history and memory within the United States. Finally, this assessment develops the recent trends within First World War historiography to analyse the 'city at war'. By taking this study beyond the dominance of a European agenda, the examination of the urban experience of conflict can be extended to understand how the war shaped culture, society and politics from an alternative perspective. In this manner, New York provides a highly appropriate example; as a nominally neutral city, in keeping with the policies of the United States, from the outbreak of the war to its place as the major disembarkation point for men and materials being shipped to the front, the metropolis encompasses an entire spectrum of the war experience. It was this experience that also affected a change in the city's politics and society, as the presence of the conflict, despite the fighting occurring thousands of miles away, was felt keenly by all aspects of the city's population.

New York's role in this conflagration, the world's first global war which was fought at an industrial level, has been largely overlooked within histories of the city. The city's place in the American Revolutionary War (1775–1783), the United States Civil War (1861–1865) and even the Second World War (1939–1945) has been the subject of sustained academic and popular historical studies.[58] Indeed, despite the memorials, monuments and associations towards the First World War across the city, the conflict of 1914–1918 is strangely absent from the collective memory of citizens and the institutional memory of the city authorities. Such an oversight obscures how the 'European War' implicated the city from the very beginning of hostilities after the breakdown in diplomacy following the assassination of Archduke Franz Ferdinand in Sarajevo in June 1914. As one of the pre-eminent trading, shipping and financial centres, as well as being home to immigrants from all the combatant nations, New York was drawn into the First World War by association, in a comparable fashion to the way in which treaty obligations drew in the nation states of Europe towards the conflict. As the war enveloped the city, its authorities sought to establish issues of identification, allegiance and control as the concern that the citizens of New York would fall into nationalistic, ethnic or religious rivalry was palpable. These concerns reflected the pre-war fears expressed by national, political and religious groups that the city, after decades of immigration from across the European peninsula, did not represent the fundamental tenants and ideals of the United States.

New York was viewed as a haven for social and political malcontents, subversives and radicals. Indeed, after 1914, the city's disparate communities

---

[58] S. Jaffe, 2013. *New York at War: Four Centuries of Combat, Fear, and Intrigue in Gotham.* New York, NY: Doubleday.

were asked to demonstrate their allegiance to the United States, a process which was heightened with the entry of the nation into the war and the introduction of the draft in 1917. As the city's residents were increasingly subject to surveillance and suspicion, official and unofficial organisations took it upon themselves to turn New York from an 'immigrant city' into an 'American city'. This alteration in identity was reaffirmed with the work of veterans' association groups such as the American Legion and the Gold Star Mothers, as well as the city authorities, the Parks Department and the Arts Commission after the cessation of hostilities. These groups contributed to a distinctly 'American' memory of the war through remembrance activities and public memorials. However, this process was utilised by communities, as both during the war and in the immediate period after the conflict, the city's residents redefined themselves in the context of the conflict. Therefore, a city which had been so influenced by European attitudes, its peoples and its cultures, began to reflect the ideas of the wider continental United States. The city became American through the process of war. The metropolis turned away from the ethnic, religious and social divisions of the 'old world' and effected a movement towards an 'American' identity.

Outline of the Book

The book will be divided into six chapters of analysis, each addressing particular thematic elements such as authority, charity and identity, but within a chronological framework. This will enable the study to detail how the First World War was perceived and represented within the city and the effect that the conflagration had on the metropolis's politics and society. Through this structure the changes wrought by the war on New York can be assessed as fully integrated into the nexus of the conflict. Therefore, this is not a study of the city as the war raged on some faraway battlefields: this is a study of the city at war. New York should not be disregarded as an object of study on the basis of the later entry of the United States into the war. This study will demonstrate the varied ways in which the conflict can be regarded as present in New York from August 1914 to its difficult denouement and remembrance. Too often the post-war isolationism of the United States has barred a consideration of the impact of the First World War on the United States. An insistence upon looking at the American experience of the war through a European framework has also hindered the development of analyses which focus on the unique position of the history and memory of the United States during the war of 1914–1918. As wartime concerns of citizenship, ethnicity, violence, authority and control were to be located on the battlefields and the home front across Europe, so too were these issues brought to bear on the United States. This investigation seeks to rectify these absences of analysis by placing the city of New York at the centre of study, to demonstrate how the urban experience of the war was not a European phenomenon, but a global issue that shaped municipalities through the contexts of the conflict.

The book's analysis begins in Chapter 2, which examines New York before the war, focusing on the disparate identities and the perception of un-American attitudes within the metropolis. This section will assess the context of the city before the alterations in society and politics which emerged with the conflict in August 1914. New York had experienced decades of immigration since the nineteenth century which had resulted in areas of the city that were distinctly 'German', 'Jewish', 'Irish' and 'Italian'. African American immigration into the city after the Civil War also saw the development of Harlem as a particular locale of business, culture and politics. These various ethnic and national groups constituted a diverse city, which by the beginnings of the twentieth century was home to more people born outside of the United States than those within the boundaries of the city of New York. These groups faced the same problems of housing and employment that characterised New York in the 1900s. However, the management of these problems by city and federal officials reflected the growing concern that this diverse populace was the haven of dissent, moral corruption and dubious attachment to the United States. As the city became a global industrial and economic hub, its international population was increasingly subject to fears that it lacked an appropriate 'American' identity.

Chapter 3 will follow from this contextual assessment by focusing upon the beginnings of the war the response to the conflict from the diverse communities in the city. At every level of society, the attachment to one belligerent nation or another was expressed. Cultural commentators espoused the values of German culture over French decadence, politicians affirmed the principles of democracy within Britain and France, whilst the city's émigré populations sided for or against their nation of origin. Eastern European Jews who had fled the pogroms expressed their favour for the Kaiser against Tsarist Russia, many Irish immigrants stated their opposition to Britain and some of the city's large German population favoured their attachment to the Fatherland. The outbreak of war brought greater focus to the issue of national self-determination for the homelands of many of New York's émigré population. The plethora of ethnic newspapers catering for the Irish, Czech, Hungarian and Slav immigrants in the city reported how these groups responded to the conflict with a resolve that it would mark a means of establishing independence for their country. However, this claim was not undertaken as a disavowal of their loyalty to the United States. Indeed, such demands were regarded to be entirely in keeping with their 'American' identity as the democracy and liberty of their adopted nation were to be exported back to the 'old country'. Similarly, African American writers in newspapers and periodicals in New York utilised the war and the stories of atrocities to highlight their own absence of representation and full citizenship in the land of their birth. Viewed through the prism of events in Europe, the war revealed the tensions surrounding identity within the metropolis.

Chapter 4 examines the aftermath of the start of the war in the city to 1916. New York was immediately implicated in the conflict as its economic and financial connections to the European powers ensured the city held a peculiar position in an otherwise neutral United States. The assets of combatant nations, held by institutions and companies in New York, were subject to scrutiny and the immediate withdrawal of finances from Europe caused a minor recession in the city. However, as the expectation of a small conflict soon evaporated, New York profited from the requirements of the warring nations as equipment, munitions, food and finance was bought on the city's markets. The wealth generated by this exchange only profited the city's merchant and financial elite, whilst the poorer sections of society were afflicted by ever-increasing prices for foodstuffs. These tensions were managed by the city's authorities under Mayor John Purroy Mitchel, who feared that such inequalities could exacerbate difficulties and ensure the conflict in Europe would become a street battle in New York. The response to this issue reveals how central the conflict had become for the city. Indeed, as different groups and supporters launched opposing charitable bodies to support the cause of belligerent nations, concerns were expressed that the loyalty to the United States was becoming diluted. The need for a strong national identity was also reinforced through an increasing fear of foreign subversives in the city and even the threat of attack from a hostile power. Throughout 1915 into the summer of 1916, increasing pressure was placed on 'hyphenated Americans' to declare their absolute commitment to the United States.

Chapter 5 continues the assessment of identity within the city as the metropolis was gripped first by a major incident at Black Tom Island during July 1916 and then by a fiercely presidential mayoral election in November 1916. The issues of 'preparedness' and 'Americanisation' were the principal points of conflict between political groups in the city as President Wilson and his rival, Republican Charles Hughes, each sought to garner votes in the metropolis. The eventual national victory of President Wilson was mirrored in his success in the city as citizens were swayed by the campaigns that tarnished Hughes as pro-German. In this manner, a vote for Wilson was a vote for the American loyalty that immigrants within the city were increasingly placed under pressure to affirm. These campaigns were led by private groups such as the National Security League, which had formed in New York during August 1914 and now led a vociferous campaign to ensure the city of immigrants was '100 per cent American' and ready to fight for the principles of the nation. In such an atmosphere of suspicion and control, allegiance to 'suspect' ethnic or political identities was subject to public opprobrium. With the declaration of war issued by the United States against Germany in April 1917, widespread surveillance of groups was carried out by the authorities and the police force.

Chapter 6 details the way in which these concerns of identity, citizenship and authority within the city were placed into greater focus after the declaration of war by the United States in April 1917. Even before the official entry of the nation into the conflict, a number of the city's political elite had begun to organise officer training and drill sessions in anticipation of the entry of the United States on the side of the Entente. This process was accompanied by a desire for the city to represent its attachment to the United States, rather than to any other cultural, political or religious attachments that the city's immigrant groups might possess. This was accelerated after the entry of the nation into the war and the introduction of the draft in 1917. This conscription fell onto the city's African American and immigrant population, who were required to register with the draft board for service. Police and private groups, such as the National Security League, worked to police this requirement, with potential 'draft dodgers' subject to arrest and possible deportation. The radical politics of the city were also restricted, as military service for the nation was enforced and considered an efficient means to 'Yank' out the hyphen of the multiform American identities that existed in the metropolis. The appeals for donations, volunteers and charity drives reinforced the place of identity. Communities were encouraged to invest and donate in the war effort through the Liberty Loans Scheme which was accompanied by parades and celebrations in the city as a means of encouraging patriotic affiliation. The imagery and symbolism associated with these campaigns reflected the ideal of military service as an instructional device for inculcating the values of the nation.

Chapter 7 assesses the aftermath of the conflict and the manner in which the war was forgotten but remembered in the city. As troops returned home they were met with a series of planned celebrations which marked their service and sacrifice to the nation. Parades on Fifth Avenue were used to welcome home soldiers, remember the dead and state their allegiance to the United States. However, not all groups were accorded the same opportunity to claim this affiliation, as African American troops were not met with the same trappings of citizenship and liberty as their comrades. This inclusion of groups with a limited framework of 'American' identity was continued with the construction of memorials and monuments across the city. The design of these structures was strictly controlled by the city authorities and the sponsoring of memorial schemes, whilst devolving to local communities, frequently relied upon the resources of veterans groups who increasingly used the memory of the war to reaffirm a singular 'American' identity. However, whilst memorials to the service of New York's citizens adorn the parks and boulevards of the city, the place of the conflict in the history of the metropolis is largely obscured in the history of the twentieth century. This forgetting to remember is not assumed to be a lapse in civic duty or a response to the hegemonic nature of official forms of remembrance. Rather, forgetting the First World War in New York has been part of a process of civic and national identification. The use of the First World War in promoting an 'American' identity was an entirely successful enterprise within the city, incorporating diverse cultures into an acceptance of an American identity. The politics of the post-war years, which stressed restrictions on immigration, anti-radicalism and isolationism, ensured that the memory of the conflict within the city was not required to reaffirm the principles of national identity. New York had become American.

Chapter 2
New York Before the War

Introduction

On the cold night of 23 January 1917, a group of bohemian performers and actors, including the avant-garde artist Marcel Duchamp (1887–1968), broke into the Washington Arch, located in Washington Square in Greenwich Village, lower Manhattan, New York. This group, who would be named by the artist and participant John Sloan as the 'Arch Conspirators', ascended the internal staircase of the monument, which was built in 1892 to mark the centennial of George Washington's inauguration. Atop the arch, this collective began celebrating their proclamation of a 'Free and Independent Republic of Washington Square'.[1] As cap guns were fired, lanterns lit and hot water bottles distributed, the group announced their declaration of autonomy, a document composed entirely of the word 'whereas'. This nonconformist venture went largely unnoticed by the residents of Washington Square, let alone the rest of the city. However, the gesture was not without meaning; the area of Greenwich Village was the home to an alternative society, not just in the performers and political radicals that inhabited the lower-cost housing, but also to the immigrant communities that had settled in New York over the preceding century.[2] In this context, Greenwich Village represented the city of New York in direct contrast to the wider continental United States; an island of 'another America' where expressions of place, belonging, identity and citizenship were far more fluid. This declaration must also be regarded in the context of the war that was at that moment raging on the battlefields of Europe, the Middle East and Africa. In a conflict fought for the preservation of the independent rights of small nations, a cause to which Woodrow Wilson, 28th President of the United States, would pledge his country's full support, the statement of a small group of artists and intellectuals can be seen to be reflective of the causes of the First World War.

The way in which this event was embedded in the conflict of 1914-1918 can be demonstrated in another mock attempted revolution which took place a year after the 'Arch Conspirators'. Ellis Jones, a journalist in the city, attempted to organise a 'Second American Revolution' in December 1918. Jones proclaimed that citizens were labouring under a union that offered 'dead liberty'. In response,

---

[1] J. Sloan, 1978. *New York Etchings*. Edited by Helen Farr Sloan. New York, NY: Dover.

[2] R. Wetzsteon, 2002. *Republic of Dreams: Greenwich Village, the American Bohemia, 1910–1960*. New York, NY: Simon and Schuster, pp. 2–3.

Jones called for a mass protest within the city, urging citizens to join together in Central Park to push forward for a new revolution. Whilst Jones perhaps meant his attempted putsch as a humorous stunt, it failed to attract widespread support from the populace. It did succeed in ensuring a strong police presence to meet the small crowd that gathered at Jones's request and who promptly arrested the ringleader for the public disturbance.[3] This full-forced reaction to a probable prank also reflected the impact that the First World War had upon the city. Fearful of the national agendas that were tearing apart the nations of Europe, the city authorities were sensitive to the threat of separatism as well as the possibility that such movements might be hijacked by radical political groups. These minor incidents reveal how a conflict thousands of miles away had an impact upon the lives of citizens and the operation of power within New York. In this manner, the conflict of 1914–1918 placed existing tensions within the city into greater focus and brought to light new concerns.

City of Greater New York: Origins and Development

Whilst the city of New York can trace its origins to the colonial outpost founded in the seventeenth century with its rapid industrial and demographic growth charted throughout the eighteenth and nineteenth century, the modern metropolis, however, was born at the cusp of the twentieth century.[4] In 1898, a new city emerged from the districts and municipalities that had grown up alongside the East River and the Hudson. The City of Greater New York encompassed the five boroughs of Manhattan, Brooklyn, Queens County, the Bronx and Staten Island (Figure 2.1).[5] This was a union that was demanded by the city's financial and mercantile class and executed by its politicians. The integrated city offered far greater opportunities for a controlled and ordered expansion from which profits could be derived from real estate speculation.[6] It also enabled an extension of control over the populace than had hitherto been possible. For city politicians, concerned with the task of reforming the city, socially, politically and materially, imposing order upon the ever-growing metropolis presented an unprecedented opportunity. This incorporation of the outlying boroughs into the city was in many ways the culmination of the processes that had fuelled New York's growth but had also questioned its status in the United States: mass immigration.

---

[3]   Ibid.

[4]   E.G. Burrows and M. Wallace, 1999. *Gotham: A History of New York City to 1898*. Oxford: Oxford University Press.

[5]   M. Ash, 1897. *The Greater New York Charter as Enacted in 1897*. Albany, NY: Weed-Parsons.

[6]   E. Graves, 1894. *Greater New York, Reasons Why*. New York, NY: H.A. Rost.

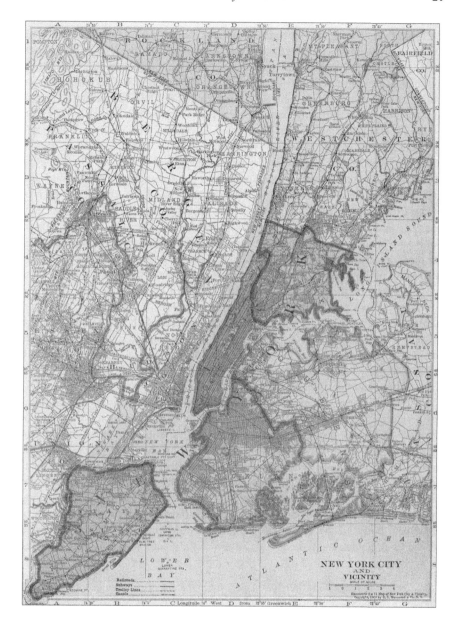

Figure 2.1   Map of the City of Greater New York, 1906. The five boroughs can be seen, with the island of Manhattan surrounded by the Bronx to the north-east, Queens to the east, Brooklyn to the south, and Staten Island to the south-west.

Source: C.S. Hammond and Company, 1906. *The Pictorial Atlas of the World*. New York, NY: C.S. Hammond.

From the early eighteenth century onwards, New York had served the United States as the nation's immigration hub.[7] From 1815 to the end of the 'open door' policy in 1920, the United States witnessed the arrival of over 30 million individuals seeking a new life in the republic. Of that total, over two thirds of those immigrants passed through the city of New York. Upon the transportation tickets of these émigrés would be the name of New York. The first experience of their new homeland would be the city on the Hudson River. On arrival, these individuals would disembark at the city's ports, where they would be processed and inspected. From the 1850s, Castle Garden, an early nineteenth-century military fort located at the southern tip of the island of Manhattan, had operated as the entrance point to the new world. After 1892, this control of immigration had passed to the full control of the federal authorities and migrants were assessed on Ellis Island, a specially built unit situated at the mouth of the Hudson River.[8] The shift of location was born out of necessity, and the sheer numbers of those seeking sanctuary ensured the development of the new site. The change was also the result of an increasing scepticism of the type of immigrant that the United States was attracting. Whereas the great wave of immigration from the 1840s had been fuelled from northern European nations and especially the German states, from the 1880s onwards a new flow of immigrants from Russia and southern Europe began to dominate the passenger lists of ships arriving in the city.[9] Eastern European Jewish communities fleeing the pogroms of Tsarist Russia or southern Italians, escaping the grinding poverty of rural Sicily, Campania, Puglia or Calabria constituted the bulk of that mass of humanity now filling the halls of Ellis Island.[10]

These new immigrant groups appeared to establish a challenge to the traditions of the nation that been set in place by the cultural and political dominance of northern European, largely protestant communities who had settled the interior of the continental United States. The unification of Germany in 1871 and the drawn-out unification of Italy between 1861 and 1871 had brought greater focus on national identity within the west. What constituted a nation, its people and its identity was the subject of concern for these newly formed states seeking the loyalty and support of a populace unaccustomed to defining themselves to a political body. In the United States, the Spanish-American War of 1898 had served to embolden the federal authority to make greater steps towards ensuring

---

[7]   This discussion has been developed from the materials provided by Fordham University. http://www.fordham.edu/academics/colleges_graduate_s/undergraduate_colleg/ fordham_college_at_l/special_programs/honors_program/hudsonfulton_celebra/homepage/ the_basics_of_nyc/immigration_32224.asp. Immigration in New York City, Fordham University Archives (accessed 11 April 2013).

[8]   N. Foner, 2000. *From Ellis Island to JFK: New York's Two Great Waves of Immigration.* New Haven, CT: Yale University Press.

[9]   R. Ernst, 1994. *Immigrant Life in New York City: 1825–1863.* Syracuse, NY: Syracuse University Press.

[10]   E. Aleandri, 2002. *Little Italy.* Charleston, SC: Arcadia Publishing.

a commitment of its diverse population towards the objectives of the state.[11] In its assumption of a world power status and the colonial possessions that victory over the Spanish Empire had brought, political leaders in Washington, DC were quick to herald the reinvigoration of the nation healing the divides of the Civil War.[12] However, the influx of Catholic Italians, Jewish Eastern Europeans and the possible arrival of political radicalism with these new groups was a source of deep concern. As such, the city of New York was placed under increasing suspicion. The majority of immigrants to the nation arrived in the metropolis and whilst a greater proportion of these individuals moved into the interior of the nation, many remained within the confines of what became the City of Greater New York. At the outset of the twentieth century, New York had come to represent both the hope and expectation of the nation as well as its deepest fears and presumed weaknesses.

The peculiar place that was held by the city was derived from its heterogeneous nature. In the federal censuses of 1890 and 1900, the metropolis's composition of a diversity of peoples was made clear. New York was undoubtedly a global city, but whether it was still an American city was a question that plagued both city politicians and national commentators. Within these surveys, respondents were asked questions regarding their country of birth, their naturalisation status and the length of time they had been resident in the country.[13] Federal auditors declared this inquiry entirely necessary and 'designed in part to afford ... a means for determining what proportion of the immigrants of each year or period of years had remained in the country'.[14] What these censuses did demonstrate was the unique qualities of New York as a city of unprecedented diversity and growth. By 1890, the city, before incorporation in 1898, was home to approximately two million individuals, from a population of little over 80,000 at the outset of the nineteenth century. It had been the steady flow of immigration which had enabled this dramatic increase. Indeed, the proportion of the descendants of late-eighteenth and early-nineteenth-century residents in the city declined during the nineteenth century.[15] It was this stream of new arrivals that ensured that by 1900, in the City of Greater New York, a population of a little under three and a half million was recorded in the census. Of this mass of people, an estimated 35 per cent were born outside of the United States. Any observer on the streets of Manhattan could observe the cosmopolitan nature of the borough; New York was undoubtedly an immigrant city (Figure 2.2).

---

[11]   P.T. McCartney, 2006. *Power and Progress: American National Identity, the War of 1898, and the Rise of American Imperialism*. Baton Rouge, LA: Louisiana State University Press.

[12]   V. Bouvier, 2001. *Whose America? The War of 1898 and the Battles to Define the Nation*. Westport, CT: Praeger.

[13]   I. Rosenwaike, 1972. *Population History of New York City*. Syracuse, NY: Syracuse University Press, p. 81.

[14]   Bureau of the Census, 1913. *Thirteenth Census of the United States Taken in the Year 1910*. Washington, DC: Government Printing Office, p. 215.

[15]   Rosenwaike, *Population History*, p. 92.

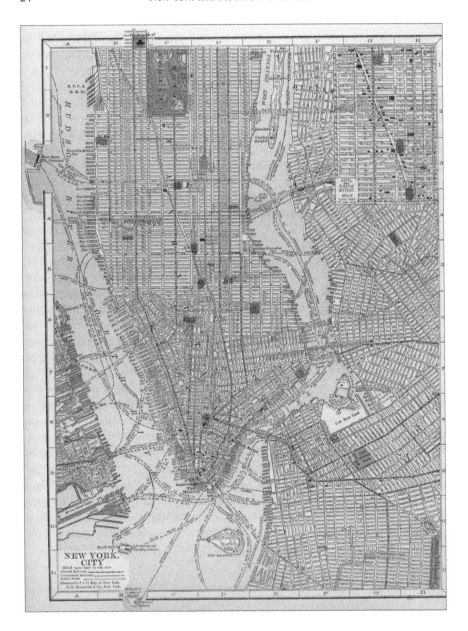

Figure 2.2   Map of Downtown Manhattan, 1906.

Source: C.S. Hammond and Company, 1906. *The Pictorial Atlas of the World*. New York, NY: C.S. Hammond.

The census records that required individuals to state their country of origin detailed how across the five boroughs, large enclaves from across Europe's ethnic and religious groups had been established. In 1900, New York City was home to over 300,000 residents born in Germany, 155,000 in Russia, 30,000 in Poland, 275,000 in Ireland, 145,000 in Italy, 117,000 from Austria-Hungary and 90,000 from Great Britain. With the movement of African Americans from the southern states after the Civil War, a population of over 60,000 resided within the boundaries of the metropolis. The city was also the residence of nearly 6,000 Chinese inhabitants, who had moved to New York from the 1840s onwards for employment opportunities and to escape the repressive measures placed upon their settlement on the west coast of the continental United States.[16] This diversity was reflected in the sounds, sights and smells of the city as definite communities were constructed in specific parts of Manhattan, the Bronx, Brooklyn and Queens, and Staten Island. The habits and lifestyles of immigrant groups were brought to the metropolis, which was increasingly taking on the appearance of a series of foreign towns, residing alongside one another with only the common dedication to their new homeland. However, it was this sense of allegiance which was questioned by those who witnessed the increasing diversity of life in New York.

A City of Many Communities

As the largest immigrant community, the German Americans were the most prominent.[17] On the Lower East Side, the German enclave, appropriately named Klein Deutschland, served as the centre of German life with bakeries, beer halls, butchers, Lutheran churches and German-language newspaper printers maintaining a strong cultural tie with the fatherland. The area occupied a substantial section of lower Manhattan, with its approximate borders being forged from Canal Street in the south, the Bowery in the West, 14th Street in the north, and the East River. Within this community, a newly arrived immigrant could quite easily acclimatise to their new home without experiencing the strain of a loss of connection to their previous life. Indeed, by 1850 the island of Manhattan could be considered the third largest 'German' city in the world after Berlin and Vienna, such was the extent of immigration into the metropolis. Politically, this community altered municipal politics, as the 10th, 11th, 13th and 17th electoral and administrative wards of the city were all within the area of 'Little Germany'.[18] Economically, this

[16] Bureau of the Census, 1902. *Abstract of the Twelfth Census of the United States, 1900.* Washington, DC: Government Printing Office, p. 107.

[17] C.T. Johnson, 1999. *Culture at Twilight: The National German–American Alliance, 1901–1918.* Frankfurt: Peter Lang.

[18] R. Haberstroh, 2014. Kleindeutschland: Little Germany in the Lower East Side. http://www.lespi-nyc.org/history/kleindeutschland-little-germany-in-the-lower-east-side.html (accessed 15 April 2013).

area was vitally important for the progression of this immigrant group with a range of German businesses centred on Tompkins Square, alongside Avenue B. This part of the neighbourhood was densely occupied by businesses of varying sizes and trades, each benefiting from the proximity of a German population desiring to purchase goods and services both familiar and familial. Every available space in the street was turned over to enterprise, with entire buildings reused to blur the lines of home and business; basements became workshops, ground floors were turned into shops to display wares, whilst the pavements outside served as a marketplace in which to buy, sell and haggle.[19] It was these developments that were frequently remarked upon by visitors and commentators as enabling the transition from resident alien to citizen, as they demonstrated the appropriate qualities for life in the republic:

> They are always endeavouring to improve their condition; and, from their constant self-seeking, they soon acquire property, carefully educate their children, ally their descendants to those of Anglo-Saxon blood, and in a few generations become as thoroughly American as the Americans themselves.[20]

German bankers and businessmen established prominent institutions in the city. The Ottman Lithographic Company, owned and operated by German immigrants, located just outside the main area of Little Germany, on Houston and Lafayette Street, provided the images for the satirical magazine *Puck* from the 1870s. The publication, originally released only in English, was also printed in German after the involvement of the Ottman Lithographic Company to cater for the tastes of the populace on its doorstep.[21] Similarly, the Germania Bank, created by German American investors in the late 1860s, placed its headquarters on the Bowery, benefiting from the financial arrangements that were developed with the German shops and businesses along the street. Nicholas Muller (1836–1917), the son of German immigrants, was one of the directors of the bank, promoting its growth as he also served as the Congressman for the 6th District, composed of the 11th and 17th wards of Klein Deutschland. The offices of the newspaper *New Yorker Staats-Zeitung* were also an integral part of this community. Located just south of the German enclave, on Chatham Street near City Hall, the newspaper's premises appeared to demonstrate the significance of the German community, close to the centre of city politics and adjacent to their audience. Oswald Ottendoerfer (1826–1900), a Sudeten German who managed the paper from the 1850s, reinvested the profits from sales into charitable organisations for the German American

---

[19]   S. Nadel, 1990. *Little Germany: Ethnicity, Religion, and Class in New York City, 1845–1880.* Urbana, IL: University of Illinois Press.

[20]   J.H. Browne, 1869. *The Great Metropolis: A Mirror of New York.* Hartford, CT: American Publishing Company, p. 166.

[21]   F.L. Mott, 1938. *A History of American Magazines, Vol. III: 1865–1885.* Oxford: Oxford University Press, pp. 521–2.

community. These profits were substantial, as this German-language paper had by the late 1880s become one of the most popular dailies in the city with an established readership amongst the German immigrants of Manhattan and a daily circulation of approximately 60,000.[22]

The success of some sections of the German American community could not overshadow the fortunes of many of their compatriots; their experiences of immigration did not bring the same level of economic or political success. Whilst the support of a German-speaking community offered employment opportunities, there was no guarantee that a secure livelihood could be found. Casper Stürenburg (1843–1909), who emigrated from Germany in 1868, recorded the harsh life of many who lived within Klein Deutschland in the late nineteenth century.[23] Originally published in the *New York Staats-Zeitung*, Stürenburg's reports detailed the privations and difficulties in the area. Stürenburg also described the issues some recently arrived German Americans faced in acclimatising both to the cultural and material life of their adopted homeland:

> "In America, they ask for such superfluous things, no human soul!" In these comfortable thoughts the women I spoke to could be divided into two. Those who moved and those who moved often. The atmosphere of the tenement houses will be fatal to such natures.[24]

The 'atmosphere of the tenement houses' certainly impacted upon the experiences of the lower classes of the German American population of New York. The area of Lower East Side, where Klein Deutschland was situated, was by far the most densely populated part of the entire metropolis. In 1890, the population density (number of people per square mile), was recorded as 57,596 for the 10th ward, 75,426 for the 11th ward, 45,834 for the 13th ward and 103,158 for the 17th ward.[25] The sheer conglomeration of humanity that dwelt within this section of the city posed innumerable problems for both the inhabitants and for the politicians seeking to govern this community.

It was not just the German community that occupied this increasingly crowded space in the city. Increasingly, southern Italian and eastern European Jewish communities were settling in the Lower East Side, as the potential for cheap housing attracted a new wave of immigrants to this part of Manhattan. These communities

---

[22] New Yorker Staatszeitung, 1997. History of a New York City Institution. http://www.germancorner.com/NYStaatsZ/history.html (accessed 12 February 2012).

[23] J. Koegel, 2009. *Music in German Immigrant Theater: New York City, 1840–1940.* Rochester, NY: University of Rochester Press, p. 512.

[24] C. Stürenburg, 1886. *Klein-Deutschland: Bilder aus dem New Yorker Alltagsleben.* New York, NY: E. Steiger Company, p. 95.

[25] Bureau of the Census, 1894. *Vital Statistics of New York City and Brooklyn: Covering a Period of Six Years Ending May 31, 1890.* Washington, DC: Government Printing Office, p. 230.

were regarded with far more suspicion by city and federal authorities as their ability to assimilate into the 'American way of life' as easily as their German American predecessors was fiercely debated. As the more prosperous members of the German American community moved to the growing suburbs in Brooklyn and Queens, eastern European Jewish immigrants took their place in the tenement housing. This immigrant group, many escaping from the pogroms of Tsarist Russia, maintained strong cultural, religious and economic ties within the community. Indeed, the Lower East Side proved to be a point where the Jewish diaspora was united:

> It is one of the most densely populated spots on the face of the earth – a seething human sea fed by streams, streamlets, and rills of immigration flowing from all the Yiddish-speaking centres of Europe. Hardly a block but shelters Jews from every nook and corner of Russia, Poland, Galicia, Hungary, Romania; Lithuanian Jews, Volhynian Jews, south Russian Jews, Bessarabian Jews …[26]

Synagogues and charitable associations in the city were prominent in acclimatising emigrants to their new homeland. For example, the Hebrew Benevolent Society, the Young Men's Hebrew Association or the United Hebrew Charities all worked to provide shelter and provisions for German Jewish families from the 1840s onwards.[27] However, by the 1880s they were also providing for the largely Yiddish-speaking Russian and Polish Jewish individuals and families. Such organisations also fostered stronger links, as fundraising initiatives brought a community together. Jewish shops and businesses, serving the needs and tastes of the inhabitants of the area, also began to thrive in these conditions. Jewish immigrant authors, theatres and publishers flourished in this environment as cultural life within the city was able to benefit from the increasing Jewish presence in New York. From the 1850s, the daily newspapers of the *Jewish Messenger*, the *Jewish Times* and the *American Hebrew* provided a conservative voice for this developing American Jewish community. However, these voices were increasingly challenged by the development of a politically active element within the city's Jewish residents. Having fled persecution and repression in Europe, radical, socialist and anarchist groups, now free to hold political assembly in the United States, began promoting their views. Sympathetic newspapers such as the Yiddish-language, socialist daily *Forverts* (*Forward*), published from the late 1890s, began to attract a much wider readership within the tenements of the Lower East Side.[28] This publication followed from the previous Yiddish-

---

[26]   A. Cahan, 1896. *Yekl: A Tale of the New York Ghetto.* New York, NY: D. Appleton and Company, p. 28.

[27]   N. Kaganoff, 1986. The Jewish Landsmanshaftn in New York before World War I. *American Jewish History* 76, 56–67; N. Kaganoff, 1966. Organized Jewish Welfare Activity in New York City, 1848–1860. *American Jewish Historical Quarterly* 5, 27–61.

[28]   R.E. Park, 1922. *The Immigrant Press and Its Control.* New York, NY: Harper and Brothers, p. 89.

language radical newspapers, *Di Arbeter Tsaytung* (*The Workman's Paper*), *Di Nyu Yorker Yidishe Folkstsaytung* (*The New York Yiddish Peoples' Newspaper*) and *Di Varhayt* (*The Truth*). Immigrant Jewish American socialists from New York, such as author and editor of the Yiddish newspaper *Forverts*, Abraham Cahan (1860–1951), and labour lawyer and politician Morris Hillquits (1869–1933) promoted the socialist cause within their community.[29]

The degree of sympathy that such socialist politics evoked within the Jewish émigré population in New York was conditioned by the experience of immigration which had placed a large section of low-skilled men, women and children within the exploitative workshops which were part of the city's economy.[30] Jewish women in particular formed a substantial part of the working population in the city's highly profitable but poorly governed garment industry. Unsafe working conditions, long hours and low wages fuelled the development of a strong trade union movement within the Jewish community which found support in newspapers such as *Forverts*. For example, the development of labour organisations, which were aided by industrial action in the 1890s that secured union rights for employees, provided a platform for the development of the International Ladies' Garment Workers' Union (ILGWU) in 1900.[31] Led by committed socialists, largely from the Jewish immigrant community in the city, such as Clara Lemlich Shavelson (1886–1982), the ILGWU led a successful strike action both in 1909 and in 1910, which brought a greater degree of accountability from employers with regard to their treatment of workers. In this manner, politics, religion and culture were fused in a demonstration of the ideas and values of this section of the immigrant Jewish community.[32]

Whether as a result of this political activism, religious difference or ingrained anti-Semitism, the Jewish community of the Lower East Side were frequently portrayed as corrupt, untrustworthy and dangerously 'un-American' by some sections of the city's populace. The Jewish community of New York were, therefore, regarded in contrast to their German Protestant predecessors, as not of

[29]   T. Michels, 2002. *A Fire in Their Hearts: Yiddish Socialists in New York*. Cambridge, MA: Harvard University Press, p. 3.

[30]   D. Katz, 2011. *All Together Different: Yiddish Socialists, Garment Workers, and the Labor Roots of Multiculturalism*. New York, NY: New York University Press; D. Soyer, 1997. *Jewish Immigrant Associations and American Identity in New York, 1880–1939*. Detroit, MI: Wayne State University Press.

[31]   L. Levine, 1924. *The Women's Garment Workers: A History of the International Garment Workers' Union*. New York, NY: Huebsch, pp. 120–25.

[32]   Hadassa Kosak, 2009. *Cultures of Opposition: Jewish Immigrant Workers, New York City, 1881–1905*. Albany, NY: State University of New York Press, p. 2; Annelise Orleck, 1995. *Common Sense and a Little Fire: Women and Working-Class Politics in the United States, 1900–1965*. Chapel Hill, NC: University of North Carolina Press, pp. 4–5.

a 'natural' line of immigration into the American continent.[33] Despite the efforts of many new arrivals to endear themselves to their new nation, commentators regarded the eastern European Jewish community as too different to be incorporated into the republic. This was not an outright objection, but that the mores and habits of this immigrant group were not immediately translatable into American traditions. In time, perhaps these differences could be ameliorated, but this was a process in which Jewish communities would have to abandon distinctive practices to become 'American'.[34] This process was challenged somewhat by the flourishing Yiddish theatre movement within the city, where dramas depicting the life of the immigrant family and their adjustment to their new life within the context of established traditions were a frequent occurrence.[35] Within these theatres, popular song writers plied their trade, fusing Yiddish lyrics with uplifting anthems that promoted patriotic ideals towards the United States. Examples such as 'Leben Zol Amerika' ('Long Live America') or 'Zei gebensht Du Freie Land' ('Long Live the Land of the Free') revealed a far more complex construction of identity than a simplistic demand for assimilation.[36]

However, such a blending of traditions was not demanded by some within the community, perhaps demonstrated by the Jewish British playwright Israel Zangwill's *The Melting Pot*.[37] The drama is set in New York and follows the fortunes of an immigrant Jewish family as their son proclaims America to be the place where former associations are renounced and everyone is remade in the same image. Aside from this idealised position, what existed within the recent émigré Russian and Polish Jewish communities in the Lower East Side was an ongoing process of adjustment. A situation exemplified in the self-help literature designed to assist the immigrant such as the New York published *Harkavy's Amerikanisher Briefenshteler* (*Harkavy's American Letter Writer*).[38] Within this guide, the Yiddish-speaking immigrant is provided with models in

---

[33]   G. Ribak, 2012a. *Gentile New York: The Images of Non-Jews among Jewish Immigrants*. Piscataway, NJ: Rutgers University Press, p. 3.

[34]   H. Szold, 1904. Elements of the Jewish Population in the United States. In C.S. Bernheimer (ed.), *The Russian Jew in the United States*. Philadelphia, PA: J.C. Winston Co., pp. 9–17.

[35]   S. Haenni, 2008. *The Immigrant Scene: Ethnic Amusements in New York, 1880–1920*. Minneapolis, MN: University of Minnesota Press, pp. 95–7.

[36]   L. Rosenberg and M. Rubinstein, 1909. *Leben Zol Amerika*. New York, NY: A. Tores; S. Smulewitz and J.M. Rumshisky, 1911. *Zei gebensht Du Freie Land*. New York, NY: Hebrew Publishing Company; Library of Congress, 2004. *From Haven to Home: 350 Years of Jewish Life in America: A Century of Immigration, 1820–1924*. http://www.loc.gov/exhibits/haventohome/haven-century.html (accessed 14 March 2014).

[37]   I. Zangwill, 1909. *The Melting Pot*. New York, NY: The Jewish American Book Company.

[38]   A. Harkavy, 1902. *Harkavy's Amerikanisher Briefenshteler*. New York: Hebrew Publishing Co.

both their native tongue and in English to guide the learning process and enable their communication with others in their new homeland. Tellingly, the majority of these examples are obtained from the business world, demonstrating the requirement to secure employment, to sustain an income and to adjust to life within the city.[39]

The Italian community held a similarly suspect place within the city.[40] The majority of Italian immigration into the United States after 1840 had been from the poorer, rural southern regions and new arrivals were frequently unskilled, occasionally illiterate manual labourers with large families. The scale of immigration from these areas was substantial, increasing to 340,765 residents born in Italy and living in the city by 1910. Indeed, Italian immigrants were the majority ethnic group in the 14th Ward in Manhattan.[41] The explosion in this population ensured the development of a number of distinctive Italian American communities in the city.[42] The earliest and the largest enclave focused upon the Mulberry Bend area of the city, close to workshops and factories, to the south-west of Klein Deutschland in Lower Manhattan.[43] This area of dense, poor quality housing, served to reflect ideas about this emigrant group as an ungovernable mass, increasing in number and prone to criminal activity.[44] In this sense, the Italian immigrant group was regarded as ultimately impossible to incorporate into the wider nation, culturally or indeed racially.[45] The Welsh American scholar Thomas Jesse Jones (1873–1950) described this situation in his study, *The Sociology of a New York City Block*:

> At present there is not another nationality in New York City so given to aggregation as the Italian. For this reason there is scarcely another nationality that so thoroughly stamps as foreign the district which it occupies … This fact, together with their brief period of residence in America and their continual association with one another, results in much ignorance of American ways and manners.[46]

---

[39]   Katz, D. (ed.) 1988. *Yiddish English Hebrew Dictionary.* New York, NY: Schocken Books, pp. 6–23.

[40]   C. Cianfarra, 1904. *Il diario di un emigrato.* New York, NY: Tipografia dell'Araldo Italiano.

[41]   C.A. Beard, 1913. *Municipal Year Book of the City of New York.* New York, NY: J.W. Pratt Co., p. 171.

[42]   D. Ward, 1989. *Poverty, Ethnicity and the American City, 1840–1925: Changing Conceptions of the Slum and Ghetto.* Cambridge: Cambridge University Press.

[43]   M.A. Jones, 1992. *American Immigration.* Second Edition. Chicago, IL: University of Chicago Press, p. 191.

[44]   E.A. Steiner, 1906. *On the Trail of the Immigrant.* New York, NY: Fleming H. Revell Company, p. 271.

[45]   E.A. Ross, 1914. *The Old World in the New.* New York, NY: The Century Co.

[46]   T.J. Jones, 1904. *The Sociology of a New York City Block.* New York, NY: Columbia University Press, p. 323.

Such perceptions misinterpreted the way in which Italian émigré communities imported kinship networks onto the geography of their new homeland.[47] Families from the same regions, towns and villages frequently lodged together, maintaining bonds and associations that resulted in entire tenement blocks or series of blocks being inhabited by individuals tied to one another by blood, marriage or culture. Therefore, the denotation 'Little Italy' was more than a description of the inhabitants but a means to portray the wholesale difference that was experienced within this area. Within these close communities in the city, a vibrant cultural and political life was formed. Italian theatre, literature and newspapers provided this immigrant community with a means to sustain their ties and promote businesses and political representatives within the metropolis. The Italian-language New York dailies, *L'Eco D'Italia*, published from 1850, and *Il Progresso Italo-Americano*, published from 1880, provided a forum for forwarding Italian American agendas within the city. This work was assisted by organisations such as the L'Ordine Figli d'Italia in America (The Order of the Sons of Italy in America), which was founded in New York's Little Italy in 1905.[48] This collective sought to raise funds for poorer members of the community, assist recently arrived immigrants and assist in demonstrating the place and value of the Italian American in the institutions of the United States.[49]

Such close associations within the immigrant group gave further rise to the concerns that within Italian American enclaves a burgeoning organised crime network was fostered. This served to exacerbate the negative perception of the émigré group within the city as a whole, a situation which was not assisted by the association between Italian immigrants and political radicalism. Socialist and anarchist Italian migrants promoted change in the political system within the United States and within New York, particularly where the disparity between rich and poor seemed to grow evermore apparent.[50] Italian socialist organisations were founded in the 1890s as *circoli operai* (workers circles), which challenged the operation of *padrones* as well as the exploitative labour bosses in the city. Socialist and anarchist newspapers such as *Il Proletario* (*The Proletariat*) or *Il Grido degli Oppressi* (*The Cry of the Oppressed*), published in New York, advocated the communal ownership of private property, the removal of landlords and the promotion of labour activism.[51]

---

[47]   E. Lord, 1905. *The Italian in America*. New York, NY. B.F. Buck, p. 66.

[48]   O. Øverland, 2000. *Immigrant Minds, American Identities: Making the United States Home, 1870–1930*. Champaign, IL: University of Illinois Press, p. 34.

[49]   B. Aquilano, 1925. *L'Ordine Figli d'Italia in America*. New York, NY: Societa Tipografica Italiana.

[50]   M. Bencivenni. 2011. *Italian Immigrant Radical Culture: The Idealism of the Sovversivi in the United States, 1890–1940*. New York, NY: New York University Press.

[51]   J. Guglielmo, 2010. *Living the Revolution: Italian Women's Resistance and Radicalism in New York City, 1880–1945*. Chapel Hill, NC: University of North Carolina Press.

The political effect of immigrant groups is perhaps best demonstrated with the prominence associated with the Irish community within the municipal political scene after 1850. Indeed, the high number of immigrants fleeing starvation and economic desperation that arrived in the port from Ireland ensured that by the end of the nineteenth century, the Irish vote provided a strong political representation in the city. This was reflected in the dominance of Tammany Hall which, after the mid-nineteenth century, organised the Democratic Party nominations and dominated the city's mayoral elections.[52] However, successive scandals had reduced the power of this party machine after the 1870s. The election of John Purroy Mitchel (1879–1918) as New York Mayor in 1913 as an anti-Tammany candidate demonstrated its decline. However, whilst Tammany Hall politicians were concerned with the acquisition of power and wealth, they also fostered Irish Republican sympathies. The Fenian Brotherhood was inaugurated outside Tammany Hall, near Union Square, in 1858, and dedicated itself to 'wrest the liberties of our country from her oppressors'.[53] This idealism led to the failed Fenian Raids on British Canada by Irish Americans from 1866 to 1870 to force the issue of Irish independence. It also saw the creation of the other pro-independence movements such as *Clan na Gael*, which supported Irish immigration and the development of national consciousness amongst Irish Americans. Therefore, the promotion of anti-British, Republican sentiment was strong in the city and facilitated through an array of newspapers and periodicals, some of which were printed in Gaelic. *The Irish News*, *The Irish-American* and the *Gaelic American* succeeded in bringing awareness of the Irish Diaspora in New York to the issues and concerns of Irish Republicanism.

Greater political representation was also sought by minority elements of New York within the municipality itself. The African American community in the city was relatively small compared to other ethnic groups, perhaps borne out of the attacks suffered by African Americans 40 years previously. Indeed, at the outset of the twentieth century, the memory of the Draft Riots of 1863 was still present. During this event, rioters had sought out African Americans to take reprisal against the imposition of conscription to assist in the war against the Confederacy. Over a hundred individuals were killed in this attack on the city's African American populace and its legacy was one of separation and fear. Although segregation was not an official policy, African American schools, churches and public meeting places ensured prominent enclaves within the city. With a comparatively small population of approximately 60,000, equating to nearly two per cent of the population of the city, representation to forward the cause of African Americans was thwarted by the power of Tammany Hall. Organisations such as the Afro-American League (1889) and the Afro-American Council (1898) all called for

---

[52]   W.C. Gover, 1875. *The Tammany Hall Democracy of the City of New York: And the General Committee for 1875, Being a Brief History of the Tammany Hall Democracy from 1834 to the Present Time*. New York, NY: M.B. Brown.

[53]   J. O'Neil and J. Savage, 1868. *To the State Centres, Centres of Circle and Members of the Fenian Brotherhood*. New York, NY: s.n.

racial solidarity and the promotion of self-sufficiency within the community.[54] The newspapers serving the metropolis's African American populace, the *New York Age* and the *New York Amsterdam News*, promoted agendas of change in the city and attempted to harness support towards greater political representation. However, racial tensions within New York can be evidenced with the outbreak of rioting in August 1900, when African American citizens were attacked after the death of a white police officer.[55] In the aftermath of the violence, with rumours of police and political conspiracy, the Citizens' Protective League was formed to 'afford mutual protection' to African American New Yorkers.[56]

For some commentators this diversity meant the city at the outset of the twentieth century appeared overwhelmingly divided. Indeed, its assessment as a 'modern Babel' reflected this fragmentation. Approximately 20 per cent of the city's population possessed English as a native tongue. Yiddish formed the first language for 19 per cent of the city, whilst German constituted the other major linguistic group with 18 per cent of New Yorkers speaking it as an arterial language. Increasingly, New York seemed to bear the appearance of a series of unfamiliar and insular communities which served to prevent the integration of minority populations; as activist Mary White Ovington (1865–1951) observed in her study of the status of African Americans in the metropolis:

> I suspect that to many Europeans New York seems still a great overgrown village in "a nation of villagers," pronouncing with narrow, dogmatic assurance upon the deep unsolved problems of life.[57]

In the city of immigrants, the issue of whether foreign-born individuals were 'Aliens or Americans' evoked deep concern across society as the nature of identity within the city and the nation were brought to the fore.[58] How far New York and its diverse residents could claim to be American was increasingly questioned.

The Fear of the City and its Reform

At the outset of the twentieth century, the city occupied a suspect place within the wider continental United States. It was seemingly a city populated by foreigners,

---

[54] S.L. Alexander, 2012. *An Army of Lions: The Civil Rights Struggle Before the NAACP*. Philadelphia, PA: University of Pennsylvania Press.

[55] A. Lorini, 1999. *Rituals of Race: American Public Culture and the Search for Racial Democracy*. Charlottesville, VA: University Press of Virginia, p. 173.

[56] Citizens' Protective League of New York, 1900. *Story of the Riot*. New York, NY: Arno Press.

[57] M.W. Ovington, 1911. *Half a Man: The Status of the Negro in New York*. New York, NY: Longmans, Green and Co., p. 227.

[58] H.B. Grose, 1906. *Aliens or Americans*. New York, NY: Young People's Missionary Movement.

without the requisite 'American' singular identity; the residents of New York were seemingly tied to their previous homelands, cultures, religions and possibly possessing radical political sympathies which could unsettle the Republic. Such was the potential disruption that was assumed to emanate from the city that New York became the subject of a body of literature, novels and travelogues that were published in an attempt to explain the metropolis to the wider nation. These accounts could sensationalise the vice and vivacity of the city, emphasise the fundamental 'otherness' of the population of the municipality or condemn New York and its citizens for their presumed laxity in cementing themselves to the values of the United States. Accounts such as George Foster's *New York in Slices: By an Experienced Carver*, or *New York by Gas-Light and Other Urban Sketches*, focused on the oddities of the city to attract outside interest and thereby reaffirm their suspicions of the peculiarity of New York.[59] Similar works expressed a fascination with the cosmopolitan nature of the metropolis, focusing on the salubrious aspects of existence within the city and thereby reaffirming the concept of New York as a foreign island within the United States.[60] In these accounts, it was the alien character of the city and its residents that were the causes of the ills of New York:

> Upon the foundation of ignorance and helplessness found in this diversity of population, constantly fed by arriving emigrants, all that we have of turbulence, poverty, vice and crime has been reared … we have this diversity of races, this constant influx of poverty and ignorance to thank for it.[61]

However, this dire set of circumstances, frequently characterised as an 'illness' or 'malaise' which was perceived to beset the city was not without an apparent remedy. From the 1890s onwards, politicians and reformers within the city worked to alleviate the consequences of unrestricted capitalism and immigration in New York which had cast many into penury. Progressive politics sought to remake the city, clear the slums, such as those within the Lower East Side, provide sanitation and health services to prevent the spread of diseases within the densely populated areas and educate the inhabitants of the city, many of whom lacked English language skills.[62] The need for reform was highlighted most famously by

---

[59]   G. Foster, 1849. *New York in Slices: By an Experienced Carver*. New York, NY: W.F. Burgess; G. Foster, 1850. *New York by Gas-Light and Other Urban Sketches*. New York, NY: DeWitt and Davenport.

[60]   J. McCabe, 1882. *New York by Sunlight and Gaslight: A Work Descriptive of the Great American Metropolis*. Philadelphia, PA: Douglass Brothers; M.H. Smith, 1868. *Sunshine and Shadow in New York*. Hartford, CN: J.B. Burr and Co; M.B. Booth, 1891. *New York's Inferno Explored: Scenes Full of Pathos Powerfully Portrayed*. New York, NY: Salvation Army.

[61]   E. Crapsey, 1872. *The Nether Side of New York; or, The Vice, Crime and Poverty of the Great Metropolis*. New York, NY: Sheldon and Company, p. 6–7.

[62]   D.E. Burnstein, 2006. *Next to Godliness: Confronting Dirt and Despair in Progressive Era New York City*. Urbana, IL: University of Illinois Press; J.L. Recchiuti,

the work of the investigative journalist Jacob Riis (1849–1914). In his account of the destitute of the city, *How the Other Half Lives* (1890), Riis details the appalling conditions endured by the city's immigrant communities and the parlous state of many districts within New York. Within this exposé is also a commentary for the concerned middle classes that the city's identity as 'American' was being gradually diluted by successive waves of immigration without integration into society:

> One may find for the asking an Italian, a German, a French, African, Spanish, Bohemian, Russian, Scandinavian, Jewish, and Chinese colony. Even the Arab, who peddles "holy earth" from the Battery as a direct importation from Jerusalem, has his exclusive preserves at the lower end of Washington Street. The one thing you shall vainly ask for in the chief city of America is a distinctively American community. There is none; certainly not among the tenements.[63]

Motivated by Riis' characterisation of New York's destitute populations as a foreign mass of potential malcontents divorced from American society by the forces of capitalism, reform movements within the city attempted to alleviate the symptoms of poverty whilst ordering and reshaping the populace.[64] Where this programme was most apparent was within the campaign to reform the high-density tenement housing of the Lower East Side.[65] In this area, long dominated by successive migrant communities seeking low-cost housing and the support of kinsfolk, the threat to American society was seemingly palpable through ignorance, vice and despair.[66] To survey the conditions of habitation within the city, the Tenement House Committee of the Charity Organization was formed in 1900 and ran a series of exhibits which demonstrated not only the social and health problems caused by the poor quality housing but the heterogeneity of the area's population. Surveys carried out across New York in the early 1890s for the state legislature had also revealed the diverse composition of the city. The results of these inquiries were published as cartographic evidence for wider public perusal by the magazine *Harper's Weekly*.[67] Within these maps, the varied nationalities of the migrant city were plotted out for assessment, by colour and cross-hatch,

---

2007. *Civic Engagement: Social Science and Progressive Era Reform in New York.* Philadelphia, PA: University of Pennsylvania Press.

[63]   J. Riis, 1890. *How the Other Half Lives*. New York, NY: Charles Scribner's Sons.

[64]   B.P. De Witt, 1915. *The Progressive Movement: A Non-Partisan, Comprehensive Discussion of Current Tendencies in American Politics*. New York, NY: The Macmillan Company, p. 343–4.

[65]   L. Veiller, 1900. *Tenement House Reform in New York, 1834–1900*. New York, NY: Evening Post Job Printing House.

[66]   R.W. DeForest and L. Veiller, 1903. *The Tenement House Problem: Including the Report of the New York State Tenement House Commission of 1900*. Cambridge, MA: Harvard University Press, p. 10.

[67]   *Harper's Weekly*, January 19, 1895; Blake, *How New York Became American*, p. 33.

enabling the audience to draw conclusions regarding the relationship between poverty and ethnicity. The development of ethnic enclaves within New York was thereby presented as a scientific and quantifiable element. The diversity of the city was assessed as a problem alongside the issues of sanitation, health and housing. In this manner, it was rendered into a solvable conundrum, a difficulty to be remedied and a 'disease' which could be cured. The quandary of New York, its status as a city composed of 'foreign villages' and its lack of apparent connection to the wider nation became an object for reformers.

Education, housing, sanitation, fire and police reforms reshaped the city from the 1890s onwards as campaigners and charitable organisations sought to turn 'Aliens' into 'Americans'. Despite these efforts, the fear that immigrants and their children were not properly inculcated into the values of their adopted homeland was an ever present feature of social and political life within the metropolis at the beginning of the twentieth century. To reinforce the 'self-evident' tenets of the United States, of life, liberty and the pursuit of happiness, and to inform the disparate population of their responsibilities, a range of public programmes were initiated. This included large-scale celebrations of American history and culture as a means of developing these values within a diverse body politic. One of the most prominent of these was the Hudson-Fulton Celebration of 1909, which was designed to commemorate both the discovery of Manhattan in 1609 by Henry Hudson and the successful operation of the steamboat by Robert Fulton in 1809.[68] The event, first mooted in 1902, was supported by some of the wealthiest industrialists, bankers and retailers in the city, including Andrew Carnegie (1835–1919), J.P. Morgan (1837–1913) and Isidor Strauss (1845–1912). The Hudson-Fulton Celebration Commission met regularly from 1906 and set to work on an event which would arouse civic pride and enthusiasm.[69] From its outset the event was designed to be 'educational' rather than 'commercial', serving to instruct the city's population in the origins of the metropolis and their place within this 'American' narrative:

> It requires but little reflection to perceive the great value of acquainting our adopted citizens with the fact that we have a body of worthy traditions and attaching them to those traditions. The power of tradition has been one of the most fundamental and conservative forces of all peoples of all times ... a people naturally tends to follow the impulses of the past and to adhere to tradition unless turned therefrom by other influences. Therefore the ingrained history of a nation, which in a broad sense we call tradition, serves as a balance wheel, tending to

---

[68]   Hudson-Fulton Celebration Commission 1905. *Official Minutes of the Hudson-Fulton Celebration Commission, Together with the Minutes of its Predecessor, The Hudson Tercentenary Joint Committee.* Albany, NY: J.B. Lyon; Lorini, *Rituals of Peace*, pp. 208–12.

[69]   Hudson-Fulton Celebration Commission 1909. *Historical Pageant: Hudson-Fulton Celebration, September 25 to October 9, 1909.* New York, NY: Redfield.

restrain sudden and spasmodic departures from the normal mode of progress. Historical culture thus materially promotes the welfare of the Commonwealth.[70]

This sense of history which would bind the population together, make it more homogenous and enable those who had adopted American citizenship to assume the traditions and values of the nation was demonstrated through reconstructions, flotillas and parades from 25 September to 9 October. The historical parade, including specially-commissioned floats, detailing the various stages of the city's history, was a significant part of this educational process to impress clearly upon the minds of spectators. This was undertaken with the support and assistance of some immigrant groups within the city, desiring to state their own connections and prominent place within their adopted nation. Indeed, Herman Ridder (1851–1915), editor of the *New Yorker Staats-Zeitung* and a child of German immigrants, significantly contributed to the organisation of the celebration as a demonstration of his 'American' values.[71] The Hudson-Fulton Celebration attempted to achieve what other social reforms also aspired towards; an amelioration of the differences within the city.

Conclusions

The tensions and concerns regarding the status of New York and the identity of its citizens would be exacerbated by the events after August 1914. What had once been an issue for debate in the provision of housing, education, sanitary reform and public celebration, now became of vital importance for municipal and national security. The ideals and values of New York's citizens would be of considerable significance in guiding the metropolis and the wider nation through the difficulties of wartime. The city, therefore, occupies a unique place within the United States when considering the history of the war of 1914–1918. Its constitution, peopled by various communities, ensured that it faced the conditions wrought by war in a manner quite unlike any other metropolis. On the eve of war, New York was a city divided. Its disparate populace had created distinct areas for themselves, fostering links, cultural connections and economic networks which established their presence within districts of Manhattan, Brooklyn, Queens, Bronx and Staten Island. The success with which populations had carved out a place for themselves in their new homeland was tempered by an ever-increasing fear that this influx of migrants had diluted the sense of 'American' identity within the city. Émigré

---

[70] Hudson-Fulton Celebration Commission 1910a. *The Fourth Annual Report of the Hudson-Fulton Celebration Commission to the Legislature of the State of New York.* Albany, NY: J.B. Lyon, p. 4.

[71] Hudson-Fulton Celebration Commission, 1910b. *Testimonials of Appreciation to Herman Ridder, Acting President and Henry W. Sackett, Secretary of the Hudson-Fulton Celebration Commission, March, 1910.* New York, NY: The De Vinne Press.

groups were viewed with suspicion as previous allegiances to other nations, cultures and religions were regarded as a barrier to assimilation.

The majority of these migrants had arrived from a European continent which after August 1914 was engulfed in a conflict largely born and sustained from national and ethnic division and competition. In such conditions, the alarm evoked at the consideration of a potential spread of this violence to the United States was palpable and it was the streets and communities of New York where this eruption was considered most likely. A city which had been viewed as suspect, as 'un-American', as harbouring potentially dangerous political and social agendas, was now cast as the entry point for a war which quickly appeared all-consuming, as nations, colonies and dependencies attached themselves to the Entente of Britain, France and Russia or the Central Powers of Germany and Austria-Hungary. In New York, the associations, charities, newspapers and networks established by immigrant groups would communicate this conflict in Europe to audiences whose loyalty was questioned both within their own communities and by an anxious civic and national government in the United States. In this respect, the First World War in New York marks the advent of the modern city, where citizenship was defined and policed within the metropolis.

Chapter 3
The Outbreak of Conflict

General opinion here connects the assassins with the Servian faction, and it is feared that it will lead to serious complications with that unruly kingdom, and may have far-reaching results. The future of the empire is a subject of general discussion. It is felt that the Servians have been treated too leniently, and some hard words are being said about the present foreign policy. All the public buildings are draped in long black streamers and the flags are all at half-mast.[1]

Introduction

The scenes described in the above quotation report on the city of Vienna after its residents had received the news of the events in the Balkans on 28 June 1914. It demonstrates the ways in which the conflict of 1914–1918 began to draw in communities into the war. Towns and cities that were physically removed from the fighting were nevertheless mobilised for the war effort. Each of these locales formed their own relationship to the conflict, finding meaning, values and associations in the conditions wrought by the clash of nation states. Indeed, despite the distance, the city of New York was enmeshed in the politics and processes that took place across Europe from June 1914. This reflected the metropolis's unique constitution as a hub for industry, politics and immigrants, and also ensured that its response to the developments that emanated from the Balkans demonstrated the intimate relationship between the war and the city from the very beginning.

The Murder in Sarajevo: The Response of New York

The announcement of the assassination of Archduke Franz Ferdinand, heir to the Empire of Austria-Hungary, on the streets of Sarajevo, first reached the citizens of New York through the city's newspapers.[2] The range of responses to this event in the Balkans presaged the struggles that New York would encounter as the war in Europe progressed and encompassed ever more of the world's capital, material and people. The Jewish socialist daily *Forverts* declared the murder to be inevitable in what had become an imperialistic struggle for power in the Balkans.[3]

---

[1]   *New York Times*, June 29, 1914.

[2]   This work has been developed from the study conducted within Kevin O'Keefe, 1972. *A Thousand Deadlines: The New York City Press and American Neutrality, 1914–1917*. The Hague: Martinus Nijhoff.

[3]   *Forverts*, July 4, 1914.

In this assessment, the scion of the Habsburg family was justly reaping the rewards of the propaganda of 'hate-patriotism' that he had helped to forge.[4] Such assessments were not unusual within the radical political communities of the city, particularly the anarchist organisations who expressed sympathy for the action taken in Bosnia. The Yiddish-language newspaper *Fraye Arbeter Shtime*, which was highly influential for anarchist groups in the city, accepted the death of the Archduke as a step forward, stating the danger that the successor to Emperor Franz Josef would have eventually posed to liberty and freedom within the Empire.[5] In this respect, the killing of the Archduke was an advancement of the anarchist cause, even if the perpetrators were perhaps not in complete unison with their ideological goals. Similarly, the Italian-language anarchist paper *Il Proletario* stated their unequivocal support and solidarity for the action taken.[6]

German-language anarchist publication followed a similar argument, declaring international commonality against the forces of industry and business.[7] Similarly, the anarchist publication *Mother Earth* marked their first edition since the escalation of hostilities with a front cover illustration, by the Dada artist Man Ray (1890–1976), of a double-headed monster of capitalism and government tearing a figure of humanity asunder. Articles within this volume, edited by the renowned anarchist Emma Goldman (1869–1940), denounced the war as a capitalist endeavour and called for public action against the industrial–military–national complexes that oppressed the proletariat.[8] However, such attitudes were challenged elsewhere within the various ethnic presses within the city. The Orthodox Jewish newspaper *Morgen Zhurnal* was far more conciliatory in its reporting.[9] Its assessment of the Archduke as a man of humanity was born from the limited emancipation afforded to Jewish groups within the newly-formed dual kingdom of Austria-Hungary.[10]

---

[4]	J. Rappaport, 1957. The American Yiddish Press and the European Conflict in 1914. *Jewish Social Studies*, 19(3): 113–14.

[5]	*Fraye Arbeter Shtime*, July 14, 1914.

[6]	E. Vezzosi, 1985. Class, Ethnicity, and Acculturation in *Il Proletario*: The World War One Years. In C. Harzig and D. Hoerder (eds), *The Press of Labor Migrants in Europe and North America, 1880s to 1930s*. Bremen: Labor Migration Project, Labor Newspaper Preservation Project, Universität Bremen, pp. 443–55.

[7]	T. Goyens, 2007. *Beer and Revolution: The German Anarchist Movement in New York City, 1880–1914*. Urbana, IL: University of Illinois Press, pp. 206–7.

[8]	C.A. Breckenridge, 1914. Down with Militarism! Up with the Rights of Man. *Mother Earth*, 9(6): 185–7; G. Herve, 1914. Insurrection Rather Than War. *Mother Earth*, 9(6): 188–90.

[9]	G. Ribak, 2012b. "A Victory of the Slavs Means a Deathblow to Democracy": The Onset of World War I and the Images of the Warring Sides among Jewish Immigrants in New York, 1914–1916. In Y. Levin and A. Shapira (eds), *War and Peace in Jewish Tradition: From the Biblical World to the Present*. London: Routledge, pp. 203–18; J. Rappaport, 2005. Hands Across the Sea: Jewish Immigrants and World War I. New York, NY: Hamilton, p. 31.

[10]	*Morgen Zhurnal*, June 30, 1914.

Indeed, the Habsburg family and their rule was regarded favourably amongst the Orthodox communities within New York and compassion for the murdered heir and his father Emperor Franz Josef I was evident.[11] The Orthodox community were not alone in their perspective; other religious ideals also influenced the response to the assassination within the city. The Jesuit periodical *America*, published in New York, regarded the piety of those affected by this tragedy in their support for the Habsburgs.[12]

The complex attitude towards the events in the Balkans was also demonstrated in the other foreign-language presses within the city. The assassination was covered in the conservative German American newspapers as a demonstration of the skill and diplomacy of Kaiser Wilhelm II, as the German Empire provided the necessary diplomatic cure to the affront committed against the Empire of Austria-Hungary. The *New Yorker Staats-Zeitung* celebrated the work of the Kaiser in his mediation whilst censuring the radicals within the dangerous arena of the Balkans for this outrage.[13] Whilst these papers used the event and its aftermath as demonstrations of national virtue, other groups within the city were also motivated to highlight how the incident also served as a timely reminder for those in power in the United States to look to issues in their own country. The African American newspaper *New York Age* compared the injustice which drove the murder of the Archduke and his wife to the situation faced across the nation:

> The mixed population of the United States, that styles itself white and is far from being such, is storing up more wrath for the future than it will be able to control when it gets to it, unless it shall be saved by a miracle; and miracles are no longer common manifestations.[14]

Similar connections were made within the Irish American newspapers in the city as parallels between the repression of national self-determination in Ireland and the Balkans afforded a means to criticise the failure of the British government to initiate Home Rule. The Howth Gun Running of July 1914, which saw the shooting dead of three unarmed citizens by troops on Bachelors Walk in Dublin, also served to place the events in Sarajevo into a relevant context for New York's Irish Republican-supporting residents.[15] Therefore, New York's ethnic press used the turmoil that emanated from June 1914 as a means to understand their own cultural, national, ethnic and religious affiliations. The crisis that erupted was a mirror in which they could observe their own place in a national and international context.

---

[11]   L.P. Bénézet, 1918. *The World War and What Was Behind It*. New York, NY: Scott, Foresman and Company, p. 5.

[12]   *America*, October 17, 1914.

[13]   *New Yorker Staats-Zeitung*, July 30, 1914.

[14]   *New York Age*, July 9, 1914.

[15]   *Gaelic American*, August 1, 1914.

Such a variegated response was perhaps the inevitability of a diverse democracy and a thriving independent press. However, the ways in which communities began to align themselves with presumed victims or aggressors began a process which would witness a change in the governance and character of the metropolis. The difficult nature of authority and identity within such a complex city was noted by the very individual whose death sparked the crisis in Europe after June 1914. Twenty years before the fateful journey to Sarajevo, the Archduke had made a far more uneventful visit to the United States. Arriving in New York on 6 October 1893, he was greeted by the Austro-Hungarian Ambassador to the United States, Ernst Ritter Schmit von Tavera (1839–1904). A banquet at the Windsor Hotel in downtown Manhattan afforded an opportunity to meet prominent members of the Austrian community in the city. However, this experience of the United States served as a moment for Franz Ferdinand to reflect on the issues of identity that were evoked in the process of emigration.[16] The Archduke stressed the racial and ethnic bonds between the peoples of the United States and those of the empire, but he also noted the way in which notions of belonging and place (*heimat*) had been shaped by their adopted homeland:

> The descendants of those sent from Europe to the West, those who were led there by a stream of migration, are strangers to us today, although they are flesh from our flesh, blood from our blood. It is not the ocean that separates the citizens of the United States from us, it is the nature of the country which has achieved this separation … which however sometimes turns into the strange or grotesque.[17]

As the events in Europe progressed, the pressure on New York's populace to choose sides, to favour one interpretation over the other, to argue for the cause of one nation, intensified. This émigré urge to 'rush to the colours' was problematised by the increasing determination of the United States government to maintain neutrality, in President Woodrow Wilson's phrase, 'in thought as well as action'. Such a position was regarded by the President as a necessity, to avoid war in the United States between 'our mixed populations'.[18]

The Outbreak of War: The Response of New York

The escalation of ultimatum, mobilisation and eventual declaration of war in Europe was viewed within the mainstream press in the city firstly as an exotic

---

[16]   R. Agstner, 2012. *Austria (-Hungary) and its Consulates in the United States of America since 1820*. Zurich: Lit Verlag GmbH & Co. KG Wien, p. 241.

[17]   Franz Ferdinand, Archduke of Austria-Hungary, 1896. *Tagebuch meiner Reise um die Erde, 1892–1893, Volume II*. Vienna: A. Hölder, p. 536.

[18]   A. Link, 1960. *The Struggle for Neutrality, 1914–1915*. Princeton, NJ: Princeton University Press, p. 65.

adventure to intrigue its readers during the summer months and then as an unfolding tragedy. The *New York Times*, the *New York Herald*, the *Brooklyn Daily Eagle* and the *New York Sun* all addressed the daily developments in the diplomatic circles of Europe from the initial shot on June 28 to the announcement of war between Austria-Hungary and Serbia on 29 July.[19] The tone of these reports throughout the fraught period of July 1914 was a marked difference with the partisan nature of the foreign-language press within the city. Rather than ascribe blame or guilt to one particular party at this stage, New York's most prominent newspapers regarded the war as a tragic, collective responsibility.[20] Strict neutrality and objectivity in reporting was rigidly enforced during this time as newspapers attempted to avoid the wrath of their readership or the increasingly concerned politicians both in New York and Washington. This approach has been interpreted as a *laissez-faire* attitude towards the impending crisis in Europe or even a marked indifference by the mainstream press in New York. Indeed, Herbert Hoover (1874–1964), an industrialist and aspirant politician who sought to involve himself in charitable work in Europe as hostilities escalated, was moved to enquire in August 1914 as to whether anyone in New York might realise what was occurring across Europe:

> So well informed a newspaper as the *New York Times* from July 1st to July 22nd carried no alarming European news on the front page – Austria got only a minor mention from time to time on the fourth page inside.[21]

Such a reading of the response of the New York press mistakes the careful tread of neutrality for nonchalance. The city's newspapers engaged with the events in Europe in a dispassionate manner as a careful policy of objectivity. Indeed, it would appear the desire to avoid partisan reporting presaged the official line of non-intervention from the White House. The response towards the assassination of Archduke Franz Ferdinand was detached in tone, with the *Brooklyn Daily Eagle*, the *New York Evening Mail* and the *New York Tribune* ruminating on the possible implications for the Habsburg succession rather than the effect it might have on the tinderbox of Balkan politics.[22] The diplomatic wrangling across Europe was accorded attention but New York's press reports appeared careful to avoid the accusation of bias.[23] This impartiality was also noticeable in the assessment of the intensification of the assassination after late July, where readers were impressed upon to realise the seriousness of the situation after Austria-Hungary's demands

---

[19]   K. O'Keefe, 1972. *A Thousand Deadlines: The New York Press and American Neutrality, 1914–17*. The Hague: Martinus Nijhoff.

[20]   *The Nation*, August 6, 1914.

[21]   H.C. Hoover, 1951. *The Memoirs of Herbert Hoover: Years of Adventure 1874–1920*. New York, NY: Macmillan Co., p. 137.

[22]   *Brooklyn Daily Eagle*, June 29, 1914; *New York Evening Mail*, June 29, 1914; *New York Tribune*, June 29, 1914.

[23]   *New York Sun*, June 29, 1914.

to Serbia were reported. The *New York Herald* demonstrates this urgency with the bold headline:

> War Devil Hangs Over Europe as Austria and Servia Sever Diplomatic Relations
> and Russian and Serv and Austrian Armies are Mobilised for the Field.[24]

As opposing armies readied themselves for conflict, New York's mainstream newspaper maintained a studied tone of neutrality whilst citing the role of competitive nationalism and militarism as the cause of the conflict rather than attributing blame to a specific nation.[25] Indeed, the reports that were presented to New York's citizens focused on the efforts made by Kaiser Wilhelm II to press for a peaceful resolution to the apparent ease with which Europe's great powers would launch themselves into war.[26] It was also to the Kaiser that a number of appeals were made to use the German Empire's influence over Austria-Hungary to step back from the brink of war or to contain the conflict to the Balkans.[27] However, all sides in the struggle were urged to find a diplomatic solution as the assassination in Sarajevo appeared to be turning from a personal and family tragedy into an international disaster.[28] As the alliances between nations were stated and war took upon the air of inevitability, the tragicomic nature of European politics was reported by the city's press as a lesson in folly.[29] The wider failings of nation states to prevent European conflict were reported with a series of sombre headlines within New York's press after the announcement of hostilities in early August 1914:

> Germany declares war on Russia, First Shots are Fired; France is Mobilizing
> and may be Drawn in Tomorrow; Plans to Rescue the 100,000 Americans Now
> in Europe.[30]

The fate of stranded Americans holidaying in the resorts of Europe or participating in the summer events of high society concerned the mainstream press of the city but it did not prompt any calls for intervention or a deviation from a policy of neutrality.[31] Indeed, as the declarations of war were passed and troops mounted the first offensives of the conflict, the city's press were noticeably dispassionate in their assessments. In this manner, New York's majority press 'policed' the doctrine of neutrality in the city and in the wider United States. This tendency is evidenced

---

[24] *New York Herald*, July 26, 1914.

[25] *New York Herald*, July 27, 1914.

[26] *New York World*, July 29, 1914; *New York Evening Post*, July 27, 1914.

[27] *New York Sun*, July 27, 1914; *Brooklyn Daily Eagle*, July 28, 1914.

[28] *New York Times*, July 28, 1914; *New York Herald*, July 28, 1914.

[29] *Brooklyn Daily Eagle*, August 2, 1914.

[30] *New York Times*, August 2, 1914.

[31] *New York Herald*, August 3, 1914.

by the reaction of the city's press to developments in Washington, when the extent of the nation's neutrality and its economic and political involvement was debated. When the delicate issue of selling arms and war material was raised in government circles, the city's press were quick to denounce any restrictions as 'un-neutral' and placing the country under the flag of one nation or another; strict neutrality could only be guaranteed by an open market.[32]

The city's newspapers attempted to maintain a distinct impartial assessment of the conflict, even after the actions of belligerent nations roused dissent for harming the interests of the city. Britain's disabling of the transatlantic submarine cables connecting Germany's telecommunications service to the United States on 5 August 1914 brought condemnation from the New York press.[33] This criticism was heightened with the evident doctoring of reports from Europe which arrived in New York via London.[34] However, the disconnection from reports of the battlegrounds did not ensure that the Entente was treated more favourably within New York's newspapers, nor did it entail that attitudes towards the German Empire were skewed. Indeed, the mainstream press in the city used their neutral status as a means to judge the war that had descended upon Europe. Even before the disruption of the news service from Europe, elements of the New York press had judged the German Empire as the belligerent power and the prominent guilty party in the development of the war. The *New York World* lambasted 'German autocracy' as the enemy of peace and humanity.[35] Similarly, the *New York Herald* criticised the German leadership for their irresponsible actions to the events which presaged war in a 'seeming disregard' of the consequences.[36] This assessment was supported by the flood of reports after the invasion of Belgium, where lurid tales of atrocities, murder and looting were presented to the city's readers. Sympathetic accounts of 'poor', 'defenceless' Belgium, a nation which professed its neutrality in the face of war, promoted the view of German responsibility for the conflict.[37]

However, in the early part of the war after August 1914, the Entente were also criticised for their military strategies. The relatively small military force sent by Britain was assessed by some sections of the New York press as insufficient to prevent the suffering of French and Belgian civilians.[38] However, the criticism of British inaction paled in response to the widespread discontent amongst the city's press over the declaration of the North Sea as a military zone in early November. This unilateral action riled the press as accounts of British detain and search operations on vessels from the city were regarded as potentially causing a serious

---

[32]   *New York Times*, August 7, 1914; *New York Herald*, August 7, 1914.

[33]   *New York World*, August 6, 1914; *New York Sun*, August 6, 1914.

[34]   *New York Times*, August 6, 1914.

[35]   *New York World*, August 17, 1914.

[36]   *New York Herald*, August 9, 1914.

[37]   *New York Sun*, August 9, 1914; *New York Times*, August 9, 1914.

[38]   *New York Times*, August 13, 1914.

rift in Anglo-American relations.[39] The British naval restriction on shipping from the port of New York as part of their blockade of the German Empire was regarded as a challenge to the wider nation's neutrality in the European conflict.[40] The actions of the Entente were subject to the same level of analysis as those of the German Empire and its allies. Indeed, reports of Russian war crimes against non-combatants and the targeting of Jewish communities by advancing Tsarist forces which drew attention to the brutality of the conflict in Europe received the same prominence as Germany's dismissal of Belgian neutrality.[41]

Readers of New York's press, therefore, placed citizens in a unique role of that of witnesses. The columns of the city's newspapers can be regarded as frames through which readers regarded both the events in Europe and their position regarding the war. This provided a view from afar, a detached and unbiased assessment of the conflict, which was not clouded by militarism, jingoism or overt patriotism. As witnesses, readers were asked to take a judgement upon the actions of the combatant nations, to observe the suffering of minorities and civilians of invaded territories and to join in the testifying against the abuses of power highlighted by the city's newspapers. This can be observed in the publication and reporting in the city's newspapers of the respective views of the combatant nations in their official documents. Within the space of a few months, the German White Paper,[42] the Russian Orange Paper,[43] the Belgium Grey Book,[44] the British Blue Book,[45] the French Yellow Book[46] and the Austrian Red Book[47] had been made available to readers for assessment. Certainly, this at times struck a self-congratulatory tone, as the press praised the good fortune and sound political judgement that had ensured the United States had remained removed from the crisis in Europe. A sense of 'American exceptionalism' characterised the reports on the war, which provided the city's populace with a means to pronounce their rights and liberties as individual Americans, as opposed to their European counterparts who were the subjects of Kings and Emperors.[48] New York's press were certainly neutral in their assessment of the conflict, but they were judgemental in other respects; the war presented an opportunity to use their position in the United States to draw a verdict on European affairs.

The popular newspapers in the city were certainly not the mouthpieces of neutrality for the city or indeed for the nation; contrary to post-war assessments,

---

[39] *New York World*, November 4, 1914; *New York Times*, November 4, 1914.
[40] *New York Herald*, November 4, 1914.
[41] *New York Times*, November 2, 1914.
[42] *New York Times*, August 24, 1914.
[43] *New York Times*, September 27, 1914.
[44] *New York Times*, October 18, 1914.
[45] *New York Times*, October 27, 1914.
[46] *New York Times*, December 13, 1914.
[47] *New York Times*, February 28, 1915.
[48] *New York Herald*, August 8, 1914.

New York's press did not necessarily control and direct the populace towards an acceptance of impartiality to the events in Europe. Indeed, it can be regarded that the wider public opinion within the city sided with a non-interventionist policy as the sabre-rattling of European states reached a cacophony. Surveys taken by periodicals that were published in New York at the outset of the crisis revealed a popular commitment to absolve the United States from the squabbles of the belligerent nations of the 'old world'.[49] However, despite this neutrality, the war was not an abstract event for the city's press. Fears were expressed within New York's newspapers about how the outbreak of war would shape global, national and even municipal politics.[50] This new situation was regarded as potentially troubling for the city. The overthrow of the established order and the revolutionary politics involved in the assassination of the heir to the Habsburg Empire concerned some newspapers as a source of inspiration for socialists and anarchists based in New York.[51]

In a city that had already witnessed bombings connected to radical political groups from the nineteenth century onwards, the perception that the war might cause disruption to New York was present in the city's press but was not the overriding concern with the advent of hostilities.[52] Indeed, one of the primary concerns expressed within these neutral reports was the potential economic boom brought about by a European conflict that the city might benefit from.[53] The increase in industrial output, the manufacturing demand and the expansion in shipping that a port city such as New York might benefit from tempered any moral and political concerns that were expressed by the city's press. Indeed, the economic boom that might arise from the conflict in Europe was actively encouraged by the media and the opportunity to advance the city beyond the markets of Europe was greeted with enthusiasm.[54] From the very outset of the crisis, newspaper reports noted how the increase in demand for raw materials and manufactured products would boost the economic condition of the city. Great riches were predicted for the city's merchants and financiers with an additional boost for the workers and labourers of New York through supply contracts with the belligerent powers. E.H. Gary (1846–1927), Chairman of the United States Steel Corporation and prominent New Yorker, wrote in the *New York Times* shortly after the war had begun that the qualities of 'patience, economy, prudence and courage' would result in a substantial profit from the war, provided that 'entanglements' with other nations were avoided.[55]

The notion of avoiding associations with combatant nations and maintaining 'clear heads' to benefit from the seas of riches that were forecast for New York's

---

[49] *Literary Digest*, November 14, 1914; *Outlook*, August 15, 1914.

[50] *New York Times*, June 29, 1914.

[51] *New York Times*, July 30, 1914.

[52] *Journal of Commerce*, October 15, 1914.

[53] *New York Times*, October 25, 1914.

[54] *New York Herald*, October 25, 1914.

[55] *New York Times*, September 20, 1914.

economy was made clear by a number of the city's prominent newspapers.[56] New York would in this respect be mobilised for the war, ready and willing to meet the demands of the conflict and benefit from the self-destruction of Europe.[57] In this estimation, New York would supplant London as the international trading hub and financial market. Such optimism appeared well-founded as the disruption caused by the war to European economies was soon evidenced by substantial investment in the stocks and commodities of New York. The city's press reported with unrestrained glee that the coffers of the city were being filled by European investors fleeing the uncertainty of war. Speaking on 29 July, Henry G.S. Noble (1859–1933), President of the New York Stock Exchange, drew upon the growing feeling of the unique position that the metropolis and the wider nation benefited from, as opposed to the control witnessed over European economies:

> The fact that the New York Stock Exchange alone had a free and un-restrained market today is a tribute to the social conditions of American finance.[58]

Such was the effect of the war on the market that share prices fluctuated violently after 28 July, with several hundred thousand shares traded in an hour and the first 'million share' day on Wall Street for nearly two years.[59] However, the panic conditions experienced on the markets after 29 July, created by foreign investors attempting quick sales of stocks to raise capital for the conflict, prompted fears of a run on the exchange and on 31 July the Board of Governors of the New York Stock Exchange followed their European counterparts and closed.[60] Rather than regard this move as an impediment to the profits that could be garnered from the war, this was regarded by the city's press as a necessary action to safeguard the economy and preserve the neutrality of the United States.[61] Regardless of this closure, the war still meant potentially substantial profits for the city and reports from Europe became a regular feature of the mainstream press.

The development of the war from this perspective was regarded as a degree removed; the gathering storm in Europe was a point of political and economic interest but divorced from any individual connection which placed the city in the context of the developing crisis. Regardless of how the war could shift markets, encourage the economy and provide points of comparison between the values and merits between the old world and the new world, the conflict was nevertheless still

---

[56] *New York Herald*, August 3, 1914; *New York World*, August 3, 1914.

[57] *New York Sun*, July 27, 1914; *New York Herald*, July 30, 1914.

[58] *New York Herald*, July 30, 1914.

[59] H.G.S. Noble, 1915. *The New York Stock Exchange in the Crisis of 1914*. Garden City, NY: Country Life Press.

[60] W.L. Silber, 2006. *When Washington Shut Down Wall Street: The Great Financial Crisis of 1914 and the Origins of American Monetary Superiority*. Princeton, NJ: Princeton University Press.

[61] *New York Times*, August 1, 1914.

'over there'. This apparent absence of concern was altered dramatically by the rapid turn of events that saw the declaration of war by Austria-Hungary on Serbia on 29 July, followed by the declaration of war by the German Empire on the Russian Empire on 1 August, France on 3 August and Britain's announcement that it was at war with Germany on 4 August. The outbreak of war in Europe immediately placed New York's émigré communities alongside the combatant nations as the city encountered the effects of the conflict on its politics, its economics and its society. The city's newspapers were fascinated by the declarations of loyalty and the denunciations of enemies voiced by the city's residents who had left their original homelands. Nowhere was this more aptly demonstrated in the congregations that formed in 34th Street, Herald Square, where the *New York Herald* had placed a large bulletin board outside their offices. The board would be regularly updated to reveal the issuances of nation states, the ultimatums of governments and the details of troop manoeuvres. With the declarations of war, for those citizens with recent ties to a home country, strong familial connections to their ancestral land of origin or even the purely intrigued, Herald Square became the place to hear news of the conflict. The newspaper covered the scenes outside its office as a spectacle of city life as individuals with connections to combatant nations 'rubbed elbows' with one another:

> Each bulletin carried more meaning, perhaps between the lines, than it did to those who exalted merely over the strategic advances to be gained by each country.[62]

Rather than give the impression that Herald Square could become a potential point of conflict within the city, the newspaper was keen to represent the scenes as peaceful, demonstrating the neutral status of the city and the calming influence of American citizenship or residence. Similar gatherings took place further uptown on 42nd Street Times Square, where the *New York Times* had their bulletin boards. At these sites, estimates of several hundred thousand people assembled. Initial reports praised the way in which supporters of opposing nations were able to hear news of the developing war without causing strife.[63] The *Herald* reported this amiable nature of the crowds:

> Conflict of emotions stirs great cosmopolitan throng in Broadway that learns of progress of the events in the capitals of Europe – cheers as Germany's declaration is posted – great self-control shown as portentous news is known.[64]

The condition described as 'war fever' swept across the city as the enthusiasm for the conflict exhibited by the émigré communities was matched by New York

---

62 *New York Herald*, July 30, 1914.
63 *New York Times*, August 5, 1916.
64 *New York Herald*, August 2, 1914.

citizens without the same direct connections. However, in the days after the initial declarations the fear that these gatherings could spark trouble and transfer the strife of the European battlefields onto the city streets was particularly troubling for the city's police force. The crowds of British, French and Belgian expatriates singing anthems and waving national flags near the vicinity of German Americans who were equally vociferous in their support for the Kaiser necessitated police control around the intersection of Broadway and Herald Square.[65] Alongside Times Square and Herald Square, reports of confrontations between New York's communities and their partisan politics also featured as a means to inform a general readership of the divisions and alliances that were being mirrored in the city.[66] News of church sermons, community hall meetings and political gatherings revealed the strong emotions with which some in New York regarded the war:

> Excited discussions in thickly populated streets on the east side and meetings of compatriots of those engaged in the European war kept New York's foreign colonies alive with interest.[67]

Mass meetings of German Americans, Austrian Americans and Hungarian Americans across the boroughs, where funds were raised for war widows and orphans, were eagerly detailed as part of the 'war fever'.[68] This reporting was not part of a denunciation of foreign-born residents and their attachment to their homeland, but as a means of connecting the New York readership with the conflict. If this passionate support conflicted or transgressed the ideals and values expected by the city's press then the 'foreign' nature of those responsible was stressed over their status in the United States.[69] The city's press, therefore, whilst quick to report the intriguing sight of foreign residents celebrating and singing as a means of connecting the metropolis to the events occurring in Europe, were, nevertheless, equally keen to censure and suppress any expression of nationalism that would disrupt the function of New York's business and complicate the neutral status of the United States.

What these news reports do demonstrate is that a far greater and a more invested approach to the conflict existed in the city beyond the steadfastly neutral confines of mainstream newspapers. It was the diverse ethnic presses in the city and their associated publications in which it was demonstrated that New York and its inhabitants were undoubtedly part of the war. In these forums, issues of the war, of independence, patriotism, nationality, representation and citizenship, which underscored the war in Europe at the outset of the conflict in August 1914, could be encountered. Just as the neutrality of the city's majority press formed

---

65   *New York Times*, August 6, 1914.
66   *New York Herald*, August 9, 1914.
67   *New York Times*, August 3, 1914.
68   *New York Times*, August 24, 1914; *New York Times*, September 28, 1914.
69   *New York Times*, August 7, 1914.

a frame through which residents could dispassionately assess the conflict, the foreign-language presses constituted a medium through which New Yorkers could align themselves with the fervour that had gripped Europe.

Extending the Battlefields: The Foreign-Language Press in New York

For the diverse communities of New York, the metropolis was thrust into the complex political ramifications of the war, before the declarations had been issued, with the visit of foreign dignitaries to the city who spoke to the émigré communities of their homeland. On 4 July 1914, Count Mihály Károlyi (1875–1955) arrived in New York as part of a deputation from Hungary, having crossed the Atlantic on the Hamburg-American liner *Vaterland*. Karolyi, as a prominent member of the Hungarian opposition party, advocated political reform in the Empire of Austria-Hungary and opposed the Dual Monarchy. The delegation sought to acquire support, both financial and political, from Hungarian emigrants within New York and the United States for the progress of democracy in their motherland. Such a venture proved highly popular in New York with over 10,000 Hungarian Americans attending a rally in Washington Square to receive Count Károlyi. However, the death of the Archduke during the passage of the ship ensured that this mission became highly sensitive in regard to the neutral status of the United States and the cohesion of the populace of New York.[70] Károlyi expressed sadness at the assassination, calling the Archduke a friend of the reform movement, as opposed to his father, but expressed deep concern at what might occur in the aftermath of the shooting, predicting 'grave disturbances' and warning of reactionary influences at the court of Franz Josef I.[71] Károlyi's presence in the city and his campaign for Hungarian independence from the 'colonial' power of Austria provoked a strong reaction from the Slovak population in New York and the wider United States.[72] This minority ethnic group in Hungary opposed the Magyar domination of an independent Hungary. New York's émigré Slovaks had previously stated their rights as Americans and their obligations as Slovaks to highlight the oppression of their people within Austria-Hungary:

> We consider this our right not only as American citizens who know what a real democratic government consists of, but also as our birth-right as brethren of those Slovaks who now live within the dominion of Hungary.[73]

---

[70] *New York Times*, July 5, 1914.

[71] *New York Tribune*, July 5, 1914.

[72] G.C. Ference, 1995. *Sixteen Months of Indecision: Slovak American Viewpoints toward Compatriots and the Homeland from 1914 to 1915 as viewed by the Slovak Language Press in Pennsylvania*. Selinsgrove, PA: Susquehanna University Press.

[73] Committee of the Political Federation of Slovaks, 1914. *An Open Letter Addressed to Count Michael Károlyi, Member of Hungarian Parliament on the Occasion of His American Voyage*. New York, NY: s.n.

Any conflict which engaged the forces of the Habsburg Empire was regarded as an expedient towards the objective of an independent Slovakia by sections of the city's Slovakian residents.[74] Slovakian-language newspapers in New York encouraged the hopes and aspirations of their readers with the potential outcomes of a war which could fragment the multi-ethnic composition of Austria-Hungary.[75] *New Yorský Denník* and *Slovák v Amerike*, the prominent Slovakian titles in the city, both edited by leading American Slovakian nationalists, promoted this viewpoint in their reporting during July 1914.[76] New York's Slovakians were joined in this ambition for independence by their fellow émigré Bohemian community in the metropolis.[77] With both communities perceiving a sense of common suffering under the imperial yoke of Austria-Hungary, a natural alliance between the two appeared to offer the opportunity to aid both causes.[78] Slovak and Bohemian groups across the United States used the opportunity presented by the crisis to express long-held objectives as a plan for a unified state between the two peoples emerged.[79] The Slovak League of America and the Bohemian National Alliance, both of which had significant numbers of followers in New York, had by September 1914 issued a joint memorandum stating their right to self-determination.[80] This memorandum identified the common cause of the two peoples and set an agenda for a post-war unification of Bohemian and Slovakian peoples into a single state. Therefore, it was in New York that the European War began to construct new national consciousnesses; the American city of diversity became a centre of nationalism that had been fired by the events after July 1914:

> Nothing now separates us, except that we owe political allegiance to two different states, one to Austria, the other to Hungary. Remove that barrier, and it

[74]   M. Getting, 1933. *Americkí Slováci a vývin československej myšlienky v rokoch 1914–1918*. Masaryktown, FL: Slovenská telocvičná jednota Sokol v Amerike.

[75]   J. Pauco, 1969. Slovak Pioneers in America. *Slovakia*, 19(42): 108–124; J. Pauco, 1973. Slovaks Abroad and Their Relationship with Slovakia. In J. Kirschbaum (Ed.) *Slovakia in the 19th and 20th Centuries*. Toronto: Slovak World Congress, pp. 333–42.

[76]   J. Alexander, 2004. *Ethnic Pride, American Patriotism: Slovaks and Other New Immigrants in the Interwar Era*. Philadelphia, PA: Temple University Press, pp. 14–19.

[77]   T. Capek, 1921. *The Čech (Bohemian) Community of New York*. New York, NY: The Czechoslovak Section of America's Making, Inc.; Bohemian National Alliance of America. 1915. *The Position of the Bohemians (Czechs) in the European War*. Chicago, IL: Bohemian National Alliance of America.

[78]   M. Stolarik. 1968. The Role of American Slovaks in the Creation of Czecho-Slovakia, 1914–1918. *Slovak Studies*, 7: 7–82.

[79]   K. Miller, 1922. *The Czecho-Slovaks in America*. New York, NY: George H. Doran.

[80]   A. Mamatey, 1915. The Situation in Austria-Hungary. *The Journal of Race Development*, 6(2): 203–217.

will be seen that the Bohemians and Slovaks are one in language, one in blood, one in national faith, indissoluble and indivisible.[81]

This desire was further encouraged by the news of August 1914 that Tsar Nicholas II had announced a desire for a degree of self-government for the ethnic communities of both the Russian Empire and the Empire of Austria-Hungary. The Tsar's declaration was principally aimed at securing the loyalty of the Polish people in the struggle with the German Empire but the promise of autonomy was regarded highly by some Polish Americans within New York:

> There are many thousands of Poles in England and 3,000,000 in America. They will all make a supreme effort to return to the European Continent and do their share towards the accomplishment of Poland's liberation.[82]

The Tsar's promise of autonomy for Polish peoples was given a cautious welcome by the New York Polish National Alliance, who were wary of the persistence of Russian influence, but who named the war a racial struggle between Slavs and Germans. Kazinirz Jaworowski, leader of the Polish National Alliance, stated immediately after the Russian declaration in 1914:

> For my own part, I would do anything to defeat Germany ... The Poles are Slavs. The fight is between the Germans and the Slavs. I hope that if the Czar is successful, he carries out his promises to reunite Poland and grant it autonomy. That would not mean Poland would be free, but it would enjoy more freedom than now. The Czar would be the King of Poland and the Government of Poland undoubtedly would be carried on largely by men appointed by the Czar. However, if Poland got the right to have a share in its Government, even if the Czar remained supreme, the country would be greatly benefited.[83]

However, for the Slovak and Bohemian newspapers in New York, this signalled the end of colonial rule as they regarded the manifesto as statement of intent to support the independence of their motherland. Indeed, *Slovák v Amerike* directed a telegram to St Petersburg to complement the Tsar on his humanitarian promise to the Polish peoples in the hope that similar arrangements would be made to the Slovakian peoples. The telegram ended with a plea to 'remember the Slovaks',

---

[81] T. Capek, 1915. The Slovaks of Hungary. In T. Capek (ed.) *Bohemia under Hapsburg Misrule: A Study of the Ideals and Aspirations of the Bohemian and Slovak Peoples, as they Relate to and are Affected by the Great European War.* New York, NY: Fleming H. Revell, pp. 113–22.

[82] *New York Times*, August 17, 1914.

[83] K. Jaworowski, 1915. Polish American Opinion. *In New York Times Current History: The European War from the Beginning to March 1915. Vol. 1, No. 2: Who Began the War, and Why?* New York, NY: New York Times, p. 360.

before wishing success to the Russian Empire and its allies in the forthcoming war.[84]
The opportunities that were seemingly presented to the immigrant communities in
New York for furthering their home country's cause for independence was not
perceived by all within the city. Indeed, the radical plans espoused by Slovak and
Bohemian newspapers and periodicals were opposed by conservative voices from
other ethnic presses. The desire not to disturb or exacerbate conditions in Europe
can be detected in the response to the crisis within the Croat-language newspaper,
Narodni List. Published in New York and forming one of the most popular Croat
titles in the city, the paper called for calm and conservatism in the city's Croat
population in the aftermath of the events in Sarajevo.[85] The reluctance of the editors
of *Narodni List* to promote Croatian statehood prompted its New York readership
to turn to the more republican-minded papers *Hrvatski svijet* or *Ilustrovani List*.
Within this paper, the war was once again seized upon as an opportunity to
achieve liberty from the Habsburg Empire.[86] Associations with other Croatian and
Slavic groups across the United States, in cities such as Pittsburgh, Chicago and
Cleveland which were home to significant émigré communities from the Balkans,
were formed to promote a Pan-Slavic Brotherhood to support their cause in the
United States.[87] Indeed, in July 1914, an array of ten Slavic-language newspapers
issued a joint declaration from the Sokol Hall, a community centre for the Slavic
population of the city, located in Manhattan's Upper East Side, which denounced
the Empire of Austria-Hungary and called for Slavic peoples in New York to resist
any attempt by the Habsburg monarchy to call up reservists in the city:

> The representatives of the Slavonic papers in New York ... met this 27th day
> of July at Sokol Hall ... with the intention of calling a mass meeting of protest
> of all the Slavs ... to express their indignation at the brutal step of the Austro-
> Hungarian Government against our brethren in the free and cultured Kingdom
> of Servia.[88]

The complexity of the political, ethnic and religious issues of the Balkans which
had been agitated by the events of June 1914 was reflected in the equally intricate
and diverse communities within New York. This is particularly evident in the
Serbian response to the conflict which prompted conflicting attitudes within the
city's Serbian immigrant residents. Whilst some expatriate Serbians in the city
may have held a degree of loyalty to the Habsburg Empire, a far greater desire for

---

[84]   Ference, *Sixteen Months of Indecision*, p. 70.

[85]   *Narodni List*, July 30, 1914.

[86]   I. Čizmić, 1970. Dobrovoljacki pokret Jugoslovenskih iseljenika u sad u Prvom
svjetskom ratu. *Historijski Zbornik*, 23–24: 21–43.

[87]   C. Pergler, 1916a. *Bohemian (Czech) Hopes and Aspirations*. Chicago, IL:
Bohemian National Alliance in America; C. Pergler, 1916b. *Bohemia's Claim to
Independence*. Chicago, IL: Bohemian National Alliance in America.

[88]   *New York Times*, July 30, 1914.

the self-determination of Serbia and commitment to their adopted homeland of the United States were all expressed within the city's newspapers and social institutions that represented the Serbian people in New York. The Serbian daily papers in the city *Srpski Dnevnik* and *Srbobran* attempted to mobilise their readers to speak up for Serbia, raise funds for charitable organisations working in Serbia and to detail the abuses suffered by the Serbian people which had been carried out at the behest of the Dual Monarchy.[89] Pan-Slavic celebrations of unity were held in New York as a means to denounce Habsburg rule over central and south-eastern Europe. One such event, held at the Central Opera House in Manhattan on 2 August, raised over $1,000 for charitable causes.[90] At this meeting, Serbians, Croats, Slovaks and Bohemians called for the principles of liberty and independence to be enjoyed by Slavic peoples in Austria-Hungary as well as reminding New York Slavs of their responsibilities:

> Fierce attacks on Austria and appeals to the men in the audience to go over to Servia and fight were repeated again and again.[91]

These responses were also influenced by the efforts made by the diplomats of Austria-Hungary within the Consular-General office in New York to cast Serbian radicals as the guilty party of the turmoil in Europe.[92] To counter these organised programmes against the Serbian cause, the Serbian National Defense League was established in New York in July 1914 by the Columbia University Professor, Mihajlo Pupin (1858–1955).[93] Pupin organised émigré Serbians whilst also embarking on an early propaganda war within New York's mainstream press to rebut the accusations of the Austro-Hungarian Consulate in the city as to the guilt of Serbia and the complicity of Serbian politicians in the death of the Archduke. In these claims, Pupin made direct use of an appeal to American virtues of democracy and liberty as opposed to Austrian tyranny.[94] Such statements enabled Pupin to reinforce support for the Serbian cause and his organisation, which formed associated chapters in other American cities and began countering claims of Serbian aggression against Austria-Hungary, whilst initiating support schemes for Serbian American men of military age to return to defend the Serbian

---

[89]   Z. Vasilijevic, 1976. *The American South Slav Attitude to the Creation of Yugoslavia, 1914–1918*. Madison, WI: University of Wisconsin, pp. 71–2.

[90]   J. Goričar, 1915. *Political Intrigues of Austria and Germany Against Balkan States*. New York, NY: New Yorské Listy.

[91]   *New York Tribune*, August 2, 1914.

[92]   C.T. Dumba, 1914. Ambassador of Austria-Hungary to the United States. *The Outlook*, August 29: 1028–9.

[93]   A. Mitrović, 2007. *Serbia's Great War, 1914–1918*. West Lafayette, IN: Purdue University Press, p. 84.

[94]   *New York Times*, July 30, 1914; *New York Herald*, July 30, 1914.

homeland.[95] Such a scheme immediately placed New York under scrutiny as the nation's pre-eminent point of departure for Europe, and the prospect of thousands of patriotic men of numerous nations descending upon the city raised concerns amongst New York's majority press and politicians.

The New York voices of disapproval towards a disintegrating empire were not answered by a sustained counterpoint delivered by the supporters of the Habsburgs in the city's press. This was largely due to the fact that German-language Austrian newspapers in the city had not managed to stake a claim in the crowded marketplace of New York's ethnic press before the war.[96] The *Osterreichish-Ungarische Zeitung* had ceased publication in the early twentieth century and its revival in the form of *Die Oesterreichisch-Amerikanische Zeitung*, published by the expatriate Austro-Hungarian journalist Karl Hugo Tippmann (1875–1942), had failed to excite the émigré community. Tippmann had served in the Imperial Army and the tone of his publication was overwhelmingly supportive of Franz Josef, an approach which did not attract a wider audience and which resulted in the renaming and eventual lampooning of the publication by its opponents as 'Der Patriot'.[97] The absence of any significant support for the Empire of Austria-Hungary from a sympathetic German-language press was certainly evident.[98] The only avenue in which the Habsburg agenda could be promoted was through the work of the Consul-General in New York which published tracts declaring the innocence of the Dual Monarchy and the righteousness of their cause in 1914.[99] However, use was also made of the various Austrian and Hungarian community and charitable organisations in the city that provided support and familiarity to new immigrants. Dr Fritz Fischerauer, Vice-Consul General of Austria-Hungary in the city, spoke at the New York section of the Austrian Fleet Society on 1 August 1914 to ask for contributions to the war effort from New York's Austrians:

> We, who, far away from our beloved Fatherland, are spared the horrors of war, have a sacred duty: to provide for the families of our brave soldiers.[100]

---

[95]   Serbian National Defense League of America, 1918. *For Freedom: A Manifestation of Oppressed Slavic Nationalities of Austria-Hungary in Honor of the Serbian War Mission to the United States.* New York, NY: Serbian National Defense League of America.

[96]   E.W. Spaulding, 1968. *The Quiet Invaders: The Story of the Austrian Impact upon America.* Vienna: Österreichischer Bundesverlag, pp. 155–6.

[97]   H.K. Tippman, 1942. *Amerikanische balladen und andere gedichte.* New York, NY: Arrowhead Press, p. 16.

[98]   T. Giant, 1993. The War for Wilson's Ear: Austria-Hungary in Wartime American Propaganda. *Hungarian Studies Review*, 20(1–2): 25–51.

[99]   Austro-Hungarian Consulate-General. 1916. *Austria-Hungary and the War.* New York, NY: Austro-Hungarian Consulate-General.

[100]   *New York Times*, August 1, 1914.

The various Austro-Hungarian Missions placed across the United States also began to follow the example of their New York counterpart by issuing the Emperor Franz Josef I's call for reservists as part of the mobilisation of the Empire for war that was made on 31 July 1914.[101] Printed in the English-language presses and pasted on the offices of the Consular-General on State Street, Manhattan, the call for reservists required all Austro-Hungarians of military age who were eligible for military service to report to their nearest consul:

> Personal considerations must fade while the old native soil, the country of our childhood and of our forefathers, needs its sons.[102]

Residents of the United States who were born in Austria-Hungary were thereby compelled to return to their homeland. In this action, New York had been made a recruitment ground for the belligerent armies of the European War. The naturalisation convention passed by the United States and the Empire of Austria-Hungary in 1871 had proclaimed that citizens of the Austro-Hungarian monarchy, who had resided in the United States for five years or more and had become naturalised citizens of the United States, would be regarded as such by the Habsburg Empire. This agreement would bar all but the most recent immigrants from the requirements of mobilisation. However, with the naturalisation process in the United States, which was standardised after 1906 across the nation, taking over five years to complete, residency would not always be a means of removing the requirements of their previous citizenship. In these circumstances, fears regarding mobilisation impacted upon the city, as some within the expatriate community believed that they would be liable for military service regardless of their status in their adopted homeland, whilst the employers and industries in New York feared the potential fall in their labour force with a large-scale migration to fight in Europe:

> Foreign orders for mobilization in this country affect therefore not only un-naturalized citizens, but in many instances, even American voters, if they fail to respond to their old allegiance.[103]

For many Austrians and Hungarians in New York, such a relinquishing of duties to the homeland would be anathema, whilst those born to Austro-Hungarian immigrant parents in the United States could also be swept along by a patriotic fervour, and whilst not legally bound to serve the Dual Monarchy would draw

---

[101]   Agstner, R. 2006. *Austria (-Hungary) and its Consulates in the United States of America since 1820*. Zurich: Lit Verlag GmbH and Co. KG Wien, p. 51.

[102]   *New York Tribune*, August 2, 1914.

[103]   M. Chamberlain, 1914. The Clutch of Militarism: Some Reactions of the War upon Our Immigrant Population. *The Survey*, 33: 44–72.

upon idealised visions of a homeland and culture they had never visited.[104] With compulsory military service in place in Austria-Hungary, reservists in New York and elsewhere within the United States represented a potentially valuable addition to the armies of the Austria-Hungary. Such was the drive for reinforcements and the desire to utilise the romantic hold of the homeland over the immigrant that the Emperor Franz Josef I's declaration of an amnesty for deserters from the imperial army and navy or those who had emigrated to escape military service was publicised by the Consular-General office in New York.[105] As the Consular-General office became the magnet for crowds of New York's Austrians both celebrating the declaration of war and offering their services for the war effort, whether charitable or military, the city was increasingly taking a partisan appearance. The various communities in the metropolis connected to the events in Europe through their own ethnic, political and religious connections. In this way, the islands and peninsula that constitute the sprawling city of New York were becoming part of a battleground of a war that had quickly engulfed Europe.

A similar situation faced another imperial regime: Tsarist Russia. Under the rule of the Romanovs, political dissidents and minority populations had suffered. This legacy had been transported to the United States and impinged upon the attitudes of Russian émigré New Yorkers towards Russia's declaration of war. Despite the large-scale immigration from the areas of Tsarist Russia into the United States during the nineteenth century, the Russian-language presses in the city had been slow to develop into well-established and thriving institutions.[106] However, the escalation of tensions in 1914 had provoked some of the Tsar's former and current citizens who were residing in the city to take different perspectives on the issues presented by the call to arms. Depending on politics and religion, the opinions of Russian émigrés on the pursuit of war in Europe was highly divisive. For example, the left-leaning Russian-language daily *Russkoe Slovo* had taken an anti-war stance from the outset but was also highly critical of the actions of Germany.[107]

The Russian independent weekly *Novyi Mir* also gave a sceptical assessment of the conflict, siding with the Social Democratic exiles within New York in calling for reform in their homeland, not conflict.[108] These responses to the conflict were countered in the *Russkii Emigrant*, which served as a vehicle for the Russian Orthodox Church in New York and the wider United States, with articles that promoted the actions of the Tsar and the righteousness of the war.[109] Patriotic calls

---

[104] V. Horčička, 2006. The United States of America and Austria-Hungary on the Eve of the First World War. *Prague Papers on the History of International Relations*, 2006: 163–80.

[105] *New York Times*, July 29, 1914.

[106] R. Karlowich, 1991. *We Fall and Rise: Russian-Language Newspapers in New York City, 1889–1914*. Metuchen, NJ: Scarecrow Press.

[107] Karlowich, *We Fall and Rise*, p. 282.

[108] *Novyi Mir*, August 4, 1914.

[109] Karlowich, *We Fall and Rise*, p. 191.

to fight for the home country were met with enthusiasm by some in the Russian communities in New York. This call for loyalty from Russian émigrés was framed within the strong religious ties with the Orthodox Church. Indeed, on 9 August, a special service was held at Saint Nicholas Russian Orthodox Cathedral on 59th Street in Manhattan, to celebrate the war effort and to praise the soldiers of the old country.[110] With the cathedral filled with prominent Russian politicians and expatriates, nearly 8,000 people congregated around the vicinity to celebrate the glory of the Russian Empire and the fight for 'Faith, Tsar and Fatherland'.[111] During the ceremony, Archbishop Nevelovsky, flanked by both American and Russian flags besides the altar, delivered his appeal to the Russian community of the city:

> Blessed be the hour that the Czar of the Russians signed the proclamation of war
> ... The Russian eagle will fly into Austria and will open the prison doors where Russians are kept unjustly suffering, and will rescue these who are our people. Now my countrymen, should the Czar so order it, I know that you all, for you are all Russians, will fight for Russia ...[112]

Attending the service was the Russian Ambassador to the United States George Bakhmeteff (1850–1928) and Michael Oustinoff (1862–1942), Consul General of Russia in New York, who were feted outside the cathedral by the assembled crowds. However, the efforts of the Russian Embassy to promote the cause of their country to exiles and émigrés within the city lacked sufficient coordination during the development of the crisis after the assassination of Archduke Franz Ferdinand.[113] The diversity of their audience and the tendency for recent Russian immigrants in New York to have fled political and religious persecution ensured a muted response to calls from the Russian consular staff to unite.[114] Indeed, despite the appearance of unity of the service at St Nicholas in August 1914, the cosmopolitan nature of the Russian Empire ensured that domestic tensions underscored their war effort; this internal strife was also mirrored in the attitudes of Russian émigré communities in the city (see Young 1915).[115]

As well as dissident political groups, largely composed of Russian exiles who advocated political revolution and an overthrow of the Tsarist autocratic rule, the Russian Jewish emigrants also influenced the perceptions of the war. Yiddish-language newspapers sympathised with the Central Powers rather than

---

[110] *New York Tribune*, August 10, 1914; *New York Herald*, August 10, 1914.

[111] N.E. Saul, 2001. *War and Revolution: The United States and Russia, 1914–1921*. Lawrence, KS: University Press of Kansas, p. 27.

[112] *New York Times*, August 10, 1914.

[113] M. Gaiduk, 1918. *Utiug: materialy i fakty o zagotovitelnoi dieiatelnosti russkikh vooennykh kommissii v Amerikie*. New York, NY: M. Gaiduk.

[114] *New York Times*, September 6, 1914.

[115] C.C. Young, 1915. *Abused Russia*. New York, NY: Devin-Adair.

the Entente in the preparations for war.[116] Even those such as *Die Varheit*, edited by the Russian Jewish immigrant Louis Miller (1866–1927), launched fierce critiques at the onset of the war of the anti-Semitism of Tsarist Russia which had forced many from their homes to the new world.[117] Such opinions were not placated by the Russian Embassy in order to win support from the city's Russian expatriates. Indeed, comments attributed to Ambassador George Bakhmeteff, who later denied them, were reported in the *New York Sun* after the initial manoeuvres of the war, suggesting that Jewish communities in Russia could expect no equivalent declarations of due liberties in return for support, which had been offered to Russia's Polish citizens.[118] However, it was not purely religious persecution that drove these Russian exiles from supporting the land of their birth in the conflict. Political sentiment amongst Russian Jewish areas of New York favoured the socialist and democratic movements within Germany. Russian socialists in the city shared and disseminated these anti-Tsarist sentiments. Representatives of the Russian Socialist Revolutionary Party in New York advocated non-intervention in what was styled as a 'capitalist war' and called for solidarity with the German working classes. Indeed, Paul Kaplan (1848–1918), the New York based secretary of the party and a prominent supporter of the revolutionary cause of Russia in the United States, viewed the outbreak of war as an opportunity to overthrow the Tsarist regime:

> We will carry out an active campaign ... All the revolutionary factions in Russia will unite. Although we will not openly talk against what is generally looked on as patriotism in a monarchical government, we will work together to make converts to the cause. The war will give the chance we never had before to make a demand for a constitutional form of government.[119]

New York's Russian expatriates, who sought political change in the home country, were encouraged to believe that conflict would topple the established structures of power. Russian socialist and German socialist opinion had previously come together in the form of the *New Yorker Volkszeitung* newspaper, which served as a platform for political dissidents in the city. However, any notion of class solidarity within this German-language paper was doubtful with the publication of German Socialist opinion that sided with the Kaiserreich and placed blame on the Tsar.[120] In this manner, American Russian socialists were urged to forego nationalistic impulses and remember that Germany was the birthplace of Marx and therefore the spiritual home of socialist politics. Despite this appeal of

---

[116]   J. Rappaport, 1957. The American Yiddish Press and the European Conflict in 1914. *Jewish Social Studies*, 19(3): 113–28.

[117]   *Die Varheit*, August 8, 1914.

[118]   *New York Sun*, October 12, 1914.

[119]   Anon., 1915. Russian Revolutionists and the War. *The Melting Pot*, 3(3): 20.

[120]   *New Yorker Volkszeitung*, September 10, 1914.

nationalism, meetings of the socialist movement in the city emphasised solidarity across the nation states of Europe. In one of the first major gatherings after the start of hostilities of the city's socialists on 21 September at the Harlem River Casino in Manhattan, an event which was organised by the Russian Socialist Revolutionary Party to collect funds for exiled political dissidents featured New York's prominent labour lawyer and leader of the Socialist Party in America, Morris Hillquit (1869–1933), who proclaimed universal 'brotherhood' from New York to Constantinople.[121] The meeting reflected the way in which socialist politics could be used as a bridging point for New York's diverse population with Hillquit himself a Jewish Russian émigré.[122] The socialist newspaper the *New York Call*, which had developed from the German and Yiddish socialist papers in the city, had made an earlier similar plea in August 1914 for workers to unite against the machinations of Kings and Emperors.[123] However, a clear demonstration of this collective effort was made on 8 August, where a large socialist anti-war protest was organised to take place in Union Square. Thousands attended the rally, where speakers clamoured for a rejection of the conflict behind a banner which read 'War is hell, Socialism alone stands for brotherhood, Working men of the world will work for Socialism'.

The Union Square rally against the war had attracted socialist politicians from the across the city, and the massed crowds had heard orations in English, German, Italian, Yiddish as well as Russian. The rejection of the war was based on its perception within New York's socialist groups as a capitalist, imperial endeavour. Nevertheless, the war was also noted for the possibilities it presented for change in both Europe and the United States.[124] The city's socialist newspapers noted that whilst Europe was ruled by monarchies, the United States was equally restrained by the empires of business and industry.[125] Therefore, a connection was formed with the conflict that appeared to offer an opportunity for change, a particularly attractive proposition for left-leaning Russian Americans in New York. The onset of war in August 1914 presented Russian émigrés in the city with cause for reflection. Whilst nationalistic endeavour spurred some on to celebrate 'Faith, Tsar and Fatherland', for political and religious exiles the war presented an opportunity to rid or revenge themselves against the oppressive government. Therefore, the Russian Empire can be seen to have already been broken in New York with the mobilisation of the Tsar's forces. The war was part of a continuing struggle for Russian migrants in the city and offered the possibility of effecting change. Their status within America provided an

---

[121] N.F. Pratt, 1979. *Morris Hillquit: A Political History of an American Jewish Socialist*. New York, NY: Greenwood Press, p. 130.

[122] M. Hillquit, 1914a. Murderous War in Europe is the Inevitable Culmination of Murderous European Capitalism. *The American Socialist*, 1(8): 1–3.

[123] *New York Call*, August 12, 1914.

[124] I.H. Hourwich, 1914. Socialism and the War. *The New Review*, 2(10): 561–78.

[125] *New York Call*, November 5, 1914.

opportunity to critique the policies of Tsarist Russia whilst promoting the forces of change and the opponents of the government from the city of New York.

Tsarist Russia and the Dual Monarchy of Austria-Hungary were not the only empires whose status was being questioned through the ethnic presses of New York. With the rights of small nations at the forefront of campaigns of Slavic communities in the city, the entrance of Britain into the war on the basis of the infringement of Belgian's sovereignty by the German Empire encouraged Irish nationalists within New York.[126] The position of Britain's supposed hypocrisy was lampooned by the satirical *Catechism of Balaam,* published in New York and written by the Irish American Hugh Masterson using the pseudonym 'Shamus O'Sheel'. Though *Catechism* decries Britain's role as the defender of honesty and 'fair play':

> Q. But England is fighting for Liberty, Progress, Enlightenment, Democracy ... that sort of thing ... isn't she?

> A. Oh, certainly. To be sure. She always fights for them. You'd think she'd achieve them sometime!

> Q. What example have we of British freedom, etc.?

> A. Well, there's Ireland. Superior civilization gradually worn down by seven centuries of murder, pillage, arson, bribery, poisoning; culture rooted out by imposition of alien language.[127]

New York's role in this issue was heightened by its place as a centre of Irish Nationalism in the United States.[128] Publications from prominent Irish American citizens were distributed in the city from August 1914 which raised the question of Ireland's independence and support for the German Empire over the Entente of Britain and its allies.[129] These arguments, which developed from the Irish American press and politicians from the outset of the war, state that the opportunity presented by the war of demonstrating the liberties and rights acquired in the United States should be applied to the people of Ireland.[130] Prominent Irish newspapers in the

[126]   J.E. Cuddy, 1967. Irish-American Propagandists and Neutrality, 1914–1917. *Mid-America*, 49: 252–75; J.E. Cuddy, 1976. *Irish America and National Isolationism, 1914–1920*. New York, NY: Arno Press.

[127]   S. O'Sheel, 1915. *The Catechism of Balaam*. New York, NY: H.H. Masterson, p. 8.

[128]   J.P. Buckley, 1976. *The New York Irish: Their View of American Foreign Policy, 1914–1921*. New York, NY: Arno Press; C.C. Tansill, 1957. *America and the Fight for Irish Freedom: 1866–1922: An Old Story Based upon New Data*. New York, NY: Devin-Adair.

[129]   K. McGuire, 1915. *The King, the Kaiser and Irish Freedom*. New York, NY: Devin-Adair.

[130]   K. McGuire, 1916. *What Could Germany do for Ireland?* New York, NY: Wolfe Tone Company.

city, such as the *Irish American* and the *Gaelic American*, took the opportunity that had been created by the war to denounce British imperial rule in Ireland, its hypocrisy in its defence of Belgian sovereignty and the potential gains that could be made through an alliance between Ireland and the German Empire.[131] The *Gaelic American* pronounced Austria-Hungary to be the ally and friend of the Irish people whilst Germany was promoted as the natural ally of the United States in the aftermath of the declarations of war in Europe.[132]

John Devoy (1842–1928), an émigré Irish nationalist in the city, prominent member of *Clan na Gael* and editor of the *Gaelic American*, worked with his nationalist counterparts in New York and in Ireland to arm and support the cause for Irish independence in the turmoil of August 1914. Devoy exchanged correspondence with nationalist leaders in the wake of Britain's entry into the war in 1914, urging the mobilisation of Irish Americans in the city to further the cause of Ireland, to thwart Britain's war aims and to promote Germany as a supporter of their mission.[133] The role of New York in the ethnic, cultural, political and religious maelstrom that constituted Anglo-Irish relations, which had been exacerbated by the onset of conflict in Europe, was reiterated with the arrival of the former British civil servant and Irish Nationalist Sir Roger Casement (1864–1916) in the city on 20 July. With the European diplomatic crisis erupting whilst he was at sea, Casement had been a careful observer of events and assessed the impact of conflict in Europe after the assassination of Archduke Franz Ferdinand whilst residing in New York. In this assessment, Casement deliberated on its potential effect regarding Irish independence and the role of Irish Americans in the war. These thoughts were collected and published in January 1915 as a means of fostering support for the Central Powers through sympathy with the cause of Irish independence:

> And now, to-day, it is the great free race of this common origin of peace-loving peoples, filling another continent, that is being appealed to by every agency of crafty diplomacy, in every garb but that of truth, to aid the enemy of both and the arch-disturber of the old world. The jailer of Ireland seeks Irish-American support to keep Ireland in prison; the intriguer against Germany would win German-American good-will against its parent stock. There can be no peace for mankind, no limit to the intrigues set on foot to assure Great Britain "the mastery of the seas".[134]

---

[131] *Gaelic American*, August 1, 1914.

[132] *Gaelic American*, August 8, 1914.

[133] W. O'Brien and D. Ryan (eds), 1953. *Devoy's Post Bag, 1871–1928, Vol. II.* Dublin: C.J. Fallon, pp. 455–65.

[134] R. Casement, 1915. *The Crime Against Europe: A Possible Outcome of the War of 1914.* Philadelphia: Celtic Press, p. 86.

In New York, from his residence on Central Park West, Casement wrote numerous letters to friends and supporters, promoting the cause of the Irish Volunteers, denouncing the actions of the British government in soliciting a war with Germany and raising Irish American support for the Kaiser. The sympathy for Casement's argument was also assisted in the wave of outrage within the Irish American community in New York for the murder of civilians during the Howth Gun Running of July 1914. Casement and Devoy also solicited German support in late August 1914, meeting with the German Empire's military attaché Franz Von Papen (1879–1979) at the German Club in Manhattan to discuss the formation of an Irish Brigade constituted by Irish prisoners of war.[135] The machinations of Casement and Devoy in New York placed the city directly into the struggles that were taking place in Europe. Indeed, Casement actively sought the support, financial, moral and physical, of New York's Irish American residents in the struggle for freedom against the British Empire. Whilst in New York during August 1914, Casement and Devoy sought to publish this clarion call for Irish Americans in the city to resist the overtures of Britain and side with their 'natural' allies, Hohenzollern Germany. Published in 1914, *The Crime Against Ireland and How the War May Right It* was an adaptation from Casement's earlier tracts against Britain and for an Irish–German alliance. However, this version was specifically targeted at the Irish American residents of the metropolis:

> Let Irishmen in America stand ready, armed, keen and alert. The German guns that sound the sinking of the British Dreadnoughts will be the call of Ireland to her scattered sons.[136]

The opportunity presented by the war was, therefore, represented as a moment when American liberties and democracy could be provided for the citizens of Ireland. Irish Americans in the city were encouraged to use their status as Americans to further the cause of Ireland during the war in the same manner as the peoples of the Balkans and their representatives in the city had also forwarded their nationalist aims. Indeed, the *Gaelic American* implored its readers in the city not to forget the history of British colonial rule in Ireland and the successive failures of the Parliament in Westminster to grant 'Home Rule' to Dublin.[137] The events of the summer of 1914 were, thereby, represented in a distinctive fashion for Irish American New Yorkers; this community was provided a vision of the war as direct participants in the politics and processes that were engulfing Europe, but they were also witnessing this conflict from the vantage point of the United States,

---

[135] R. MacColl, 1956. *Roger Casement: A New Judgment.* London: Hamish Hamilton, p. 149.

[136] R. Casement, 1914. *The Crime Against Ireland and How the War May Right It.* New York, NY: s.n., p. 6.

[137] *Gaelic American*, October 31, 1914.

where their identity as 'Americans' was used to understand the problems of the old world.

The fermenting of Irish American insurrection in the city was encouraged by a highly organised campaign led by German-language newspapers and German organisations in New York.[138] From the outset of hostilities to the declaration of war, New York's German-language press, especially the *New Yorker Staats-Zeitung*, had promoted the politics of the German Empire with unabashed and unrestrained loyalty. This work was undertaken to ensure that New Yorkers negative perceptions of autocracy and imperialism in the German Empire as opposed to their democratic republic could be successfully countered. The *New Yorker Staats-Zeitung* was, therefore, reporting both for its readership but also for a far wider audience. The image of the German Empire within the city was a longstanding point of contention. Nevertheless, only the previous year had seen favourable and honorific reports in the mainstream city press that accompanied the celebrations for the silver jubilee of the reign of Kaiser Wilhelm II.[139] This representation of Germany within New York public life was underlined by the actions of patriotic German Americans in the city who through the 'German Society' had organised the 'Kaiser Memorial Fund' to erect the Kaiser Wilhelm Pavilion at the German Hospital and Dispensary located on 77th Street and Fourth Avenue.[140]

However, loyal German-language papers quickly censured any critical comment on the Kaiserreich. This was clearly demonstrated in the outcry that followed the production of the play *Zabern* in the city in January 1914, written by the Jewish German theatre impresario Adolf Phillip (1864–1936).[141] The production took its material from the Zabern Affair of 1913, where German troops stationed in Alsace Lorraine had used illegal measures including violence and detention as reprisal against civilian discontent in the French-speaking area of the German Empire. The actions brought international rebuke and were unfavourably covered in the New York press.[142] The play also took a critical perspective on the actions of the soldiers and presented a German Empire that was militaristic and dictatorial. Such slurs against the Kaiser and the German nation were forcefully rejected within the *New Yorker Staats-Zeitung*, which viewed the production as an affront to German values and aimed at detracting from the positive image of Germany in the United States.[143] The same strong defence by the newspaper of the actions of the German Empire after the declarations of war can be observed.[144] Robust arguments for the

[138]   H. Falcke, 1928. *Vor dem eintritt Amerikas in den weltkrieg deutsche propaganda in den Vereinigten Staaten von Amerika 1914/1915*. Dresden: C. Reissner.

[139]   *New York Times*, June 8, 1913.

[140]   *New York Evening Post*, May 22, 1913; *New York Sun*, May 23, 1913.

[141]   Koegel, *Music in German Immigrant Theater*, p. 339.

[142]   *New York Times*, January 11, 1914.

[143]   *New Yorker Staats-Zeitung*, February 7, 1914.

[144]   *New Yorker Staats-Zeitung*, August 11, 1914.

GERMAN RESERVISTS 'N BROADWAY 8|4|14

Figure 3.1   German Reservists Marching Down Broadway, Manhattan,
                  August 1914.

Source: Grantham Bain Collection, Library of Congress (LC-B2-3171-4).

necessity of the invasion of Belgium, the treatment of civilians in the warzones and the position of civilised Germany as the bulwark against the forces of barbarism were regular features in during August 1914.[145]

As the German-language newspapers encouraged their readership to actively participate in the war and to promote the cause of the 'fatherland' within the city, German social organisations also began organising charitable events to raise funds for widows and orphans whilst the German Consul in New York encouraged German Americans to volunteer for the reserve forces in the homeland. Numerous German community groups existed in the city, from the venerable German Society founded in the late eighteenth century to the German American Chamber of Commerce in New York, all of which were mobilised by individual accord or through the coordinated encouragement of individuals such as Herman Ridder, President of the *New Yorker Staats-Zeitung*. With the announcement of war, parades of German Americans took place across New York, with thousands attending events in Manhattan, Brooklyn and Queens (Figure 3.1). The German–American Alliances of these boroughs, largely composed of business owners and prominent citizens, organised large-scale

---

[145]   *New Yorker Staats-Zeitung*, September 2, 1914.

Figure 3.2   Henrietta Mielke Giving Iron Ring to Contributor Outside her
Father's Shop on Broadway, Manhattan, August 1914.

Source: Grantham Bain Collection, Library of Congress (LC-B2-3270-4).

events in the beer halls and parks of the city where both American and German anthems were sung and the flags of both nations displayed.[146] The charitable efforts of organisations such as these became a significant feature of German American contribution to the war effort as the British blockades prevented the return of reservists. Indeed, contemporary observers estimated that the number of reservists in the city numbered as much as 50,000.[147] During August 1914, the German Consul was inundated with recent immigrants from Germany as well as naturalised citizens who desired to return to fight. Their presence in the city offered an opportunity to raise the profile of the German cause but ultimately was not able to fill the ranks of the Imperial Army.

Regardless of this inability to effect proceedings on the battlefields of Europe, prominent German Americans in New York actively contributed to the development of charitable groups and organisations committed to promoting Germany in the United States. For example, the German Literary Defense Committee was formed in the city in August 1914 and chaired by Henry Weismann of the Brooklyn branch

---

[146]   *New York Herald*, October 19, 1914.
[147]   *New York Times*, August 14, 1914.

of the German–American Alliance. The Committee possessed the expressed aim of publishing materials which undermined the cause of the Entente and demonstrated the necessity of Germany's actions to the citizens of the United States.[148] The German Historical Society of New York, formed in 1890 to promote German American history, took upon a new direction after the declaration of war and drew upon the events within Germany, which saw the return of the Napoleonic War appeal for the exchange of gold for iron to raise funds for war widows and orphans (*Gold gab ich für Eisen*). This programme of activity, which was operated by Henry Mielke from his premises on 2nd Avenue, saw the donation by German American New Yorkers of precious objects in return for an iron ring decorated with a Maltese cross and the inscription 'Loyalty to the Fatherland to evidence, gave I, in troublous time, gold for this iron'. A report of this activity in the *New York Times* estimated that over 10,000 of the iron rings were being worn across the city by October 1914.[149]

Despite the activity of German American charitable organisations and the patriotism demonstrated in the parades and gatherings professing support for the Kaiser, prominent figures within the city deemed that because of the connection in the language of the city's mainstream press, there would automatically follow a bias for Britain and thereby the Entente. This perception encouraged the development of a dedicated German propaganda machine from August 1914 to influence the New York press and the city's populace towards a sympathetic regard for the Central Powers and the maintenance of neutrality in the wider United States.[150] The function of this initiative was to publish, distribute and to promote pro-German reporting across the city.[151] The initial lead in coordinating this effort was held by Bernhard Dernburg (1865–1937), a liberal politician and New York-based banker who was detailed by the German government to install a German Information Service in New York. Leaflets, pamphlets and booklets were quickly distributed through Dernburg's office which quickly focused on dismissing claims of German brutality over the invasion of Belgium.[152] A steady stream of publications was continued over the first few months of the war which put Germany's case as well as demonstrating the close connection between the United States and Germany.[153] The German American

---

[148]　A. Szarski, and F. De Walsh, 1914. *The Great Conspiracy*. New York, NY: German-American Literary Defense Committee.

[149]　*New York Times*, October 18, 1914.

[150]　G. Alphaud, 1914. *L'action allemande aux États-Unis de la mission Dernburg à l'incident Dumba*. Paris: Payot et Cie.

[151]　Anon., 1914. *Truth About Germany: Facts about the War*. New York, NY: Trow Press.

[152]　B. Dernburg (ed.), 1914. *The Case of Belgium in the Light of Official Reports Found in the Secret Archives of the Belgian Government After the Occupation of Brussels*. New York, NY: International Monthly, Inc.

[153]　B. Dernburg, 1915a. *Germany and the War: Not a Defense but an Explanation*. New York, NY: The Fatherland; H. Frobenius. 1914. *Germany's Hour of Destiny*. New York. NY: International Monthly, Inc.

population of the city were key to demonstrating this unity between the nations, as Dernburg consistently highlighted the similarities of the two 'races' and the success of New York as the direct effect of their collaboration.[154] Alongside Dernburg, prominent German American academics were mobilised by the German Information Service to provide impassioned defences of German culture after the outbreak of war and themselves serve as emblems of unity.[155]

The objectives of this organised campaign to influence the ideas of the citizens of New York are made clear in view of their publication in English. Seemingly confident of the German American support in the city, a focused effort was made to ensure that the English-reading populace were able to learn of the Kaiserreich's efforts to ensure civilisation in Europe.[156] This was conducted under the plea for 'fair play' for the Central Powers and coordinated from August 1914 through the offices of the *New York Staats-Zeitung* and Herman Ridder. Partly this was driven from an agenda within the German American Embassy and Germany's New York Consul that to influence the New York press would be to influence opinion in the United States, but it also reflects a strong belief in the dominance of Britain over the English-language press in the city. Count Johan Heinrich von Bernstorff (1862–1939), the German Ambassador to the United States, revealed this perception in his post-war memoirs:

> As is known, American public opinion at that time had been given a one-sided view of the causes and course of the war, for England, who, immediately after the declaration of war, had cut our Transatlantic cable, held the whole of the Transatlantic news apparatus in her hands. Apart from this, however, our enemies found from the beginning very important Allies in a number of leading American newspapers, which, in their daily issue of from three to six editions, did all they could to spread anti-German feeling.[157]

Despite the prominence given to the cutting of the transatlantic cable service, reports from Germany were still relayed to the city through the wireless transmitting station in Sayville, Long Island, 40 miles from New York. Built in 1912 by the German Telefunken Company, its partner site was located just outside Berlin and regular war reports were communicated to the German Consul after August 1914.[158] With a reliable source of information, Ridder ensured that

---

[154]   B. Dernburg, 1915b. *Search-lights on the War*. New York, NY: The Fatherland.

[155]   H. Münsterberg, 1914. *The War and America*, New York, NY: D. Appleton and Company; E. von Mach, 1914. *What Germany Wants*. Boston, MA: Little Brown; K. von Wiegand, 1915. *Current Misconceptions about the War*. New York, NY: The Fatherland.

[156]   G.S. Viereck, 1931. *Spreading Germs of Hate*. London: Duckworth.

[157]   J.H von Bernstorff, 1920. *My Three Years in America*. New York, NY: Charles Scribner's Sons, p. 35.

[158]   J.P. Jones and M. Hollister, 1918. *The German Secret Service in America*. Boston: Small, Maynard and Company, pp. 44–5.

translations of his editorial pieces in the *New York Staats-Zeitung* were published in the mainstream press in the city.[159] This attempt to gain the attention of a far wider readership in the city was reinforced with the publication of a collection of articles from the *New York Staats-Zeitung* in English.[160] In August 1914, through the New York Consul and the activities of the Commercial Attaché Heinrich Albert, the German government funded supportive German and English-language press in the city.[161] One of most prominent of these was that edited by the German American writer, George Sylvester Viereck (1884–1962), who published the English-language magazine *The Fatherland*, which was launched and distributed in New York. Declaring 'Fair Play for Germany and Austria-Hungary', the publication possessed the three aims of placing forward the 'German side' of the events of the war, reviewing the 'truthful' aspects of the conflict and reviewing the American press for negative sentiments towards Germany and its allies.[162] In its early editions one of the significant aspects of the articles was a stress on the shared values of Germany and America and the contributions of Germans to the building of New York.[163] Indeed, one contributor was keen to remind the readers of the *Fatherland* of the proud response of German Americans in the city with the declarations of the war in Europe:

> The streets of New York at the outbreak of the war, when thousands and thousands of German reserves in America gathered here and sang the songs of the Fatherland (demonstrate) ... to what extent the German-American element has been aroused for enthusiasm for the cause of the Fatherland (this) may (also) be judged by the enormous sums contributed by them to the various relief funds.[164]

Alongside these celebrations of German Americans was a celebration of past German Americans and their achievements, from the initial settling of the United States to the sacrifices of the Civil War and the Spanish–American War, the loyalty and steadfastness of German immigrants to the United States was illustrated.[165] Commentators compared this historical presence to the absence of British

---

[159] *New York Times*, August 26, 1914; *New York Sun*, August 26, 1914.

[160] H. Ridder, 1915. *Hyphenations*. New York, NY: Max Schmetterling.

[161] J. Reiling, 1997. *Deutschland, safe for democracy? Deutsch-amerikanische Beziehungen aus dem Tatigkeitsbereich*. Stuttgart: Franz Steiner Verlag, pp. 85–7.

[162] G.S. Viereck, F.F. Schrader and L. Sherwin, 1914. Preamble. *The Fatherland*, 1(1): 3.

[163] P. Keller, 1979. *States of Belonging: German-American Intellectuals and the First World War*. Cambridge, MA: Harvard University Press, p. 5.

[164] F.F. Schrader, 1914b. German-Americans. *The Fatherland*, 1(16): 7–10.

[165] F.F. Schrader, 1914a. A Question for German-Americans. *The Fatherland*, 1(3): 7–10; J.W. Burgess, F.F. Schrader and W.M. Sloane, 1914. *Germany's Just Cause, as Viewed by Eminent Native American Writers & Thinkers*. New York, NY: The Fatherland.

American identity in the city; German Americans were forwarded as 'true' citizens of the United States and the wider nation was shown to possess a harmony with the economics and culture of Germany. *The Fatherland* provided non-German speaking citizens with a frame through which to regard German-Americans, a tool for understanding the city's composition as well as its position towards the European war.

Despite the presumption of an anglophile tendency within the New York mainstream press, German propagandists were able to rely to a degree upon the support of the newspapers of William Randolph Hearst (1863–1951), particularly the *New York Evening Journal* and the *New York American*. Hearst also owned the German-language newspaper the *Deutsches Journal*, thereby forming a powerful press block in the city.[166] Whilst reports in these papers were capable of criticising the German government, after the outbreak of war they cultivated a rebuking tone towards the British pursuit of the conflict in Europe and with its dealings towards the United States.[167] However, where all the Hearst papers were united was in the demonstration of German American values and the significance of American neutrality in the war.[168] The tendency of stressing the place of German Americans within municipal society provided a means of both highlighting the perversity of any conflict between the two nations and the assistance of Germany's enemies whilst also ensuring that the readership of Hearst's newspapers could associate Germans as Americans.

This process was also undertaken by the *New Yorker Staats-Zeitung*, which encouraged its readers to realise the role of Germans in political and cultural life within the United States.[169] The demonstration of the 'American' character of the German population of the city was evidently emphasised to counter the perception that the Anglo-American identity was the norm and any variations were deviations whose loyalty was suspect.[170] This German-language paper, therefore, reinforced an identity that could be both German and American, providing a particular frame through which to view the war.[171] Indeed, the later publication of the *New Yorker*

---

[166] P. Conolly-Smith, 2009. Transforming an Ethnic Readership Through 'Word and Image': William Randolph Hearst's *Deutsches Journal* and New York's German-Language Press, 1895–1918. *American Periodicals: A Journal of History, Criticism and Bibliography*, 19(1): 66–84.

[167] *New York American*, September 1, 1914; *New York Evening Journal*, August 12, 1914.

[168] O. Carlson and E.S. Bates, 1936. *Hearst: Lord of San Simeon*. New York, NY: The Viking Press, p. 186.

[169] G.A. Dobbert, 1967. German-Americans between New and Old Fatherland, 1870–1914. *American Quarterly*, 19(4): 663–80.

[170] J. Goebel, 1914. The German-American and the President's Neutrality Proclamation. *The Fatherland*, 1(7): 10; K. Francke, 1915. *A German-American's Confession of Faith*. New York: B.W. Huebsch.

[171] B. Wiedemann-Citera, 1993. *Die Auswirkungen des Ersten Weltkrieges auf die Deutsch-Amerikaner im Spiegel der New Yorker Volkszeitung und der New York Times*

Staats-Zeitung's 'Kriegs Album', which provided supplementary material on the war, was titled 'Deutsch-Amerika'; to follow the progress of the conflict was thereby accorded a dual loyalty.[172] Readers of the pro-German press were also reminded of the more difficult moments of British American relations whilst they were asked to question whether 'blood was thicker than water' and whether there could be such a thing as a joint union either racially or culturally between the two nations:

> Was blood thicker than water when England sent the Iroquois to burn and torture women and babies in the borders of the struggling thirteen colonies? When Americans rotted alive in the prison-ship of the Brooklyn shore? When Buford's men were killed or mutilated living during a truce?[173]

This attempt to ensure the recognition of the validity of German American identity and to undermine the presumption of a singular Anglo-American identity drove greater alliances between German American groups and Irish American communities in the city, both of whom found common ground in the burgeoning pacifist movement in New York after August 1914. Indeed, financial arrangements between the German Information Service and Irish periodicals and individuals were investigated after the war. The extent of the shared objectives and agendas can be observed in the example of the *American Truth Society*. This organisation was founded in New York before the war in 1912 by Irish and German émigrés as a means to disrupt any Anglo-American alliance, and the society undertook a concerted campaign after the onset of hostilities in Europe to promote pacifism and neutrality. Led by the onetime Irish independence campaigner and New York lawyer Jeremiah O'Leary and promoted by the German–American Alliance leader Alphonse Koelble, the organisation held large public meetings in the city to raise the profile of their cause.[174] Although religious ties through Catholicism between Irish American and sections of the German American communities in the city brought a degree of harmony, it was through a strong verification of their status as Americans against British intrigue that constituted the majority of this discourse.[175]

Whilst the *New Yorker Staats-Zeitung* used the conflict to proclaim the German American character in the city, it also negated other roles and identities in the city. In an attempt to ensure support from a majority ethnically European population,

---

1914–1926. Frankfurt am Main: Peter Lang.

[172]　*Deutsch-Amerika*, February 27, 1915.

[173]　G.S. Viereck and F.F. Schrader, 1914. Editorial. *The Fatherland*, 1(10): 2.

[174]　American Truth Society, 1914. *Plan and Scope of American Truth Society*. New York, NY: American Truth Society.

[175]　D.R. Esslinger, 1967. American German and Irish Attitudes toward Neutrality, 1914–1917: A Study of Catholic Minorities. *The Catholic Historical Review*, 53(2): 194–216; D.H. Tolzmann, 1995. *German-Americans in the World Wars, Vol. 1: The Anti-German Hysteria of World War One*. Munich: K.G. Saur, p. 40.

other minority communities in New York were denigrated. As the European powers mobilised the colonised populations for the war effort, the reports of African and Asian men participating in the conflict as soldiers and labourers drew criticism from the *New Yorker Staats-Zeitung* as it had from within Germany itself.[176] The employment of this use of manpower within Europe was used as evidence by German American publishers in the city to convince their readership of the civilising mission of the German Empire which fought against the 'savagery' of the Entente. An early issue of *The Fatherland* published a poem which denounced the use of 'barbarian' troops against the Germany Army by the Entente:

> And out of Britannia's gigantic lap
> Forth come the Negro, the Hindu, the Jap;
> And as the English bagpipes play
> Five hundred million slaves will prey
> Upon one and crave for the loot.[177]

In this way, the tensions within American identity and race relations were used to cultivate support and sympathy for the German position. The use of this racial politics in the city was strongly criticised by the African American press in New York, which provided a distinctive means to understand the European War and its meanings for those within the metropolis.[178] The contributors to these newspapers acted quickly to condemn the attempt to play upon the racial divisions both within the city and the wider nation when mob violence and lynchings were murdering African Americans across the nation.[179] These accounts were also met with an increasing use of the war from August 1914 onwards as a means to elevate the role of Africa and African people across the world.[180] This was accompanied by a critical perspective on the 'European values' presented by the combatants that were seen to have failed; in this manner, the promotion of African culture took centre stage:

> The European war is much to be deplored, as being too savage and cruel to be tolerated, by intelligent human beings, but it will change the map of the world and give the people of Africa and Asia a better and more respectable standing with the races and powers of Europe and America, so that out of weakness may come strength, and out of the stench of battlefields may come sweetness, in new and better conditions of mankind.[181]

---

[176] *New Yorker Staats-Zeitung*, September 12, 1914.

[177] H.H. Ewers, 1914. We and the World. *The Fatherland*, 1(7): 9.

[178] W.G. Jordan, 2001. *Black Newspapers and America's War for Democracy, 1914–1920*. Chapel Hill, NC: University of North Carolina Press, p. 40.

[179] National Association for the Advancement of Colored People. 1919. *Thirty Years of Lynching in the United States, 1889–1913*. New York, NY: Negro Universities Press.

[180] *New York Age*, August 20, 1914.

[181] *New York Age*, September 10, 1914.

The accusation of barbarism levelled by Germany towards the Entente for the deployment of African and Asian men provided an opportunity for the African American press in the city to regard the war as an extension of the imperial aims of European nation states. This reflected the socialist influence in some sections of the African American intellectual circle in New York and it was also promoted by the scholar and activist W.E.B. Du Bois (1868–1963), who was based in the city after 1910, through the National Association for the Advancement of Colored People (NAACP) publication *Crisis*.[182] In this way, a direct link was made between the situation of African American individuals in New York and those who suffered under the colonial rule of European powers and segregation in the United States. The war was presented as fought in Europe, but impacting upon the lives of African American New Yorkers too. The NAACP asked its readers to contemplate these issues:

> Is it not the disgrace of the century, a disgrace even greater than the present
> European war that the foremost republic on earth should be directing its greatest
> battle not against war and poverty and prejudice, but against these dark little
> babies? More than this, it is dark children like these that in a sense are the
> cause of the present barbarous war in Europe. The rivalry of leading European
> countries in their lust for colonies is the underlying cause of this war.[183]

Similarly, the deployment of African labourers and troops in the war in Europe was promoted in *Crisis* as a point of pride for the achievements of African peoples, but also as a means of exposing the hypocrisy of European nations who would subjugate African people and deny them self-determination whilst using them to protect their own national borders.[184] In the December edition of *Crisis* a photograph of an African soldier on the Western Front provided a convenient illustration of the point:

> A Black Heathen of the Congo, fighting to protect the wives and daughters of the
> white Belgians, who have murdered and robbed his people, against 'Christian'
> Culture represented by the German trophy in his hand![185]

The war also provided an opportunity to reflect upon the actions of the United States as questions of citizenship, identity and human rights were evoked by Germany's invasion of Belgium. The news reports of atrocities committed against civilians, which followed the initial onset of hostilities, provided a point of unfavourable comparison to both the colonial rule of Belgium in the Congo and the brutality

---

[182]   W.E.B. Du Bois, 1914a. World War and the Color Line. *The Crisis*, 9(1): 28–30.

[183]   Anon., 1914. Our Baby Pictures. *The Crisis*, 8(6): 298–303.

[184]   Anon., 1914. Out of Africa I have Called my Son! *The Crisis*, 9(1): 26–7.

[185]   Anon., 1914. Men of the Month. *The Crisis*, 9(2): 68.

of the lynch-mob faced by African Americans.[186] Indeed, the *New York Age* ranked the European combatant countries by virtue of their treatment of colonised peoples; France was lauded for its presumed benevolent imperial rule, Britain was below its partner in the Entente, whilst Germany was criticised for its subjugation of people in Africa and Asia.[187] Belgium was offered no sympathetic quarter in this assessment as its 'unspeakable' crimes in the Congo were considered to have evaporated any goodwill from the African American readership in New York.[188] The outcry caused by the atrocities of the German Army in the city was condemned whilst the actions of lynch-mobs in the United States went unpunished:

> The bogey of race prejudice, again brought to the fore by those who seek to disguise the real issues of the ghastly war now raging and to justify its awful carnage, we are pledged to defy. It is our constant experience to deal with its hideous effects. Within the last month lynchings have occurred within our borders which equal in barbarism any of the atrocities which are reported from the theatre of war in Europe.[189]

The conflict in Europe was thereby brought home to the streets of New York. This was an international, imperial conflict but its effects were used to illustrate the condition of African Americans in the United States. The war was used to mobilise opinion in this respect; to reframe issues of identity and citizenship. The conflict offered an opportunity to recast the world for the 'betterment of mankind'; the African American population of New York were informed through the press that this was the war that was being fought in Europe and in their city too.

The use of identifying with the war through national, cultural, ethnic or religious connections was also used to stress the close association between the Entente and the citizens of New York. Pro-British sentiment was largely the driver of this mobilisation of identity as authors and sympathetic presses attempted to associate the United States with the values and ideals of Britain. Concepts of shared 'Anglo-Saxon' institutions of law and government were voiced in this regard as notions of familial relationships between the two nations as 'cousins' and 'brothers' were promoted.[190] The perception of an anglophile elite in New York's publishing circles by the German-language press and the German Consul was over-stated, but British press officers were dispatched to ensure a favourable representation in the city's media.[191] This included the mobilisation of well-known

---

186   *New York Age*, October 1, 1914.

187   *New York Age*, October 15, 1914.

188   *New York Age*, October 28, 1914,

189   W.E.B. Du Bois, 1914b. Of the Children of Peace. *The Crisis*, 8(6): 289–91.

190   H. Ringrose, 1914. *Why is America Neutral?* New York: The Marlow Press, Inc.

191   J.D. Squires, 1935. *British Propaganda at Home and in the United States from 1914 to 1917*. Cambridge, MA: Harvard University Press; H. Peterson, 1935. *Propaganda for War: The Campaign Against American Neutrality, 1914–1917*. Norman, OK: Oklahoma

British authors to state their case in the *New York Times* for Britain's war effort and appeal to the sense of 'common justice' within the 'English-speaking race'.[192] Some of New York's publishers, such as the British-supporting G.P. Putnam's, focused on releasing material that held sympathy with the Entente's position.[193]

Similarly, anglophile New York businessmen, lawyers and politicians were encouraged to present the unity between the two nations and the peaceful conduct between the United States in Britain since the war of 1812.[194] Supportive British pieces frequently highlighted the atrocities of the German Army, thereby emphasising the 'difference' of German culture over the concepts of decency and justice within Anglo-Saxon sentiment.[195] Accounts of the destruction of Louvain, the bombardment of Antwerp and the attack on Rheims provided a means for readers to measure their qualities as Americans by comparing the savagery of the war from their own position of neutral judgement.[196] However, this neutral assessment could align itself with a presumed sense of Anglo-Saxon chivalry and nobility which set citizens apart from the supposed Teutonic barbarity.[197] The publication of favourable reports, tracts and pamphlets in the city from the onset of the war onwards emphasised the Entente's position as similar to the ideals of the United States.[198] The function of these accounts demonstrates the ways in which these materials served as tools through which readers could associate themselves with the events of the war.

Conclusions

With the escalation of hostilities leading to the outbreak of war in August 1914, New York's citizens were immediately placed in the context of the 'European War'. Despite the fighting occurring thousands of miles away, the diverse residents of the city were implicated in the issues at stake as numerous associations from nationality to political, ethnic to religious, all drew New Yorkers to contemplate the war. Overwhelmingly, the conflict was viewed for its potential; whether for its capacity to grant national self-determination, patriotic glory, economic expansion,

---

University Press; J.M. Read, 1941. *Atrocity Propaganda: 1914–1919*. New Haven, CT: Yale University Press.

[192]   *New York Times*, September 18, 1914; *New York Times*, October 18, 1914.

[193]   G.H. Putnam, 1915. *Memories of a Publisher, 1865–1915*. New York: G.P. Putnam's Sons, p. 435.

[194]   F.W. Whitridge, 1914. *One American's Opinion of the European War: An Answer to Germany's Appeals*. New York: E.P. Dutton.

[195]   *New York Times*, October 25, 1914.

[196]   *New York Herald*, August 9, 1914.

[197]   *New York Times*, November 29, 1914.

[198]   Anon., 1915. *Germany's War Mania: The Teutonic Point of View as Officially Stated by her Leaders*. New York, NY: Dodd, Mead and Company.

religious freedom or civil rights, either in the United States or in Europe, the war was regarded as an agent of change. The manner in which this possible change was encountered demonstrates how issues of identity and belonging were negotiated and how the city was affected by the war. Whilst immigrant communities, whether recent or well-established, were mobilised by the outbreak of war, they met the prospect of conflict with an understanding of their role as Americans. Whilst pledging loyalty to the cause of another country, this was undertaken with the liberties and freedoms granted to them in the United States. Indeed, in the case of the movement for Slavic independence from the rule of the Habsburgs, this involved a desire to import these 'American' values back to their homeland. An ability to occupy multiple allegiances allowed New York's citizens to observe the war as an event which was happening to them. Rather than assume the neutrality of the United States, resulting in a tentative engagement with the conflict by its citizens, a survey of the ethnic press in the city indicates a passionate engagement with the war.

However, this should not be regarded as a tendency present only in the city's émigré community. New York's mainstream press utilised a position of judgemental neutrality in their reporting of the war, a means to exercise a particular vision of the conflict which emphasised a perception of 'American exceptionalism'. This can be regarded as part of the same negotiation that was taking place within the immigrant press in the city: a mobilisation of identity to meet the challenges presented by the conflict. Different versions of what constitutes an American can thereby be located in relation to the outbreak of the war in August 1914. This was a continuation of debates that had accompanied the waves of immigrants into the city since the nineteenth century, but their association with a war of unprecedented scale and ferocity cast such issues into a potentially disruptive context. With the advent of 'war fever' in the city, the metropolis was placed into a troubling context: the potential of rival factions continuing the conflict of Europe on the streets of New York, which would thereby add a further indictment on its status as a 'foreign city' in the United States. The municipal and national authorities would be drawn to dealing with this issue as New York posed particular problems for maintaining the United States' neutral stance and for ensuring the loyalty of its citizens. As the progress of the war continued, the authorities took an increasingly interventionist strategy to manage the diverse population of the city and develop a singular concept of identification with the nation.

The assassination of 28 June 1914 not only marked the beginning of the tumultuous events that led to war in Europe, it also marked the beginning of New York's own conflict; a war which would witness the redefinition of the city's residents and alter the identity of the city itself. The changes that would mark New York during the Great War can be observed at the very outset in a sermon given by William Thomas Manning (1866–1949), Rector of Trinity Church in Downtown Manhattan in August 1914, where the city was called upon to bear witness to the war:

That we may feel the shame which we share with all Christians that in spite of our Lord's own power and presence in this world, such strife is still possible; That our hearts may be touched with sympathy for all who suffer and with the desire to render them our aid; That we may feel due thankfulness for the blessings which we enjoy as citizens of this republic.[199]

It was the 'due thankfulness' of citizens that would be formed as the war implicated all aspects of life in the city. A conflict which mobilised the complex identities of the residents of New York would be used to affirm their place as Americans. As opposed to the wider United States, the First World War began in 1914 in New York.

---

[199]   W.T. Manning, 1914. A Form of Supplication and Intercession for the Restoration of the World's Peace and for Divine Guidance for All Men. *Year Book and Register of the Parish of Trinity Church in the City of New York, 1914.* New York, NY: Trinity Church, p. 456.

Chapter 4
Charity and Suspicion

The effect of the European War on social traditions in New York will be strongly in evidence this week. About this time of the year, for a long, long time, the annual Horse Show in Madison Square Garden has been mentioned in the same breath with the opening of the grand opera season ... Now that it has been abandoned owing to the war, fad and fashion are realizing the fact that the affairs of the day are closely allied to the history-making events on the other side of the ocean.[1]

Introduction

The impact of the war was experienced by all sections of New York's society. The city's elite were brought into the conflict just as much as the city's poor. Prominent businessmen, industrialists and publishers, with strong links to Europe, either financial or familial, could be embroiled in the war just as much as the recently arrived migrants from the war-torn continent. Each would be influenced by the representations of the war through the various city presses, as they framed the events in relation to specific identities, values and ideals. However, all sections of society would be implicated in the agendas set by the city authorities to take a greater control over its citizens, their perceptions and their loyalties. After the accusations of atrocities, the debates over culpability and the consideration of the repercussions of the conflict for national, political and religious identities, the war began to shape New York and its residents in other ways. As the war in Europe formed into a bloody stalemate across the battlefields, the citizens of the metropolis built new associations to the war, serving to draw attention to issues of citizenship within the city. With a populace that was drawn to opposing combatant nations, which could potentially lead to civil disruption as well as a challenge to the nation's neutral status, the city authorities were moved to begin controlling the expression of identity within the body politic. The war was being fought on the streets of New York in the form of a struggle to shape and maintain the loyalty of both émigré and established populations who, whilst not renouncing their place as 'Americans', were increasingly using this status to draw parallels with what was becoming an all-consuming conflict in Europe, Africa and the Middle East.

---

[1] *New York Times*, November 15, 1914.

Economic Effects of the War

Despite the expectation of an economic boom in the city, as European powers purchased much-needed materials in New York for their war-effort, the desertion of European capital that presaged the closure of the Stock Exchange brought crisis and uncertainty to the metropolis after August 1914. An economic downturn, with a decline in industrial output and exports, caused a rise in the level of unemployment in the city. By December 1914, an eight per cent reduction in the employment rate from the previous year ensured that 200,000 of New York's workforce, mainly its common labourers – a field traditionally held by the city's immigrant poor and an occupation highly sensitive to swings in demand – were out of work.[2] The potential disruption that this could cause within the delicate social fabric of the city was highlighted by a number of commentators.[3] Such was the level of concern, the civic authorities and Mayor Mitchel responded by initiating the Mayor's Committee on Unemployment in December 1914. Led by E.H. Gary, the committee was composed of civic reformers and business leaders, who advocated a limited intervention within the employment market to encourage businesses to offer 'steady work' to employees. The social and political benefits of an occupied workforce were regarded as paramount in the city's survival of the economic conditions wrought by the European war. The committee also encouraged the development of charitable organisations to meet the needs of the poor and to provide occupation for unemployed men.[4] This combination of private and public concern for the welfare of the city's residents served to inculcate a sense of loyalty to the city and to the nation and would become a key feature of how the city authorities responded to the pressures regarding identity and citizenship.

However, regardless of the ulterior motives for the greater involvement of authorities within the lives of the populace, it was a remedy for a very real and pressing problem. Whilst the economic depression had created a rise in unemployment, the tumultuous markets created by panicked buying and selling of materials and reserves had the effect of substantially increasing the price of foodstuffs and their availability. Across the city, vast swathes of the New York's citizens came under increasing pressure as they struggled to afford to purchase staples, thereby contributing to the potential points of tension in the city. From August 1914, the effect was significant and exacerbated by a poor harvest in the mid-western United States. Prices rose by as much as ten per cent between July and August 1914; eggs, meat, beans, butter and bread became scarce and

---

[2]   United States Department of Labor, Bureau of Labor Statistics. 1915. *Unemployment in New York City, New York*. Bulletin of the United States Bureau of Labor Statistics, 172(10): 6.

[3]   *New York Herald*, September 6, 1914; *New York Times*, September 8, 1914.

[4]   G. Elbert, 1916. *Report of the Mayor's Committee on Unemployment*. New York, NY: C.S. Nathan, Inc.

highly-priced commodities as supplies became increasingly difficult to obtain (Table 4.1).[5] The pressures placed upon the city's populace were noticeable, as appeals for action on food prices were directed towards City Hall.[6] The issue was perhaps inevitably tied into the wider debates about the war within New York, as stories of hoarding, price fixing and the practice of the refusal of sale between national and ethnic groups in the city gathered apace. In Blissville, Queens, a large-scale demonstration erupted and arrests were made on Saturday 15 August 1914, when several German butchers' shops in the area refused to extend credit to Polish, Russian and Slavic customers, with the reason that the men of the households would leave to fight in Europe, leaving families unable to pay their bills. The shop owners were dragged from their premises by the crowds and assaulted, as were attending policemen who arrived to restore order.[7] Such was the intensity of the incident that over the next few weeks, policemen were stationed outside the butchers in Greenpoint (Brooklyn), Bradley Avenue (Staten Island), and Review Avenue (Brooklyn) to protect premises which were described as a 'war zone'.[8]

Table 4.1   Wholesale Price of Beans in New York City, January to December 1914

Month	Price (per 100 pounds)
January 1914	$3.60–$3.65
February 1914	$3.55–$3.60
March 1914	$3.50
April 1914	$3.65
May 1914	$3.75–$3.80
June 1914	$3.75–$3.80
July 1914	$3.70
August 1914	$3.85–$3.90
September 1914	$5.15–$5.25
October 1914	$4.65–$4.70
November 1914	$4.35–$4.40
December 1914	$4.65–$4.70

Source: Bureau of Labor Statistics, 1915. *Wholesale Prices, 1890 to 1914*. Washington, DC: Government Printing Office, p. 47.

---

5   *New York Tribune*, August 15, 1914.
6   *New York Herald*, August 27, 1914.
7   *New York Herald*, August 15, 1914.
8   *New York Times*, August 16, 1914.

Therefore, the response to the problem of food supply and high prices was paramount for the security of the city and immediately dealt with by the municipal authorities. In July 1914, the Mayor's Committee on Food Supply was initiated, led by the politician and businessman George W. Perkins (1862–1920). The group had been working on issues of food supply before the advent of war, but with the conflict, their remit altered substantially.[9] Since supplying the city's food shops had become a problem after August 1914, ensuring a free and open market for necessities was vital.[10] A city-operated market, liberated from political or cultural bias, had been suggested in January 1914 as a means to alleviate supply problems to the poorest sections of the city, but the scheme was rapidly set up to address the conditions brought about by the war.[11] Perkins announced plans in late August to organise a series of 'free market' sites in the city, where farmers and traders could sell their produce at cost price and not with the significant mark-ups seen on foodstuffs since the outbreak of war.[12] The markets were sited with both economy and politics in mind, taking their place at the main thoroughfares of the city; they were located within the populous areas of Manhattan, largely inhabited by the poorer members of the city's émigré communities. Markets were eventually organised at eight locations in the city by September 1914, four held on new sites and four constructed on previous sites: Washington Market on the west of Lower Manhattan; West Washington Market to the west of Midtown Manhattan; Gansevoort Market to the west of Midtown Manhattan; Jefferson Market in Greenwich Village; Manhattan Bridge Market in the Lower East Side; Williamsburg Bridge Market in the Lower East Side; Queensboro Bridge Market in the Upper East Side; and Harlem Bridge Market in the north of Manhattan.[13] With the Lower West Side traditionally associated with Irish immigrants and the Lower East Side connected to German and more recently Russian Jewish immigration, the markets, operated and monitored by the city authorities, reflected the progressive political agenda for public works, but also provided a means to ameliorate tensions within the city socially and economically:

---

[9] Mayor's Committee on Food Supply, 1914a. *Reports of the Executive Committee of Mayor Mitchel's Committee on Food Supply*. New York, NY: C.S. Nathan, Inc.

[10] Merchants' Association of New York, 1918. *Report of the Food Problem Committee. March, 1918*. New York, NY: Food Problem Committee, p. 18.

[11] M. Marks, 1915. *Report on Market System for New York City and on Open Markets Established in Manhattan*. New York, NY: M.B. Brown.

[12] New York State, 1917a. *Joint Report on Foods and Markets of Governor Whitman's Market Commission, Mayor Mitchel's Food Supply Committee and the Wicks Legislative Committee. Transmitted to the Legislature January 3, 1917*. Albany, NY: J.B. Lyon, pp. 13–14.

[13] H. Bruére, 1916. *New York City's Administrative Progress, 1914–1916: A Survey of Various Departments under the Jurisdiction of the Mayor*. New York, NY: M.B. Brown, p. 40.

The widespread publicity of the free public markets recently established in New York City is responsible for the countless hundreds of consumers that frequent those markets and for the fact that ladies in automobiles come down to buy shoulder to shoulder with the wash-woman of the slums.[14]

The public markets were hugely successful, attracting large crowds on their opening and serving to reduce the price of food in the city.[15] Alongside the public markets, the Mayor's Committee on Food Supply also began attempting to change the dietary and purchasing habits of the city's residents in an organised leaflet and pamphlet campaign. Materials were distributed to schools throughout the city, in the hope that children would be enlightened and inform their possibly non-English speaking parents through this information.[16] Ostensibly, the programme was undertaken to educate citizens to protect food supplies, but it also provided a means of engaging with sections of the population as a process of 'Americanisation'.[17] Whilst benevolent in outlook, the programmes of wartime reform, just as their pre-war counterparts, were conducted under the auspices of reforming the populace, politically, socially and nationally.[18] As part of this process, the Committee of Food Supply's literature drew attention to the reader as to what should be done with food and how it could be conserved as part of an attempt to change values and ideals in the city.[19] Through the new economic conditions brought about by the war, an attempt was made to reshape the city's residents.[20] In this manner, well-established cultural traditions which did not suit the prevailing climate were criticised:

The habit of eating fish on Fridays only is absurd, and should be stopped. Fish are just as appetizing and nourishing on Tuesdays and Thursdays as on Fridays, and if you and your neighbours will buy fish any day in the week you will get cheaper fish and better fish. Hundreds of carloads of fish are sent from New York to other cities because the people living here do not appreciate the value of fish as a food, and do not buy it as often as they should.[21]

---

[14] National Municipal League, 1915. *Report of a Committee of the National Municipal League, November 19, 1914*. Philadelphia, PA: National Municipal League, p. 24.

[15] *New York Herald*, September 3, 1914.

[16] *New York Herald*, September 15, 1914.

[17] Recchiuti, *Civic Engagement*, p. 12.

[18] Burnstein, *Next to Godliness*, p. 8.

[19] Mayor's Committee on Food Supply, 1914b. *Substitutes for Meat*. New York, NY: Brooklyn Eagle Press.

[20] Mayor's Committee on Food Supply, 1914c. *Preparation of Vegetables for the Table*. New York, NY: Brooklyn Eagle Press.

[21] Mayor's Committee on Food Supply, 1914d. *Information about Fish and How to Use Them, Issued by Mayor's Committee on Food Supply*. New York, NY: G.W. Pratt, p. 5.

However, this was not a simple process of incorporation; indeed, there were aspects of 'European' society that were regarded as highly useful by the Committee of Food Supply. These were recommended to householders in order to cut down waste and to save money, but were offered as alien to New Yorkers, as practices to be borrowed not ones that were already present.[22] The place of authority within public life was thereby extended as the city authorities, through the jurisdiction of the mayor's committees, sought to take a greater role in the lives of citizens. These bodies, headed by appointees of Mayor Mitchel and staffed by reformers, politicians and prominent citizens were formative in shaping the city's response to the war. As pressures of unemployment, food supply and questions of loyalty and defence became of increasing concern to a city during wartime, the mayor's committees would formulate the municipal response. One of the first directives issued by the mayor's office was to control the 'war fever' and parades of reservists and patriotic émigrés on the city streets. To maintain order and to prevent any points of friction between communities, Mayor Mitchel, with a proclamation of 6 August 1914 issued through the New York press, ordered the removal of foreign flags from public display, banned processions for combatant nations and stated that only the national flag of the United States could be exhibited:

> The population of this city is cosmopolitan. In it we have people of German, of French, of English, of Italian, of Austrian, and of Russian blood. Public demonstrations of sympathy by people of a particular race, while natural from their point of view, are calculated to breed ill feeling upon the part of their fellow-citizens of other blood and sympathies and should not take place in this cosmopolitan and entirely neutral city. Furthermore, such demonstrations are calculated to breed disorder, and it is the duty of all of us, particularly at this time, to conserve the peace and order of this community.[23]

Mayor Mitchel reminded the city's population of where their loyalties should lie, stating that they were, after all, American citizens first and sympathisers with their respective fatherlands second.[24] Despite this proclamation of New York as a 'neutral city', its status as a global trading point ensured that it was implicated and compromised by its financial arrangements on the outbreak of war. The city of New York had borrowed extensively from the markets in Britain and France before 1914 to fund infrastructure development and owed a total of $80,000,000.[25] The European crisis that engulfed the continent accelerated the due date of these

---

[22] Mayor's Committee on Food Supply, 1915. *How to Use Left-overs, Issued by Mayor Mitchel's Committee on Food Supply*. New York, NY: G.W. Pratt, p. 7.

[23] *New York Herald*, August 7, 1914.

[24] *New York Times*, August 7, 1914.

[25] M. Harris, 2011. Full Faith and Credit: The United States' Response to the Panic of 1914. *Tempus*, 12(2): 1–22.

loans and the city was only saved by an appeal to the 'patriotism' of prominent city financial institutions. In particular, J.P. Morgan and Company and Kuhn, Loeb and Company, who provided the majority of the capital for a buy-out of the city's debts, thereby maintaining a neutral balance sheet as Europe descended into war.[26] Whilst the city's appearance of impartiality had been spared, J.P. Morgan and Company's other activities were placing the question of neutrality under far greater scrutiny.[27] After August 1914, the bank had become the purchasing agents for the Entente, a situation which was legalised and cemented by January 1915 with the Commercial Agency Agreement.[28] Under this arrangement, J.P. Morgan would procure and supply materials for use by Britain and France for the war effort, thereby benefiting from a highly lucrative trade:

> The commercial agents undertake in respect of the said purchase of goods and supplies to use their best endeavours to secure for His Majesty's Government the most favourable terms as to quality, price, delivery, discounts, and rebates, and also to aid and stimulate by all the means at their disposal sources of supply for the articles required.[29]

Regardless of political sentiments held within the firm by its partners, the agreement with the belligerent states was not regarded within New York's mainstream press as a tacit admission of support but a reflection of the 'American' values. Indeed, ensuring that the city profited from the war in Europe was sensed as a demonstration of national character.[30] In a self-proclaimed 'neutral city', such actions could be framed as part of a usual process of business. However, for readers of the ethnic press, the seemingly implicit or evidently explicit support for Entente was self-evident. Such a perception was not born purely out of a sense of an Anglophone conspiracy, but rather from the conditions which had developed as the war progressed. With the relaxation of trade embargos with belligerents in the United States and the operation of Britain's maritime blockade, any trade, whether material or financial, was inevitably weighted towards the Entente.

---

[26] T.W. Lamont, 1915. *Discussion of Financial Administration Budget and Tax Rate: The Government of the City of New York*. New York, NY: The New York State Constitutional Convention Commission, pp. 162–4.

[27] M. Horn, 2002. *Britain, France, and the Financing of the First World War*. Montreal: McGill-Queen's University Press, p. 12.

[28] M. Horn, 2000. A Private Bank at War: J.P. Morgan and Co. and France, 1914–1918. *Business History Review*, 74(1): 85–112.

[29] *Hearings before the Special Committee Investigating the Munitions Industry, United States Senate, Seventy-third (Seventy-fourth) Congress, Pursuant to S. Res.* Washington, DC: Government Printing Office, p. 8092.

[30] *New York Herald*, October 15, 1914.

The Origins of the City's War Charities

In a comparable manner to the city's financial institutions, the population of New York were nevertheless similarly implicated in the conflict through financial arrangements. As the declarations of war were issued and troops began crossing enemy territory, accounts of refugees fleeing the fighting or suffering at the hands of soldiers became commonplace in both the mainstream newspapers and the city's ethnic presses. These piteous stories served to galvanise public opinion into action and a series of charitable organisations were rapidly developed to meet the needs of those in Europe.[31] Charitable work and donations became a means for New Yorkers to associate with the war, either as a neutral or as a sympathiser with a combatant nation. Opportunities for this work abounded, with a number of small-scale organisations in the city beginning 'relief funds' in September 1914.[32] However, from October onwards, a coordinated newspaper campaign featuring adverts for the financial or material relief of Belgian civilians who had suffered from the effects of the war was enacted across the city:

> Belgian Relief Fund: Children starving in Belgium. You saw that, no doubt, in the war news. There is a good deal of war news – pages of it – every day. But that, somehow, stood out black from the page. Children starving. No meals in war-wreaked little Belgium for hundreds – yes, thousands of children – and mothers.[33]

The Belgian Relief Fund, or the Commission for Relief in Belgium, had its origins in London, where concerned American expatriates led by Herbert Hoover had begun to raise funds for widows and orphans left homeless after the German invasion. However, it was in New York that the organisation's main office was located and where the purchasing of goods and the raising of funds was coordinated. It was also in New York that the majority of the organisation's literature was printed and distributed.[34] These pamphlets informed the city's residents of the condition of Belgian refugees as well as providing information on how donations to the cause could be made.[35] The collections raised in the city were substantial, with

---

[31]   *New York Tribune*, October 11, 1914.

[32]   G.I. Gay and H.H. Fisher, 1929. *Public Relations of the Commission for Relief in Belgium*. Stanford, CA: Stanford University Press, p. 238.

[33]   *New York Herald*, October 25, 1914.

[34]   T.B. Kittredge, 1918. *The History of the Commission for Relief in Belgium, 1914–1917*. New York, NY: Commission for Relief in Belgium, pp. 52–3.

[35]   Commission for Relief in Belgium, 1915a. *General Instructions*. New York, NY: Commission for Relief in Belgium, pp. 5–6; Commission for Relief in Belgium, 1915b. *General Instructions for Making Contributions of Food, Clothing and Money*. New York, NY: Commission for Relief in Belgium, p. 7; Commission for Relief in Belgium, 1915c.

nearly $500,000 collected by November 1914.[36] The collections made in New York on behalf of the Belgian Relief Fund enabled the city's residents to connect themselves to the conflict in a more concrete term than following the news reports. Giving to the organisation was also represented as a patriotic act of a citizen of a neutral country; to come to the aid of a suffering 'little' nation was unquestionably 'American'.[37]

> We, as Americans are enlisted for the war to serve seven million men, women and children. It is the greatest commissary undertaking in the history of the world, and in the lexicon of America there is no such word as fail.[38]

Intriguingly, this was also accomplished with a mixture of private and public enterprise, which was regarded as unique to the nation and especially the city of New York.[39] Indeed, the New York-based Rockefeller Foundation, backed by the oil wealth of the Rockefeller family, lauded its own war relief work as an example of the uniquely American approach of business providing charitable works.[40] As the Commission, backed by the First National City Bank and the Guaranty Trust Company recommended that cash donations from the public were to be made out to J.P. Morgan at their Wall Street address, the relationships between war, profit and patriotism were somewhat obscured through the charitable endeavours of New York's institutions and citizens.[41]

The formation of the Women's Division of the Belgian Relief Fund in New York during November 1914 also provided an opportunity to engage with the conflict; to be part of the European War and to assist its victims. The Women's Division was primarily charged with organising the collection and distribution of clothing and foodstuffs for the widows, women and children of occupied Belgium and northern France.[42] Staffed by some of the wives of the businessmen, philanthropists and

---

Clothe Belgium and Northern France. New York, NY: Commission for Relief in Belgium, p. 5.

36 *New York Times*, November 17, 1914.

37 *New York Times*, November 3, 1914.

38 Commission for Relief in Belgium, 1915d. *The Need of Belgium*. New York, NY: Commission for Relief in Belgium, p. 32.

39 G. Birmingham, 1915. *Crowns for the Valiant*. New York, NY: Commission for Relief in Belgium, p. 10.

40 Rockefeller Foundation, 1915. *The Relief of Suffering Non-combatants in Europe: Belgian Refugees in Holland*. New York, NY: Rockefeller Foundation War Relief Commission, pp. 5–6.

41 Commission for Relief in Belgium, 1915e. *Financial Statement*. New York, NY: Commission for Relief in Belgium.

42 Commission for Relief in Belgium: Woman's Section, 1915. *History of the Woman's Section of the Commission for Relief in Belgium*. New York, NY: Commission for Relief in Belgium.

reformers who had propelled the Belgian Relief Fund, the Women's Division also served as a means for New York's suffragettes to connect to the patriotic movements. Indeed, with the advent of conflict in Europe and the development of 'war fever', a diversion of energy from the campaign for the extension of the franchise to the 'patriotic' work of American benevolence. The shift in focus was also the result of anti-suffrage campaigners who publically equated the avoidance of war work with a dereliction of national duty.[43] For example, in Annie Nathan Meyer's (1867–1951) drama *The Spur*, performed at the Cort Theatre in October 1914, with all profits being pledged to the Belgian Relief Fund, the issue of female emancipation was explored but found wanting as an apparent contrast between industrious patriotism and self-indulgence was drawn.[44] Suffragists in New York were compelled to remind supporters and detractors alike that it was their fellow female campaigners such as Florence Nightingale who had pioneered charity and nursing work in wartime; to align oneself to the cause of female suffrage was not to lapse into self-interest.[45]

Therefore, the suffragette movement in the city was beset by the same conundrum faced by émigré communities. Indeed, within the highly politically active section of the suffrage-supporting, Yiddish-speaking female population of New York the issues of gender, politics, ethnicity and nationalism were indistinguishable. The representation of the self was framed by a representation of the wider collective; a wider representation that, even at outset of the war, was restraining aspects of self-expression within the city. This can be clearly observed in the 'Peace Protest' of 29 August 1914, which witnessed a crowd of over a thousand, of the vast majority of whom were women, march through Fifth Avenue. The protestors focused upon the stories of crimes and atrocities from the warfront and marched dressed in black in solemn time to the beat of a drum. Disavowing nationalist identities, protestors hoped to attract pacifists to the cause which stressed the shared, global concerns of womanhood. Whilst attracting coverage of the event, the organisers were compelled to defend the utility of their actions from criticism that such efforts did not aid those they proclaimed to support. Whilst the 'Peace Protest' served as the basis for the formation of the national Women's Peace Party, its debated function emphasised the increasing sense of compulsion, moral, political and social, for individuals within the city to conform to an expected set of norms. Indeed, these issues were brought to the attention of suffrage campaigners with the speech of Christabel Pankhurst (1880–1958) at Carnegie Hall, 24 October 1914.[46] In this oration, the British suffragette was heckled by pro-German sections of the audience as she propounded the righteousness of the British cause and proclaimed

---

[43] *New York Times*, September 4, 1914.

[44] *New York Times*, October 27, 1914.

[45] *New York Times*, September 4, 1914.

[46] C. Pankhurst, 1914. *America and the War: A Speech Delivered at Carnegie Hall, New York*. London: Women's Social and Political Union.

the duty of American women to be dedicated to the service of the war.[47] It was these values, characters and loyalties that were focused through the prominence of the war charities in the city.

The organisation that provided an opportunity to serve and which drew the majority of female participants from the suffragette movement in the city was the Red Cross.[48] Whilst undertaken for an international organisation, the work completed in the city for the Red Cross from the very start of the war was a point of immense satisfaction and pride for the city's press. The self-congratulatory tone of these reports was well-justified; by October 1914, over $250,000 had been raised by in New York alone. Individual newspapers would keep their readers informed of the amounts donated to the Red Cross through their donations.[49] Such was the scale of public and private donations to the cause, that by September 1914, the American Red Cross had collected enough to charter the ship SS *Hamburg* to carry $10,000 worth of clothing, foodstuff and medical equipment as well as doctors and nurses from New York to Europe. The SS *Hamburg*, a passenger ship and part of the Hamburg-America Line, which had been interned by the United States Government after the British blockade ensured that Atlantic routes were no longer possible for German shipping, was renamed *Red Cross* and decorated with the liveries of both the organisation and the United States. Before sailing on 13 September the ship was moored off Manhattan to enable citizens to inspect the fruits of their benevolence. The departure of the vessel marked an opportunity for the mainstream press to marvel at the rapidity with which the contents and the vessel had been organised; a demonstration of the private and public spirit of New York's citizens.

It was New York's financial institutions and prominent businessmen who were to make the sizable donations to the cause of the Red Cross. J.P. Morgan and Company donated $10,000 in September 1914, a gift which was accompanied by a separate donation from Kuhn, Loeb and Company of $5,000. Smaller donations raised by dances, performances and shows across the city added to the organisations funds. For a 'neutral city', the Red Cross seemingly provided a fittingly impartial means of connecting oneself to the war. Indeed, German, Austrian and Hungarian donors in New York were reassured that their gifts would find their way to the soldiers, widows and orphans of the 'old country'. One was able to express association but this was conducted under the remit of a larger national effort. All gifts to the cause, whether large or small, were managed by the Treasurer of the New York Section of the Red Cross, Jacob Schiff (1847–1920). Through the active work of Schiff, the Red Cross in New York were able to promote the act of donating to the 'European Fund' for war relief as an American duty.

Jacob Schiff represents the division of association that marked New York at the outbreak of the war. Whilst a long-standing financier with Kuhn, Loeb and

---

[47]   *New York Herald*, October 25, 1914.

[48]   J.F. Irwin, 2013. *Making the World Safe: The American Red Cross and a Nation's Humanitarian Awakening*. Oxford: Oxford University Press, p. 101.

[49]   *New York Herald*, October 30, 1914.

Company, Schiff was born in Germany to a prominent Ashkenazi Jewish family and was also a prominent member and benefactor of the New York Yiddish community.[50] Schiff, like a number of his fellow Russian and German Jews in the city, had opposed the actions of Tsarist Russia for their anti-Semitism before August 1914.[51] After the start of hostilities, Schiff had proclaimed himself to favour the German cause and he asked his fellow Jewish New Yorkers to consider the sufferings of fellow Jewish peoples in Europe:

> It is hardly possible to exaggerate the horrors of the Jewish conditions in the war-stricken countries ... conditions in Russian Poland are such that Belgium's plight is a mere bagatelle in comparison. The Jewish people there have been outraged in the most terrible manner, both by the Poles who denounced them to the Russians as enemies and spies and then by the Russians themselves, who treated them as such. It is only after the Russian armies are forced to leave that the Jews are given protection by the Germans. In saying this I do not want to be misjudged, for it is well known that I am a German sympathizer. But the fact is that the Russians and the Poles alike have been inhumane to the Jewish population.[52]

As such, Schiff had become closely associated with the Abraham Cahan, the editor of the Yiddish socialist newspaper *Forverts*.[53] This degree of cooperation between two seemingly unlikely allies enabled the development of Jewish war relief charities in the city, providing a means for New York's Jewish communities to connect to the war and express solidarity with others in Europe. The impetus for action emerged after reports of anti-Semitic attacks in both Eastern Europe and Palestine. As a response to these, in October the American Jewish Relief Committee for Sufferers of the War was formed with Jacob Schiff's son-in-law Felix Warburg (1871–1937) and lawyer Louis Marshall (1856–1929) at its head. Constituted predominantly by German Reform Jews in the city, with other chapters located across the United States, the committee sought donations from citizens to aid 'fellow Jews'.[54] This organisation would be united in November 1914 with the Central Relief Committee, which had been largely formed through the Orthodox Eastern European Jewish communities of the city.[55] The Central Relief Committee

---

[50]   C. Adler, 1921. *Jacob Henry Schiff: A Biographical Sketch*. New York, NY: American Jewish Committee, p. 43.

[51]   *Forverts*, January 22, 1914.

[52]   J. Schiff, 1915. The Jewish Problem Today. *Menorah Journal*, 1: 75–8.

[53]   E. Manor, 2009. *Forward: The Jewish Daily Forward (Forverts) Newspaper: Immigrants, Socialism and Jewish Politics in New York, 1890–1917*. Brighton: Sussex Academic Press.

[54]   F. Warburg, 1918. *A Message from Felix M. Warburg, Chairman: Jewish War Relief 1918 Campaign, New York City*. New York, NY: Jewish War Relief.

[55]   M. Engelman, 1918. *Four Years of Relief and War Work by the Jews of America, 1914–1918*. New York, NY: Schoen, p. 5.

had also launched its efforts in October 1914 with a plaintive cry to citizens of New York and Jewish residents across the United States:

> Our brethren are dying. Widows and orphans are wandering, homeless, naked and hungry. Women, old and young, with their little ones, and the aged find no refuge. In every land that we or our father once called home, bloody war with all its unspeakable horrors stalks abroad: thousands of villages have been ravaged and great cities laid waste. Mourning, they lift up their eyes, whence shall come their help![56]

The combined work of the two, together with wider national partners, was coordinated through the American Jewish Joint Distribution Committee (JDC).[57] The JDC apportioned funds collected from musical performances, recitals, fundraisers and ordinary donations to the various Jewish communities across Europe and the Middle East, who were reported to require assistance.[58] The varied range of activities launched by the JDC from their inception onwards provided Jewish New Yorkers, whether Yiddish, German, Russian or English-speaking, socialist or conservative, émigré or nativist American, Zionist or anti-Zionist, with a means to establish a common response to the war.[59] This was exemplified with the initiative launched in December 1915, when the JDC sought to specifically mobilise the general Jewish population of the city; programmes such as 'Women of the Hour' and Men of the Hour' were used, encouraging residents to devote one hour a week for ten weeks for work towards raising war relief funds.[60] Jewish New Yorkers were encouraged to complete these actions as an act of 'self-sacrifice' to assist their brethren abroad.[61] However, this charitable work was not undertaken to acquire the presumption of difference by the Jewish enclaves within the city; such charitable actions were defined as being distinctly American and for the service of the United States.[62]

The relationship between an American identity that expresses benevolence and a religious or ethnic identity that expresses solidarity was a feature of other groups within the city who sought to develop organisations to support, both financially

---

[56]   H.S. Goldstein, 1928. *Forty Years of Struggle for a Principle: The Biography of Harry Fischel*. New York, NY: Bloch Publishing Company, p. 126.

[57]   F. Warburg, 1916. *Reports Received by the Joint Distribution Committee of Funds for Jewish War Sufferers*. New York, NY: C.S. Nathan, p. 7.

[58]   Y. Bauer, 1974. *My Brother's Keeper: A History of the American Jewish Joint Distribution Committee, 1929–1939*. Philadelphia, PA: Jewish Publication Society of America, p. 7.

[59]   J. Jacobs, 1916. The Federation Movement in American Jewish Philanthropy. *American Jewish Year Book*, 17: 159–98.

[60]   *New York Times*, December 26, 1915.

[61]   Schiff, *The Jewish Problem Today*, p. 78.

[62]   H.M. Kallen, 1915a. Nationality and the Hyphenated American. *The Menorah Journal*, 1: 79–85; H.M. Kallen, 1915b. Democracy Versus the Melting Pot: A Study of American Nationality. *The Nation*, February 25, pp. 217–19.

and materially, those affected by the war in Europe. The conflict brought a surge of charitable efforts in New York; during the first year of the war, a diverse array of altruistic causes made their claim on the goodwill of the city's residents. These causes aligned themselves with aspects of the conflict which enabled citizens to proclaim allegiance and to feel connected to the events on the battlefields and behind the lines. Alongside the calls for support for the Red Cross and the Belgium Relief Fund, appeals were made for the British Fund, the British War Relief Association, the Austrian Relief Fund, the French Fund, the Prince of Wales Fund, the Paris Ambulance Fund and the Committee of Mercy.[63] These organisations arose from the personal, cultural or political allegiances that their founders held and offered supporters within the city to exercise their own moral, cultural or ideological stances. Their spread was phenomenal, testifying to the eagerness with which New Yorkers associated with the conflict. By December 1914, at least 50 organisations had been registered in the city as undertaking work associated with 'war relief'.

This process was definitely noticeable in the campaigns to raise money and attention for Britain, its soldiers and civilians, during the war.[64] For example, the British War Relief Association (BWRA) was founded in August 1914 to aid military and civilian hospitals both in Britain as well as France and Belgium.[65] Its mission was to collect money, clothing and surgical dressings from New York's residents who were sympathetic to the British cause.[66] The organisation issued instructions to potential donors as to how to contribute materially as well as financially, as knitting patterns for soldiers' socks, headgear and undergarments were distributed.[67] Headquartered at the British Imperial Club on 132 West 27th Street, the fund was presided over by Beatrice Forbes-Robertson Hale (1883–1967), a British expatriate married to a prominent New York lawyer. This particular fund reflects the potential tensions between differing roles and identities, as Forbes-Robertson Hale had been an active member of the suffragette movement before the war, proclaiming the rights of women as a mark of civilised society and war as a brutal expression of contemporary man's vicious nature.[68] During the conflict her position on these matters was complicated by the demands of a patriotic impulse and the work of the Association (BWRA);

---

[63] *New York Times*, September 4, 1914; *New York Tribune*, September 12, 1914.

[64] K. Burk, 1979. The Diplomacy of Finance: British Financial Missions to the United States 1914–1918. *The Historical Journal*, 22(2): 351–72; W. Lyddon, 1938. *British War Missions to the United States, 1914–1918*. Oxford: Oxford University Press.

[65] I. Clarke, 1918. *American Women and the World War*. New York, NY: D. Appleton and Company, p. 492.

[66] British War Relief Association, 1917. *How to Make Surgical Dressings*. New York, NY: British War Relief Association, p. 5.

[67] *New York Herald*, October 24, 1914.

[68] B. Forbes-Robertson Hale, 1914. *What Women Want: An Interpretation of the Feminist Movement*. New York, NY: Frederick A. Stokes.

her novels, written during wartime, portray the conflict within an uplifting and enlightening context which enables cooperation both between nations and the sexes.[69] Nevertheless, her role with the BWRA, similarly to the act of giving by the thousands of the association's donors, served as a means to allow an expression of identity and affiliation.

The organisation proved highly successful, benefitting from the donation of a sizeable property for the duration of the war, from which volunteers prepared packages for delivery and organised the collection of materials.[70] Despite a minor scandal that was caused by the departure of the owners of the British Imperial Club, allegedly with a proportion of the association's funds in February 1915, after three years of operation the BWAR had processed nearly $250,000 worth of goods to Europe. Other British charitable donations were also able to rely upon generating a sense of fellow-feeling amongst sections of the city's population. Whilst the British and Canadian Patriotic Fund held charity cricket matches and gymkhanas to develop funds for British Empire servicemen and organisations such as the British-American War Relief Fund sought to collect funds for hospital supplies for soldiers through subscriptions, both assumed the role as an instrument of expression for New Yorkers.[71] Despite the development of offices across the United States, their origin in New York reflected the tensions present in the city.

The mobilisation of New Yorkers' sentiments was particularly vigorous with regard to raising funds for the relief of French victims of the war. Indeed, with that raised for the widows and orphans of Belgium, the French Fund attracted a significant section of the city's population, undoubtedly helped by powerful accounts of the condition of the nation which were reported in New York's newspapers:

> In France I saw a pastoral land overrun by soldiers and racked by war until it seemed the very earth would cry out for mercy. I saw a country literally stripped of its men in order that the regiments might be filled. I saw women hourly striving to do the ordained work of their fathers, husbands, brothers, and sons, hourly piecing together the jarred and broken fragments of their lives. I saw countless villages turned into smoking, filthy, ill-smelling heaps of ruins. I saw schools that were converted into hospitals and factories changed into barracks.[72]

Spurred on by these descriptions, New Yorkers provided generous donations to French widows, orphans, wounded soldiers and serving soldiers. Indeed,

---

[69]   B. Forbes-Robertson Hale, 1916. *The Nest-Builder*. New York, NY: Frederick A. Stokes.

[70]   *New York Herald*, January 18, 1915.

[71]   National Allied Relief Committee, 1915. *Some of America's Contributions to European War Relief*. New York, NY: Herald Square Press, p. 50.

[72]   *New York Evening Post*, December 2, 1914.

as a direct response to the reports of orphaned children in France, funds were raised in the city by prominent French American businessmen, lawyers and organisations, such as the international law firm, the Coudert Brothers. These fundraising ventures culminated in 1915 with the organisation in New York of the Fatherless Children of France.[73] Whilst the Red Cross donations were used to provide for the orphans and widows in France, a number of private charities were formed in the city to relieve their plight. These charities were formed by individuals with cultural, political and intellectual ties to France. For instance, the Society of Beaux-Arts Architects, founded in 1894, which had promoted the teachings of the Parisian École des Beaux-Arts in the United States, responded to the war by forming charitable ventures for French artists and their families. The French Artists War Relief Fund was supported by *soirées artistiques*, concerts, pantomimes and exhibitions of art, which exhibited both American and French works, to provide sustenance for artists and their families during the war.[74] Similarly, the Duryea Relief Fund, which was founded by Francophile Americans with strong ties to the city, ran their operations from New York to provide supplies to French hospitals, calling upon the goodwill of individuals towards the French 'victims' of the war.[75]

Rather more problematic, with regard to issues of neutrality, were the organisations that sought to directly help the French Army. The Lafayette Fund, named after the celebrated French officer, was formalised in December 1915 in New York and specifically reminded New Yorkers of the close association between the two republics of the United States and France dating back to the War of Independence.[76] The organisation was focused on the conditions of troops in the field and organised the production and shipping of equipment kits, predominantly warm clothing and rubber ponchos to serving French soldiers.[77] Within a year of its formation, 50,000 'comfort kits' had been supplied to French soldiers.[78] Inevitably, such activities brought criticism from German and pacifist elements for seemingly breaking the neutral status of the United States by directly assisting a combatant nation:

---

[73]   Fatherless Children of France, 1915. *The Fatherless Children of France*. New York, NY: National Executive Office.

[74]   American Artists' Committee of One Hundred, 1916. *Exhibition of Contemporary French Art: For the Relief Fund for the Families of French Soldier Artists. Ritz-Carlton Ballroom, New York, January, 1916*. New York, NY: Knickerbocker Press.

[75]   Duryea War Relief. European War Scrapbooks, 1914–1918. New York Public Library, MSS Col 952.

[76]   *New York Times*, December 7, 1914.

[77]   W. Guthrie, 1916. *America's Debt to France: The Most Unalterable Gratitude*. New York, NY: American Society for the Relief of French War Orphans.

[78]   *New York Sun*, May 2, 1915.

Do you realise fully what that means, you vociferous criers-out in the cause of humanity, you members of the Lafayette League … and other mushy beldames who are making themselves a party of the murder of mothers and infants?[79]

Nevertheless, the Lafayette Fund continued in their fundraising, defending their role in supplying materials to troops as a charitable donation which was conducted in the spirit of American traditions.[80] This was reaffirmed with the decision to annually mark Lafayette Day from September 1915, an event which would be coordinated by the Lafayette Fund and intended as a national celebration of the alliance between the United States and France.[81] The coincidence of Lafayette Day with the anniversary of the Battle of the Marne in September 1914 provided a crucial context in which to stress support for both the civilians and the soldiers of France. Indeed, placing it into this context ensured the direct engagement of New York's residents with the conflict in Europe. Parades, speeches, banquets and concerts were held as part of the celebrations. Within New York, Lafayette Day became a notable event during the conflict, with the city marking the event with further celebrations of American–French amity.[82] As part of the events, congratulatory dinners were held for ambassadors and dignitaries, both American and French, to further the sense of cooperation and to promote the work of the Lafayette Fund.[83] Through the patronage of the charity and participation in the commemorative events, individuals could express their support and their sympathies whilst overtly stating their loyalty to the United States.[84] Within this context, a critical perspective on the politics of the neutrality of the United States could emerge, with former President Theodore Roosevelt (1858–1919) remarking after a children's performance organised by members of the Lafayette Fund that, 'never be neutral between right and wrong'.[85]

Across the city, similarly large sums were being raised for seemingly partial causes with their contributors still able affirm their status as Americans in the process. As the war progressed, charitable groups such as these were forced to change, both from the pressures of the industrialised war in Europe and from

---

[79]   F.F. Schrader, 1915b. Warring on Women and Children. *The Fatherland*, 3(17): 291–3.

[80]   *New York Times*, September 3, 1916; *New York Tribune*, September 6, 1916.

[81]   *New York Times*, September 7, 1915; Lafayette Day Citizens' Committee of New York, 1916. *Lafayette Day, 1916*. New York, NY: Law.

[82]   Lafayette Day National Committee, 1917. *Lafayette Day Exercises in Commemoration of the Double Anniversary of the Birth of Lafayette and the Battle of the Marne: September 6th, 1917*. New York, NY: Law.

[83]   France-America Society, 1916. *Lafayette Day Dinner of the France-America Society, in Honor of His Excellency, the Ambassador of France, on the Evening of September 16th, 1916, at the Waldorf-Astoria Hotel, New York*. New York, NY: McGuire.

[84]   France-America Society, 1918. *Lafayette Day*. New York, NY: McGuire.

[85]   *New York Times*, April 16, 1915.

changing political attitudes within the city. This process can be identified with the Mayfair War Relief Committee. The organisation was formed in September 1914, principally to serve as a small-scale collection and distribution depot for clothes, food and necessities for the destitute of Belgium and France.[86] By 1916, after the mass death that had occurred on the battlefields of the Somme, Vimy, Verdun and Gallipoli, the organisation was forced to increase its efforts to meet the demand.[87] In contrast, the Austrian Relief Fund similarly altered not through external pressure but through the alterations in the political climate in the city. Formed in September 1914 by Ambassador Constantine Dumba (1856–1947), representative of the Dual Monarchy to the United States, the organisation proclaimed its humanitarian mission in its call for donations which, as the call stated, would be delivered specifically to the peoples of Austria-Hungary.[88] The donations received by the fund were relatively minor compared with the larger organisations in the city, though it attempted to raise funds through dances, card parties and soirées for a sympathetic New York elite.[89] However, its efforts were hampered by the difficulties of presenting its case to New York's residents as the campaigns for independence from representatives from Bohemia, Hungary and Slovakia in the city sought to sway public opinion.[90]

Demonstrating Identity

Where the supporters of the Central Powers in New York could express their loyalties and contribute to the efforts led by these combatant countries in the war in Europe was through a series of dedicated events, which allowed citizens from all across the social spectrum to donate money to the cause of Germany and Austria-Hungary. During the autumn of 1914, representatives of the consuls of the Central Powers within the city encouraged the formation of a single German, Austrian and Hungarian War Relief Fund. Leading members of the city's German American communities were prominent in the organisation of the fund, connecting the importance of their place in the United States with the promotion of the Fatherland. Initially, this fund was based in New York, but offices were created in cities across the United States with significant émigré populations. The primary aim of this charity was to promote collections for widows and orphans of soldiers killed on the battlefields. In New York, this aim was accomplished with the formation of bazaars, where traditional German, Austrian and Hungarian goods and food were sold in order to raise funds. Those sympathetic citizens of the

---

[86]   J. Williams, 1918. *The Voluntary Aid of America*. New York, NY: Williams, pp. 98–9.

[87]   *New York Times*, September 9, 1917.

[88]   *New York Evening Telegraph*, September 4, 1914.

[89]   *New York Times*, March 21, 1915.

[90]   *New York Times*, May 18, 1915.

city, who favoured the Kaiser or Emperor Franz Josef I, were able to express their loyalties and participate in the war, both whilst performing the American character of the consumer. Just as businesses and organisations raised funds through private finance, the aid for the Central Powers would be similarly acquired.[91]

The location and size of the first of these bazaars is telling; the 71st Armory on 34th Street and Park Avenue was leased for the occasion and advance admission ticket sales alone had provided an estimated $10,000 for the fund. The opening of the market was oversubscribed, with large crowds turned away from the event on 5 December 1914.[92] Undoubtedly, some parts of these large crowds were enticed by the spectacle as much as the show of solidarity, as the interior of the bazaar was lavishly decorated, echoing the streets, buildings and monumental architecture of Germany, Austria and Hungary.[93] The significance of the cultural contribution of the Central Powers was reinforced through the bazaar; indeed, visitors were welcomed with the sight of a re-creation of the Nürnberg Gate. However, the creators of this spectacular stressed the significance of German American identity.[94] As such, the avenues that stretched out from this structure were named after prominent German officers who fought during the War of Independence.[95] Therefore, visitors would peruse the wares on offer as they strolled DeKalb, Steuben or Leisler Streets. American flags were predominantly displayed throughout the bazaar whilst a parade of German American Civil War veterans cemented the association between pride for a cultural or ethnic Fatherland and loyalty to the adopted homeland of the United States. Herman Ridder and Alphonse Koelble spoke to the crowds after the veterans' parade, stating that the bazaar demonstrated how German Americans could express 'love and sympathy' for both nations.[96]

Such sentiments were repeated in the second bazaar held by the German, Austrian, Hungarian War Relief Fund, which was held in the larger venue of Madison Square Garden in March 1916 (Figure 4.1). Again, the spectacular decorations were intended to communicate or to affirm the significance of the relationship between the Central Powers and the United States. The main entrance to the site, on Madison Avenue, was once again the replica of the Nürnberg Gate, which led to the 'Market Platz', where radiating streets bore the names of German

---

[91]   G.S. Viereck, 1914. For Widows and Orphans. *The Fatherland*, 1(20): 12.

[92]   *New York Tribune*, December 14, 1914.

[93]   *New York Tribune*, December 15, 1914.

[94]   F. Luebke, 1974. *Bonds of Loyalty: German-Americans and World War I*. Dekalb, IL: Northern Illinois University Press.

[95]   *New York Times*, December 6, 1914.

[96]   German, Austrian, Hungarian and Their Allies War Relief Fund, Inc., 1914. *Charity Bazaar for the Benefit of the Widows and Orphans of German, Austrian and Hungarian Soldiers Under the Auspices of the German, Austrian and Hungarian War Relief Fund, Inc: 71st Regiment Armory, New York City, December 5th to 20th, 1914*. New York, NY: J.F. Geis.

Figure 4.1   Charity Bazar for the Widows and Orphans of German, Austrian,
              Hungarian and their Allied Soldiers, March 1916.

Source: Hegeman Print, 1916. Library of Congress (LC-USZC4-9854).

American figures. However, symbolically, the grand processional way, which bore
the name 'Washington Avenue', led directly to the appropriately named 'Peace
Plaza'. To wander the bazaar was to be offered a lesson in the current political
drive from Germany to maintain the neutrality of the United States. The centre
of the 'Peace Plaza' was a sculpture depicting the landing of German pilgrims
in America in 1695. The venue was completed with the addition of over 300
booths, from Hungarian stalls selling both traditional foods and crafts, to Benz
automobile vendors and Zeppelin Airship displays, whilst a 'Munich' restaurant

provided visitors with a taste of Bavaria.[97] Throughout the venue, great stress was placed on the loyalty of German Americans to the United States, and the bazaar was also used as an opportunity to affirm the importance of the attachment to the Fatherland as part of this 'American' identity. Emanuel Baruch, Chair of the organising committee, drew explicit reference to this effect:

> We do not believe in the loyalty of any citizen to our own country, who finds no place in his heart for the land of his fathers. Prove yourself worthy of your new fatherland, by proving yourself worthy of your old.[98]

Henry Weismann, President of the German–American National Alliance, in New York also spoke at the bazaar, reassuring the audience that their 'duties as Americans' were entirely in unison with their sympathies for the 'war sufferers' of the Central Powers.[99]

Before the second bazaar for the Central Powers, the requirement to stress the attachment of German Americans to the United States and to maintain the neutrality of both the city of New York and the wider nation was becoming of increasing concern after the spring of 1915. The sinking of the passenger liner RMS *Lusitania* in May 1915 by German U-boats off the coast of Ireland, which had set sail from New York and carried on board both passengers and sailors from the city, with the loss of over a thousand lives, had caused outrage in some sections of the metropolitan press. Mainstream newspapers were outraged by the brutality of an attack which was considered a clear display of militarism against a civilian target.[100] The horror of the large-scale loss of life was communicated to readers in clear detail, as the terrifying accounts of death caused by the explosion or drowning occupied the front page of the majority of the city's newspapers.[101] However, whilst these publications levelled their anger at the German Navy, a strong rebuke of British naval policies which had placed the lives of passengers in danger was also expressed.[102] The German-language papers also used this supposed dereliction of responsibility by Britain, a point reinforced by claims that the vessel represented a legitimate target because of

---

[97]   G.S. Viereck, 1916a. The Significance of the War Bazaars. *The Fatherland*, 4(7): 105.

[98]   German, Austrian, Hungarian and Their Allies War Relief Fund, Inc., 1916. *Charity Bazaar: For the Benefit of the Widows and Orphans of German, Austrian, Hungarian and Their Allied Soldiers under the Auspices of the German, Austrian, Hungarian and Their Allies War Relief Fund, Inc. Madison Square Garden, New York City, March 11th to 23rd.* New York, NY: J.F. Geis, p. 1.

[99]   *New York Times*, March 13, 1916.

[100]   *The Evening World*, May 7, 1915; *New York Sun*, May 8, 1915.

[101]   *New York Tribune*, May 8, 1915; *New York Times*, May 8, 1915; *New York Herald*, May 8, 1915.

[102]   *New York Evening Telegraph*, May 7, 1915.

the war contraband on board.[103] Intriguingly, the incident did not contribute to an overwhelming embrace of the Entente and a rejection of the Central Powers; indeed, it cemented the position of neutral judgement amongst the city's press and a desire for peaceful resolution. However, the sinking of the *Lusitania* did clarify the role of charitable works and war relief work in the city. The status of the war's 'victims' was a cultural currency within the city; to promote the suffering of innocents at the hands of the enemy enabled the promotion of the cause across the various ethnic enclaves in New York.

This process of competitive and political suffering can be assessed with the Jewish War Sufferers Relief Bazaar, which was held after the Central Powers Bazaar at Grand Central Palace in March and April 1916.[104] The event was billed as a 'democratic' effort, with Jewish New Yorkers from across the social scale in attendance; from the poor residents of the Lower East Side to the wealthy financiers of Wall Street. The fair focused on German and Russian Jewish victims of the war on successive nights as a particular effort was made to recognise the effect of the war on these communities. Days were also dedicated to the particular boroughs of the city, so Jewish residents from all parts of the city could exhibit both patriotism and loyalty to two separate identities at the same time by attending 'Bronx Day' or 'Brooklyn Day'. To raise money for these worthy causes, raffles, donations and cash gifts were accepted. The bazaar was also noticeable for the presence of German and Irish delegates alongside Jewish representatives as the association with the victims of the conflict formed valuable political capital in a city whose citizens were being increasingly drawn into the conflict.[105] The connections between Ireland and Germany and the role of 'the victim' was further demonstrated with the news in April 1916 of the Easter Rising in Dublin.[106] The attempt by Irish Republicans to seize power for an independent Ireland and the subsequent suppression and execution of the leaders by the British Army reinforced the position of the Irish American papers as favouring a victory for Germany in the hope of aiding their cause for Home Rule.[107] The attempt to overthrow colonial rule in Ireland was also used by *The Fatherland* to remind Irish American New Yorkers of Britain's hypocrisy and brutality.[108] This mode of representation was also evident in the coverage afforded to the trial and eventual execution of Sir Roger Casement in August 1916 for his role in attempting to land

---

[103]   *New Yorker Staats-Zeitung*, May 22, 1915.

[104]   Peoples Relief Committee for the Jewish War Sufferers, 1916. *The Book of the Exile: Souvenir of the Bazaar and Fair Held under the Auspices of the Peoples Relief Committee for the Jewish War Sufferers, March, 1916*. New York, NY: Peoples Relief Committee for the Jewish War Sufferers.

[105]   G.S. Viereck, 1916b. The Jewish Bazaar. *The Fatherland*, 4(10): 158.

[106]   *Gaelic American*, April 29, 1916.

[107]   *Gaelic American*, May 6, 1916.

[108]   G.S. Viereck, 1916c. War's Great Irish Hero. *The Fatherland*, 4(13): 122.

a cargo of weapons from Germany in Ireland in advance of the Easter Rising.[109] In these accounts, Casement was presented to sympathetic New Yorkers as not only a victim of the war, brutalised and demeaned by the chief warmonger 'perfidious Albion', but as an 'American' hero: an heir to those who fought against British rule in the War of Independence.[110]

Just as the city witnessed markets and fairs for the cause of Germany, Austria-Hungary and the Jewish victims of the war, the supporters of the Entente, including prominent industrialists, politicians and reformers, also used large-scale events to attract supporters in New York. After the bazaars of the Central Powers and the Jewish sufferers of the war from March to April 1916, the Allied Bazaar was held in June 1916, once again at the Grand Central Palace and organised by three major relief charities in the city for the Entente: the National Allied Relief Committee, the War Relief Clearing House, and the Commission for Relief in Belgium. The National Allied Relief Committee had emerged in New York during July 1915, at the instigation of prominent businessmen who sought to assist the combatant nations, as a means of centralising the efforts for the relief of the victims of the war in Belgium, Britain, France and Russia. Similarly, the War Relief Clearing House, which was formed in June 1915 by shipping merchants in the city, coordinated the movement of charitable donations from New York to the warzone for the benefit of Allied forces. From these organisations, the Allied Bazaar emerged as a spectacular to rival the preceding events held at the Grand Central Palace.

The bazaar was an opportunity to reiterate the status of France and Belgium as the victims of the war. Indeed, the naming of the bazaar for 'the blinded, starving and homeless' was ideally placed to maximise the attention of the mainstream New York press and their particular mode of neutral judgement with regard to the war. Adverts for the bazaar were placed across prominent newspapers in the city:

> Will you help us raise a million dollars for the Allies next June? Not for munitions
> of war, but for millions of innocent, unoffending people who are in pitiful need
> … we have given an American pledge to do it.[111]

Organisers of the event hoped that through this appeal, the citizens of the city would be moved and thereby mobilised to contribute to the war relief effort for the Allies. The ten-day bazaar featured a fusion of European and American ideals, with images and materials from Britain, France and Russia used to convince the visitors to the fair. Recreations of picturesque scenes from the countries of the Entente also added an element of European exoticism to attract New Yorkers. Part of this appeal was also enabled by the first large-scale exhibition of 'war trophies' in the United States, which was displayed in the bazaar through the special permission

---

[109] G.S. Viereck, 1916f. Casement and Liebknecht. *The Fatherland*, 4(23): 232.

[110] C. Collman, 1916a. Who Betrayed the Irish People? *The Fatherland*, 4(14): 211–12.

[111] *New York Times*, May 7, 1916.

of the French Government. This included examples of 'trench art' made by soldiers and disabled ex-servicemen, medals, uniforms, war art (landscape and portraiture), the remains of the fighter plane belonging to the first fighter ace Adolphe Pégoud (1889–1915) and a selection of souvenirs from the battlefields of Verdun, including spent shell cases, which the public were encouraged to place bids upon as a fundraising venture.[112] The bazaar was opened with a parade down Fifth Avenue and an 'invasion' of Wall Street by operatic and theatrical stars in automobiles, each vehicle decorated with the liveries of one of the Allied nations. A young woman, dressed as Joan of Arc, atop a white horse, declared the pageant open to visitors, which proved to be a highly popular society venue amongst the wealthy elite of the city.[113] It was this association with the prosperous sections of New York society that drew criticism from sources which were close to the German cause; the exclusivity of the event was compared to the democratic nature of the German and Jewish bazaars where 'ordinary people' participated and where the loyalty towards the United States was proclaimed so vehemently.[114] In contrast, participants of the Allied Bazaar proclaimed that their loyalty to the United States was affirmed in their work to aid the Allied cause; being an American, expressing the rights of life, liberty and the pursuit of happiness, was therefore accomplished through aiding the cause of Belgium, Britain, France and Russia.[115]

Municipal Responses to the War

As the representatives and supporters of the opposing combatant nations were increasingly using charitable works in the city to both alleviate the suffering of civilians and promote their political cause, prominent individuals, local politicians and the city authorities themselves were being pressed to attend events and offer their support for a particular group. The responsibility of managing a potentially factious city's diverse responses to the condition of wartime was a task that Mayor Mitchel employed all the powers of the office to achieve. As a response to the growing economic, social and political pressures placed upon the city by the conflict, Mayor Mitchel attempted to organise the city's response through a single administrative unit, creating the Mayor's Committee on National Defense in October 1915. The committee quickly formed into a complex, multi-faceted organisation with sub-committees and bureaus, and with a range of responsibilities in the field of labour, industry, immigration, food, transportation,

---

[112]   National Allied Relief Committee, 1916. *The Allied Bazaar Under the Auspices of National Allied Relief Committee, War Relief Clearing House for France and Her Allies, and the Commission for Relief in Belgium, Grand Central Palace, June 3 to June 14, 1916.* New York, NY: Herald Square Press.

[113]   *New York Times*, June 4, 1916.

[114]   G.S. Viereck, 1916e. The Allied Bazaar. *The Fatherland*, 4(22): 347.

[115]   *New York Times*, June 25, 1916.

law and, significantly, civic loyalty. The committee emerged from the developing concern, held by Mitchel, regarding the influence of disruptive political and ethnic elements in the city which would seek to undermine or influence authority both in New York and in the wider nation. Preparation and defence were developing into powerful political issues both for the United States Government in Washington, DC and particularly for the diverse, multi-lingual and divided city of New York. For Mitchel, the control of the city in wartime was a continuation of the battle with the politicking he had fought since his election; as an anti-Tammany candidate, he had opposed the crude electioneering that had garnered the votes of immigrants in the city.[116]

This administrative system was founded from a call issued by Mayor Mitchel for a 'committee of 1000' of the city's 'finest', whether industrialists, politicians or reformers, to serve on the various bureaus and sub-committees of the organisation.[117] The zeal with which volunteers donated their time and money to the cause was encouraged by President Wilson's visit to the city and his speech to the Manhattan Club in November 1915. In this address, President Wilson called for the development of both the army and the navy of the United States as a response to the war in Europe in order to defend the interests of the nation.[118] However, President Wilson also used the occasion and the venue of the city of New York to decry the presence of dissenting voices within the nation:

> The only thing within our borders that has given us grave concern in recent months has been that voices have been raised in America professing to be the voices of Americans which were not indeed and in truth American, but which spoke alien sympathies, which came from men who loved other countries better than they loved America and had forgotten that their chief and only allegiance was to the great government under which they live.[119]

The issue of alien influences within the city was also brought to attention with the speech in October 1915 by former President Theodore Roosevelt.[120] Roosevelt's tacit support for the Entente's efforts, expressed through articles written for the New York *Metropolitan Magazine*, had brought criticism, but his focus of attention

---

[116] E. R. Lewinson, 1965. *John Purroy Mitchel: The Boy Mayor of New York.* New York, NY: Astra Books, pp. 191–3.

[117] *New York Herald*, October 29, 1915.

[118] H. Watterson, 1915. *History of the Manhattan Club: A Narrative of the Activities of Half a Century.* New York, NY: De Vinne Press, p. 123.

[119] W. Wilson, 1915. *Address of President Wilson at the Fiftieth Anniversary Dinner of the Manhattan Club (Biltmore Hotel) New York City, November 4, 1915.* Washington, DC: Government Printing Office, p. 7.

[120] T. Roosevelt, 1916. *Fear God and Take Your Own Part.* New York, NY: George H. Doran.

on 'hyphenated' Americans had a particular resonance in a city of immigrants.[121] For Roosevelt, the status of those who proclaimed allegiance to a 'Fatherland' whilst stating their loyalty to the United States was inconceivable and potentially traitorous. Speaking to the charitable group, the Knights of Columbus, who had been prominent in war relief themselves, he stated:

> There is no room in this country for hyphenated Americanism. When I refer to hyphenated Americans, I do not refer to naturalized Americans. Some of the very best Americans I have ever known were naturalized Americans, Americans born abroad. But a hyphenated American is not an American at all ... The one absolutely certain way of bringing this nation to ruin, of preventing all possibility of its continuing to be a nation at all, would be to permit it to become a tangle of squabbling nationalities ... each preserving its separate nationality, each at heart feeling more sympathy with Europeans of that nationality, than with the other citizens of the American Republic ... There is no such thing as a hyphenated American who is a good American. The only man who is a good American is the man who is an American and nothing else.[122]

The response from municipal and national authorities, as well as some charitable organisations, to the profusion of support for the various combatant nations in the war was to insist upon a singular nature of being an 'American' that could be instilled within an immigrant population and accepted without recourse to other ethnic, religious or cultural affiliations. This process was not unique to New York, with other American cities experiencing similar tensions that had been exacerbated by the war.[123] However, what was distinct about New York's experience of these changes was its size, its density of population, its diversity and the city's wartime prominence, culturally, politically and economically, both in the United States and across the world. National agendas, therefore, magnified in New York as campaigns to 'Yank out the hyphen' from American society, gathered apace. This movement is demonstrated in the development of the National Americanization Day Committee (NAC), which formed in May 1915 in New York, with its headquarters on 95 Madison Avenue, Manhattan. Its mission was stated as promoting general education in citizenship and civic affairs. The organisation emerged from the various reform groups, such as the Committee for Immigrants in America or the League of Foreign-Born Citizens, arguing for greater assistance for newly arrived migrants. However, the war brought greater significance to their work, and under the leadership of New York-based campaigner Frances Kellor (1873–1952) a strong emphasis on loyalty and patriotism to the United States was

---

[121] T. Roosevelt, 1915a. Americanization Day. *Metropolitan Magazine*, 42(3): 3–4.

[122] T. Roosevelt, 1915b. *Americanism. Address before the Knights of Columbus, Carnegie Hall, New York, October 12, 1915*. New York, NY: s.n.

[123] Philadelphia War History Committee, 1922. *Philadelphia in the World War, 1914–1919*. New York, NY: Wynkoop Hallenbeck Crawford.

issued under the slogan 'many peoples, one nation'.[124] The organisation did not seek to advance an anti-immigration agenda, but to assert the failings of the nation in dealing with immigrant identity; to ensure through education, occupation and recreation, that all immigrants became 'Americans'. The war was used to assert this position as readers were informed that with their charitable donations to war relief funds of Jewish, Slavic and Polish peoples, they neglected the sufferings of those same groups in the city:

> He has served us well in our industrial trenches, standing shoulder to shoulder with us to maintain the democratic institutions for which all Europe is battling. He is our immediate neighbour and we shall not better care for the wounded in Europe by failing to recognise the need of the alien here.[125]

The group came to prominence in July 1915, when the inaugural 'Americanization Day' was promoted for the Independence Day celebrations on 4 July. The day was organised in New York, as well as other cities, with patriotic readings and songs, delivered by recent arrivals, who were encouraged to demonstrate their loyalty to their new country and the curtailment of ties to their native lands.[126] From the summer of 1915, the NAC began a programme of engagement with immigrant groups in the city, using education initiatives, English-language lessons and leisure pursuits to inculcate a sense of American values and identity amongst the metropolis's diverse population.

With the questions raised as to the nature of the 'hyphenated' American in the city, the NAC became increasingly concerned with promoting an 'American' character that communicated strength and singularity of purpose. Operating under the assumption that 'foreign influences' were weakening civic society, the NAC increasingly equated a 'strong' society with a militarised society, promoting the expansion of the army and navy as a means of instilling unity amongst the populace.[127] Despite its status as a charitable body, the NAC was reliant on raising funds for their cause through subscription and donation. The aims of this group contributed significantly to the formation of the Mayor's Committee on National Defense, as from within the sub-committees emerged the same belief that a diverse city was a weakened city. Therefore, to strengthen the bonds between the city and its citizens, to demonstrate loyalty and to cultivate the singular character of an 'American' within New York's ethnic enclaves, the city and the wider nation

---

[124]   F. Kellor, 1915b. Immigrants in America: A Domestic Policy. *The Immigrants in America Review*, 1(1): 9–15.

[125]   F. Kellor, 1915a. The Trenches of Peace. *The Immigrants in America Review*, 1(1): 5.

[126]   F. Kellor, 1915c. National Americanization Day: July 4th. *The Immigrants in America Review*, 1(3): 18–29.

[127]   F. Kellor, 1916a. *Straight America: A Call to National Service*. New York, NY: Macmillan, p. 153.

should be prepared for defence.[128] Prominent members of this call to arms which became known as the Preparedness Movement were based in New York.[129] Whilst the effect of the Preparedness Movement had a significant impact on the wider nation, it emerged in New York as a specific response to the tensions and conflict within the city.

This desire for an expression of American identity and democracy and its entwining with the Preparedness Movement led to the formation of the Plattsburg Camp in August and September 1915.[130] Located several hundred miles away from the city in upstate New York, the camp provided officer training courses and facilities for businessmen, professionals and college graduates who hailed mostly from the city.[131] The camp was attended by nearly 1,300 volunteers who had responded to calls in the press to join up for this patriotic duty.[132] Funded by private donations and sponsored by the United States War Department, the camp continued a pre-war tradition of providing limited military training to college graduates.[133] With the escalation of the war in Europe, the divisions between opposing groups within the metropolis and now the training provided to the elite of the city in the summer of 1915 at Plattsburg, the Preparedness Movement began to possess significant influence upon New York's potentially turbulent wartime politics. The camp was represented as a physical manifestation of the singular 'American' character that disavowed previous loyalties to affirm the principles of 'liberty' and 'democracy'.[134] Indeed, prominent New York citizens including Mayor Mitchel attended the camp, which was extensively reported by the city's press, thereby lending their direct support to the association between preparedness and American identity.[135] This connection was bluntly reinforced by former President Theodore Roosevelt, who visited the camp and gave a widely-reported speech that emphasised the American ideals represented by those present at Plattsburg and the nefarious 'hyphenated Americans':

---

[128] H. Croly, 1916. The Effect on American Institutions of a Powerful Military and Naval Establishment. *Annals of the American Academy of Political and Social Science*, 66(1): 157–72.

[129] S. Strunsky, 1916. Armaments and Caste. *Annals of the American Academy of Political and Social Science*, 66(1): 237–46.

[130] H.D. Wheeler, 1915. Plattsburg: How it Works. *Harper's Weekly*, 61: 248–50.

[131] Roster of Company 'F', 1st Training Regiment, 1915. *A Military Training Camp for Business and Professional Men Held Near the U.S. Army Post, Plattsburg Barracks, N.Y., August 10 to September 6, 1915*. New York, NY: s.n.

[132] *New York Times*, August 13, 1915.

[133] Committee on Regimental Affairs, 1915. *Bulletin of the First Training Regiment: The Business and Professional Men's Military Training Camps, Plattsburg, N.Y.* New York, NY: New York, NY: Wynkoop Hallenbeck Crawford.

[134] Plattsburg Military Training Camp, 1917. *The Plattsburger*. New York, NY: Plattsburger, Inc.

[135] *New York Times*, August 10, 1915; *New York Tribune*, August 28, 1915.

In any crisis the hyphenated American is an active force against America, an active force for wrongdoing. The effort to hoist two flags on the same flagpole always means that one flag is hoisted underneath and the hyphenated American invariably hoists the flag of the United States underneath.[136]

The way in which the Preparedness Movement and the Plattsburg Camp had reframed issues of 'hyphenated Americans' was roundly criticised within the foreign-language presses and particularly within pro-German newspapers, who viewed it as further evidence of the complicity of the city's elite with the Allies.[137] However, this did not deter the support for the expansion of the United States armed forces amongst elements of the foreign-language press; with Germany's pre-war programme of rearmament offered as an example for the nation, it was regarded as a necessity to protect the state's interests against the 'aggressors' of Britain and Japan.[138]

The fear of the hyphenated identity increased tensions within New York. As the authorities cast aspersions on those who did not declare themselves to be fully American, accusations of unpatriotic, disloyal or even traitorous behaviour could be levelled at those who sought to promote their attachment to both their home country and their homeland. These tensions were heightened by the growing number of 'scare stories' after the summer of 1915, which revealed alleged German espionage to disrupt the ever-increasing and highly-profitable trade conducted with the Allies. With New York's status as the main depot of international commerce and finance, the city began to be viewed as a potential target for alien saboteurs, or even native seditionists. With the attempted murder of J.P Morgan at his Long Island mansion just outside the city in July 1915, by a disgruntled German émigré angry at the financial arrangements that Morgan had reached with Britain, the war in Europe was viewed by the authorities as a battle that was to be fought at home. With the outrage that followed the sinking of the *Lusitania* in May 1915, the wider threat of German U-boats to American passenger liners and cargo ships and the fear which was promoted through the stories of German subterfuge in the city, a climate of suspicion prevailed within the municipal authorities of New York. Unbeknownst to the wider populace, this period also witnessed the intensification of German-sponsored propaganda in the city, with the secret purchase in May 1915, made by the German government through their agent Heinrich Albert, of the New York daily the *Evening Mail*.[139] The newspaper was, thereafter, notably committed

---

[136] *New York Times*, August 26, 1915; *New York Evening Telegraph*, August 25, 1915.

[137] F.F. Schrader, 1915a. German Sympathizers, Roosevelt and Others. *The Fatherland*, 3(5): 84–6.

[138] G.S. Viereck, 1915. From G.S. Viereck, Editor, The Fatherland. In H. Maxim (ed.), *Leading Opinions Both For and Against National Defense*. New York, NY: Hearst International, pp. 20–21.

[139] United States Senate, Committee on the Judiciary, 1919. *Brewing and Liquor Interests and German Propaganda: Hearings Before a Subcommittee of the Committee*

to providing supportive accounts of the German war effort, encouraging American neutrality and criticising both the Allies and the Preparedness Movement.[140]

Fear and Suspicion in the City

Support for the removal of the hyphenated identities within New York and the consequent distrust which was beginning to form regarding the loyalty of German Americans in the city was also fuelled by the scandal caused by the disclosure of the use of agents by the German government to sabotage profits made by trading with the Allies.[141] Documents detailing German efforts to disrupt business networks, purchase vital industries and ferment labour disputes within the city and the wider United States were published in the *New York World*.[142] These details implicated the German Consul in New York, including Heinrich Albert, Naval Attaché Karl Boy-Ed (1872–1930) and Franz von Papen, and thereby the German Americans in the city who had expressed support for the cause of the Fatherland.[143] To compound the problem, German American businesses in New York were also involved in the scandal, with evidence that the Hamburg-American Line had supplied German ships in a direct contradiction of the neutral policies of the United States.[144] The damage to the image of German Americans was compounded by the publication in New York's mainstream newspaper of letters obtained by the British authorities from an American journalist, J.F.J. Archibald in September 1915.[145] Archibald was revealed to be a courier for the Austro-Hungarian Ambassador to the United States, Konstantin Dumba (1856–1947). The letters also confirmed the operation of German and Austrian agents in the United States and the intention to disrupt financial or industrial activity that could contribute to the war.[146] Dumba, Von

---

on the Judiciary, United States Senate, Sixty-fifth Congress, Second and Third sessions, Pursuant to S. Res. 307, Vol.1. Washington, DC: Government Printing Office, p. 1454.

[140]   *New York Evening Mail*, October 27, 1915; *New York Evening Mail*, November 19, 1915.

[141]   National Americanization Committee, 1917. *A Partial Record of Alien Enemy Activities, 1915–1917: A Compelling Appeal for a War Policy for Aliens to Be Adopted by the Government and Citizens of the United States*. New York, NY: National Americanization Committee.

[142]   *New York World*, August 15, 1915.

[143]   *New York Sun*, August 17, 1915.

[144]   E. Sperry and W. West, 1918. *German Plots and Intrigues in the United States During the Period of our Neutrality*. Washington, DC: The Committee on Public Information, p. 24.

[145]   *The Evening World*, September 22, 1915.

[146]   *New York Herald*, September 10, 1915; *New York Evening Telegraph*, September 8, 1915.

Papen and Boy-Ed were all recalled by their respective governments after official complaints from Washington.

Despite these diplomatic expulsions, stories of bombs and other incendiary devices placed on board ships departing from or arriving into New York by German agents were highly prominent towards the end of 1915. From the spring of 1915 onwards, suspicious fires on vessels leaving New York, bound for France or Britain, had been attributed to German or Austrian infiltrators in the city.[147] The threat to the city's economy was clear and the conclusion that alien seditionists were to blame was exemplified in the example of the SS *Kirk Oswald*; the vessel had departed New York harbour in May 1915, and was found to contain a series of ill-made incendiary devices in four sacks of sugar upon docking in Marseille. The effect of this discovery served to galvanise the city's Police Department into action and the Bomb Squad division was employed in the investigation of native and foreign seditionists across New York.[148] The investigation into the bombs found on the SS *Kirk Oswald* enabled the prosecution of a number of individuals attached to the German Consul in New York. Those arrested also included a number of German ship captains and to the city's agitated press it was these individuals who posed a threat. Whilst the German vessels had been kept in the docks in New York after the declaration of war by the British blockade, their captains were now, unlike their ships, unrestricted in their movement in the city.[149] In this manner, through the machinations of agents operating to undermine industrial and financial institutions in the city, German Americans were viewed as potential sources of sabotage and intrigue. This development, coupled with the growing campaign for unhyphenated identities and dedications of loyalty to the United States after October 1915, ensured there was no doubt that what was once classed as the 'European War' was being fought in the city.[150]

It was from this context that the National Security League (NSL) grew to prominence in New York in 1915. Its original formation in December 1914 emerged from a concern that the city had become a haven for aliens and subversives which the United States, let alone the municipal authority of New York, was ill-equipped to address.[151] The organisation's influence was far-reaching; by October 1915 it had secured the membership and subscription of over 40,000 individuals from all parts of the United States.[152] Despite its spread to other cities across the nation, the organisation remained governed and influenced by the financial, industrial

---

[147] H. Landau, 1937. *The Enemy Within: The Inside Story of German Sabotage in America*. New York, NY: G.P. Putnam's Sons, p. 36.

[148] T. Tunney, 1919. *Throttled! The Detection of the German and Anarchist Bomb Plotters*. Boston, MA: Small, Maynard and Company, p. 10.

[149] *New York World*, November 19, 1915.

[150] *New York Herald*, August 17, 1915; *New York Times*, August 17, 1915.

[151] R.D. Ward, 1960. The Origin and Activities of the National Security League, 1914–1919. *The Mississippi Valley Historical Review*, 47(1): 51–65.

[152] H. Pulsifer, 1915. The Security League Conference. *Outlook*, 111: 853–4.

and political elite from within New York. From its headquarters in the city, the NSL promoted military preparedness and civic educational policies to encourage integration; according to the organisation, this would be most easily achieved through the introduction of universal military training.[153] Military training across all sections of society would, therefore, 'Americanise' the disparate nature of New York. Speaking in the city at the NSL's 'Peace and Preparedness' conference on 14 June 1915, in Carnegie Hall, former Secretary of State for War Henry Stimson outlined the importance of military preparedness for national unity.[154] Such sentiments were also detailed in the 'war exhibit' held by the NSL in the Hotel Astor as part of the 'Peace and Preparedness' convention (Figure 4.2). The opinions expressed in these displays were countered on 15 June at the Cooper Union in downtown Manhattan, during a meeting of the Women's Peace Party, where pacifists and socialists condemned the 'anti-American' stance of the NSL.[155] Certainly, the composition of the leadership of the NSL also drew criticism from supportive, pro-German sources in the city, which attacked the organisation as a capitalist endeavour that sought to ensure the profits of industrialists rather than the security of the American people.[156] Therefore, German-sponsored propaganda in the city could smear the NSL for their apparent disloyalty, as to profit from the war was to assist the Allies; of 'standing with foreigners against your own countrymen'.[157]

As a means of countering these claims and demonstrating the patriotic nature of their objectives, the NSL situated itself in the traditions, values and identity of the United States, issuing a call in November 1915 for a trained citizenry, ready to defend the nation just as the militias of the War of Independence had done in the late eighteenth century.[158] Whilst the NSL supported the neutrality policy of President Wilson and encouraged the administration's movements towards increasing the army and navy, a more direct branch of the organisation had broken away to form

---

[153]   United States Congress, Special Committee to Investigate the National Security League, 1918. *Hearings Before a Special Committee of the House of Representatives, Sixty-fifth Congress, Third Session on H. Res. 469 and H. Res. 476, to Investigate and Make Report as to the Officers, Membership, Financial Support, Expenditures, General Character, Activities and Purposes of the National Security League, a Corporation of New York, and of Any Associated Organizations, Parts 1–13.* Washington, DC: Government Printing Office, p. 314.

[154]   H. Stimson, 1915. *The Duty of Preparedness Today: Address of Henry L. Stimson before the National Security League at Carnegie Hall, June 14, 1915.* New York, NY: National Security League.

[155]   *New York Call*, June 15, 1915.

[156]   C. Collman, 1915a. The Scandal of the Navy League. *The Fatherland*, 3(16): 271–3.

[157]   C. Collman, 1915b. *The War Plotters of Wall Street.* New York, NY: The Fatherland Corporation, pp. 35–6.

[158]   National Security League, 1915. *Report of the Committee on Militia.* New York, NY: National Security League.

Figure 4.2   War Exhibit at Hotel Astor, Held by the National Security League, June 1915.

Source: Grantham Bain Collection, Library of Congress (LC-B2-3513-8).

the American Defense Society (ADS) in August 1915.[159] Similarly compiled of New York's elite, the ADS was more vigorous in its criticism of President Wilson and urged the direct involvement of the United States in the war on the side of the Allies.[160] Where both organisations found common ground was in the use of the fear present in the reports of sabotage in the city to promote the belief that New York itself was under threat from invasion, whether through alien dissidents or foreign aggressors.[161] Such visions were seemingly not so far beyond the realm of possibility; indeed, the 1915 film *The Battle Cry of Peace* depicted terrifying scenes of barely disguised Teutonic invaders quickly overcoming the city and oppressing the populace.[162] In place of Belgium and France, the location of the

[159]   J. Edwards, 1976. Playing the Patriot Game: The Story of the American Defense Society, 1915–1932. *Studies in History and Society*, 1(1): 54–72.

[160]   J. Street, 1915. *Our Next War*. New York, NY: American Defense Society; R.M. Johnston, 1915. *The Ounce of Prevention: Switzerland Versus Belgium, with a Lesson for the United States*. New York, NY: American Defense Society; A.P. Gardner, 1915. *Gardner or Daniels?* New York, NY: American Defense Society.

[161]   H. Maxim, 1915. *Defenseless America*. New York, NY: Hearst International.

[162]   W. North, (Dir.) 1915. *The Battle Cry of Peace*. Vitagraph Company of America.

atrocity reports which had so consumed the mainstream press of the metropolis, the city of New York now stood in their place. Such depictions were designed to infuse the public with a sense of dread, to fear the outsiders who plot against the state and to associate with the organisations that promoted preparedness.[163]

Such thinly-veiled depictions of German aggression on New York, whilst drawn from the recent scandals of alien saboteurs, were inevitably countered by New York's German press, who regarded such allusions as a threat to their status as 'Americans'.[164] Such denunciations of stereotyped images of Germanic militarism demonstrated that debates within the city had become focused upon the issue of identity.[165] This issue was clearly delineated with the outrage that followed the disclosure that Hungarian Jewish émigré Marcus Braun (1852–1921), a former Immigration Official, President of the Hungarian Republican Club, political ally of Theodore Roosevelt and prominent member of the Hungarian American community in New York had received payment for his 'American' values of fair play towards the reporting of the war from the German Ambassador.[166] The case disturbed sections of the media, as a seemingly 'naturalised' immigrant could be seen to be working for the cause of their original fatherland.[167] The status of American identity in the city was, therefore, beginning to appear in a state of flux, with individuals required to justify through their actions that they were loyal citizens.

Just as charitable organisations for the Central Powers had proclaimed their status as Americans and their benevolent actions as 'American', now organisations such as the NSL and the ADS sought to delineate what constituted the character of the nation. Increasingly, politics in the city was being drawn along the same lines as representatives sought to respond to the concerns of voters. The status of the security of New York and the status of the loyalty of its citizens were thereby entwined as the city authorities sought to adjust to the demands of governing a city which by the end of 1915 appeared far from 'neutral'. The threat to the city was now measured not only in the internal divisions between its populace, but rather a fear from the 'enemy within'.[168] The external danger was a prominent concern at the outset of the war; indeed, the coastal defences protecting New York's harbour had been tested in August 1914, with the large battery sited on Fort Hamilton in south-west Brooklyn at the mouth of New York's harbour, firing rounds as part of the installation's routine exercises.[169] However, by the end of 1915, the far more

---

[163] *New York Times*, August 7, 1915.

[164] H. Münsterberg, 1915. Hugo Münsterberg Defines Theo. Roosevelt as a Presidential Possibility. *The Fatherland*, 3(20): 346–8.

[165] *New York Times*, September 19, 1915.

[166] *New York World*, August 21, 1915.

[167] *New York Times*, October 2, 1915.

[168] *Brooklyn Daily Eagle*, May 8, 1915.

[169] *New York Herald*, August 16, 1914.

troublesome prospect of domestic insurrection or disruption was the fear of New York's Police Commissioner Arthur Hale Woods (1870–1942).[170]

Woods, who was elected to the post in 1914, had begun a process of reforming the city's law enforcement, providing guidance to officers on how to interact and control a diverse, multilingual population in New York.[171] The advent of the war had not immediately placed any extra burden onto the force, bar the policing of patriotic crowds that had convened in public places during August 1914.[172] Despite this early reticence, Police Commissioner Woods directed the New York police department towards increasing involvement in the investigation of bomb plots and threats of sabotage after the spring of 1915. The harbour patrols were increased by early 1915 and equipped with machine guns, with police squads manning the vessels trained by members of the US Navy in their use. However, the most significant aspect of policing after the outbreak of war was the formation of the 'Neutrality Squad'. This division had been established within the city's police force after the onset of hostilities to counter both alien and domestic insurgency and to preserve the appearance of the city's impartiality. This group became increasingly occupied in their work and were significantly enforced to meet their varied tasks. For example, in May 1915, arrests were made after threats were received by the Cunard Steamship Company which stated that their ships would be targeted by bombers in New York; this was followed by a series of arrests in August 1915, when the Fabre Steamship company was targeted by would-be bombers.[173] The division also foiled a plot in October 1915 which aimed to detonate explosives on board ships docked in New York's harbour that were bound for Britain and France.[174] Working with the national security services, the New York Police Department became increasingly embroiled in a war on its own territory. This work was almost exclusively targeted at the threat posed by German agents or saboteurs sympathetic to Germany.

Investigations continued apace throughout the end of 1915. In December, officers from the squad had arrested the Austro-Hungarian immigrant Anton Mente in his tenement apartment on the Upper East Side. Mente was found with bomb-making chemicals, equipment and pamphlets that supported American neutrality, critiqued the support of some of New York's financiers for the Entente and stressed the righteous cause of the German war effort.[175] Early in 1916, after extensive surveillance, police officers arrested six German agents in New York

---

[170]   A.H. Woods, 1919. *Policeman and Public*. New Haven, CT: Yale University Press, pp. 17–19.

[171]   C. Cahalane, 1914. *Police Practice and Procedure*. New York, NY: E.P. Dutton.

[172]   A.H. Woods, 1915. Police Administration. *Proceedings of the Academy of Political Science in the City of New York*, 5: 54–61.

[173]   New York Police Department, 1915. *Annual Report*. New York, NY: Bureau of Printing, City of New York, p. xii.

[174]   *New York Times*, November 21, 1915; *New York Herald*, November 21, 1915.

[175]   *New York Times*, December 29, 1915; *New York Herald*, December 29, 1915.

who were charged with conspiring to procure explosives, weapons and associated equipment to destroy the Welland Canal in Ontario, Canada.[176] The investigations into espionage plots in 1916 brought further arrests of confessed German agents who had targeted shipping in New York, to ensure that cargoes were destroyed during transit from the city to Europe, using bombs that were manufactured in the metropolis's own harbour. In the spring of 1916, German agents were also charged with working with Indian nationalists to smuggle weapons to the British colonial possession, in order to ferment rebellion and distract Britain from the war in Europe.[177] The division also responded to calls from the public with concerns about individuals or situations, with thousands of reports filtering to the officers, the majority of which were found to be without any basis in fact. The number of these false claims was perhaps reflective of the level of concern experienced within the populace, as an apparently palpable threat was felt across the city.[178]

At the outset of 1916 the 'Neutrality Squad' was, therefore, overwhelmed by the efforts to investigate and contain the threat of German subversives. The scale of the operation was substantial and complicated by the city's place as a global trading point and its status as the home of a diverse population. The Police Department of New York were also aided in their work within the city with the formation of the Citizens Home Defense League (CHDL) in the autumn of 1915.[179] This programme, which originally started in the Bronx before being employed across the city, was part of Woods' reforms which recruited ordinary residents to assist the main police force in their duties. Whilst initially small in number, the total number of citizens registered had reached 20,000 by April 1916. The CHDL were a uniformed and drilled organisation which, despite not being issued with firearms, did carry truncheons and could act to disperse crowds, make arrests and respond on the suspicions and reports they received.[180] Therefore, whilst the original objective of the initiative was to encourage cooperation between the police and citizens, the CHDL became an important part in policing the populace. The CHDL were also tasked with protecting the populace, as their brief also included organising the defences in the event of any invasion by a foreign power. However, it was within the more day-to-day business of policing that the CHDL had their most significant effect. This volunteer body acted as a means to report on the activities of potential suspects and take upon the role of controlling the expression of potentially disruptive sentiments; in effect, as the suspects of sabotage were German agents or sympathisers, the CHDL acted to police the identity of citizens

---

[176] *New York Herald*, March 31, 1916.

[177] F. Strother, 1918. *Fighting Germany's Spies*. New York, NY: Doubleday, p. 236.

[178] New York Police Department, 1916. *Annual Report*. New York, NY: Bureau of Printing, City of New York, pp. iii–iv.

[179] A. Kates, 1916. New York's Home Defense League. *The Review: Prison Association of New York*, 6: 4–6.

[180] W. Dawkins, 1918. *Police Reserve and Home Defense Guard Manual*. New York, NY: E.P. Dutton and Co.

within the city. Indeed, their voluntary status was regarded as emblematic of the 'American' spirit itself, which 'responds to the call in a time of need'.[181]

The CHDL were able to attract significant numbers of recruits through the growth of the Preparedness Movement in the city as reports of bombs and espionage were reported by the city's press.[182] Indeed, an indication of the fear of domestic subversives and alien saboteurs can be obtained through the public demonstrations of support for the call of an increase in the nation's army and navy.[183] This popular opinion was expressed most clearly during the Preparedness Parade in the city on 13 May 1916. An estimated 130,000 individuals participated in the event, which was organised to express support for national defence schemes by members of the Executive Committee of the Citizens' Preparedness Parade. This committee was composed of some of the prominent members of the city's political and financial elite, including William L. Barbour of the Linen Thread Company as Chairman and New York lawyer and lobbyist Charles H. Sherrill as Treasurer. Considering this composition, it was perhaps inevitable that the city's leading businesses took a prominent part in the parade. Although official displays of logos and company standards were prohibited and only the American flag was allowed to be displayed, the economic interests of the city were represented by over 40 trades in the procession through Manhattan from the Bowling Green in the south to Central Park on 59th Street.[184] Indeed, the parade provided an opportunity for businesses to advertise their wares through the patriotic display and reap the reward of an economic stimulus that rearmament would potentially provide.[185]

The incongruous nature of this parallel display of patriotism and business acumen was criticised by pacifists, socialists and the German-language press.[186] *The Fatherland* referred to the participants as 'Morgan's Guards' and reminded its readers that nearly 5,000 financiers had pledged their commitment to the cause whilst enriching themselves on the profits of the war.[187] The events of the

---

[181] H.J. Case, 1916. How Organization Helps. *The American Red Cross Magazine*, 11: 396–401.

[182] *New York Times*, April 16, 1916; *New York Herald*, April 14, 1916.

[183] W. Carter, 1916. *The Necessity of Preparedness: An Address on National Preparedness by Rev. Wm. Carter in a Debate with Rev. Washington Gladden at the Broadway Tabernacle, New York City, February 8th, 1916*. New York, NY: National Security League.

[184] Executive Committee of the Citizens Preparedness Parade, 1916. *Official Program: Citizens Preparedness Parade, New York City, May 13, 1916*. New York, NY: Citizens Preparedness Parade.

[185] United States Mortgage and Trust Company, 1916. *Preparedness Parade New York City, May 13, 1916: Views Along the Line and Other Preparedness Pictures*. New York, NY: Mortgage and Trust, Co.

[186] *New York Call*, April 30, 1916.

[187] C.A. Collman, 1916b. Morgan's Great War Parade, May 13, 1916. *The Fatherland*, 4(15): 227–9.

Easter Rising in Dublin earlier in April 1916 were used to place the 'Preparedness Parade' into perspective, by highlighting the presumed self-evident absurdity in the assistance now supplied to Britain when citizens from America and Ireland had once fought 'the same foe once before for the same reason'. This was not to suggest that the issue of preparedness did not have support from supports of the Central Powers in the city – it was to proclaim that preparedness should be in the 'name of democracy' and not 'in the name of Wall Street'.[188] These dissenting voices were suppressed somewhat by the sheer size of the Preparedness Parade, which also provided a forum for the expression of an unhyphenated national identity as participants affirmed their loyalty to the principles and traditions of the United States. Favourable reports stressed that the march provided an egalitarian union across the classes, as all the city's residents came together to celebrate their national identity.[189] Indeed, to advocate preparedness was expressed as a patriotic act in itself.[190] This was most clearly indicated by the content, structure and route of the parade. As the marchers made their way uptown along Fifth Avenue they moved beneath a large sign that proclaimed: 'Absolute and unqualified loyalty to our country'.[191]

This is clearly represented in the painting by Frederick Childe Hassam (1859–1935) entitled *The Fourth of July, 1916*, but which is also known as *The Greatest Display of the American Flag Ever Seen in New York, Climax of the Preparedness Parade in May*. Hassam represents the scenes of the parade, with Fifth Avenue bedecked with the national flag, flying from every level of every building along the thoroughfare.[192] The flag was also used to identify the members of the parade, with badges decorated with the 'stars and stripes' provided to sectors of businesses included in the parade.[193] Accompanying the marching bands of the parade were members of the National Guard and veterans of previous conflicts, all of whom were reviewed by Mayor Mitchel, Colonel Leonard Wood and Rear Admiral Nathan R. Usher at Madison Square. The entirety of the parade took 12 hours to process through New York, with ornate floats of patriotic scenes and martial endeavour serving as an instructional device to proclaim the meaning of the nation to the audience.[194] In case the audience forgot the purpose of the event, a biplane, decorated to mimic those flown by the Imperial German Flying Corps, was flown repeatedly across Governor's Island in the harbour to demonstrate the ease by which an invasion of the city

[188]   G.S. Viereck, 1916d. Editorial. *The Fatherland*, 4(16): 250–52.

[189]   *New York Herald*, May 14, 1916.

[190]   J.H. Holmes and C.A. Eaton, 1916. War, Religion and Preparedness. *The Advocate of Peace*, 78(6): 174–5.

[191]   *New York Tribune*, May 14; 1916; *New York Times*, May 14, 1916.

[192]   F.C. Hassam, 1916. *The Fourth of July, 1916*. Frederick Hassam Private Collection.

[193]   Real Estate – Citizen Preparedness Parade, May 13, 1916. Museum of the City of New York, 96.79.13.

[194]   *New York Times*, May 14, 1916.

could take place.[195] The display provided a useful foil to demonstrate the key to preventing the eventuality of any such attack, a commitment to unity and loyalty to the nation. The apparent inclusivity offered by this dedication to the nation belied the way in which the 'Preparedness Parade' in the city vaunted one image of what constitutes an 'American' over others. Indeed, whilst African Americans in the city could support the issue of preparedness, providing that it served the needs of their community not hindered their progress, they could still find themselves excluded from the civic platform provided by the parade.[196]

Others who were also excluded from this event were political dissidents whose opinions on the point of preparedness were marginalised as 'un-American' within the mainstream press.[197] Socialist and anarchist resentment towards preparedness stemmed from the understanding of conflict as the continuation of the imperialist, capitalist machine; the profiteering that occurred in the city was regarded as a demonstration of the rule by a business oligarchy in New York.[198] These sentiments drove the organisation of an anti-preparedness parade to coincide with and disrupt the large-scale event on 13 May 1916. Members of the Women's Peace Party joined socialist radicals and anarchists in moving through the crowds gathered on the sidewalk, distributing leaflets which called for an end to New York's 'sponsorship' of the European War. The first floor of a Fifth Avenue building opposite the reviewing platform on Madison Square was rented for the purpose of launching tirades against the 'Morgan Guard'. Intriguingly, this dissent was framed not as a critique of 'American' identity but of its subversion in the name of preparedness.[199] On their platform, the protesters held up their own banner which proclaimed:

> There are only 100,000 of you. You are not the only patriots. Two million families, 500,000 mine workers and organized labor of America are opposed to what you and Wall Street are marching for. Are you sure you are right?[200]

The presence of the anarchist and reform campaigner Emma Goldman, a vociferous opponent of the preparedness movement, at the parade also increased the high police presence that the protesters were controlled with. Goldman had stated her aim to disrupt the parade, which she later termed not a demonstration of preparedness but one of people's own 'degradation and servitude'.[201] To combat any potential public spectacle, the building used by the protestors was cordoned

[195] *New York Sun*, May 14, 1916.

[196] *New York Age*, April 16, 1916; *New York Age*, May 17, 1916.

[197] *New York Tribune*, May 14, 1916.

[198] E. Goldman, 1915. *Preparedness: The Road to Universal Slaughter*. New York, NY: Mother Earth Publishing.

[199] *New York Call*, May 15, 1916.

[200] Anon., 1916. New York's Parade for Preparedness. *The Survey*, 36: 196–7.

[201] E. Goldman, 1916. Observations and Comments. *Mother Earth*, 11(4): 497–503.

off by police officers and its occupants prevented from any overt expressions of dissent.[202] However, this did not prevent members of the minority radical socialist organisation, the Church for Social Revolution, interrupting the parade before the review just south of Madison Square on Fifth Avenue where they distributed leaflets and hoisted aloft the church's red banner. This action, regarded as highly disrespectful towards the national flag as the only symbol on display, was swiftly broken up by the police and the offenders given prison sentences.[203] Such actions were not regarded as heavy-handed in the context of the anarchist bombing of the San Francisco 'Preparedness Parade' in July 1916. However minor in comparison to the events in California, the activities of a few dissenting voices during the parade of May 1916 highlighted a new development within the city of New York.

Conclusions

By the summer of 1916, across the city, the fear of the war had galvanised the authority of both business and the mayoralty to take greater control of the populace. The expression of loyalty and patriotism was requisite, and any deviation beyond the prescribed boundaries of this evocative, powerful but nevertheless ill-defined concept of an 'American' identity was policed and punished. Even before the United States had officially declared war, the conditions of wartime had served to reshape New York's politics, its economics and its society. Whilst the city's residents had once been able to express regard for both their adopted nation and their cultural or original homeland, a demand for complete loyalty to the United States was now made. After the 'Preparedness Parade', the campaign to 'Yank out the hyphen' from American identity grew to even greater prominence. As the city descended further into wartime conditions, the attempt to recast New York as a purely 'American' city would have a substantial impact upon the lives of its citizens. As the war of European nations had spread to the Middle East and Africa, the effects of the conflict were now felt on the streets of New York. Just as combatant nations increased their control of their populations to sustain the efforts required for a 'total war', residents of the metropolis were also subject to the same processes.

---

[202] *New York Evening Telegraph*, May 13, 1916.
[203] *New York Times*, May 14, 1916.

Chapter 5
Preparedness and Identity

As we look back over the records of history we see the downfall of nations
coterminous with the decline of military virtue and the abandonment of thorough-
going systems of universal service ... Universal military training is the only way to
yank the hyphen out of America. With German and English, Russian and Austrian,
Italian and Turk, all rubbing elbows in common service to one country out comes
the hyphen, up goes the Stars and Stripes and in a generation the melting pot will
have melted.[1]

Introduction

The statement above was part of a wider speech given by former Assistant Secretary
of War Henry Breckinridge (1886–1960) at the Academy of Political Science at
Columbia University, New York in May 1916.[2] Breckinridge and the Secretary of
War Lindley Miller Garrison (1864–1932) had both resigned their posts in February
1916 at the failure of Congress in Washington to back their proposals to strengthen
the military and reserve forces of the United States. Breckinridge's speech took
place a few days after the 'Preparedness Parade' in the city and built upon the
link between the demonstration of 'American' values and rearmament. For New
York, Breckinridge's comments were particularly pointed, as the city's diasporic
population was becoming the target of suspicion and reform campaigns from the
authorities, the police and volunteer organisations such as the NSL. Indeed, the
latter's prominence in the metropolis significantly increased throughout 1916,
as it intensified its campaign for loyalty amongst the émigré population in New
York.[3] In this work, each citizen was required to express complete dedication to
the nation and reject any previous association as part of the movement towards
'preparedness'.[4] The range of national, cultural or political identity expressed in
the city noticeably narrowed, even before the entry of the United States into the
war in April 1917.[5] By the summer of 1916, New York was firmly embedded in

---

[1]   *New York Times*, May 19, 1916.
[2]   H. Breckinridge, 1916. Universal Service as the Basis of National Unity and
National Defense. *Proceedings of the Academy of Political Science*, 6(4): 436–41.
[3]   O. Straus, 1916. *Address of Oscar S. Straus at the National Security League Mass
Meeting at the Century Theatre, February 29th, 1916*. New York, NY: National Security
League.
[4]   H.K. Love, 1916. *'National Security': As It Involves the Preparation and Use of the
Citizenry*. New York, NY: National Security League.
[5]   *The Nation*, April 27, 1916.

the conflict which had engulfed Europe, Africa and the Middle East. As the war intensified, with reports of extensive casualties on the battlefields of the Somme, Flanders and Verdun, New York experienced an escalation in the concerns for its security and its role in the conflict. Therefore, the threat of espionage and the work of saboteurs were combated with an affirmation of loyalty within the city and the development of volunteer and public committees to ensure New York was an 'American' city.

Black Tom Island Explosion

These issues of preparedness and patriotism in the metropolis were brought under greater scrutiny after the large-scale explosion at the transport docks on Black Tom Island, located south of Manhattan Island in New York's harbour, off the coast of Jersey City, during late July 1916. The proximity of Black Tom Island to New York's docks, both on Manhattan and in Brooklyn, had ensured that the site had been transformed with the onset of hostilities in Europe. The site was also connected to the mainland through a railway line constructed by the Lehigh Valley Railroad Company, which brought significant amounts of traffic to the promontory. With the development of commercial contracts with the Allies and the shipment of munitions, food and materials to Europe, Black Tom Island had become a hub for international trade and a depot for goods entering and leaving New York. The weaponry that constituted part of this exchange, whilst constituting the significant contributor to the profits of the city's trade with the Allies, also made the site extremely dangerous and a significant target for saboteurs. Nearly two million pounds of explosives were stored on Black Tom Island in one form or another. Unsurprisingly, the blast that emanated from the site on the night of 30 July 1916 was colossal. Reports stated that a series of small fires across the depot were first noticed after midnight by guards who fled the scene but alerted the local Fire Department to the issue. Although attempts were made to extinguish these, just after two o'clock, a violent explosion caused by shrapnel shells reverberated through Black Tom Island, followed by a series of smaller blasts which illuminated the city harbour.[6]

The damage caused by the incident was substantial, with barges, piers, ships and infrastructure wrecked by the fireball caused by the munitions stored on the site.[7] However, despite the ferocity of the explosion only nine individuals were reportedly killed. These included guards, firemen and dockworkers at the site itself as well as an infant in Jersey City who was thrown from its crib by the force of the blast. It was this aftershock which caused the majority of the damage in New York with windows blown out in buildings in Manhattan from Battery Park to Times

---

[6]   *New York Times*, July 31, 1916.

[7]   Fire Department of the City of New York, 1916. *Annual Report*. New York, NY: Fire Department, p. 73–4.

Square on 42nd Street. Similar structural damage was also sustained in homes and offices across Brooklyn. The force of the blast launched shrapnel across the harbour, causing significant damage to the Statue of Liberty and forcing the evacuation of the immigration processing unit at Ellis Island, which was shifted to the original point of immigration in the nineteenth century, Castle Clinton in Manhattan.[8] The explosion was immediately placed within the context of the sabotage committed by German agents against shipping interests in New York harbour. A degree of suspicion was placed upon a presumed German American fifth column or German infiltrators thought to be operating in the city at the behest of the German Government. However, the mainstream press were careful not to incite problems between communities in the city by openly accusing a particular group.

Nevertheless, in a city which was already fearful of attack, the explosions heightened the sense of dread that an aggressive power could wage war against the metropolis. Despite the sensitivities of the issue, the event was couched in the terms of martial endeavour, implicitly laying blame with an aggressive and militaristic Germany. Indeed, the blast from Black Tom Island provided an opportunity for the city's press to place the city directly into the war, as the incident was likened in one report to the battlefields of the Western Front:

> … the manifestation of an American Verdun. Bombs soared into the air and burst a thousand feet above the harbour into terrible yellow blossom. Shrapnel peppered the brick walls of the warehouses, plowed the planks of the pier, and rained down upon the hissing waters. Shells shot hither and thither, exploding under the touch of the terrific heat and shooting their missiles at random. Some of the shrapnel shells fell even in Manhattan. On the pier arose a white glare as of a million mercury-vapor lights.[9]

Similarly, Ellis Island was described by commentators as a 'war-swept town' as the munitions that were pummelling armies across the Atlantic had now wreaked havoc across city.[10] However, the connection between the explosion on Black Tom Island and the European War remained a purely literary device for the majority of the city's mainstream press as, despite suspicions, issues of safety and management were forwarded as contributing factors as much as German agents.[11] Confirmation of the incident as an act of German espionage did not occur until after the war; however, arrests were made during August 1916 and though no charges were brought, rumours of German complicity did circulate within the mainstream press.[12] This sentiment was not helped by reports in publications sympathetic to the German position that the explosion was the inevitable product

---

[8] *New York Herald*, July 31, 1916.

[9] *New York Sun*, July 31, 1916.

[10] *New York Times*, July 31, 1916.

[11] *New York Herald*, July 31, 1916.

[12] *New York Herald*, August 2, 1916.

of the city's involvement in the trade of war materials.[13] In the context of the Preparation Parade that had taken place only a few weeks before, the event served to focus attention on the nature of identity in the city and the issue of preparedness. Regardless of whether it was accident or espionage, the framing of the explosion through martial analogies served to remind citizens that their city was under threat. The war had most definitely been brought home.

Preparedness and Identity in the City

The issue of preparedness had succeeded in securing the passing of the National Defense Act in June 1916 by both houses of the legislature in Washington, which provided for an expansion of both the United States Army and the National Guard. This had an immediate effect on New York, as the legislation saw an increase in New York's National Guard to nearly 30,000 men, with a number of these trained reservists attached to the garrisons in the city. However, in response to this expansion, Mayor Mitchel's Committee on National Defense established a survey of reservists in August 1916 and whilst concurring that there was a need for a force to repel potential invaders, a more substantial force was required to sustain 'American democracy'.[14] However, the potential loss of income for city employers from reservists who were obliged to undergo regular training and drills could also have been influential for a committee overseen by business-owners and financiers.[15] The issue of preparedness and security did still form a significant point of debate within New York. Whilst the Sussex Pledge of 1916 between the United States and Germany, regarding the restrictions on submarine warfare, had lessened the opportunity for outrage expressed by the city's majority press regarding Germany's pursuit of the war, the war continued to structure political and social life within the city.

The issues of identity, preparedness and loyalty were particularly exercised during the campaigning in the city for both the Presidential and Congressional Elections of November 1916. The run-up to the election was marked by the discussion of hyphenated identities and their dedication to the United States; a debate that was particularly pointed in New York. The challenger to President Wilson was the Republican candidate was Charles Hughes (1862–1948), a former Governor of New York State and current Associate Justice of the Supreme Court. Hughes had proclaimed himself a supporter of both the programme of Americanisation and preparedness. Whilst Wilson's stance on the issues had shifted, his presidency was still associated with neutrality and his claim to have

---

[13] G.S. Viereck, 1916g. Editorial. *The Fatherland*, 5(1): 10.

[14] W.D. Straight, 1917. *The Mobilization of the National Guard, 1916: Its Economic and Military Aspects*. New York, NY: Mayor's Committee on National Defense.

[15] *New York Times*, August 2, 1916.

kept the nation out of the war was used to attract voters.[16] Hughes' campaign was boosted in the city by the endorsement given to him by former President Roosevelt and his Progressive Party. In his acceptance speech for the Republican nomination delivered at Carnegie Hall, Hughes called upon the sense of American identity as an ideal that should be extended and defended as part of the nation's security.[17]

> In this land of composite population, drawing its strength from every race, the national security demands that there shall be no paltering with American rights. The greater the danger of divisive influences, the greater the necessity for the unifying force of a just, strong and patriotic position. We countenance no covert policies, no intrigues, no secret schemes. We are unreservedly, devotedly, whole heartedly for the United States. That is the rallying point for all Americans, that is my position, I stand for the unflinching maintenance of all American rights on land and sea.[18]

Rather than just the traditional division between Democrat and Republican, the city's residents were obliged to decide upon the candidates on the basis of their commitment to loyalty. However, dealing with ethnic politics in the city could cause problems with candidates, with the danger of particular ethnic enclaves voting *en masse* for one candidate over another. In an attempt to combat this, both candidates appeared in the mainstream press as courting the hyphen vote of German and Irish Americans particularly, but also at other times indicting the 'Hyphenated Americans' for their lack of patriotism. For example, Hughes repeatedly both distanced himself from but also congratulated the speeches of Roosevelt, who was far more adamant in his demand for the Americanisation of immigrants, preparedness and a confrontation with Germany.[19] Such prevarication could be interpreted as both shrewd politics but also pandering to the 'hyphens'. This certainly served to frustrate political allies. Writing to Charles Hughes in August 1916, from the office of the *Metropolitan Magazine* in the city, Roosevelt had suggested to the presidential candidate that loyal New Yorkers desired a harder line to be taken with the pro-German publishers in the city.[20] However, the complexity of electioneering in the city was also compounded by the conflicting messages of support coordinated by German American propagandists in the city

---

[16]   W. Wilson, 1916. *Address of President Wilson before the Press Club in New York City, June 30, 1916.* Washington, DC: Government Printing Office.

[17]   *New York Herald*, July 31, 1916; *New York Sun*, July 31, 1916.

[18]   C. Hughes, 1916. *Speech of Acceptance at Carnegie Hall, New York, July 31, 1916. Republican Campaign Text-book.* Washington, DC: Republican Party, National Committee, pp. 2–19.

[19]   *New York Times*, August 18, 1916; *New York Herald*, August 18, 1916; *New York Times*, September 3, 1916; *New York Sun*, October 13, 1916.

[20]   *Letter from Theodore Roosevelt to Charles Evans Hughes. August 9, 1916.* Theodore Roosevelt Collection. MS Am 1540 (381). Houghton Library, Harvard University.

undertaken in order to ensure the continuation of the nation's neutrality.[21] This itself derived from the increasing perception, communicated and promoted by such publications as the *New Yorker Staats-Zeitung* and the Fatherland, that German American identity was becoming vilified not just within the city, but across the wider nation.[22] The 'hyphen' was becoming the object of suspicion:

> The hyphen, however is dangerous only in certain combinations. You may be an Anglo-Saxon, or a British-American, or Scotch-Irish, or a score of other things with hyphens, and the hyphen will be a mark of distinction and a badge of honor. But if you are a German-American – that is, during the past two years – the hyphen is as dreadful as the brand of Cain.[23]

The motivation for supporting either of the candidates was drawn around issues of the war as much as domestic concerns. Some German Americans would favour opposition candidates on the basis that under the policy of neutrality, President Wilson had tacitly accepted the support of the United States for the war effort of Britain, France and Russia.[24] Conversely, some sections of the Yiddish press in the city had sided with President Wilson as the preserver of peace and stable foreign policies.[25] However, the socialist elements within the New York Jewish community had been left frustrated by the failure of the current administration to secure peace or to reign in the war profiteering of Wall Street financiers.[26] Similarly, Irish American sentiment in New York was also drawn upon the perceived leanings towards Britain and the failure to recognise the cause of independence during the Easter Rising of 1916.[27] The inevitability of a plethora of opinion in a diverse, democratic municipality ensured that the outcome of the city's vote in the Presidential Elections was far from certain.

New York and the 1916 Presidential Election

The nature of identity politics was most clearly drawn by the lobby groups within the city that sought to influence the nature of American politics with regard to the

---

[21]   *New York Times*, October 12, 1916; *New Yorker Staats-Zeitung*, October 11, 1916; F. Koester, 1916. America's Perilous Position. *The Fatherland*, 4(23): 357–9.

[22]   F.F. Schrader, 1916a. *Handbook: Political, Statistical and Sociological, for German Americans and All Other Americans who have Not Forgotten the History and Traditions of their Country, and who Believe in the Principles of Washington, Jefferson and Lincoln.* New York, NY: The Fatherland Corporation.

[23]   G. Seibel, 1916. *The Hyphen in American History.* New York, NY: New Yorker Staats-Zeitung, p. 2.

[24]   *New Yorker Staats-Zeitung*, April 24, 1916.

[25]   *Forverts*, October 2, 1916.

[26]   *New York Call*, October 1, 1916.

[27]   *Gaelic American*, October 21, 1916.

war.[28] One of the most vociferous groups in this respect was the 'American Truth Society'. Founded in 1912 in New York, its membership was largely comprised of Irish Americans who promoted independence for Ireland and rejection of Anglo-American relations. However, after 1914 its membership had been swelled by German Americans who shared the antipathy towards Britain.[29] The society proclaimed itself to be organised on the spirit of 'Americanism' and dedicated to the prevention of 'one race', loosely interpreted as Anglo-Saxon, dominating the institutions of the state.[30] After the outbreak of war, the society had embarked on a programme of publications designed to undermine the cause of the Allies and expose the machinations of Britain towards the United States.[31] Under the direction of the chairman, Jeremiah A. O'Leary (1881–1972), a New York lawyer, the society launched a direct attack on President Wilson. On 29 September, a telegram to the White House was sent by O'Leary and published across the Irish press in the city.[32] The missive accused President Wilson of disloyalty to the United States through his perceived support of the British, his 'autocratic' rule over Congress and absence of support for the Easter Rising in Ireland.[33] The response from the President, received by the society and which was subsequently published across both the Irish American press in the city and the mainstream newspapers, was cutting:

> Your telegram received. I would feel deeply mortified to have you or anybody like you vote for me. Since you have access to many disloyal Americans and I have not, I will ask you to convey this message to them.[34]

The President's reply was immediately seized upon by the American Truth Society as an attack, not just upon their organisation and their chairman, but upon all the Americans in the city who did not align themselves with the Anglo-Saxon elites

---

[28] W. Leary, 1967. Woodrow Wilson, Irish-Americans, and the Election of 1916. *Journal of American History*, 54(1): 57–72; J.E. Cuddy, 1969. Irish-Americans and the 1916 Election: An Episode in Immigrant Adjustment. *American Quarterly*, 21(2): 228–43.

[29] American Truth Society, 1914. *Plan and Scope of American Truth Society*. New York, NY: American Truth Society.

[30] G.W. Mead, 1915. *The Conquest of the United States: A Book of Facts – The Remedy*. New York, NY: American Truth Society.

[31] D. Wallace, 1916. *The Revelations of an American Citizen in the British Army*. New York, NY: American Truth Society; J. O'Leary, 1916a. *The Slave-mind in the United States*. New York, NY: American Truth Society.

[32] *Gaelic American*, September 30, 1916.

[33] American Truth Society, 1916a. *The Telegram to Woodrow Wilson, President of the United States, and the Answer to Jeremiah A. O'Leary, President of the American Truth Society*. New York, NY: American Truth Society.

[34] *New York Times*, September 30, 1916; *New York Herald*, September 30, 1916; *New York Sun*, September 30, 1916.

that were perceived to be in control of the metropolis.[35] The correspondence was reported in the sections of the press who were specifically against the policies of Britain, especially the Hearst-owned newspapers in the city, not only as a slander but an admission of his support for a narrow definition of American identity:

> Mr. Wilson regards any American who expresses opposition to these policies of his as a disloyal person, whose vote and support he would be ashamed to have.[36]

This exchange appeared to lay bare the issue of the election in New York as that of identity and loyalty. Publications that were sympathetic to the Irish or German reported Wilson's message as an act of hostility towards émigré communities.[37] In response to this, the American Truth Society organised a campaign to remove President Wilson from office by coordinating attacks against the policies of the White House and on prominent Democratic Representatives in the city.[38] On 4 October, the American Truth Society began its mission with a fundraising event held in the Garden Theatre, Manhattan, where O'Leary presented himself as a loyal, ardent, young American patriot, appealed to the same principles of liberty and unity from the assembled crowds of nearly 5,000. Attending the event were prominent members of the Irish and German communities in the city, including the editor of the *New Yorker Staats-Zeitung*, Bernard Ridder, and members of the Friends of Irish Freedom, an organisation formed in New York in March 1916 by Clan na Gael to promote the cause of independence.[39] During the meeting, anti-British sentiments were cheered, whilst President Wilson was roundly booed and hissed at every available opportunity. When the name of his challenger to the office, Charles Hughes was called, the crowd cheered and voiced their approval of the candidate.[40] The crowd was also informed of the plan by the American Truth Society to ensure all the Democratic Party candidates for Congress in New York would not be elected. Excepting Henry Bruckner (1871–1942), Democratic candidate for the 22nd District, located in northern parts of Manhattan and the Bronx, the American Truth Society vowed to use the Irish and German vote to remove Democratic Party influence in the city.[41] Indeed, both the *New Yorker Staats-Zeitung* and the *Fatherland* also advised their readers of acceptable

---

[35]   American Truth Society, 1916b. *A Statement Issued by the American Truth Society in Defense of Its President against An Unjust Attack Made upon Him by the President of the United States*. New York, NY: American Truth Society.

[36]   *New York American*, September 30, 1916.

[37]   *Gaelic American*, October 7, 1916.

[38]   J. O'Leary, 1919. *My Political Trial and Experiences*. New York, NY: Jefferson Publishing, p. 465.

[39]   Friends of Irish Freedom, 1920. *Constitution and State, Local and Branch By-laws of the Friends of Irish Freedom*. New York, NY: Friends of Irish Freedom.

[40]   *New York Times*, October 5, 1916.

[41]   *New York Times*, October 3, 1916; *New York Herald*, October 1, 1916.

candidates for the Congressional Elections, in particular those who had voiced their displeasure at the United States trading with the Allies, the British blockade system and whose 'Americanism' was beyond reproach:

- Walbridge Taft, 16th District
- George Francis, 18th District
- Walter Chandler, 19th District
- Martin Ansorge, 21st District
- Henry Bruckner, 22nd District
- William S. Bennet, 23rd District
- Benjamin Fairchild, 24th District[42]

The *New York American*, part of Hearst's pro-German publications, also commented that these candidates should be 'proud' to attract the votes of Irish and German Americans, as it was these individuals who were 'amongst the best of our American citizens'.[43] This direct play of ethnic politics in the city was roundly denounced in the majority mainstream press, who regarded O'Leary's telegram to President Wilson as insulting to the office and to the individual.[44] The publication of Wilson's retort to the accusations levelled by the American Truth Society was widely acclaimed across the mainstream press in the city, with both Republican and Democrat leaning newspapers regarding the statement as a well-calculated move to undermine the 'hyphen' vote in the city.[45] The Democratic Party also presented the incident as a victory against the alien elements in the city that were determined to undermine the nation.[46] Such was the strength of feeling that some remarked that the President's response to New York's 'hyphens' was perhaps one of the few communiqués which received almost unanimous approval in a fiercely-fought and extremely close election.[47] The *Brooklyn Daily Eagle* suggested that the actions of the President communicated a desire amongst New Yorkers to reject the machinations of 'hyphenated Americans'. Therefore, Wilson's telegram was highly lauded:

> … a sentiment to which all Republicans as well as all Democrats who resent the intrusion of alien sympathies and alien issues into American politics will cordially respond.[48]

---

[42] F.F. Schrader, 1916b. N.Y. Congressional Candidates Worthy of Support. *The Fatherland*, 5(14): 2–3.

[43] *New York American*, November 6, 1916.

[44] *New York Sun*, October 1, 1916.

[45] *New York Sun*, October 6, 1916; *New York Herald*, October 2, 1916; *New York Times*, October 2, 1916.

[46] Democratic National Committee, 1916. *The Democratic Text Book*. New York: Democratic National Committee, p. 86.

[47] *New York Evening Post*, October 2, 1916.

[48] *Brooklyn Daily Eagle*, October 2, 1916.

Within the city's newspapers, the vigorous manner in which President Wilson had challenged the 'disloyal' elements in the city was contrasted with the hesitant communications of his challenger:

> At what time will Charles E. Hughes send such a message to the disloyal Americans who cheer him when he utters his careful platitudes.[49]

Therefore, the incident had the effect of associating the 'hyphen' vote, especially that of German and Irish Americans, with the Republican Party and Charles Hughes. Hughes was vociferously backed by the German press in the aftermath of the campaign led by the American Truth Society. Despite his associations with Roosevelt and his claims to the contrary, his candidacy was presented in the city as both a protest against the incumbent and as a means of maintaining 'American' rights. Campaigning in the city revolved around these issues for both candidates. On 2 November, during the final part of the election campaign, President Wilson spoke at the Cooper Union and Madison Square Garden to large crowds at both venues, with many more gathered on the street outside, to reaffirm his policies of neutrality and of Americanisation.[50] The event was marked by a parade, organised by the Democratic Party in the city, to accompany the President's journey between the venues, with a processional of young people dressed as Uncle Sam, George Washington and Native Americans. Along the march, banners were carried that endorsed the President's policy towards the war and criticised his opponent's views on the war. Slogans such as, 'British losses on the Somme 3,000 a day; Hughes says Wilson's peace policy is wrong' and 'Our honor is safe with Wilson'.[51] This rally was swiftly followed by a Republican event held the next day at the Cooper Union where Theodore Roosevelt spoke to a considerable gathering of the significance of the forthcoming election in a speech entitled 'The Soul of the Nation'.[52] Roosevelt endorsed Hughes as the candidate as a man who was straightforward and 'courageous in his actions', whilst damning President Wilson for the dilution of the values of the United States through his foreign policy and neutrality.[53] In a city where ethnic sentiments had been mobilised for political action, the proclamation by Roosevelt of 'American' principles served to heighten tensions in the metropolis and draw further restrictions on the expression of identity.

Similar appeals were also made by Charles Hughes in the city, who used the final days of campaigning in New York to proclaim himself as neither a warmonger nor a friend of alien influence in the United States. Rather, he was a candidate

---

[49]   *New York Times*, October 1, 1916.

[50]   *New York Times*, November 2, 1916.

[51]   *New York Times*, November 3, 1916.

[52]   T. Roosevelt, 1917. *Americanism and Preparedness*. New York, NY: Mail and Express, p. 135.

[53]   *New York Herald*, November 4, 1916.

committed to 'an American administration with an exclusive American policy'. Speaking to labour groups in Brooklyn and to an assembled crowd of over 15,000 at Madison Square Garden on 4 November, Hughes defended the rights of America and Americans. Drawing a direct link to the furore regarding the exchange between President Wilson and Jeremiah O'Leary, Hughes justified the rights of American citizens to differ from the policies emanating from the White House and remain American citizens.[54] Such sentiments were designed to appeal to a broad spectrum of voters in New York, including those who were critical of the impartiality of the United States in the European War as well as those who resented the perceived favouritism towards the Allies.[55] Therefore, the casting of votes in the election on 7 November became an expression of identity as much as political alliance. The results from the city can be viewed as an indication of the dialogue that the metropolis had witnessed regarding the issue of 'Americanisation'.

The day of the election had passed relatively peacefully, with only a number of arrests made for voter fraud and a demonstration by suffragettes. By the evening, crowds had gathered in the city's theatres, bars and restaurants to await news of the election. Early reports were contradictory, with declarations for both Wilson and Hughes being met with approval or despair by rival supporters. Indications that the vote had passed to Hughes were regarded by some sections of the press who were preparedness advocates as a fitting rebuke to a President who had stood idly by as war engulfed Europe.[56] However, the news that President Wilson had been defeated was received with great solemnity by newspapers that were supportive of the programme of Americanisation and regarded the policies of Hughes as 'made in Germany':

> The American people have decided that unity of citizenship is not essential to the nation and that a divided allegiance involves no peril to the Republic.[57]

The crowd of German Americans who had gathered on election night at the Garden Theatre, the Irving Place theatre and Yorkville Theatre, all of which were associated with the German cultural scene in the city, had welcomed the news of Hughes' apparent victory and the defeat of Wilson. Attendants at the gathering remarked upon the reasons for the rejection of President Wilson being his perceived aggression towards 'hyphenated Americans'. Rudolf Erbsloh, business owner and resident of Manhattan, remarked upon these issues:

> I returned from Germany a few days ago in time to cast my vote for Mr. Hughes. It is not necessary for me to say that I am glad my party won. The German-Americans have been displeased with President Wilson in many ways, but

---

54   *New York Times*, November 4, 1916.
55   *New York Sun*, November 6, 1916; *New York Tribune*, November 6, 1916.
56   *New York Tribune*, November 7, 1916.
57   *New York World*, November 7, 1916.

particularly because we think that he has done much by act and deed to stir up a race hatred in this country which should not exist. We hope that Mr. Hughes will do better, and hope that he will not find it necessary to place Colonel Roosevelt in his cabinet.[58]

This sentiment of favouring the candidacy of Hughes over Wilson, whilst rejecting Roosevelt was a frequently expressed sentiment within the German American press in the city. Before the election, the Fatherland expressed its concerns over Roosevelt but its belief in the power of the 'hyphen vote':

If Mr Wilson is defeated the hyphen is the hatchet that has decapitated his hopes. If Mr. Hughes is defeated he is defeated because he permitted his Machiavellian advisor, Theodore Roosevelt, to drive the German-American vote into the Wilson camp.[59]

The conflicting reports of victories and defeats for both candidates continued apace throughout the evening into the following day. However, by 9 November, the result was clear. Whilst New York State had voted convincingly for Hughes and the Republican Party, the city of New York had voted for President Wilson and the Democrats. On a national level, by the narrowest of margins, President Wilson had also defeated his challenger.[60] The city's vote was not an overwhelming endorsement of the incumbent. However, with 351,539 votes cast for the President compared to 311,470 for Hughes, the city's decision was clear. The results also raised issues about the potential impact of the 'hyphen vote'. All the boroughs of the city, bar Queens County, had sided with President Wilson. Brooklyn, home to a large section of German Americans, though notably third or fourth generation immigrants, had voted by a margin of over 6,000 ballots to elect Wilson. The Bronx, which also had a well-established German American community, as well as more recent German immigrants, also voted by a more substantial margin of over 7,000 ballots for President Wilson. Queens, home to both German and Irish émigrés, which had traditionally voted for Democratic candidates with the influence of the Tammany Hall machine, had swung by a margin of 3,000 votes to back the Republican Hughes's candidacy.

The Congressional Election results had also appeared to dispel the belief that the 'hyphen vote' could influence the politics of the metropolis. Indeed, it is within these elections that the voting patterns of émigré communities could have the greatest impact. The metropolis was divided into 24 electoral districts, with boundaries arranged by area and population.[61] As such, with several significant

---

[58]   *New York Times*, November 8, 1916.

[59]   G.S. Viereck, 1916h. Editorial. *The Fatherland*, 5(13): 202.

[60]   New York State, 1917b. *The New York Red Book*. Albany, NY: J.B. Lyon, p. 478.

[61]   Board of Elections, 1916. *Maps Showing the Assembly Districts of the City of New York*. New York, NY: Board of Elections.

German, Irish and Russian Jewish communities across Manhattan, Brooklyn, Queens and the Bronx, the potential for these enclaves to shape the result of the election was highly probable. Despite the anger of the American Truth Society and the dissatisfaction expressed by some groups at the policies of President Wilson, who had hoped to use their influence to prevent Democratic candidates from gaining seats, the overall effect of their campaigning was seemingly minimal or even non-existent. Indeed, where elections had been held, the sitting candidates had all successfully defended any opposition regardless of the presumed 'hyphen' vote. As in the contest between Hughes and Wilson in the city, these results were most notable in Brooklyn, where the presence of a large German American community could have been presumed to have shaped the outcome, if not for a Presidential Election then at least for a Congressional Election. However, Frederick Rowe (1863–1946), Republican, had retained his seat for the 6th District in Queens; John J. Fitzgerald (1872–1952), Democrat, had retained his seat for the 7th District in Brooklyn; Daniel J. Griffin (1880–1926), Democrat, had retained his seat for the 8th District in Brooklyn; Oscar Swift (1869–1940), Republican, had retained his seat for the 9th District encompassing parts of Brooklyn and Queens; Reuben Haskell (1878–1971), Republican, had retained his seat for the 10th District in Brooklyn; Daniel Riordan (1870–1923), Democrat, had retained his seat for the 11th District in Brooklyn; Meyer London (1871–1926), Socialist, had retained his seat for the 12th District in Manhattan's Lower East Side; Christopher Sullivan (1870–1942), Democrat, had retained his seat for the 13th District in Manhattan; Michael Conry (1870–1917), Democrat, retained his seat in the 15th District in the Bronx.

The major reversal of a sitting candidate saw the reform politician Fiorello LaGuardia (1882–1947), Republican, win the 14th District from the Democratic candidate and Tammany Hall man Michael Farley (1863–1921). LaGuardia, of Jewish and Italian heritage, triumphed in an electoral territory which was highly diverse and located in the poverty-stricken area of Harlem; campaigning in English, Yiddish, Italian and Slovenian, LaGuardia mobilised voters to reject the perceived corruption of his political opponent. However, this was seemingly the only incident where issues of identity affected voters. Of the Republican candidates that were endorsed by the *New Yorker Staats-Zeitung* only two had managed to overturn Democratic incumbents. Of the 24 districts across the city, 14 had voted for Democratic candidates with majority retaining their current representatives. Therefore, despite the ethnic politics that had marked the run-up to the election, New York remained a largely Democratic-voting city.

The result was lauded as evidence that the fear of voting *en masse* by particular ethnic groups to influence the outcome of elections was nothing but hysteria that had been concocted by a press within the city that were sympathetic to the cause of the Central Powers.[62] Indeed, commentators were left to wonder whether the 'hyphen vote' was purely a chimera, or perhaps whether it had been

---

[62]   *New York Times*, November 9, 1916.

negated by those voters motivated to act against the perceived influence of émigré populations.[63] Inevitably, the apparent absence of the émigré vote in the city had perplexed those seeking to use the elections as a means to demonstrate the opposition to the perceived bias against 'hyphenated Americans'. *The Fatherland* rebuffed the suggestion that the result represented the weakness of the German American position, declaring that, 'the entirety of the German-American vote can not be, and never will be, delivered to any one candidate'.[64] Both the *Irish World* and the *Gaelic American* highlighted the effect that the 'hyphen vote' had in areas of Queens County, where a swing to the Republicans had overturned a previous Democratic majority.[65]

Alphonse Koelble, President of the New York Branch of the German–American Alliance, claimed that the majority of German American votes had been for Hughes and a smaller proportion of Irish Americans had voted Republican.[66] The majority mainstream press were, however, convinced that the result demonstrated the work of patriotic Americans who had turned out to ensure victory against a foreign-backed political group.[67] However, the number of those voting in both the Presidential and Congressional elections in the city in November 1916 was not significantly different from previous contests. Therefore, rather than the disappearance of the 'hyphen vote', New York's émigré communities with close cultural, familial and political ties to their former homelands in Europe had opted to express their identities as Americans. Rather than a campaign based upon identity and an election result based on pragmatism, this was a result which had been developed and completed as a means of expression. In a city which had witnessed the narrowing of national identification, individuals were responding accordingly and redefining themselves within this restricted definition.

Increasing Wartime Involvement

By the end of 1916 the war had reshaped New York's society, culture, economics and its politics. The effect of the conflict in Europe was to place the city on a wartime footing whilst remaining, however nominally, a 'neutral city'. Indeed, such was the extent of the metropolis involvement with the war that the Thanksgiving Day sermons in the city's churches and synagogues during November 1916 focused upon the conflict and the nature of patriotism.[68] Reverend William Manning of the Episcopalian Trinity Church fused the concern for preparedness with the principles

---

[63] *New York Times*, November 12, 1916.

[64] F.F. Schrader, 1916c. The Presidential Election Reviewed. *The Fatherland*, 5(16): 243–4, 255.

[65] *Gaelic American*, November 18, 1916.

[66] Anon., 1916. How the Hyphen Voted. *The Literary Digest*, 53(22): 1394.

[67] *New York Sun*, November 12, 1916; *New York Herald*, November 12, 1916.

[68] *New York Sun*, November 25, 1916.

of national character in a manner which appeared to follow the campaign message of President Wilson in the city a few weeks previously:

> An opportunity without precedent in history has been given to us to take the moral leadership of the world, and we have not accepted it. And out of our enormous profits we have not even given generously for the help of those suffering from the war. Individuals and groups have given heroic help, but our people as a whole have given pitifully little.[69]

The admonition to congregations was common across the city; as war relief charities were the beneficiaries of the collection at Protestant, Catholic and Jewish services, religious leaders took the opportunity to remind individuals of their religious duties, obligations of service and sacrifice which frequently took upon the mantle of national virtues. For example, Rabbi Samuel Schulman (1864–1955), of Temple Beth-El on Fifth Avenue, had previously spoken of the role of religion in inspiring patriotism.[70] However, the occasion of Thanksgiving provided a further occasion on which to outline a commitment to the policies of the United States.[71] Rabbis, Pastors and Priests across the city proclaimed themselves neither to be 'pro-Allies' or 'pro-German' but rather concerned with the spiritual state of citizens if the nation continued to stand apart and profit from the conflict.[72] As part of this distillation of national expression, a campaign for a United War Relief organisation to operate in the city beyond religious and ethnic boundaries was also voiced by religious leaders and philanthropists alike.[73] Within the city of immigrants a mobilisation of American values was underway, spurred on by a drive to commit to the process of 'Americanisation'.

Beyond the religious and charitable impulses the forces of conformity were experienced in other ways across the city. Indeed, the enthusiasm of religious leaders to admonish the charity and dedication of the faithful within New York was matched by the near religious zeal with which patriotic organisations in the city were requiring the end of 'hyphenated' American identity. The NSL had forged ahead after August 1916 to begin a campaign to raise awareness of the security risks of 'hyphenated Americans' both in New York and across the wider nation.[74] The issues of loyalty and patriotism, which were observed in the elections of November 1916, were also championed by the NAC in New York.[75]

---

[69] *New York Times*, November 25, 1916.

[70] S. Schulman, 1916a. War, Religion and Preparedness. *The Advocate of Peace*, 78(6): 136–8.

[71] S. Schulman, 1916b. *Gratitude with Apology: A Thanksgiving Sermon, Sunday, November 26th, 1916*. New York, NY: Chambers.

[72] *New York Herald*, November 25, 1916.

[73] *New York Times*, December 28, 1916.

[74] *New York Times*, August 21, 1916.

[75] *New York Times*, April 2, 1916.

Indeed, the organisation had embarked upon a programme of public information throughout 1916 to coincide with the election, detailing how 'Americanisation' would reshape industry, education and the relationship of citizens to the state.[76] Within this assessment, what being an American meant began to be defined; though frequently this was expressed as what this sense of identity was not, just as much as what it actually constituted.[77] As an example of this, Royal Dixon (1885–1962), a member of the NAC and a lecturer in the city for the Board of Education, in his attempt to define the concept, drew upon the war and the perceived attacks upon American ideals that had been made by alien subversives as the catalyst for national consciousness:

> So far as any national consciousness has been found to exist, it has stirred from this stupor to fits of indignation only when groups of people calling themselves Americans committed outrages against life and property, or propagandists of the Prussian creed were found trying to beguile and persuade the rest of us into espousing the cause of tyranny and falsehood.[78]

The work of the NAC within New York's Board of Education was particularly significant as from 1915 onwards they had drawn upon the philanthropy of their backers to ensure programmes of instruction were in place across the nation's cities to educate and 'Americanise' the immigrant.[79] In New York, this mission was regarded as especially difficult, since the sheer size of the 'immigrant tide' had overwhelmed the schools and resulted in not only 'feeble minded' alien children but individuals lacking in the appropriate knowledge and respect for American traditions.[80] The New York Board of Education had used the opportunity presented by the war to further their work to integrate the foreigner through schooling and tuition.[81] With the lobbying of the NAC and their parent organisation, the Committee for Immigrants in America, imposition of a greater focus on English-language teaching, the politics of the United States and the figures of national

---

[76]   F. Kellor, 1916b. Americanization: A Conservation Policy for Industry. *Annals of the American Academy of Political and Social Science*, 65(1): 240–44.

[77]   D.J. Hill, 1916. *Americanism: What Is It?* New York, NY: D. Appleton and Company.

[78]   R. Dixon, 1916. *Americanization*. New York, NY: Macmillan, p. 2.

[79]   National Americanization Committee, 1915. *Americanizing a City*. New York, NY: National Americanization Committee; G. Abbott, 1917. *The Immigrant and the Community*. New York, NY: Century Company.

[80]   F.J. Warne, 1916. *The Tide of Immigration*. New York, NY: D. Appleton and Company, pp. 103–104.

[81]   A. Shiels (ed.), 1916. *The School and the Immigrant: A Series of Articles*. New York, NY: Department of Education, the City of New York; A. Rhodes, 1916. Women's Organizations and Americanization. *The Journal of the New York State Teachers' Association*, 4(3): 103–104.

pride, most notably the wartime leaders George Washington and Abraham Lincoln, the schools across the city began to reflect the wider political trends in New York.[82] In 1916, through the New York State Department of Education, the Committee for Immigrants in America published a syllabus for immigrants which outlined the principles required of immigrants to 'train' the foreign-born population to become 'good, efficient and devoted' American citizens.[83] In this manner, through both religion and education the nature of identity was redefined into what was acceptable and what was liable for censure. Therefore, what the debates surrounding the election of 1916 had introduced into the city was a new discourse and a new concept of identification; the year had witnessed the rise of the demand to demonstrate and to have others represent a quality of 'one hundred per cent Americanism'.

Such a means of conformity was nevertheless presented as inherently liberating. Members of the NAC regarded their work as charitable, assisting New York's émigré population with the naturalisation process and ensuring that they were aware of the roles as citizens.[84] Whilst the notion of 'Americanisation' was presented as progressive, utilising the support of charitable and philanthropic organisations and reformers in the city, within the increasingly hostile environment created by the war, the call could appear to assert less benevolent tendencies. Indeed, the drive towards 'one hundred per cent Americanism' can be observed in the work of the New York biologist and social commentator, Madison Grant (1865–1937). Writing in the city, with the backdrop of war in Europe and fears of alien subversives in the metropolis, Grant hypothesised the fall of the 'Nordic Races' in the United States as they were diluted by miscegenation, outvoted or outnumbered by 'swarms' of 'inferior races'.[85] Grant regarded this perceived tragedy as ensuring the subsequent decline in civilisation as the nation was overrun by 'lesser peoples'. For New York, this situation posed a threat to the very existence of the city itself:

> In many countries the existing classes represent races that were once distinct. In the city of New York … there is a native American aristocracy resting upon layer after layer of immigrants of lower races, and the native American, whole, of course, disclaiming the distinction of a patrician class, nevertheless has, up to

---

[82]   Board of Education, New York, 1916. *School Library Bulletin*, 9(5).

[83]   Committee for Immigrants in America, 1916. *Citizenship Syllabus: A Course of Study and Syllabus*. New York, NY: Committee for Immigrants in America, p. 2.

[84]   Committee for Immigrants in America, 1915. *Professional Course for Service Among Immigrants: Prepared for the Use of Colleges and Universities, Schools of Civics and Philanthropy, to Fit Men and Women for Service Among Immigrants*. New York, NY: The Committee for Immigrants in America.

[85]   C. Alexander, 1962. Prophet of American Racism: Madison Grant and the Nordic Myth. *Phylon*, 23(1): 73–90.

this time, supplied the leaders of thought and the control of capital, of education, and of the religious ideals and altruistic bias of the community.[86]

The concern for the protection of American values and identities echoed the racial development of a concern for 'one hundred per cent Americanism' and offered a tool through which the figure of the immigrant could be reformed, but it also offered a means by which the foreigner could be excluded. This concept of 'one hundred per cent Americanism' was certainly present within the educational programmes in the city that were initiated throughout 1916. These served to isolate and alienate any departure from the 'norm' within the metropolis. A city that had experienced attacks, subterfuge and the potentially divisive nature of ethnic politics began to condition its citizens through various public and private operations to conform to an ideal. As 1916 drew to a close, New York was still neutral in the global conflagration, but it had declared a tacit war upon itself.

Americanisation in the City

Using the identifying framework of Americanisation, the events of early January 1917 served to reiterate the sense of American ideals and the need to protect and preserve them in the face of foreign opposition. New York's press and its wider public were able to use this perspective to offer further judgement on the conflict; however, this was now frequently made with reference to the values of the United States.[87] This is particularly evident with the decision taken by the German Empire at the start of the New Year to resume unrestricted submarine warfare on Atlantic shipping which brought condemnation from the city's majority press.[88] In New York, for the German American community, this military action was feared greatly, predominantly for the fuel it would provide for an already virulent campaign for 'Americanisation'.[89] Indeed, the announcement that the Atlantic would once again be regarded as an arena of war by the Germany Navy appeared to indicate all the hallmarks of 'Prussianism', defined in opposition to the values of the United States.[90] The aggression and militarism of Germany was regarded as being expressed in this act and indicative of the nature of the people; Germany had seemingly declared war on the nation and created German Americans as the emblems of a hostile foreign power.[91] Such was the antipathy towards this action within the city, that even the Hearst-owned and previously German-leaning

---

[86]   M. Grant, 1916. *The Passing of the Great Race; or, The Racial Basis of European History*. New York, NY: Charles Scribner's Sons, p. 5.

[87]   *New York World*, December 28, 1916; *New York Tribune*, December 28, 1916.

[88]   *New York Times*, February 9, 1917; *New York Herald*, February 9, 1917.

[89]   *New Yorker Herold*, December 27, 1916.

[90]   *New York Herald*, February 1, 1917.

[91]   *New York Sun*, February 1, 1917; *New York Times*, February 2, 1916.

newspaper, *The American*, felt compelled to declare its support for the President, even to the point of conflict.[92] In effect, the war was creating a consensus in the city, a union that was formed and understood through the context of 'one hundred per cent Americanism'. The extent to which this had galvanised the populace can be assessed in the petition organised by the Mayor's Committee on National Defense as a consequence to the return of German submarine warfare.[93] Beginning in early February, after only three weeks, over one million signatures had been collected from New York citizens pledging their support to President Wilson and the defence of 'American' values:

> As an American, faithful to the American ideals of justice, liberty and humanity, and confident that the government has exerted its most earnest efforts to keep us at peace with the world, I hereby declare my absolute and unconditional loyalty to the Government of the United States and pledge my support to you in protecting American rights against unlawful violence upon land and sea, in guarding the Nation against hostile attacks, and in upholding international right.[94]

The petition was placed in hotels, bars, telegraph offices, municipal offices, political party branches, as well as police stations.[95] The normalising of this proclamation of loyalty in New York was thereby complete as citizens were able to state their allegiance whilst completing their daily tasks.[96] The reference to 'hostile attacks' struck a particular note within the city as fears of German agents or subversives contributed to the desire to protect and defend the identity and principles of the nation. This framework of understanding was also exercised by the news in early March of the telegram made by the Secretary of State for Foreign Affairs, Arthur Zimmermann (1864–1940), to the German Ambassador to Mexico. This communication offered the proposition of Mexico's alliance with the Central Powers in the event of the United States joining the war on the side of the Allies. As a reward for declaring war on the United States, Mexico was offered territory in the states of Texas, New Mexico and Arizona as part of any future peace settlement. The offer intended to exacerbate the border disputes between Mexico and the United States, which had been a source of tension from 1914.

News of the telegram was met with strong denunciations within the city's press of Germany's attempts to disturb relations within the North American continent and to undermine the policies of the United States.[97] This subterfuge of German politicians, attempting to ferment war in North America, was linked to

---

[92]   *New York American*, February 1, 1917.

[93]   *New York Times*, March 13, 1917; *New York Herald*, March 13, 1917.

[94]   *Daily Standard Union*, March 13, 1917.

[95]   *New York Tribune*, March, 13, 1917.

[96]   *New York Times*, March 15, 1917.

[97]   *New York Herald*, March 3, 1917; *New York Sun*, March 3, 1917.

the sabotage of German agents in New York; the fear of alien sedition was thereby intensified.[98] The effect of these events, both the resumption of submarine warfare and the Zimmermann Telegram, on a national level, was to ensure the break in diplomatic relations between Germany and the United States and to precipitate the declaration of war. However, within the specific locale of New York, these events served to focus attention on the issues of identity. The initial response within the German-language press of the city to the Zimmerman Telegram was incredulity, suspecting the work of British forgers.[99] Nevertheless, with the acknowledgement of its authenticity, recognition of the difficult position of German Americans in the city was made.[100] No longer was a hyphenated identity acceptable in the city, nor were expressions of associations with a former homeland; now only a commitment to the values of the United States and a declaration of 'one hundred per cent Americanism' was permissible in New York. Just as it had declared war on itself, the metropolis began to police itself; to regulate the expression of identity.

The extent of the city's embrace of Americanisation, even before the entry of the United States into the war, can be witnessed in the final publication of *The Fatherland*. The weekly issue which had done so much from the start of the conflict to represent and reiterate the significance of both German and German American values could no longer continue in the current climate of New York's politics. The final issue reflected the tensions within the city, as a journal that only three months earlier had harangued the political establishment and had demanded the recognition of the significance of 'hyphenated' identities, was obliged to conform to the dictum of 'one hundred per cent Americanism'. The cover of *The Fatherland* for 14 February stated:

> America First ... The Fatherland has always emphasized that it is an American publication. Its original name was adopted as a graceful tribute to the country of our fathers. Our Fatherland is America ... We cannot champion Germany's cause if our country is at odds with Germany.[101]

For this reason, the name of the publication was altered from the February issue onwards to reflect this commitment to the United States; *The Fatherland* became *The New World*. The tenor of the articles maintained a desire to avoid war and to protest against British policies, but these were framed as in the interests of the United States; readers were encouraged to desire the continuation of neutrality but to support the nation if arms were taken. The charitable efforts undertaken by concerned citizens, the bazaars organised to assist war widows and orphans and the numerous church and community events held to express support for Germany

---

[98] *New York Tribune*, March 4, 1917; *New York Times*, March 4, 1917.

[99] *New Yorker Staats-Zeitung*, March 2, 1917; *New Yorker Volkszeitung*, March 2, 1917.

[100] *New Yorker Herold*, March 2, 1917.

[101] G.S. Viereck, 1917. America First. *The Fatherland*, 6(2): 1.

were advised to be halted in order that individuals do their duty to themselves and their country. As if to affirm the new dedication to the nation, the publication changed its name again towards the end of February, taking the patriotic moniker *The American Weekly*. These changes were indications of the wider perception within the city that regarded attachment to any other nation or cause beyond that of the primary allegiance to the United States as suspicious. This perception in the city was summarised most succinctly in the words of the popular song, *Let's all be Americans now*, published in New York in February 1917. Written by the Russian Jewish immigrant New Yorker, Irving Berlin (1888–1989), the song asked its listeners to consider where their loyalties should really lie:

> It's up to you! What will you do?
> England or France may have your sympathy, over the sea,
> But you'll agree
> That, now is the time, To fall in line,
> You swore that you would so be true to your vow,
> Let's all be Americans now.[102]

The demand for conformity was also extended to the radical political elements in the city, as the requirements of Americanisation began to alter issues of expression and representation beyond the confines of the ballot box.[103] Socialists and anarchists in the city had opposed any involvement in the war and campaigned against the profiteering by New York's industrialists and financiers since the outbreak of the conflict.[104] The elections of 1916 had brought the re-election of the only Socialist Representative in the city, Meyer London. With a strong backing from the Russian Jewish community of the Lower East Side, London had won the election in 1914 on the basis of his socialist politics and support for the working classes.[105] Within this context, London had maintained a consistent approach to the issues of neutrality and had campaigned for a peaceful resolution to the conflict.[106] He had been joined in this policy by the New York lawyer and leader of the Socialist Party in America, Morris Hillquit. Both politicians had used the elections in the city to emphasise the manner in which huge profits had been procured from the death and suffering in Europe.[107] London's election victory had demonstrated a strong support for continuing the non-interventionist approach taken by President Wilson.

---

[102]　I. Berlin, E. Leslie and G. Meyer, 1917. *Let's All Be Americans Now*. New York, NY: Waterson, Berlin and Snyder.

[103]　J. Weinstein, 1959. Anti-War Sentiment and the Socialist Party, 1917–1918. *Political Science Quarterly*, 74(2): 215–39.

[104]　E. Goldman, 1917a. The Promoters of the War Mania. *Mother Earth*, 12(1): 5; M. London, 1915. There Must Be an End. *The Masses*, 6(8): 18.

[105]　M. London, 1917. *Speeches of Congressman Meyer London*. New York, NY: s.n.

[106]　*New York Call*, January 20, 1916.

[107]　*New York Call*, September 13, 1916.

The socialist party were highly sympathetic to the pacifist movement, which had secured a great deal of public support in New York during 1916. Indeed, the song, *I didn't raise my boy to be a soldier*, written and distributed in the city's fast-growing music-producing district, Tin Pan Alley, had become a popular success across the music halls and theatres in the city from 1915 onwards:[108]

> I didn't raise my boy to be a soldier,
> I brought him up to be my pride and joy.
> Who dares to place a musket on his shoulder,
> To shoot some other mother's darling boy?
> Let nations arbitrate their future troubles,
> It's time to lay the sword and gun away.
> There'd be no war today,
> If mothers all would say,
> I didn't raise my boy to be a soldier.[109]

The sentimental lyrics mask somewhat the significant political agenda within the appeal to pacifism and neutrality, that the involvement of the United States in a large-scale conflict could necessitate the mobilisation of the populace for war.[110] As the socialist politicians of the city were keen to highlight through the election campaign of 1916, this would be a burden which would fall overwhelmingly upon the working classes.[111] However, the figure of the pacifist or the neutral was one that increasingly evoked the ire of campaigners for Americanisation. Pacifists were associated with immigrant communities who desired peace for their own self-interest rather than for the benefit of the United States and who seemingly lacked the martial qualities represented by the nation. This was illustrated in the 1916 film *Fall of a Nation*, based upon the book by Thomas Dixon, Jr (1864–1946).[112] In Dixon's rendering, a prominent New York businessman, who espouses pacifist views, is revealed to be a foreign dignitary who engineers and then takes advantage of New York's weakened defences to capture the city with a hidden army of

---

[108]   C. Gier, 2013. War, Anxiety, and Hope in American Sheet Music, 1914–1917. *Music and Politics*, 7(1). http://dx.doi.org/10.3998/mp.9460447.0007.102 (accessed 21 April 2013).

[109]   A. Piantadosi and A. Bryan, 1915. *I Didn't Raise My Boy to Be a Soldier*. New York, NY: Leo Feist.

[110]   M. Hillquit, 1914b. Socialism and War, I. *Metropolitan*, 28: 56–7; M. Hillquit, 1915a. Socialism and War, II. *Metropolitan*, 36: 51–2; M. Hillquit, 1915b. Socialism and War, III. *Metropolitan*, 37: 39–41.

[111]   *New York Call*, November 9, 1916.

[112]   T. Dixon, 1916. *The Fall of a Nation*. New York, NY: D. Appleton and Company; T. Dixon, 1915. *The Clansman*. New York, NY: Doubleday. Dixon was also the author of the overtly racist novel *The Clansman*, which was filmed in 1915 as *Birth of a Nation*.

foreign supporters posing as New York citizens.[113] The account provides a graphic rendering of the rape and slaughter of the city as it falls to a vicious army who swiftly succeed in overpowering the populace and conquering the metropolis.[114] Through depictions such as these and the campaigns for preparedness, the socialist platform of pacifism was undermined as unpatriotic and deleterious to the nation.

Representing the position of the Socialist Party in America in the city became increasingly difficult despite the efforts of such publications as *The Masses*. The periodical had begun in 1912 as an outlet for socialist views and artistic expression emerging from the bohemian and radical communities which had begun to inhabit Greenwich Village. After the outbreak of war, *The Masses* had rejected the conflict and the involvement of New York's businesses with it as a clear demonstration of the abuse of the capitalist market.[115] This position was to become far harder to defend after the elections of 1916 had signalled a movement towards the 'Americanisation' agenda.[116] Faced with an onslaught of 'one hundred per cent Americanism', the editors of the journal felt compelled to retain their socialist dedication to the international, foregoing the appeal to patriotism:

> I do not believe many people will ever be led to feel unpatriotic. To argue against these tribal and egoistic instincts is like arguing against gravitation. But I do hope that a fair proportion of the intelligent may be persuaded to resist the establishment, in their own minds or in American society, of patriotism as a religion.[117]

Despite these hopes that the 'religion of patriotism' would be disavowed within the city, the declaration of war by the United States Congress on 6 April brought an inevitable tightening of control over political and cultural expression in New York.[118] The place of socialism within the accepted tenets of the American character came under greater focus with the vote placed by Meyer London in the House of Representatives against the pronouncement of war with Germany.[119] The tone of the reporting of London's actions within New York's press was vitriolic. The socialist politician was immediately regarded as having betrayed the nation and that his refusal to support the resolution shamed the city whilst sacrificing

---

[113]   P. Conolly-Smith, 2008. Casting Teutonic Types from the Nineteenth Century to World War I: German Ethnic Stereotypes in Print, on Stage, and Screen. *Columbia Journal of American Studies*, 9: 48–73.

[114]   *New York Times*, June 24, 1916.

[115]   M. Becker, 1914. Hearst: 'My, What Inhuman Brutes these Europeans Are!'. *The Masses*, 5(12): 14.

[116]   F. Bohn, 1917. The Re-election of Wilson. *The Masses*, 9(3): 15–16.

[117]   M. Eastman, 1917b. The Religion of Patriotism. *The Masses*, 9(9): 8–12.

[118]   W. Wilson, 1917. *Why We are At War*. New York, NY: Harper Brothers, p. 35.

[119]   *Congressional Record*, House, 65th Congress, April 6, 1917, pp. 2815–50.

American values for the benefit of foreign powers.[120] However, the declaration of war and London's vote against it mobilised the socialist opinion in the city towards a renewed action, condemning the conflict once again as a capitalist exercise.[121] *The Masses* launched a strong anti-war campaign, urging its readers to resist the expected militarisation of society and to maintain their socialist ideals.[122]

Tensions Wrought by War

The support of the working classes and critique of the war as a means to enrich the city's businessmen and financiers was more than a commitment to principles; it was a means to represent the working classes in the city who had been significantly disadvantaged by the conflict. Whilst employment had risen after the initial slump in economic productivity after the onset of war in August 1914, the rise in demand for raw materials and foodstuffs had caused a steady increase in prices. Indeed, by December 1916, the cost of living in the city had increased by nearly 20 per cent.[123] The situation was documented by the socialist campaigner Dorothy Day (1897–1980) for the *New York Call*.[124] Despite municipal efforts to alleviate the issue of 'food poverty' during the first few months of the war, the poorer sections of the city were still faced with price rises for staples, a situation that had deteriorated after Germany's recommencement of submarine warfare.[125] Despite the employment opportunities that had been created by the war, wages in the city had stagnated, exacerbating the problems that were afflicting New York's poorest residents.[126] The price for bread, meat, milk and butter rose to exponential heights, particularly from the hand-cart sellers from whom the majority of the metropolis' tenement residents were compelled to purchase from.[127] With prices

---

[120] *New York World*, April 7, 1917; *New York Sun*, April 7, 1917.

[121] *New York Call*, April 7, 1917; J. Reed, 1917. Whose War? *The Masses*, 9(6): 11–12.

[122] A. Giovannitti, 1917. Militant Pacifism. *The Masses*, 9(7): 31–2.

[123] Bureau of Applied Economics, 1920. *Changes in Cost of Living and Prices, 1914 to 1920*. Washington, DC: Government Printing Office, p. 9.

[124] *New York Call*, December 15, 1916.

[125] New York Board of Estimate and Apportionment, Bureau of Personal Service, 1917. *Report on the Increased Cost of Living for an Unskilled Labourer's Family in New York City*. New York, NY: M.B. Brown.

[126] W. Gibbs, 1917. *The Minimum Cost of Living: A Study of Families of Limited Income in New York City*. New York, NY: Macmillan, pp. 50–51; New York State Legislative, 1917. *Preliminary Report of the Joint Legislative Committee on Dairy Products, Live Stock and Poultry. Transmitted to the Legislature February 15, 1917*. Albany, NY: J.B. Lyon, pp. 928–36.

[127] Commissioners of Accounts, 1917. *The Pushcart Problem in New York City: Progress Toward its Solution and Need for Prohibition of Pushcart Peddling in the Vicinity of the Williamsburg and Manhattan Bridge Markets*. New York, NY: Brown.

rising by between 10 and 50 per cent for some items, the ability to survive and avoid starvation in areas of the Lower East Side was severely tested.[128] Despite the economy measures suggested by the Mayor's Committee on Food, it was the sheer cost that drove resentment and concerned the city authorities.[129]

The problems had become acute by early February 1917; the citizens of a city that was still ostensibly neutral and removed from the war was becoming tired and restless of wartime restrictions. The potential for these tensions to be profited upon by socialist and pacifist elements was particularly worrisome for the municipal and state authorities.[130] Before any degree of control over markets and prices could be organised, the city's residents revolted against the conditions. With sporadic outburst of protest from the beginning of the month, the violence began on 19 February, when women shoppers attempting to purchase goods from pushcart sellers in the Brownsville and Williamsburg districts in Brooklyn were confronted with what was another consecutive rise in prices. The response was dramatic; pushcarts were overturned and set alight, produce was both stolen and destroyed and police officers sent to the disturbances were attacked by crowds of women which were estimated to be numbered in the thousands.[131] Through baton charges, the protesters were dispersed, but the event was widely covered in the city newspapers the following day.[132] Despite exerting the authority of the police over the rioters, the actions taken by the women of Brooklyn inspired similar protests across the city on the following day. This included a boycott of pushcart sellers of meat, fruit, bread and eggs, who were deemed to have conspired amongst themselves to raise prices in the city.[133] The women participating in these protests were largely from the Russian Jewish communities, which had a strong tradition of unionisation and socialist politics. It was from these sources that a degree of leadership emerged among the protestors as 20 February witnessed coordinated action against profiteering food sellers, the city authorities and the police (Figure 5.1).

Members of the women's protest group who had labour and union political connections within the city had placed an advert in the Jewish social newspaper *Forverts* calling for a mass meeting on Rutgers Square in the Lower East Side. This organisation, naming themselves the Mothers' Anti-High Price League, was composed of socialists and suffragettes who were closely supported by the

---

[128] W. Mitchell, 1919. *International Price Comparisons.* Washington, DC: Government Printing Office, p. 8.

[129] *New York Times*, February 3, 1917.

[130] E. Goldman, 1917b. Hunger Demonstrations: The Outcome of National Prosperity. *Mother Earth*, 12(1): 17–19.

[131] W. Frieburger, 1984. War Prosperity and Hunger: The New York Food Riots of 1917. *Labor History*, 25(2): 217–39.

[132] *New York Times*, February 20, 1917; *New York Herald*, February 20, 1917.

[133] D. Frank, 1985. Housewives, Socialists, and the Politics of Food: The 1917 New York Cost-of-Living Protests. *Feminist Studies*, 11(2): 355–85.

Figure 5.1   Crowd Gathered Outside a Butcher Shop During the 1917
               Food Riot.

Source: Grantham Bain Collection, Library of Congress (LC-B2-995-11).

socialist party.[134] Mrs Rebecca Panken, Mrs Theresa Malklel, Mrs Bella Neumann Zilberman, Mrs Volinsky and Miss Helen Fisher were the main proponents of the League and provided a platform for protesters outside the *Forverts* offices on 20 February. They were joined by the socialist campaigner Ida Harris, whose Mothers' Vigilance Committee had also attacked the rise in food prices. The large crowds that attended the meeting were encouraged by more radical figures, such as the anarchist Marie Ganz (1891–1968), who encouraged the crowd to march to City Hall.[135] Spurred on by these leaders, a section of the protesters crowded in front of the city's main administrative building in Downtown Manhattan pleading with Mayor Mitchel to ensure lower food prices in the city.[136] Policemen detached to protect the Mayor, who was not in attendance during the protest, spoke to the crowd in German, attempting to placate what had become a plea for the authorities to feed starving children. In response, Ida Harris asserted the

---

[134]   *New York Call*, February 20, 1917.

[135]   M. Ganz, 1920. *Rebels: Into Anarchy and Out Again*. New York, NY: Dodd, Mead and Company, pp. 252–3.

[136]   *New York Herald*, February 21, 1917.

patriotism of the crowd, proclaiming that 'we do not want to make trouble. We are good Americans and we simply want the mayor to make the prices go down'.[137] The appeal to nationalism served as a pre-emptive strike to rumours that the protest was organised by German agents in the city to sow the seeds of discontent amongst the masses.[138] The war served as the catalyst for these protests, and a critical stance against the position of the United States in supplying the Allies was taken at a second mass meeting held in Madison Square on 24 February. Calls for a protection of 'American lives', 'American standards' and 'America first' were used by the Mothers' Anti-High Price League to promote their cause.[139] During the meeting, a section of the crowd had also rushed to the site of the Hotel Waldorf-Astoria, protesting outside the elite dining establishment. Police reservists and volunteers were drafted into the areas of conflict to disperse the crowd and arrest those deemed to be inciting further insurrection.[140]

To halt the spread of the protests, which had also spread to other cities in the United States and which in New York had resulted in large-scale disturbances across the city throughout February 1917, the Mayor's Committee on Food, working with the state and federal authorities, launched a series of inquiries which resulted in the move to increase the amount of foodstuffs imported into the city as well as escalating the variety of literature available to citizens regarding the preparation and preservation of consumables.[141] By the middle of March 1917, the boycotts and protests had abated somewhat, with a slight fall in prices and the pressure exerted by the city authorities reducing the tensions in the city.[142] However, what marked the protests was their use of the disputed arena that was 'American' identity in the city. Encouraged to follow the call for 'Americanisation', women from the mainly Russian Jewish areas of the city, had corresponded by demanding their rights as Americans – a demand that was met with suppression as alternative visions of what constitutes patriotic sentiment in New York was policed. The fear of socialist elements operating as a fifth column or undermining 'American' values was significant in these debates and these fears were increased with foreign radicals in New York who called for a rejection of nationalist sentiment to embrace the international movement. Leon Trotsky (1879–1940), resident in New York

---

[137] *New York Times*, February 21, 1917.

[138] *New York Sun*, February 21, 1917.

[139] *New York Herald*, February 24, 1917.

[140] *New York Tribune*, February 25, 1917; *Brooklyn Daily Eagle*, February 25, 1917.

[141] New York State, 1917a. *Joint Report on Foods and Markets of Governor Whitman's Market Commission, Mayor Mitchel's Food Supply Committee and the Wicks Legislative Committee. Transmitted to the Legislature January 3, 1917*. Albany, NY: J.B. Lyon; Mayor's Committee on Food Supply, 1917. *Hints to Housewives on How to Buy, How to Care for Food, Meats, Drippings and Butter Substitutes, Substitutes for Meat, Fish, Vegetables, Cereals, Bread, How to Use Left-overs, How to Make Soap, Fireless Cooker, Canning Fruits and Vegetables, How to Preserve Eggs*. New York, NY: I. Goldmann.

[142] *New York World*, March 17, 1917.

from January to March 1917 during the height of the food riots, had called for such a rededication amongst the Russian Jewish community in the city.[143] Trotsky returned to Russia upon receiving news of the February Revolution in Petrograd and the abdication of Tsar Nicholas II, an event which also brought celebrations within the Russian Jewish sections of the city.[144] In the Jewish-dominated Lower East Side, residents marked the removal of the Romanovs with a mass meeting sponsored by various socialist party groups in Madison Square during the evening of 20 March. This occasion was widely reported in the city's press as declarations from Meyer London and Morris Hillquit were regarded as sympathetic towards the revolutionary cause in Russia and elsewhere, seemingly advocating the overhaul of the structures of authority in the United States.[145] Indeed, Morris Hillquit, writing in the *New York Call*, sounded a particularly worrying tone for the city's bankers and investors who had profited from the trade which had been stimulated by the conflict:

> The rule of the privileged classes is bound to bring strife and war among nations. A genuine and worldwide democracy alone can and will preserve perpetual peace among nations.[146]

The perception of socialism in the city as 'un-American' was increasingly apparent. Indeed, in a rally held at Carnegie Hall on 23 March to celebrate the Russian Revolution and sponsored by the Society of the Friends of Russian Freedom, Mayor Mitchel welcomed the uprising and the spread of democracy but warned hecklers from the crowd that war was seemingly inescapable and that all citizens could be divided into two classes, 'Americans and traitors'.[147] Whilst Socialist Party members in the city may have hoped that the war, the Russian Revolution and the Food Riots would bring wider support for the socialist cause, the effect of these occurrences was a higher degree of suspicion and regulation from the authorities. These restrictions to expression would be applied to socialist activists themselves after the declaration of war in April 1917. Indeed, the only significant disturbance that occurred in the city after the announcement that war had been declared was a raid conducted by the city's police on the Labor Lyceum, located on Myrtle and Cyprus Avenues, Long Island, where the Queens County Socialist Party had gathered.[148] The group had organised an anti-war meeting in response to the actions of the United States Congress and several hundred party members were in attendance. Arrests were made and the meeting was disrupted on the basis that

---

[143] *Forverts*, January 16, 1917.

[144] J. Rubenstein, 2011. *Leon Trotsky: A Revolutionary's Life*. New Haven, CT: Yale University Press, p. 44.

[145] *New York Times*, March 21, 1917; *New York Tribune*, March 21, 1917.

[146] *New York Call*, March 25, 1917.

[147] *New York Times*, March 24, 1917.

[148] *New York Times*, April 7, 1917.

such an event in the context of the previous day's pronouncement was regarded to be bordering on treason. Certainly, what could be termed seditious material was disseminated across the city in the following days after the declaration, with the city's socialists reminded of their obligation to the international rather than their duty to the United States.[149] Such perceptions were not uncommon across New York's socialist press.[150] Indeed, the lobby group, the Emergency Peace Federation, was formed in New York from the socialist movement in the context of the potential entry of the United States into the war.[151] The organisation immediately began its campaign to reinstate a policy of neutrality and to resist the militarisation of society.[152]

The City at War

However, this was not the sole voice within the socialist party politics within the city, as the desire to defend the country from invasion and the political will of a less democratically inclined nation than the United States was regarded as a duty in the service of the working classes.[153] Regardless of its expression, the sentiment of national pride and endeavour in this response are evident. It is this exceptional state, regardless of its flaws, that was celebrated in the city after 6 April 1917. Private citizens, businesses and institutions acted simultaneously to the news of the state of war with Germany and New York was soon festooned with flags, garlands and patriotic displays.[154] Fifth Avenue was decorated along its length and the appearance of the 'Stars and Stripes' in the windows of German American businesses, such as the offices of the Hamburg-American Line on Broadway, reflected the dominance of 'Americanisation'.[155] The corollary of this expression of dedication to the values and character of the nation, a rejection of the 'hyphen', was the suppression of alternative perspectives and the exclusion of others. This was evidenced in the arrest and detention of a number of assumed

---

[149]   *New York Call*, April 8, 1917.

[150]   M. Eastman, 1917a. In Case of War. *The Masses*, 9(6): 7–8.

[151]   United States Congress: Committee on Foreign Affairs, 1917. *Emergency Peace Federation: Hearings Before the Committee on Foreign Affairs, House of Representatives, Sixty-fourth Congress, Second Session: Statements of Cedric Long and Others.* February 22, 1917. Washington, DC: Government Printing Office.

[152]   Emergency Peace Federation, 1917. *Alternatives to War: Findings of the Unofficial Commission which Met at the Holland House, New York City, March 19–24, 1917 'to Devise Ways and Means of a Peaceful Solution of Our International Crisis'.* New York, NY: Emergency Peace Federation.

[153]   *New York Call*, April 10, 1917.

[154]   *New York Times*, April 7, 1917; *New York Herald*, April 1917.

[155]   *New York Tribune*, April 7, 1917.

German agents in the city and potential sources of dissent, whether political or violent, were extinguished.[156]

This suspicion was not restricted to the German American sections of the city.[157] In April 1917, just after the news of the war had served to reinforce national identity in the metropolis, New York's mainstream press began publishing accounts of the 'San Diego Plot'. This alleged conspiracy, which was widely discredited after its appearance in 1915, involved the complicity of African American communities in Texas who were supposedly assisting Mexican insurgents into the country as part of a wider invasion sponsored by Germany.[158] Whilst Mexican plans to ferment ethnic conflict in the United States were verifiable, the recruitment of African Americans in this plan was never substantiated.[159] Nevertheless, the city's newspapers took the incident as a contemporary issue in the fervour of enthusiasm for patriotic commitment. Lurid accounts of the supposed treasonous actions of African Americans on the border were published, as individuals and groups were assumed to be operating to undermine the nation and disrupt the mission of its citizens.[160] These allegations demonstrated the operation of 'one hundred per cent Americanism', whose undertones of racial homogeny served to limit the involvement of certain groups in the demonstration of patriotism.[161] Such suggestions of disloyalty were roundly dismissed within the African American press in the city, accompanied by a use of the war to proclaim the allegiance of the community to the cause of the nation.[162] In this manner, the declaration of war was seized by some within the city as an opportunity, a means to cement the place of African Americans in the nation and thereby remove the vestiges of racial inequality.[163] Writing in the journal *Crisis*, W.E.B. Du Bois responded to the accusations of collusions between Germany and African Americans through comparisons between the effects of German militarism and southern slavery:

> War! It is an awful thing! It is hell … Bad as it is, slavery is worse; German dominion is worse; the rape of Belgium and France is worse. We fight shoulder

---

[156] *New York Sun*, April 7, 1917.

[157] *New York Age*, March 29, 1917.

[158] J. Sandos, 1992. *Rebellion in the Borderlands: Anarchism and the Plan of San Diego, 1904–23*. Norman, OK: University of Oklahoma Press.

[159] Senate Foreign Relations Committee, 1920. *Investigation of Mexican Affairs: Report of Senator Albert B. Fall to the Subcommittee of the Committee on Foreign Relations, Examining into Mexican Affairs, Reports and Hearings*. Washington, DC: Government Printing Office, p. 6.

[160] *New York Times*, April 7, 1917; *New York Tribune*, April 7, 1917.

[161] M. Ellis, 2001. *Race, War, and Surveillance: African Americans and the United States during World War I*. Bloomington, IN: Indiana University Press, p. 6.

[162] *New York Call*, April 12, 1917.

[163] M. Ellis, 1992. 'Closing Ranks' and 'Seeking Honors': W.E.B. Du Bois in World War I. *Journal of American History*, 79(1): 96–124.

to shoulder with the world to gain a world where war shall be no more ... No temptation to trust German race-hatred has ever been offered and if offered would not for a moment have been considered. Back of the German mask is the grinning skeleton of the Southern slave driver.[164]

Such comparisons were intended to affirm the dedication of African Americans to the principles of liberty and democracy that characterised appeals for 'Americanisation'.[165] However, the publication of the 'San Diego Plot' revealed how in the context of the war, any dissent or unrest, whether political or racial, was increasingly regarded as the result of German intrigue or allegiance.[166] With an increasing African American population in Harlem, resulting from migration from the southern states, the perceived threat posed by such developments fuelled the growing demands for 'one hundred per cent Americanism'.[167] Within this context, the war, therefore, served to divide political allegiances within the African American community in the city. The stance taken by Du Bois to proclaim loyalty to the nation was countered by the position espoused by the Jamaican political leader Marcus Garvey (1887–1940), based in the city after March 1916, who promoted the cause of African nationalism in New York, a political ideology which rejected the citizenship of western nation states to focus on the development and liberation of Africa.[168] Garvey had installed the New York branch of his Universal Negro Improvement Association by May 1917.[169] The presence of such potentially divisive politics in New York appeared to confirm the suspicions of both the press and city authorities that a potential problem of sedition and unrest could emerge from the African American communities of the metropolis.

Nevertheless, just as Du Bois, *The Crisis* and the *New York Age* comprehended the war as an opportunity to reiterate the democratic rights of African Americans in the city and across the nation, so too were New York's immigrant groups attracted by the role of their adopted homeland in asserting the democratic rights of their countries of origin. This was particularly relevant to New York's Irish American community, which despite misgivings and suspicions about the war in August 1914, largely drawn from hostility towards Britain's colonial rule, welcomed the entrance of the United States as a means of extending democracy to a post-war independent Ireland.[170] In a meeting at Carnegie Hall on 9 April, held to commemorate the anniversary of the Easter Rising and organised by Clan na Gael,

[164] W.E.B. Du Bois, 1917b. Editorial. *The Crisis*, 14(1): 7–10.

[165] *New York Age*, April 5, 1917.

[166] M. Ellis, 1993. Federal Surveillance of Black Americans during the First World War. *Immigrants and Minorities*, 12(1): 1–20.

[167] *New York Times*, April 8, 1917.

[168] *New York Age*, June 2, 1917.

[169] M. Garvey, 1923. *The Philosophy and Opinions of Marcus Garvey*. New York, NY: Universal Publishing House, p. 128.

[170] *Gaelic American*, April 14, 1917.

the speakers exalted President Wilson's claim that the war was fought for 'the rights of small nations'. However, the speakers were mindful of communicating their loyalties and whilst the Irish tricolour was in abundance so too were the 'stars and stripes' and proclamations of 'American first'.[171] The meeting was concluded with a telegram to President Wilson which affirmed the devotion of Irish Americans to the United States and pledged to fight for the 'honour and interests' of the nation. Such a conciliatory, respectful tone was in marked contrast to both the previous tenor of war reporting within the Irish press in the city and the vitriolic telegram to the President sent by Jeremiah A. O'Leary during the 1916 election. Indeed, O'Leary, through his satirical New York-based periodical *The Bull* and associated publications, continued to launch attacks against the foreign policies of the United States and the municipal governance of New York.[172] Whilst the Irish American response to the declaration of war still held to the goal of Irish republicanism, this was now tempered with assurances of the loyalty of the populace to the United States; the city of immigrants was now censoring itself as the metropolis prepared for war.

The appeal issued by Mayor Mitchel demonstrates this implicit compulsion for self-regulation in New York. In a proclamation made on 7 April, the mayor reminded citizens that aiding the enemies of the United States was regarded as sedition and the punishment for this treason was death or imprisonment:

> There will be some exceptional cases of malign influence and malicious purpose among you, and, as to them, I advise you all that full and timely preparation has been made adequate to the exigency which exists for the maintenance of order throughout the City of New York.[173]

The notice was placed across the city by the police, printed in the principal languages of its citizens, English, Yiddish, Italian and German, and displayed prominently in public buildings, shop fronts and offices.[174] The reminder of the definition of traitorous behaviour was reflective of the previous rejoinder that Mayor Mitchel had issued at the celebration to mark the advent of the Russian Revolution in March 1917; through this discourse, there now existed only Americans and traitors in the city. Similar reminders were offered throughout the city's churches and

---

[171] Tansill, *America and the Fight for Irish Freedom*, p. 221.

[172] J. O'Leary, 1916b. *The Fable of John Bull and Uncle Sam: A History in Prose and Picture of the Real Relations of John Bull and Uncle Sam*. New York, NY: American Truth Society; J. O'Leary, 1917. *An Open Letter to George W. Perkins Criticising His Report on the Food Question*. New York, NY: American Truth Society.

[173] W. Wilson and J.P. Mitchel, 1917. *President Woodrow Wilson's Address to Congress April 2, 1917. Proclamation of the President April 6, 1917. Proclamation of the Mayor of the City of New York, April 6, 1917. Address of the President to His Fellow Countrymen, April 16, 1917*. New York, NY: American Exchange National Bank, p. 6.

[174] *New York Herald*, April 7, 1917; *New York Tribune*, April 7, 1917.

synagogues after the declaration was issued, with thanks given to God within the context of national fervour. Indeed, for the various Christian denominations in the city who expressed their support for their nation, the coincidence of the announcement of war and the Mayor's proclamation with the festival of Easter and of Passover appeared to cement the purpose and mission of the United States for worshippers in the metropolis. For example, All Souls Unitarian Church in Manhattan, led by Reverend William L. Sullivan, issued their statement of support during services, upholding their belief in the righteousness of conflict for freedom and liberty.[175] Similarly, Reverend William T. Manning, of Trinity Church, used his Easter sermon to instruct the congregation on the religious duty of service to the nation and the exceptional moral position taken by the United States:

> But none of us has ever known an Easter Day like this one. The Easter message today has a new depth of meaning for us as our country rises to answer the clear call of God, to give itself a great service, to perform, at whatever cost, a solemn and inexorable duty.[176]

Similarly, Reverend William T. Manning of Trinity Church also spoke at a service on 22 April before the Church of the Incarnation on Madison Avenue to ask for loyalty and devotion to God and to the United States.[177] Rabbi Samuel Schulman of Temple Beth-El, Manhattan, spoke to the gathered masses of the need to sacrifice private impulses for the good of the nation:

> There is only one sane opinion today. That which urges us to give ourselves, single-mindedly to our nation until America has made its influence felt and has won a real victory.[178]

Overwhelmingly, the connection between citizenship and religion was made by religious leaders as the residents of the metropolis offered up their commitment as a sacrifice for the nation. Alongside the floral displays and religious icons were American flags, as the faithful were encouraged to continue their work for war charities with renewed rigour.[179] Dissenting voices from churches who did not preach the war message were marginalised from reporting in the mainstream press. The Reverend John Haynes Holmes (1879–1964), of the Unitarian Church of the Messiah in midtown Manhattan, had earlier preached a strong anti-war message

---

[175] *New York Times*, April 8, 1917.

[176] W.T. Manning, 1917a. *The Easter Call to America: A Sermon Preached in Trinity Church*, New York. New York, NY: Trinity Church.

[177] W.T. Manning, 1917b. *America's Part in the World-War: A Sermon Preached April 22, 1917, in the Church of the Incarnation*. New York, NY: The American Rights League.

[178] Anon., 1917. From Coast to Coast. *American Jewish Chronicle*, 3(20): 536.

[179] *New York Herald*, April 9, 1917; *New York Sun*, April 9, 1917.

to his congregation.[180] Such opinions were increasingly drowned out by a tide of religious sentiment that equated devotional duties with the national endeavour. This was further underlined by the arrival in the city during Easter 1917 of the evangelical preacher Billy Sunday (1862–1935). Already at the height of his popularity for his passionate orations, Sunday's stay in New York from April to June 1917 was used as a platform to sway the citizens of the city towards sobriety and loyalty.[181] A substantial wooden tabernacle had been built for the preacher's sermons on 138th Street, Washington Heights, Manhattan, which held a capacity of 20,000 people. Sunday's volunteers encouraged participation by contacting local church groups whilst his influential supporters in the city, which included former President Theodore Roosevelt and John D. Rockefeller (1839–1937), ensured that the preacher was assisted in his endeavours.[182] The sermons preached by Sunday took the issue of the war and provoked the crowd towards the emotional call for duty and service to the nation through the account of suffering:

> Look at the millions of poor, tortured Belgium as she turns her weeping eyes over three thousand miles of ocean, her bleeding hands outstretched toward the stars and stripes for help.[183]

Sunday declared that his message was for Christ in the service of his country, a call that he asked the citizens of New York to follow.[184] The fusion of religious and patriotic devotion struck a chord in a city that had already seen the promotion of the concept of martial endeavour and 'American' identity. Indeed, United States Army and Navy recruitment stations were located nearby to Sunday's tabernacle to provide a means to satisfy the nationalistic urge that the sermons would induce. These stations had been erected in the city in the days after the declaration of war, as the realisation that the demands of the conflict would exceed the capabilities of the United States armed forces became abundantly clear.

The lead in this recruitment drive was taken by the Mayor's Committee on National Defense, which after 6 April was rapidly transformed from a lobbying and advisory group to a fully operational unit overseeing the promotion, mobilisation and control of the city's wartime activities. The transformation was enabled by the planning of Mayor Mitchel and his recruitment of 1,000 individuals to serve on the various committees in the autumn of 1915. The committee members, constituting the business, industrial and financial elite of the metropolis, assumed responsibility

---

    [180]   J.H. Holmes, 1917. *The Messiah Pulpit: A Statement to My People on the Eve of War*. New York, NY: The Church of the Messiah.
    [181]   B. Sunday, 1917. *Billy Sunday, the Man and his Message: With his Own Words which have Won Thousands for Christ*. Philadelphia: J.C. Winston, p. 433.
    [182]   D.T. Morgan, 1973. The Revivalist as Patriot: Billy Sunday and World War I. *Journal of Presbyterian History*, 51(2): 199–215.
    [183]   *New York Times*, April 9, 1917.
    [184]   *New York Herald*, April 9, 1917.

for a host of municipal functions under the authority of the office of the Mayor. Within a matter of days, the city had been placed on a war footing, with the earlier committees reorganised to meet the new challenges of the conflict:

- Recruitment Committee – Chairman, Alexander J. Hemphill
- Committee on Industry and Employment – Chairman, Reverend Percy Stickney Grant
- Committee on Speakers and War Instruction – Chairman, Ernest Stauffen
- Committee on Hospital and Medical Facilities – Chairman, S.S. Goldwater, M.D.
- Committee on Aliens – Chairman, Archibald E. Stevenson
- Committee on Organizations – Chairman, George T. Wilson
- Committee on Relief – Chairman, Thomas Cochran

The most active of these within the first few days of the war's announcement was the Recruitment Committee, which heeded the call from Washington to enlist men to the colours. Whilst setting up Recruitment Stations within the city provided one means of encouraging the citizens of New York, the Committee also organised a municipal enlistment drive and inspired a national recruitment day on 19 April, the anniversary of the Battles of Lexington and Concord, fought against the British Army in 1775.[185] The incongruity of lauding a historical military action taken against what had been a despised enemy which was now a significant ally was seemingly disregarded.[186] As indeed was the way in which Irish American and German American publications in the city had previously mobilised the memory of the War of Independence as a means to maintain the neutrality of the United States. The Recruitment Committee designated the 19 April campaign as 'Wake up, America! Day'; serving as a clarion call for those 'one hundred per cent Americans' keen to demonstrate their loyalty to the nation. The title of the event called to mind the lyrics of a popular song, *Wake up, America*, produced and distributed in the city in late 1916, intriguingly by the same publishers as the anti-war ditty, *I didn't raise my boy to be a soldier*, which opposed the preparedness movement:

> Wake up, America, if we are called to war,
> Are we prepared to give our lives,
> For our sweethearts and our wives?
> Are our mothers and our homes worth fighting for?
> Let us pray, God, for peace, put peace with honour,
> But let's get ready to answer duty's call,
> So when Old Glory stands unfurled,

---

[185] W. Rawls, 1988. *Wake up America! World War I and the American Poster*. New York, NY: Abbeville Press, p. 5.

[186] *New York Times*, April 10, 1917.

> Let it mean to all the world,
> America is ready, that's all![187]

Patriotic songs such as these and dramatic renderings of historical scenes were part of the events of 'Wake Up, America! Day', as concerts were held in theatres across the city as well as a variety event in Carnegie Hall featuring the latest stars of the stage.[188] The event was designed as a full-scale celebration of American martial virtues. The day commenced with a recreation of the ride of Paul Revere through the city at midnight; as the chimes of Trinity Church in lower Manhattan were rung, Jean Earle Mohle, a young suffragette activist from the city, dressed in the uniform of a Continental Soldier, rode on horseback along a route through midtown Manhattan, summoning the young men and women of the nation to fight.[189] Meetings and parades were held throughout the five boroughs, but a full-scale procession was organised along Fifth Avenue with representatives from war relief charities, Broadway celebrities, patriotic organisations and boy scouts. Floats depicting scenes from American history and banners proclaiming the loyalty of citizens were part of this extensive rally, which also saw businesses and shops along Fifth Avenue decorated as part of the patriotic spectacle. This was accompanied by a flypast over the parade, which dropped leaflets onto the crowds below that encouraged citizens to assume the 'Spirit of '76' and of Paul Revere and to enlist immediately. New York's diverse communities were also encouraged to participate in this celebration, although in a reduced manner in comparison to the main events on Fifth Avenue. The League of Foreign Born Citizens paraded through the Lower East Side before their rally.[190] The African American Salem Methodist Church in Harlem also held a service to mark the enlistment drive, though the enthusiasm for this was tempered by news within the African American press of the city of the plans for segregated army camps for recruits.[191]

Just as the Recruitment Committee increased their efforts, so too were New York's police coordinating their actions against possible dissent from socialist and anarchist party members in the city. Indeed, the day before the 'Wake up, America! Day' parade, a rally attended by socialists and anarchists in the New Star Casino on 107th Street, Manhattan, was raided by the authorities, with arrests made and attendees dispersed. The group was targeted because of their discussion point, the potential refusal of any draft for the armed forces introduced into the city.[192] The meeting was significant for the fact that those attending declared themselves to be 'true patriots', that conscription was 'un-American' and that the only German

---

[187]   G. Graff, Jr and Jack Glogau, 1916. *Wake Up, America!* New York, NY: Leo Feist.
[188]   *New York Sun*, April 20, 1917.
[189]   *New York Times*, April 19, 1917.
[190]   *New York Herald*, April 20, 1917; *New York Times*, April 20, 1917.
[191]   W.E.B. Du Bois, 1917a. Editorial. *The Crisis*, 13(6): 267–71.
[192]   *New York Call*, April 18, 1917.

invasion that the city faced was one of German militarism.[193] A lone pacifist was also arrested during the parade itself for distributing anti-conscription literature; during the subsequent court case the accused pleaded the First Amendment and freedom of expression, but was nevertheless sentenced to six months' imprisonment by the city magistrate.[194] The possibility of the introduction of conscription at first appeared an unlikely event in New York, as numbers who joined up for the Army and Navy reserves in April 1917 were significant.[195]

However, the numbers attending the recruitment offices soon began to dwindle. No mass volunteering took place in the city, with a steady, but modest, several hundred men attending the recruitment offices weekly in the metropolis. 'Wake up, America! Day' was conceived, in part, to arrest this decline in numbers, but despite the ambitions of its organisers a notable increase in volunteers was not apparent. The War Department in Washington had set a target of 287,000 men as the full authorised war strength, and New York's contribution to this total was far short of expectation.[196] Indeed, in the days after the 'Wake up, America! Day', recruitment across the nation, not just New York, fell way below the expected levels; across the city, 70 men enlisted in the army and 43 men were recruited into the navy on 20 April.[197] By 24 April, an increase in volunteers had occurred which was attributed to the events of 19 April, but this had only added 107 men to the navy and 117 to the army.[198] The paucity of recruits nationwide resulted in the passing of the Selective Service Act by Congress on 28 April and its enactment on 18 May 1917, authorising the draft of all men aged 21 to 30 to register for military service.[199]

The absence of any large-scale volunteering within New York was greeted with suspicion; the city, which despite its strong support for the recruitment rally organised by the Mayor's Committee, was still regarded as a potential threat to the war effort through political radicalism and alien allegiances. The perception that 'foreign' influences were inhibiting citizens from their proper duties can be seen with the growing use of the city's police force to disrupt socialist and anarchist

---

[193]   *New York Times*, April 18, 1917.

[194]   *New York Times*, April 21, 1917.

[195]   *New York Herald*, April 8, 1917.

[196]   United States Congress, Committee on Military Affairs, 1917. *Increase of Military Establishment: Hearings Before the Committee on Military Affairs, House of Representatives, Sixty-fifth Congress, First Session, on the Bill Authorizing the President to Increase Temporarily the Military Establishment of the United States. April 17.* Washington, DC: Government Printing Office, p. 76.

[197]   *New York Herald*, April 21, 1917.

[198]   *New York Times*, April 24, 1917.

[199]   Office of the Provost Marshal General, 1917. *Selective Service Regulations Prescribed by the President: Under the Authority Vested in Him by the Terms of the Selective Service Law (Act of Congress Approved May 18, 1917).* Washington, DC: Government Printing Office.

meetings that argued against the draft.[200] Such repression was sanctioned by both the city authorities and by the national government, as within the remit of the 1917 Act was an ability to prosecute those who spoke out against federal laws. This resulted in a number of prosecutions in May 1917, as socialist, anarchist and pacifist citizens, who either spoke out against the draft or distributed literature against the legislation, were charged with preventing or disrupting the enactment of a federal law.[201] The passing of the 1917 Selective Service Act was used by radical political groups in the city to denounce the authoritarianism of the United States and the unconstitutional nature of universal conscription. The 'American Union Against Militarism', which was founded in New York in 1915 by socialists from the Lower East Side, had worked to prevent the entry of the United States in the European War and now openly opposed universal conscription.[202] However, the most prominent anti-draft campaigners in New York were the anarchists Emma Goldman and Alexander Berkman, who organised the 'No Conscription League' in April 1917. Goldman and Berkman held public meetings and also used *Mother Earth* to publicise their objection to the draft.[203] The manifesto of the 'No Conscription League' set forth the arguments for their objections, which were largely based on the infringement of the civil liberties of the nation:

> No one to whom the fundamental principle of liberty and justice is more than an idle phrase, can help realize that the patriotic claptrap now shouted by press, pulpit and the authorities, betrays a desperate effort of the ruling class in this country to throw sand in the eyes of the masses and to blind them to the real issue confronting them. That issue is the Prussianizing of America so as to destroy whatever few liberties the people have achieved through an incessant struggle of many years.[204]

The work of the Berkman and Goldman in the city was a direct challenge to the authority of the government and also represented a potential point of dissent within the city upon which radicals, socialists, anarchists and pacifists could coalesce. As a direct response to this type of potential fermenting of sedition within New York, the Espionage Act was passed by Congress on 15 June 1917.[205] The same day,

---

[200]　N. Thomas, 1917. *War's Heretics: A Plea for the Conscientious Objector*. New York, NY: Civil Liberties Bureau of the American Union Against Militarism.

[201]　*New York Times*, May 22, 1917; *New York Herald*, May 22, 1917.

[202]　American Union Against Militarism, 1917. *Conscription and the 'Conscientious Objector' to War: Facts Regarding Exemptions from Military Service Under the Conscription Act*. New York, NY: American Union Against Militarism.

[203]　A. Berkman, 1917. America and the Russian Revolution. *Mother Earth*, 12(3): 75–7.

[204]　E. Goldman, 1917c. The No Conscription League. *Mother Earth*, 12(4): 112–14.

[205]　United States Congress, Committee on the Judiciary, 1917. *Espionage and Interference with Neutrality: Hearings before the Committee on the Judiciary, House of*

Berkman and Goldman were arrested in police raids on their premises in the Lower East Side and charged with distributing literature that discouraged individuals to register for the draft and which undermined the function of the legislation.[206] Their subsequent trial in the city's district court in downtown Manhattan from 2 July to 9 July attracted widespread coverage in New York's majority press.[207] The defendants pleaded the First Amendment in response to the prosecution, and used the trial as a platform to decry the manner in which American freedoms were being eroded.[208] Goldman declared that their arrest and trial was a cruelly ironic mockery of the 'noble' and 'lofty' ambitions of the United States:

> We say that if America has entered the war to make the world safe for democracy, she must first make democracy safe in America. How else is the world to take America seriously, when democracy at home is daily being outraged, free speech suppressed, peaceable assemblies broken up by overbearing and brutal gangsters in uniform; when free press is curtailed and every independent opinion gagged? Verily, poor as we are in democracy, how can we give of it to the world?[209]

Such dissent against the spirit of Americanisation and the potential of Berkman and Goldman to foster resistance against the draft within socialist and anarchist groups in the city ensured that a harsh prison sentence of two years was given to both.[210] This prosecution was not the only effect of the Espionage Act on the city. The extent of the legislation, outlawing dissident views in speech and media, ensured that many radical political groups in New York were faced with losing the right for their publications to be carried by the United States Postal Service.[211] Indeed, the city was adversely affected by this ruling as the majority of the perceived seditious publications were those from the metropolis.[212] The editors of the socialist periodical *The Masses* and the Irish American anti-war advocate Jeremiah O'Leary, who published tracts against the conflict for the American

---

Representatives, Sixty-fifth Congress, First Session on H.R. 291, April 9 and 12, 1917. Washington, DC: Government Printing Office, pp. 58–9.

[206] E. Goldman, 1931. *Living my Life.* New York, NY: A.A. Knopf, p. 610.

[207] *New York Herald,* June 3, 1917; *New York Sun,* June 3, 1917; *New York Times,* June 3, 1917.

[208] Supreme Court of the United States, 1917. *Emma Goldman and Alexander Berkman, Plaintiffs-in-Error vs The United States.* New York, NY: s.n.

[209] A. Berkman and E. Goldman, 1917. *Anarchism on Trial: Speeches of Alexander Berkman and Emma Goldman Before the United States District Court in the City of New York, July, 1917.* New York, NY: Mother Earth Publishing Association, p. 64.

[210] *New York Times,* July 10, 1917.

[211] United States Postal Service, 1919. *Annual Report of the Postmaster General.* Washington, DC: Government Printing Office, p. 15.

[212] United States Postal Service, 1918. *Annual Report of the Postmaster General.* Washington, DC: Government Printing Office, p. 77.

Truth Society, were prosecuted under the Espionage Act. Indeed, W.E.B. Du Bois' *Crisis* was monitored for dissenting opinion, as were the activities of Marcus Garvey; even the popular Jewish socialist newspaper *Forverts* was threatened with exclusion from the mail service.[213] The policy of surveillance within the city had been enacted and legitimated by the state. Such developments marked how New York was regarded as a highly possible source of dissent and disloyalty after the declaration of war.

Conclusions

The clear expression of identity and loyalty to the United States was no longer merely a social formality but a quality that was policed by the authorities. As the war progressed and the full deployment of the draft was enacted in the metropolis, this demand for loyalty was overwhelming as through public displays, donations, activities and governance, the city was orientated towards becoming 'one hundred per cent American'. The war had brought about a fundamental change in the expressions of identity within the city. Whilst, before the war, groups had once been able to proclaim their 'American' values in relation to their immigrant identity, such concepts had now been declared anathema to the programme of affirming the city's loyalty. The Presidential Elections had illustrated how identity within New York was strictly monitored. 'Hyphenated Americans' were now called upon to make public their commitment to the United States. Any deviation from this set pattern amounted to assumed treachery; protestors against the conditions wrought by war or political dissidents in the city became the objects of surveillance. In such circumstances, citizens began to police themselves. Indeed, many residents began renouncing any allegiance to a 'foreign' power and utilising both metropolitan and federal structures to demonstrate their civic and national pride. The restrictions placed on what was regarded as seditious activities ensured that the perception of the city as a haven of radicals and 'aliens' began to alter; in this climate of war, New York was to become wholly American.

---

[213] C. Capozzola, 2002. The Only Badge Needed is Your Patriotic Fervor: Vigilance, Coercion, and the Law in World War I America. *The Journal of American History*, 88(4): 1354–82.

Chapter 6
One City, One Nation, One Loyalty

The work of local boards has been exacting but it has been faithfully executed. The consummation of this patriotic service, however, will be the prompt and complete mobilization of the national army. Curious eyes are directed toward the City of New York, and active minds are wondering what will happen here. Let the board members and the selected men therefore, inspired by their loyalty to the nation, proceed as a unit to the end that the story of the city's greatness may be told in this one sentence, 'New York City has mobilized'.[1]

Introduction

These comments were made by Assistant Attorney General Conkling during a speech in September 1917 in New York's Lower East Side. As the home of a large proportion of the city's immigrant community, particularly the Russian Jewish émigrés whose allegiances and political sympathies were particularly suspect for the authorities, the central message of an appeal to patriotism was clear. The fear of subversion and 'un-American' attitudes within the metropolis were heightened by the developing role that the United States took in the European War. The process of enacting the draft in the city extended the process of 'Americanisation' directly into the lives of the inhabitants of New York. The Selective Service Act demanded that a direct and visible commitment to the values of the nation was to be made both by individual men in registering for the draft, but also their communities in the metropolis in supporting the mobilisation.[2] This marked the introduction of a rigorous programme of surveillance of the city's populace, conducted overtly by the authorities and volunteer organisation that policed expression and identification in New York, and conducted implicitly through the various education and community initiatives that were developed after the declaration of war. The city's response to the conflict was an intensification of the processes already set in place even before the start of military operations in August 1914. The participation in the war was used to 'Yank out the hyphen' within the immigrant population and to cultivate a loyalty and dedication to the nation.

---

[1] *New York Times*, September 2, 1917.
[2] J. Whiteclay Chambers, *To Raise an Army*, p. 5.

The Draft in the City

The Selective Service Act carried a far greater organisational effect on New York City than any other part of the United States. The legislation called for the creation of draft boards within local areas where eligible recruits would register for service. The sheer size of the metropolis ensured that the management of such an endeavour was highly complex. In total, 189 local draft boards were created across the five boroughs of the city. Business owners, campaigners and patriotic volunteers who were outside the age requirements were selected to sit on these panels, where the health, status and occupation of the individual were assessed as to whether they would be enlisted into the army or navy and serve in one of the regiments with ties to the city. These draft boards were coordinated through committees from each borough as well as a central city committee, appointed by Mayor Mitchel, upon which representatives from the judiciary, the medical profession and a labour representative sat. The locations of the draft boards were set by the city's police in the same location as the polling stations so that individuals could exercise their democratic duty in the locales where they exercised their democratic rights. 5 June was selected by the government as the first day of the draft and a heavy police presence was placed across the city. Armed officers guarded the boards; a machine gun unit was also detailed to the largely Jewish-dominated sections of Brooklyn where the 1917 Food Riots had broken out. Anxieties were high as to what could be expected of asking a city, largely populated by first and second-generation immigrants, to fight for their adopted homeland.

Such fears were based on the understanding of the draft of 1917 in the context of the Draft Riots of 1863, which witnessed a large-scale revolt amongst sections of the city's immigrant communities. This incident was sparked by an undemocratic application of conscription, which saw the burden of military service during the United States Civil War (1861–1865) fall predominantly upon the poorer, émigré communities, as wealthier families could afford the financial penalties incurred through avoiding the draft. In the approach to 5 June 1917, the city's mainstream press were minded to recall the events of 1863, which saw politically and racially motivated violence throughout the city.[3] This act of remembrance was highly appropriate as the ethnic and political tensions that had contributed to the riots of 1863 were perhaps more significant in 1917. The dissent that Goldman and Berkman had provoked with their campaign against the draft had found sympathy, especially within the socialist, pacifist and anarchist supporters in the city whose stronghold in the Lower East Side was dominated by Russian Jewish immigrants. However, the reference to this historic event served both as a means to frame any potential disturbances that might occur along the lines of rebellion and sedition whilst also providing an instructional effect, as the city's population were reassured or perhaps persuaded that no dissent was expected in the metropolis.[4]

---

[3]   *New York Tribune*, June 5, 1917; *New York Times*, June 4, 1917.

[4]   *New York Herald*, June 5, 1917.

Indeed, despite the fears of insurrection, the registration day for the draft passed peacefully in all sections of New York.

The apparent ease by which the draft was enforced in the city appeared to defuse the potential tension that selective service could have brought to the city. In a metropolis with a greater proportion of immigrants and resident aliens the larger percentage of the burden of service would have fallen to the 'native' citizens of the city.[5] Despite this, the speed at which the city's quota of 39,000 men for the draft had started to be raised was significant; from its opening to early August, the city had sent over 12,000 of its men to the armed forces.[6] However, regardless of the enthusiasm, if not the acceptance of the draft, there were still concerns regarding the possible reluctance of some communities in the city to serve, with a high proportion of claims for medical exemptions supposedly received within the draft boards of the Lower East Side.[7] As if to affirm this perception, the leading members of Draft Board 99, Louis I. Cherey, S.J. Bernfeld and Kalman Gruher, who chaired the board in the area between Rivington and Lewis Streets on the Lower East Side, were arrested and eventually jailed for their part in selling medical exemptions to residents in August 1917.[8] Their trial before a grand jury in the city emphasised the particularly treacherous nature of their crime in defrauding the nation of able-bodied men.[9]

By September, the indictments of those refusing the draft were heard in the city's courts and socialists, conscientious objectors, 'slackers' and 'shirkers' were paraded in the press as traitors and enemies.[10] Through this association, the image of the 'draft dodger' or the 'slacker' began to be used within the mainstream press in the city as a definite symbol of 'un-American' values, those who live in the United States but who were not prepared to serve it.[11] Inevitably, therefore, it was the figure of the political radical, the immigrant, or the 'hyphenated American', that was associated with the 'slacker'.[12] Whilst the idea of raids for those individuals registered for the draft but neglecting to attend hearings was mooted by officials and the police, public displays of the names of those who had refused exemptions and signed up for national service were prominently printed in the city's press.[13] These conscripts were feted with a parade through the city in early September before their relocation for training outside of the city at Camp Upton on Long

---

[5] *New York Times*, July 18, 1917; *New York Herald*, July 18, 1917.

[6] *New York Times*, August 8, 1917.

[7] *New York Herald*, August 1, 1917; *New York Tribune*, August 2, 1917.

[8] *New York Times*, August 13, 1917; *New York Tribune*, August 13, 1917.

[9] Department of Justice, 1918. *Interpretation of War Statutes, Bulletin No. 19.* Washington, DC: Government Printing Office.

[10] *New York Tribune*, September 4, 1917; *New York Times*, September 4, 1917.

[11] *New York Tribune*, July 29, 1917.

[12] *New York Herald*, July 31, 1917; *New York Tribune*, August 3, 1917.

[13] *New York Times*, August 4, 1917.

Island.[14] The facility, measuring nearly 10,000 acres, located 60 miles outside the city, was part of the nationwide expansion of the military after April 1917 and housed all the draftees from New York, thereby acquiring the moniker, 'The Metropolitan Division'.[15] These men, who were recruited from all the districts of the city, represented the diversity of the metropolis, but it would be through their detailing into the armed forces that would constitute them as 'Americans'. The conscripts from the city were either formed into the 77th Division of the 'National Army', created after the declaration of war in April 1917, or used to supplement the numbers in New York's regiments of the regular army or the National Guard in order to ensure full-strength units.

The conscription and training of the 77th Division at Camp Upton was intended to reform the city's heterogeneous citizen body into a unit of 'American' soldiers. Indeed, as if to emphasise their duty and civic pride, the body of men was united under its emblem of the Statue of Liberty:

> The recruits represented all races and all creeds – men who had only recently been subjected to the pogroms of Russia, gunmen and gangsters, a type peculiar to New York City, Italians, Chinamen, the Jews and the Irish, a heterogeneous mass, truly representative both of the varied human flotsam and the sturdy American manhood which comprise the civil population of New York City. To stamp the fundamental principles of military discipline on such men was a gigantic task.[16]

Alongside this new formation of the United States Army, New York's citizens were also drafted into the older regiments of the National Guard within the metropolis, with their own histories and traditions of service and loyalty. Units such as the 42nd Infantry Division (known as the Rainbow Division from their emblem), the 27th Infantry Division, the 107th Infantry Regiment (known as the Silk Stocking Regiment due to their recruitment from the city's social and political elite) or the 69th Regiment (known as the Fighting Irish from the traditional composition of the city's Irish community), had been formed during the Civil War or later and were based in the various garrisons across the city. These sections of the National Guard were drafted into service with the entry of the United States into the war. This included the 15th Infantry Regiment, which was based in Harlem and constituted in 1916 as an African American detachment. Conscripts from the city's African American communities were also placed within 367th Infantry Regiment, with just under half the unit's number constituted by residents of Manhattan and

---

[14]   *New York Herald*, September 4, 1917; *New York Times*, September 4, 1917.

[15]   R. Batchelder, 1918. *Camp Upton*. Boston, MA: Small, Maynard and Company.

[16]   J.O. Adler, 1919. *History of the Seventy Seventh Division: August 25th, 1917 to November 11th, 1918*. New York, NY: W.H. Crawford Company, p. 8.

Brooklyn.[17] The 367th was formed within the 92nd Division and inherited the mantle of 'Buffalo Soldiers', the nineteenth-century title of African American Cavalrymen. The 15th was renamed as the 369th Infantry Regiment after their incorporation into the wider army. Nevertheless, all African American units were segregated from the European American fighting troops of the 'National Army'.[18] This separation detailed African American troops with labouring roles with some suggestion that they would even be sent to agricultural posts within the United States.[19] However, despite the absence of equality, the NAACP still proclaimed the draft as a valuable means of demonstrating loyalty and service.[20] Such perceptions within the city were not particular to African Americans. Rather, they were shared across the diverse sections of New York.[21] The mobilisation of the metropolis provided communities and the city authorities with a symbol of their loyalty.

The enthusiastic manner in which the city's residents responded to the call for men of military age to attend their local draft board was a product of the culture of 'Americanisation' that had developed within the city's institutions and wider society after August 1914. Individuals and groups were able to align themselves to the nation through their registration; a demonstration of patriotism and identity. However, this loyalty and devotion to the nation within the diverse populace of New York was also ensured through the physical presence of authority. The city's police were accompanied in their duties of overseeing the draft by both the Citizens Home Defense League and the National Security League. The NSL had grown into a wider national organisation, but its basis in the city reflected the pre-war concerns over the commitment of an immigrant population and current worries regarding preparedness.[22] By 1917 it had organised itself into a nearly 50,000 strong national force, coordinated from its New York headquarters which recruited volunteer officers into regional committees and branches.[23] The militaristic structure of the organisation was particularly prominent in its home city, with approximately 10,000 members.[24] Indeed, the vast proportion of the organisation's financial and material donations

[17] E.J. Scott, 1919. *Scott's Official History of the American Negro in the World War.* Chicago, IL: Homewood Press, p. 191.

[18] *New York Age*, August 23, 1917.

[19] *New York Age*, August 16, 1917.

[20] R.C. Jamison, 1917. Negro Soldiers. *The Crisis*, 14(5): 249.

[21] E.H. Crowder, 1920. *The Spirit of Selective Service.* New York, NY: The Century Co., pp. 298–9.

[22] National Security League, 1917a. *What It Is and Why, What It Has Done and Is Doing: A National Defense Catechism for the Busy Man or Woman.* New York, NY: National Security League; J.B. Walker, 1917. *The Great Emergency.* New York, NY: National Security League.

[23] National Security League, 1916. *Officers, Committees and Branches.* New York, NY: National Security League.

[24] J.C. Edwards, 1982. *Patriots in Pinstripe: Men of the National Security League.* Washington, DC: University Press of America, p. 8.

stemmed from New York's businesses, corporations and individual benefactors. Members were issued with badges and identity cards which testified to their loyalty and status as 'one hundred per cent American' but also gave the appearance of a state-sanctioned organisation. Such an impression was also evidenced in the role played by the NSL in distributing educational material regarding patriotism and guides for speakers to promote American ideals in the war.[25]

However, the official status of the NSL was seemingly confirmed with the registration day of June 1917, as members of the NSL were detailed by the Mayor's Committee on National Defense to organise various patriotic celebrations in the city to encourage recruits. A musical event in City Hall Park, downtown Manhattan, was opened for recruits and families to sing patriotic songs alongside the Mecca Temple Band and addresses by Mayor Mitchel.[26] Similar events at Union Square and Borough Hall Park in Brooklyn were organised by the NSL which included mass gatherings and singing of *America* and the *Star Spangled Banner*.[27] This patriotic work was reinforced with the Home Defense League, who were stationed at every draft board in the city. Through this implicit and explicit show of force, the registration day passed without incident. However, the involvement of the NSL set a precedent for the organisation's role in enforcing the process in the city. Within this remit was an unstated responsibility for ensuring the loyalty of the metropolis's diverse citizens. Indeed, by July 1917, the NSL had begun to issue letters to German American social and community groups in the city, such as the Germania Society in Brooklyn or the German Historic Society, requiring them to hold public meetings where their members could denounce the German government and declare their allegiance to the United States. This demand, issued by the Chairman of the NSL Solomon Stanwood Menken (1870–1954), stated how this process would enable a truly national character in the city to develop:

> In order that you may understand the attitude with which this resolution is presented, I would say that throughout the National Security League has taken the position that Americans of native birth should approach their fellow citizens of foreign origin with understanding and good fellowship and make the way the occasion of creating a nationality by cementing all elements into a common people.[28]

This process of creating unity within the city's populace was also promoted through a series of spectacles to promote the draft and, thereby, 'one hundred per cent

---

[25]　National Security League, 1917b. *Why We are At War. Why You Must Help. What You Can Do.* New York, NY: National Security League; A.B. Hart, 1917. *Handbook of the War for Public Speakers.* New York, NY: National Security League; H.A.W. Wood, 1917. *American, Look Into Your Heart!* New York, NY: National Security League.

[26]　*New York Herald*, June 5, 1917.

[27]　*New York Times*, June 5, 1917.

[28]　*New York Times*, July 18, 1917.

Americanism'. Indeed, before the launch of the official registration day in New York, citizens were confronted with a vivid reminder of the way in which martial service was considered a means of homogenisation.[29] In Union Square, Manhattan, from early May 1917, at the behest of the Mayor's Committee on National Defense, a model replica dreadnought named USS *Recruit* was constructed.[30] The model, measuring 200 feet in length and 40 feet in beam, was replete with gun turrets, torpedoes and weapons made from wood, whilst the entire model was staffed by a US Navy crew led by a Captain C.F. Pierce. Inside the structure, a recreation of the staff quarters was accompanied by a registration and examination room for potential recruits into the service. The USS *Recruit* was opened in late May as the initially disappointing response to the call for recruits in the city had become known. The model served as a popular site in the city, hosting patriotic parties, fundraising drives and as a meeting place for the war relief charities in the city. Whilst enabling residents to form a direct connection to the war, the USS *Recruit* was also a means of encouraging affiliation; the conflict had been brought home to the citizens of New York in the form of a warship erected in the centre of the city. Indeed, the model served as a successful tool in relaying the significance of service, with a notable rise in volunteers and later conscripts passing through the USS *Recruit* to register their allegiance. Through such initiatives, potential sources of dissent were censured, by the weight of the majority but also through a process of self-regulation.[31]

However, whilst the drive for recruits had enabled the promotion of 'Americanisation', this attempt to remove the hyphen from the nation through a universal draft operated a subtle demonstration of power of exclusion and inclusion with regard to identity. Whilst citizens who proclaimed their allegiance to the state could be enveloped, those regarded as outside the 'one hundred per cent Americanism' could be isolated from such processes. This is demonstrated in the way in which socialist and pacifist elements in the city were marginalised through their denotation as 'draft dodgers', 'shirkers' and 'traitors' by both the mainstream press and patriotic organisations such as the NSL.[32] As the Russian Jewish sections of the Lower East Side were the strongholds of the socialist movement in the city, the call for a repression of dissenting politics could be equated with ethnic or religious difference.[33] The draft also functioned as a subtle form of exclusion for African Americans with the city.[34] Whilst the Selective Service Act provided did

---

[29]   J. Merwood-Salisbury, 2009. Patriotism and Protest: Union Square as Public Space, 1832–1932. *Journal of the Society of Architectural Historians*, 68(4): 540–59.

[30]   *New York Times*, April 28, 1917; *New York Herald*, April 28, 1917.

[31]   *New Yorker Staats-Zeitung*, May 2, 1917.

[32]   *New York Times*, June 3, 1917; G.H. Mead, 1917. *The Conscientious Objector*. New York, NY: National Security League.

[33]   *New York Times*, June 10, 1917.

[34]   J. Mennell, 1999. African-Americans and the Selective Service Act of 1917. *The Journal of Negro History*, 84(3): 275–87.

not bar the service of African Americans it supported the structure of a segregated armed forces for the nation; training camps, units and facilities were to be separated. Nevertheless, the process of self-regulation which had altered political and ethnic dissent elsewhere in the city ensured the appearance of commitment within the African American press in the city; this was also undertaken to avoid the accusation of German sympathies, which led to the embrace of the draft despite the context in which it was issued.[35] Du Bois echoed this sceptical acceptance:

> We ... earnestly urge our colored fellow citizens to join heartily in this fight for eventual world liberation; we urge them to enlist in the army; to join in the pressing work of providing food supplies; to labor in all ways by hand and thought in increasing the efficiency of our country. We urge this despite our deep sympathy with the reasonable and deep-seated feeling of revolt among Negroes at the persistent insult and discrimination to which they are subject even when they do their patriotic duty.[36]

Therefore, Du Bois' NAACP evidenced how conflict within the city shaped the expression of identity. Such was the social and political exclusion reserved for those regarded as wilfully inhibiting or negligently suppressing Americanisation that a consistent form of self-definition was created in the city through the framework provided by the conflict. This association through the war served as a powerful symbolic device within the metropolis, detailing issues of place and belonging. As such it was drawn upon by members of the NAACP in their response to the continuing racial violence taking place within the southern states.[37] The organisation also utilised the concept of wartime service in their reaction to the events of 3 July 1917, when race riots erupted in East St Louis, Illinois, which saw an estimated number of 50 African Americans murdered and many more fleeing their homes in the city.[38] The incident provoked outrage in New York, especially in the growing African American area of Harlem, which saw a demand that whilst its residents were required to register for the draft to protect democracy abroad, the rights of African Americans would be upheld in the United States.[39] On 8 July, speaking at Lafayette Hall in Harlem, Marcus Garvey addressed a crowd of supporters on the subject of the riots, describing the murders as a crime against the laws of nature and of God. Through this allusion, Garvey explicitly evoked the cause for which the nation had seemingly declared war on Germany.[40]

---

[35] *New York Age*, July 12, 1917.

[36] W.E.B. Du Bois, 1917c. Editorial. *The Crisis*, 14(2): 59.

[37] Anon., 1917. The Riot in East St. Louis. *The Crisis*, 14(4): 172–6.

[38] *New York Times*, July 3, 1917; *New York Herald*, July 3, 1917; *New York World*, July 3, 1917.

[39] *New York Age*, July 12, 1917.

[40] M. Garvey, 1983. *The Marcus Garvey and Universal Negro Improvement Association Papers, Vol. I: 1826–August 1919*. Edited by R.A. Hill. Berkeley, CA:

Such a critical understanding was also expressed in the socialist movement within African American Harlem, which had been flourishing after Garvey's arrival in the city. These opposing voices regarded the war as a diversion to prevent equal rights from emerging in the city and across the wider nation.[41] A. Philip Randolph (1889–1979) and Chandler Owen's (1889–1967) *The Messenger* was founded in the city for just this purpose.[42] *The Voice*, founded in the summer of 1917 by Hubert Harrison (1883–1927), also forwarded a socialist agenda, condemning the tactics of *The Crisis* of supporting the efforts of the United States in its declaration of war in the face of continued social and racial repression across the nation.[43] These works contributed to the strengthening of the New Negro Movement in Harlem, which asserted the rights of African Americans and need for direct action to protect their interests and promote their cause.[44] Intriguingly, Harrison couched this concern in the established 'American' discourse of liberties and democracy, forming the 'Liberty League' in Harlem as a means of forwarding anti-war opinion and civil rights.[45] In this assessment, the war served no purpose but to continue the segregation present within the nation and ensure the enrichment of the city's capitalists.[46] This served as a continuation of the initial response within the African American press in New York during August 1914, which sought to use the events in Europe as a means to draw attention to situations in the United States. The conditions of war had brought a new agenda into the metropolis and the response to the violence of East St Louis demonstrated how the war served to shape the process of identification in the city. Despite the growing support for the socialist and pan-African movement, the city's African American residents were mobilised by the members of the NAACP and prominent church groups to respond to the events in East St Louis by evoking their service to the nation for the war effort.[47]

The use of the war to comment on domestic issues was achieved through the 'Silent Protest' or the 'Silent Parade' which marched upwards along Fifth Avenue on 28 July 1917. An estimated total of 10,000 to 12,000 individuals participated in the event, which saw women dressed in white and men in black, march in sombre silence, except for the beat of a muted drum, through Manhattan.[48] Thousands more lined the route of the parade, ensuring participants in the protest carried

University of California Press, pp. 221–2.

[41] A. Philip Randolph, 1917. *Terms of Peace and the Darker Races*. New York, NY: Poole Press Association.

[42] Anon., 1917. Peace. *The Messenger*, 1: 7.

[43] *The Voice*, July 4, 1917; Ellis, *Race, War and Surveillance*, pp. 102–5.

[44] H. Harrison, 1917. *The Negro and the Nation*. New York, NY: Cosmo-Advocate Publishing, Co.

[45] *The Voice*, September 19, 1917.

[46] H. Harrison, 1920. *When Africa Awakes*. New York, NY: Porro Press: p. 14.

[47] W.E.B. Du Bois and M. Gruening, 1917. The Massacre of East St. Louis. *The Crisis*, 14(5): 219–38.

[48] Anon., 1917. The Negro Silent Parade. *The Crisis*, 14(5): 241–4.

banners and placards that directly alluded to the contradiction of asking African American men to fight for freedom in Europe whilst they were being deprived of representation, assaulted and murdered in the United States. For example, signs read 'Make America Safe for Democracy' and 'Your hands are full of blood', whilst one sign which pictured an African American women pleading with President Wilson to bring democracy to the United States was regarded as objectionable by the police and removed.[49] The organising committee of the parade in New York also petitioned President Wilson with a request that a greater degree of protection should be afforded to African Americans, arguing that, 'no nation that seeks to fight the battles of civilisation can afford to march in blood-smeared garments'.[50] Leaflets distributed amongst the crowds gathered on the sidewalks also drew attention to the way in which African Americans had fought loyally for their country in all of its previous conflicts:

> The impact of this demonstration upon New York was tremendous. And it is not strange that it was so. More than twelve thousand of us marching along the greatest street in the world, marching solemnly to no other music than the beat of muffled drums bearing aloft our banners on which were inscribed not only what we have suffered in this country, but what we have accomplished for this country, this was a sight as has never been seen before.[51]

The militaristic nature of the protest which was conducted in rank and file to the rhythm of a slow drum, the references to the fight to uphold rights and liberties and the direct allusions to the war provided a powerful spectacle on the city's streets. However, it served to reinforce the position of the NAACP, which was to demand full acknowledgement of citizenship through the dedication that was offered to the nation.

The Liberty Loan and Identity

Allegiance to the principles of the United States and conformity to the ideas of 'Americanisation' was also offered in another form of public commitment beyond the draft which was open to all citizens. The first issue of war bonds was announced by the government in late April 1917, with William G. McAdoo (1863–1941), Secretary to the Treasury and New York businessman, declaring the name of this fund raising initiative to be the 'Liberty Loan'.[52] The title was chosen to reflect the cause for which the nation strove for, to bring liberty to Europe. However, such a moniker also provided an opportunity for individuals

---

49 *New York Times*, July 27, 1917.

50 *New York Age*, August 2, 1917; *New York Age*, August 9, 1917.

51 *New York Age*, August 3, 1917.

52 *New York Times*, April 29, 1917; *New York Herald*, April 29, 1917.

and communities to commit to the liberty provided by the United States; in a city where expressions of identity had been progressively monitored since the outbreak of war this was an opportunity to demonstrate your status as 'one hundred per cent American'.[53] Indeed, foreign-born residents of New York and second generation immigrants used the Liberty Loan to make their 'American' character publically known. For example, the German-born New York investment banker Otto Hermann Kahn (1867–1934), speaking at the Merchants Association in the city in June 1917, declared the Liberty Loan as a patriotic duty and the rightful course of action for German Americans seeking to extend the principles of democracy to a Prussian-dominated, militaristic Germany.[54] Similarly, the German-language press in the city demonstrated the devotion of German Americans by proclaiming the enthusiasm by which they would subscribe to the bond issue.[55] The wider city was, however, under wider attention in the campaign to raise funds for the Liberty Loan, both for its role as the financial capital of the nation but also as the home of an immigrant population which was still viewed with suspicion as to its commitment to the nation.

The national target for the Liberty Loan was set at $2,000,000,000, for which all aspects of municipal and national authorities were activated to ensure the city provided more than its quota. The loan was operated through the financial division of the nation into 12 separate Federal Reserves, with the city of New York operating as the centre of the Second Federal Reserve District. The board heading this division was comprised of the leading figures of the city's financial institutions, including J.P. Morgan and Jacob H. Schiff, both of whom had supported opposing sides in the war at its outset. Therefore, the function of the Liberty Loan in the city was as much ideological as financial. Through the work of this board, coordinated with the assistance of the Mayor's Committee on National Defense, the purchase of war bonds were represented to the city's populace as a patriotic duty.[56] To encourage this process, the several-hundred-strong volunteer Liberty Loan Army was recruited in the city, particularly from the financial services sectors and especially insurance salesmen, to go out into the metropolis to advertise the war bonds and encourage citizens to participate.[57] Speakers, leaflets, posters and large-scale rallies were organised by the committee to promote the loan through the city;

---

[53] *New York Herald*, May 3, 1917.

[54] O.H. Kahn, 1917. *Americans of German Origin and the War: Extracts from an Address Delivered before the Merchants Association of New York, at its Liberty Loan Meeting, Held on June 1, 1917.* Washington, DC: Government Printing Office.

[55] *New Yorker Staats-Zeitung*, May 5, 1917.

[56] Liberty Loan Committee, Second Federal Reserve District, 1917. *Report of the Publicity Committee on Work Done in Connection with the Flotation of the First United States Government Liberty Loan of 1917, Amounting to $2,000,000,000.* Washington, DC: Government Printing Office.

[57] L. St. Clair, 1919. *The Story of the Liberty Loans: Being a Record of the Volunteer Liberty Loan Army, its Personnel, Mobilization and Methods. How America at Home*

residents could acquire bonds not only from banks but major department stores and hotels were also encouraged to enable customers to express their patriotism through purchasing practices.[58]

The selling of bonds was also turned into a city-wide celebration of military endeavour. Every individual in the metropolis was encouraged or impelled to participate in the effort. A large sign was erected in Times Square, made from several hundred light bulbs and claimed to be the largest electrical sign in the world, which advertised the bonds and which later used electric dials to communicate the amount of loans bought by the public. The sign proclaimed to an estimated one million people a day to do 'Your Patriotic Duty – Buy a Liberty Bond'.[59] The effort to ensure the city's strong response to the drive for the war bonds was significant. Indeed, to further advertise the availability of the Liberty Loan to all citizens, on 7 June a vast air display over the city was coordinated. At the event, which was organised by the Liberty Loans Committee in conjunction with the Aero Club of America, 20 biplanes of the latest design equipped with 50-pound packages of leaflets advertising the loan were to be dropped across the city. The 'aerial rally' joined into military formation over City Hall in downtown Manhattan before dividing into teams to continue the 'bombardment' over Fifth Avenue, Harlem and onto the Bronx.[60] The promotional material which was used by this display team was specifically worded to inspire both patriotism and fear into the populace, reminding citizens of their duty but also demonstrating the potential damage that could be wrought upon the city by an enemy attack: 'This was dropped by a United States aviator. It might have been a German bomb. To avoid bombs buy bonds'.[61] These events, supported by church and synagogue sermons as well as political speeches, enabled New York to far exceed all expectations in its contribution to the Liberty Loans.

Indeed, at the close of first Liberty Loan campaign at the end of June, the amount raised by the city, from the contributions made by corporations to the bonds bought by individuals, totalled approximately one billion dollars. In effect, the city had contributed to around a third of the funds raised by the United States government through the war bonds, which was estimated at \$3,035,000,000. Such a level of financial commitment was used to demonstrate the patriotism of New York in the face of suspicion about the loyalty of the populace:

> This phenomenon is worth remembering when the next patriot mounts the stump and denounces New York as the enemy's country ... Evidence that New York

---

Backed her Armies and Allies in the World War. Washington, DC: James William Bryan Press, p. 36.

[58]   Federal Reserve Bank of New York, 1917. *Third Annual Report*. Washington DC: Government Printing Office, pp. 32–45.

[59]   *New York Times*, May 8, 1917.

[60]   *New York Herald*, June 7, 1917.

[61]   B.E. Tousley, 1917a. Bombing New York City on Behalf of the Liberty Loan. *Flying*, 6(7): 484–5, 500.

is in the Union is always to be desired. Voters in sundry states that it would invidious to specify, need to be reconvinced of it every morning. Let us hope this billion-dollar subscription to the liberty loan will come to their notice.[62]

The enthusiasm which had met the campaign was all the more impressive because of the relatively small amount of preparation time available for the organising committee to promote the initiative. Therefore, it could be regarded by the authorities that the success of the Liberty Loan was a product of the fervent commitment to the nation that had been secured through the previous efforts to promote 'one hundred per cent Americanism'. Indeed, this work had gathered pace during September 1917 when the Mayor's Committee on National Defense announced its new plan to introduce a new policy of adult education through evening classes delivered through religious and social organisations to ensure the city's diverse populace was entirely English-speaking.[63] Under the slogan, 'One city, one nation, one loyalty', the programme was designed to ensure that a city with a high proportion of foreign-born citizens would have no other commitment or allegiance except to the United States.[64] The work was undertaken by the Committee on Aliens, which was initiated in June 1917 and headed by the attorney Archibald E. Stevenson (1884–1961). Stevenson was a highly active supporter of Americanisation in the metropolis, frequently contributing to the debates on immigration and identity.[65] His committee forcefully addressed the issue of Americanisation, even purging itself of German American members in September 1917 in the wake of a controversy over the dedication of these individuals to the nation's cause.[66] The educational initiative set in place by the committee mirrored this process as it asked for the patriotic service of 'one hundred per cent Americans' in the cause of ensuring that the city maintained its character as 'American':

> The Mayor's Committee on National Defense Committee on Aliens wants good American volunteers for American service among new Americans in cooperation with schools clubs, settlements, churches, synagogues, and other agencies.[67]

---

[62] *Life Magazine*, June 28, 1917.

[63] M.R. Olneck, 1989. Americanization and the Education of Immigrants, 1900–1925: An Analysis of Symbolic Action. *American Journal of Education*, 97(4): 398–423; E.G. Hartmann, 1948. *The Movement to Americanize the Immigrant*. New York, NY: Columbia University Press, p. 167.

[64] *New York Times*, September 7, 1917; *New York Evening Telegram*, September 8, 1917.

[65] *New York Tribune*, May 20, 1917; *New York Tribune*, September 26, 1917.

[66] *New York Times*, September 26, 1917.

[67] The Mayor's Committee on National Defense, 1917a. *The Mayor's Committee on National Defense: Committee on Aliens Wants Good American Volunteers for American Service Among New Americans*. Princeton University Poster Collection, Map Case 1, Drawer 8, Folder 5.

Alongside language classes, courses in the history, government and citizenship of the United States were provided to the city's immigrant population.[68] In this work, the Committee on Aliens attempted to assuage any fears and resentments that foreign-born residents might hold towards their adopted country as a result of the war.[69] Indeed, posters advertising advice and assistance and potentially employment to 'all aliens' written in English, German, Hungarian, Czech, Hebrew, and Italian, were placed across the city during the autumn of 1917.[70] The Committee on Aliens successfully obtained the financial and political backing for this work from the New York Chamber of Commerce and the city's Merchants Association by highlighting its anti-radical, anti-socialist and 'Americanising' objectives; thereby cementing an association of political and commercial interests which could continue after the war.[71] Such was this drive for conformity that the Committee also advised businesses in the city to prioritise the employment of those who could prove their attendance at the organised classes.[72] Such situations both enabled the extension of surveillance over who could be regarded as 'troublesome' or 'dangerous' inhabitants of the city whilst also encouraging conformity within that populace.[73] The Committee on Aliens was, therefore, at the vanguard of ensuring a form of loyalty within the city that could not just be stated, but could be evidenced in the actions, habits and values of New York's citizens.

This was further demonstrated in the campaign in New York for the Second Liberty Loan, which was announced for October 1917.[74] On this occasion the metropolis was materially and ideologically re-envisioned as an altar upon which the citizen's patriotism could be offered. With a quota of $900,000,000, the city as part of the Second Federal Reserve District required a great deal of patriotism to be displayed.[75] Mayor Mitchel commenced proceedings on the steps of City Hall on 1 October, declaring how the city had always been a bastion of

---

[68] *New York Times*, October 28, 1917.

[69] *New York Times*, October 8, 1917.

[70] The Mayor's Committee on National Defense, 1917b. *To All Aliens*. Library of Congress, POS-WWI-US, no. 435.

[71] C.R. Lusk, 1920. *Revolutionary Radicalism: Its History, Purpose and Tactics with an Exposition and Discussion of the Steps Being Taken and Required to Curb it, Being the Report of the Joint Legislative Committee Investigating Seditious Activities, Filed April 24, 1920, in the Senate of the State of New York, Part 2(4)*. Albany, NY: J.B. Lyon, pp. 3178–80.

[72] New York Chamber of Commerce, 1918. *Sixtieth Annual Report of the Corporation of the Chamber of Commerce of the State of New York*. New York. New York, NY: Press of the Chamber of Commerce, pp. 142–3.

[73] J. Fronc, 2009. *New York Undercover: Private Surveillance in the Progressive Era*. Chicago, IL: University of Chicago Press, p. 141.

[74] Treasury Department, 1917. *The Second Liberty Loan of 1917: A Source Book*. Washington, DC: Government Printing Office.

[75] Liberty Loan Committee, New York, 1917. *Allotments, Second Liberty Loan, Second Federal Reserve District*. New York, NY: Liberty Loan Committee.

national pride after the onset of hostilities in Europe had begun, whilst a parade of Volunteer Liberty Loan Army through the city announced a new drive for government bonds. William A. Nash (1859–1923), Chairman of the Board of the Corn Exchange Bank, stated that it was the patriotic duty of everyone in the city to contribute to the initiative, to do otherwise would be tantamount to treachery and 'cowardice'.[76] Such encouragement once again saw New York's citizens, businesses and corporations donate considerable amounts to the cause of the nation, demonstrating their loyalty and devotion in the process.[77]

The city was decorated with patriotic posters advertising the loan which was only available for 27 days from the beginning of October 1917. The organising committee of the Second Federal Reserve District coordinated this distribution of patriotic material accompanying the promotion of the Liberty Loan to ensure the recognition amongst the populace of one's duty towards one's nation. This work was also aided by the development of the Women's Liberty Loan Committee for the Second Federal Reserve District, which whilst possessing equivalents nationwide was developed from the city's organising body and worked to develop events to promote the drive.[78] Such events included soldiers and sailors parades, which were also organised throughout October as a means of reinforcing the civic *esprit de corps*. Through such activities, the city was characterised as being 'enlisted' for the effort and strengthened by 'an army' of small investors who were eager to 'do their bit'.[79] On 5 October, Mayor Mitchel, speaking to an assembled crowd at Carnegie Hall, described the metropolis as the nation's 'first city' in its preparedness and in its dedication.[80] This association immediately framed critics of the nation's policies in the city as traitors, especially socialist and suffragette campaigners who argued over the necessity to fight for democracy abroad when it did not exist in the United States. Such extensive activities appeared to be irrelevant as even by the end of the opening day of the loan a claim was heralded that New York had raised nearly $50,000,000.[81]

Spectacles within the city encouraged participation in the war bonds scheme. Most prominently, a captured German U-boat was constructed in Central Park after being paraded through the city during the October drive for subscriptions as an exhibition for those who could prove their ownership of a war bond.[82]

---

[76] *New York Times*, October 2, 1917; *New York Herald*, October 1, 1917.

[77] Guaranty Trust Company of New York, 1917. *The Liberty Loan*. New York, NY: Guaranty Trust Company of New York.

[78] Woman's Liberty Loan Committee, 1917. *Report of the Woman's Liberty Loan Committee of the Second Federal Reserve District, Second Liberty Loan, October, 1917*. New York, NY: Woman's Liberty Loan Committee.

[79] *New York Times*, October 8, 1917.

[80] *New York Herald*, October 6, 1917.

[81] *New York Herald*, October 2, 1917.

[82] *New York Tribune*, October 26, 1917.

Renamed 'U-buy-a-bond', the vessel served as a rallying point for the municipal and national authorities to proclaim the 'spirit of the city' in 'fighting the Hun' whilst enthusing the populace with the exciting image of the war.[83] Such sentiments were reinforced with another aerial display across the city on 21 October.[84] During this show, paper Germanic Iron Crosses, measuring seven inches across, were dropped onto the city streets. These objects carried on one side a message admonishing citizens who were not participating in the drive as 'un-American':

> Don't buy Liberty bonds. I hereby award all American citizens who can afford to, and who do not buy Liberty bonds, to wear this honourable insignia in proof of their devotion and loyalty to me. Kaiser William

And upon the reverse:

> Buy, buy Liberty bonds. Bye-bye Kaiser.[85]

The bombardment was part of a wider national campaign by the Liberty Loan Committee in Washington, DC. However, the particular circumstances of the city's diverse population, as well as its perceived state of readiness for the war, was promoted by Mayor Mitchel as evidence that the metropolis had demonstrated its loyalty before any other part of the nation.[86] It was this character that was celebrated when the city took part in the national Liberty Loan parade of 25 October 1917. The spectacular, including pageants and historically-themed floats, began their journey down Fifth Avenue from Central Park to Washington Square Arch in Greenwich Village. The event was also aided by the arrival of a British Mark I tank which joined the parade to promote the cause of the Allies.[87] Estimated attendances of the event were approximated at 40,000, lessened in number by bad weather, but nevertheless celebrated as a tremendous success for the city 'of many nations' which had come together for a 'single patriotic purpose'.[88] Once again, the city met its required quota for the Liberty Loan, demonstrating Mayor Mitchel's assertion that the metropolis was not only doing more than its part for the war effort but leading the nation.

---

[83] *New York Evening Telegraph*, October 21, 1917; *Brooklyn Daily Eagle*, October 24, 1917.

[84] *New York Times*, October 21, 1917.

[85] B.E. Tousley, 1917b. Aeronautics Again Plays an Important Part in Arousing Interest in Liberty Loan. *Flying*, 6(10): 856–9.

[86] *New York Times*, October 22, 1917.

[87] *New York Herald*, October 24, 1917.

[88] *New York Times*, October 26, 1917.

The Mayoral Elections

The determination by Mayor Mitchel to emphasise the work of his administration during the Second Liberty Loan was also born out of political necessity, as the city's mayoral elections held on 6 November centred upon the issues of the war. Primary elections for the office had been held for the first time in September and had seen Mayor Mitchel narrowly lose his support in a highly-contested and fraudulent count. Mitchel had succeeded as a candidate backed by anti-Tammany and Republican Party concerns under a so-called Fusion ticket.[89] With the Republican Party choosing William M. Bennett (1869–1930) as its nominee and the Democratic Party naming John F. Hylan (1868–1936) as their candidate, Mayor Mitchel was forced to run as an Independent. The array of candidates increased the likelihood of a split vote and this scenario was almost confirmed with the announcement of Morris Hillquit as the Socialist Party contender. The electioneering throughout October was frequently framed in relation to the war. Mayor Mitchel forwarded his work in encouraging 'Patriotic Americanism', highlighting his consistent support for preparedness and the threat that the city faced from traitors and enemy sympathisers within its own boundaries. This approach damned Hylan for his supposed leniency towards those not committed to 'one hundred per cent Americanism' and his support from the former German-leaning newspaper magnate, William Randolph Hearst. Indeed, Mitchel promised to campaign against this proclaimed dangerous presence in the city by leading a fight against 'Hearst Hylan, and the Hohenzollerns'.[90] On 2 October, outside City Hall, Mayor Mitchel, who was joined on a specially-constructed platform by former President Roosevelt, stated in a rally to nearly 10,000 people that Hylan, Tammany, Hearst and the German autocracy were all part of the same system and that only he represented a candidacy of 'Americanism'.[91]

These concerns were also directed at the Socialist Party Mayoral candidate, Morris Hillquit, whose persistent campaigns against the conflict as an extension of the capitalist oppression of the workers was regarded by the city's mainstream press as open disloyalty and potentially treasonous.[92] Hillquit offered his candidacy as a demonstration of the Socialist Party's long-held anti-war position, labelling the city's industrialists as war-profiteers and the conflict as an affront to the democratic principles set forward by the nation.[93] Indeed, at a rally at Madison Square Garden

---

[89]   Fusion Committee, 1917. *Record of Fusion under Mayor Mitchel.* New York, NY: Fusion Committee.

[90]   *New York Evening Post*, October 3, 1917; *New York Tribune*, October 3, 1917.

[91]   *New York Herald*, October 3, 1917; *New York Times*, October 3, 1917.

[92]   F.C. Giftin, 1999. Morris Hillquit and the War Issue in the New York Mayoralty Campaign of 1917. *International Social Science Review*, 74(3/4): 115–28.

[93]   A. Trachtenberg, 1917. *The American Socialists and the War: A Documentary History of the Attitude of the Socialist Party toward War and Militarism since the Outbreak of the Great War.* New York, NY: The Rand School of Social Science.

on 23 September, Hillquit had led a crowd of several thousands in the cry of 'We Want Peace', as the war was held responsible for the rising food prices, declining liberties and the expanding profits of the metropolitan capitalists.[94] Hillquit's ability to promote these views was hampered by the increasing surveillance of socialist newspapers under the Espionage Act, which had effectively removed both English and foreign-language papers entirely from circulation.[95] The *New York Call*, *Forverts* and *Novyi Mir*, alongside the *New Yorker Volkszeitung*, had all fallen under suspicion for alleged defamation of the nation and overt support for the German Empire.[96] These allegations plagued Hillquit's campaign as he was frequently depicted in the mainstream newspapers as a shortcut to German domination, thereby cementing the perception that socialism was a 'foreign' element and not 'one hundred per cent American'.[97] Hillquit's refusal to participate in the Second Liberty Loan drive during the run-up to the election confirmed these fears for many within the city. Indeed, in response to this stance, Hillquit was depicted in one newspaper illustration as a bomb-wielding maniac, intent on destroying the nation's liberty, whilst his campaign was satirised as a candidacy to be 'Mayor of Berlin'.[98]

The issue of the war had also caused a rift within the ranks of the Socialist Party in the city, with fraught meetings throughout 1917 resulting in the departure of long-standing members uneasy at denouncing a war in which their nation was now an active participant.[99] Mayor Mitchel's campaign also drew upon this uneasy feeling towards policies which appeared to jar with the mood of Americanisation with their election poster, 'Remove This Menace from the Greatest City on Earth – Vote Mitchel'. Such sentiments won the support of the moderate foreign-language press and mainstream newspapers in the city, as the means to define oneself as 'American' in New York now entailed a public disavowal of any dubious or implicating associations with 'alien' elements.[100] For example, some commentators felt assured that the Lower East Side would vote for Hillquit, with its large component of Jewish voters that had traditionally been associated with socialist politics in the city.[101] However, such assumptions of bloc voting could not be relied upon as the election was frequently cast as a vote on identity with

---

[94]   *New York Call*, September 24, 1917.

[95]   *New York Call*, October 8, 1917; *New York Call*, October 21, 1917.

[96]   *New York Call*, October 5, 1917.

[97]   *Brooklyn Daily Eagle*, October 26, 1917; *New York Tribune*, October 28, 1917; *New York Sun*, November 4, 1917.

[98]   *New York Herald*, October 25, 1917.

[99]   H.L. Slobodin, 1917. The State of the Socialist Party. *International Socialist Review*, 17: 539–41.

[100]   Z. Szajkowski, 1970. The Jews and New York City's Mayoralty Election of 1917. *Jewish Social Studies*, 32(4): 286–306.

[101]   Anon., 1917. Hillquit and the Lower East Side. *The Nation*, 105(2731): 475–6; Anon., 1917. National Aspects of the Mayoralty Contest in New York City. *Current Opinion*, 63: 292–4.

direct reference to the war.[102] This aspect of the mayoral race was emphasised when Mitchel framed the election in exactly these terms a few days before polling, declaring that a vote for any of his opponents was a 'comfort to the enemy'.[103] Mitchel based these accusations on the public support that Hylan had received from both the prominent German and Irish newspapers in the city.[104] However, in response, in the approach to the election date, Hylan publicly rejected Mitchel's campaigning on the issue of loyalty and declared his unwavering support to the President and to the nation.[105]

These concerns all shaped the results of the election, which saw the surprise defeat of Mayor Mitchel as the result of the split vote between his Fusion ticket and the Republican candidate William M. Bennett. The returns of the polls highlighted the extent to which Mitchel's campaign had lost the support of wavering voters to the Democrats whilst failing to win the support of the majority of Republican voters and losing votes to the Socialist Party. In such circumstances, a resounding victory for the Democrats was secured:

Hylan – 293,386 votes
Mitchel – 148,060 votes
Hillquit – 138,793 votes
Bennett – 52,828 votes[106]

The tone of the coverage of the election amongst the majority press, most of whom had supported Mitchel, was largely one of shock.[107] Indeed, a sense of incredulity across the mainstream newspapers was apparent as an election result that was perceived to be against the interests of the city and the state was absorbed.[108] This reaction was born partially from the outcome, which saw a Tammany Hall candidate take office, but also at the success of the Socialist Party which secured approximately 21 per cent of the entirety of the votes in the metropolis.[109] The sheer size of the vote for Hillquit, nearly a 500 per cent increase compared to the socialist vote for city mayor in 1913, was immediately greeted by supporters in the city as a triumph of working-class solidarity against the spectre of militarism.[110]

---

[102] C.J. Rosenblaut, 1917. *Mitchel's Election a National Triumph*. New York, NY: Public Welfare Committee.

[103] *New York Tribune*, November 4, 1917; *New York Times*, November 4, 1917.

[104] *New Yorker Staats-Zeitung*, October 23, 1917; *Gaelic American*, November 10, 1917.

[105] *New York Times*, November 1, 1917; *New York Herald*, November 1, 1917.

[106] Board of Elections, 1917. *Annual Report of the Board of Elections of the City of New York for the Year Ending 1917*. New York, NY: Board of Elections, p. 25.

[107] *New York Tribune*, November 8, 1917.

[108] *New York Herald*, November 8, 1917; *New York Times*, November 8.

[109] *New York Sun*, November 7, 1917.

[110] *New York Call*, November 7, 1917.

Such a claim was supported by the success of seven socialist candidates in the Board of Aldermen elections which were held concurrently with the mayoral race.[111] This small but vocal minority amongst 67 members appeared to promise a new direction for the city's politics.[112] However, for others the defeat of Mitchel marked a victory against the principles of Americanism that he had so vehemently promoted during the election and his tenure as a wartime mayor.[113] These claims, that it was Mayor Mitchel's demand for public protestations of loyalty that was the cause of his downfall, were based upon the perception that it was itself fundamentally 'un-American':

> Mayor Mitchel was defeated by hundreds of citizens who sternly resented his effort to claim as his sole property the loyalty that is inherent in every American heart, and in time of war overshadows every other sentiment that Americans can feel.[114]

However, the significant vote for a socialist candidate and the loss of a sitting candidate who had so vehemently argued for a patriotic commitment in the city led commentators outside the metropolis to question directly the issue of the affinity that New York had with the United States. In such circumstances, the loyalty of the city of immigrants was judged and found to be wanting as newspapers across the nation looked upon the result as 'pro-German' and of 'great satisfaction' to the Kaiser.[115] The election result had, therefore, appeared to have undone the efforts made by Mayor Mitchel to promote the city as paramount in issues of preparedness and 'Americanisation'. Nevertheless, whilst the result of the election served to heighten suspicion regarding New York's citizens, it was far from the damning rejection of 'one hundred per cent Americanism'. A more mundane reasoning for the result could be that the success of the Mitchel administration in introducing wartime controls over the municipal economy reduced both the fear of the corruption of Tammany Hall and in turn the need for a Fusion candidate.[116] Indeed, Hylan's support as the Democratic candidate can also be regarded as the result of wartime fervour to support a Democratic President in what had traditionally been a Democrat-voting city. Hylan's rejection of Mitchel's slurs that he was 'for the Hohenzollerns' also enabled the Democrat candidate to present his views in harmony with the President's:

---

[111]　*New York Call*, November 8, 1917.

[112]　Anon., 1917. Current Affairs: The New York Mayoralty Campaign. *The Class Struggle*, 1(4): 100–101.

[113]　*New Yorker Staats-Zeitung*, November 7, 1917.

[114]　*New York American*, November 7, 1917.

[115]　*St. Louis Globe-Democrat*, November 7, 1917; *Washington Post*, November 7, 1917; *Baltimore Sun*, November 7, 1917; *Cornell Daily Sun*, November 7, 1917.

[116]　J.M. Price, 1918. Fusion Mistakes and a Way Out. *National Municipal Review*, 7(2): 183–6.

I want to make it plain to the world that there was no issue of Americanism or loyalty involved, so far as I am concerned. There could be none, for I am as good an American as any man, as loyal to my flag, as loyal to my country, and as firm and determined in support of every act of the Government in this was as any man.[117]

The victory of Hylan, therefore, did not alter the spirit of 'one hundred per cent Americanism', carried out as it was by a variety of public and private groups, rather in Mitchel it had lost one of its most vociferous supporters.

'Hero Land' and the American City

In the aftermath of the mayoral election, it was not the loyalty of Hylan that was at issue, it was the allegiance of the thousands that had voted for Hillquit's anti-war agenda that concerned the press and city politicians alike. For example, that the promotion of Hillquit amongst sections of Irish independence supporters and Jewish socialists within the city was based on his anti-war stance once again evoked issues of the fear of 'hyphenated Americans'.[118] Whilst the structures of preparedness that Mitchel had arranged remained in place for the incumbent, including the Mayor's Committee on National Defense, it was the challenge presented by the socialist vote that disturbed commentators. If such a large proportion of city's residents had voted against the war, how could they be expected to maintain allegiance, suffer further privations and accept the imposition of a draft to fight in the war in Europe?[119] Such anxieties over the city as truly 'American' had fuelled the programme of activities carried out in the metropolis after 1916 and they were also fundamental in the organisation of the largest wartime event held in the city during November 1917. Therefore, although the plans for this festival were initiated several months beforehand, only a few weeks after an election result that appeared to have revealed the alien allegiances of the city, a spectacle of patriotism and loyalty was launched under the uplifting moniker of 'Hero Land'. The event was described by some promotional materials as 'the greatest spectacle the world has ever seen for the greatest need the world has ever known'.[120] Held at the Grand Central Palace in Midtown Manhattan, this was a two-week celebration of American endeavour in the war which ran from 24 November to 12 December; whilst it was designed to

---

[117] *New York Times*, November 7, 1917.

[118] Z. Szajkowski, 1972. *Jews, Wars, and Communism*, Vol. 1. New York, NY: KTAV Publishing, p. 517.

[119] *New York Herald*, November 8, 1917.

[120] J.C. Mueller, 1917. *Hero Land: The Greatest Spectacle the World has Ever Seen for the Greatest Need the World has Ever Known*. New York, NY: The Hegeman Print.

raise funds for war relief charities it also assisted in the programme to encourage fealty towards the state.[121]

The development of 'Hero Land' set as its objective the encouragement of the spirit of unity and camaraderie that now existed between the United States and its allies.[122] The significance of such notions of harmony for the metropolis were not lost on the organisers, a voluntary body of men and women from the various war relief organisations in the city who had joined together in a fundraising effort.[123] This work was conducted under the supervision of the National Allied War Relief Committee, based in the city, which offered a checking house for war charities, overseeing their financial and administrative arrangements.[124] Throughout this 'grand bazaar' were situated booths attached to each of the Allies, where goods from that country could be purchased, their culture sampled with a dramatic or musical performance, and a donation made to their cause. Each nation was given its own day to promote itself as part of its joint military endeavour with the United States. As part of the display, a reconstructed trench system was exhibited for visitors by the French war relief body, whilst the British tank used in the Second Liberty Loan was also paraded, enabling New York's residents to experience the conflict now not as just a piece of exotica, but as a cause that their own nation was fighting for (Figure 6.1).[125] Whilst the theme of the bazaar was multinational, the tenor was ardently patriotic, as crowds gathered to see that the world had come to the United States, whose citizens could marvel at the display of power, politics and prestige.[126] Beginning with the opening night which was designated 'America Night', coinciding with Thanksgiving, over the course of its run the event proved to be highly successful, with nearly 250,000 estimated visitors and a $400,000 return from ticket sales.[127]

Such was the attraction of Hero Land that upon its opening it became a popular feature of the city's social calendar, with newspapers reporting on the parade of the higher echelons of society through the Grand Central Palace.[128] The opportunity for perusing the booths and attractions of the charitable event was not solely restricted to the metropolis's wealthy inhabitants, but it was certainly catered towards the tastes of the affluent, whose support for the war effort was a political and economic necessity. The significance of this income was reflected in the increasing controls over the operations of war charities in the city, with the National Allied War Relief

---

[121]   *The Survey*, December 1, 1917.

[122]   *New York Times*, October 19, 1917.

[123]   *New York Herald*, October, 19, 1917; *New York Times*, November 11, 1917.

[124]   National Allied Relief Committee, 1917. *Some of America's Contributions to European War Relief: A Brief Account of the Personnel and Aims*. New York, NY: Herald Square Press, p. 4.

[125]   *New York Herald*, November 23, 1917; *New York Times*, November 23, 1917.

[126]   *New York Herald*, November 25; 1917; *New York Times*, November 25, 1917.

[127]   *New York Times*, December 16, 1917.

[128]   *New York Times*, November 18, 1917.

Committee concerned over the operation of fraudulent or mismanaged benevolent drives damaging morale and confidence. Indeed, a minor scandal had erupted in the aftermath of the inexpertly designed United States Army and Navy Bazaar, also held at the Grand Central Palace, from 27 October to 3 November 1917.[129] The event had also been an extravaganza of patriotic appeal, where visitors were implored to find mercy in the 'loyal American hearts' to donate money for the provision of 'comfort kits' to 'our boys over there'.[130] Despite the apparently good intentions of the organising committee, the outlay on the venue and events, which included a shooting gallery replete with targets made from photographs of Kaiser Wilhelm II, the German Crown Prince and Grand Admiral Von Tirpitz, ensured that only a minor profit was generated to provide the packages of sweets, tobacco and clothing for United States servicemen.[131]

The unfortunate situation with the Army and Navy bazaar brought to wider attention the unregulated way in which war charities had emerged across the city since the outbreak of the conflict in Europe. After August 1914, the benevolent efforts of New York's citizens had demonstrated allegiance, cultural, ethnic and political, whilst also enabling identification with the nation state as 'one hundred per cent American'. In this manner, patriotism could be bought; 'commercialised patriotism' was in effect as nationalism was exhibited and paid for in donations to charities extolling the virtues of loyalty and preparedness.[132] As such, deceitful individuals and criminal groups seeking to make a profit from such operations could potentially not only undermine the war effort but devalue the identification with the nation state.[133] For example, organisations within the city, such as the Loyal Publicity League of America, had been founded after the entry of the United States into the war with the express intent of extorting contributions from German American residents of the city. Victims of this scam would be sent a questionnaire which when returned completed with a fee was exchanged for a 'certificate of loyalty'.[134] Such operations could be highly profitable with New York contributing the significant proportion of the nation's donations to the various war relief agencies.[135] Therefore, after December 1917, city authorities began planning greater regulations for organisations, ensuring the registration of all charitable bodies with the National Allied Relief Committee and the provision of access to all

---

[129]   Army and Navy Field Comfort Committee, 1917. *U.S. Army and Navy Bazaar, Grand Central Palace*. New York, NY: Carey Print Lith.

[130]   *New York Herald*, October 28, 1917.

[131]   *New York Times*, December 2, 1917; *New York Herald*, December 2, 1917.

[132]   See A. Miller, 2010. Rupert Brooke and the Growth of Commercial Patriotism in Great Britain, 1914–1918. *Twentieth Century British History*, 21(2): 141–62.

[133]   *New York Times*, November 29, 1917.

[134]   United States Senate, Committee on Military Affairs, 1919. *Regulating Collection of Money: Hearings Before the Committee on Military Affairs, United States Senate, Sixty-fifth Congress, 3rd Session on S.4972*. Washington, DC: Government Printing Office, p. 27.

[135]   *The Survey*, May 18, 1918.

Figure 6.1   Advertising Poster for Hero Land, November 1917.
Source: Hegeman Print, 1917. Library of Congress (LC-USZC4-9456).

financial records to ensure probity.[136] These measures were conducted as a means to secure the patriotic endeavour of the city's residents.[137] Just as the processes of

---

[136]   *New York Times*, November 25, 1917.

[137]   E. Swann, 1919. *War Charities Frauds in the City of New York*. New York, NY: M.B. Brown, pp. 20–30.

'Americanisation' and 'one hundred per cent Americanism' had encouraged the protection and elevation of a singular identification with the nation state, so now that affiliation was controlled, protected and policed.

By the end of 1917, the city had been transformed. Now firmly on a war setting, with its population mobilised and monitored, the change in the mayor's office had not dulled the drive for ensuring the loyalty of the citizenry of the metropolis. Prominent in this work, both in New York where it was founded but also nationwide, was the National Security League. The organisation had been leading a campaign within the metropolis to encourage the teaching of patriotism within the state school system throughout 1917.[138] The League had also issued a variety of leaflets and promotional material after the declaration of war to communicate the need for the intervention of the United States in the war and its positive effects on society. Indeed, the group had also been highly active in both the mayoral election campaign, favouring the candidateship of Mitchel over Hylan.[139] The winner had not deterred the agenda of the group and in December 1917, from their base in the city, they launched an initiative calling for a universal military training week across the nation.[140] However, these measures were put in place after the November mayoral race in the city, as the apparent appeal of socialist politics in the city deeply concerned the League. Such a programme was designed to support the drive for patriotic sentiment and reject what was regarded as the 'alien' and 'un-American' nature of socialist politics. The equation with socialism as a 'foreign' incursion into the nation also resulted in a campaign by the group to prevent 'suspect' languages such as German being taught in state schools.[141]

The actions of the National Security League ensured that the fear of being labelled as suspect, regarded as unpatriotic or even suspicious was at the forefront of German American individuals and businesses in the city. It was particularly significant in these circumstances not to be seen as possessing sympathies towards socialist politics. Therefore, by late 1917 and into 1918, German American New York began to disappear. What was once a highly prominent part of the metropolis began to fade away into the fabric of the city; German businesses and shops altered their frontage and trading names in the hope that they would not be tarred with the accusation of disloyalty. For example, the Germania Bank, located on the Bowery on the Lower East Side, once a strong feature of life in Klein Deutschland, had, by late 1917, filed papers with the Supreme Court of New York

---

[138] National Security League, 1917c. *Proceedings of the Congress of Constructive Patriotism: Held under the Auspices of the National Security League, Washington, D.C., January 25–27*. New York, NY: National Security League; S. Stanwood Menken, 1917. *Knowledge by the People True Basis of National Security*. New York, NY: National Security League, Inc.

[139] *New York Evening Post*, October 30, 1917; *New York Herald*, October 30, 1917.

[140] *New York Times*, December 17, 1917.

[141] *New York Times*, December 10, 1917; *New York Herald*, December 10, 1917.

County to alter its operating title to the Commonwealth Bank.[142] The request was made despite the institution's participation in the Second Liberty Loan campaign. This request was granted and by early January 1918 the new operation continued within the city without its previous associations.[143] At the same time, the German Exchange Bank of the City of New York also petitioned to have its name changed to the Commercial Exchange Bank.[144] These alterations set a precedent for other financial institutions who were fearful of their foreign connections. During the first few months of 1918 the following changes in names for the city's financial institutions took place:

- The German American Building and Loan Association of the City of New York, to, The Enterprise Savings and Loan Association;
- The German American Bank, to, The Continental Bank of New York;
- Germania Savings Bank, Kings County, to, the Fulton Savings Bank, Kings County;
- German Savings Bank of Brooklyn, to, The Lincoln Savings Bank of Brooklyn;
- Germania Life Insurance Company, to, the Guardian Life Insurance Company;
- The German Savings Bank in the City of New York, to, Central Savings Bank in the City of New York.[145]

This alteration was also mirrored across other public and private institutions within the city. The German–American Alliance of Brooklyn formerly disbanded in April 1918, as it regarded its name and function to have become perceived to be synonymous with disloyalty in the city.[146] Later in 1918, the German Hospital and Dispensary, which had constructed the Kaiser Wilhelm Pavilion just five years earlier, was renamed the Lenox Hill Hospital by its Board of Trustees.[147] This new identification was an attempt to remove its association with the city's German community as well as the role of some of its staff members in the relief effort for the Central Powers during the early years of the war.[148] Significantly, the new

---

[142] New York Senate, 1918. *Documents of the Senate of the State of New York, Volume 5*. Albany, NY: J.B Lyon, p. 92.

[143] *New York Tribune*, January 31, 1918.

[144] *New York Tribune*, January 25, 1918.

[145] State of New York, 1919. *Annual Report of the Superintendent of Banks of the State of New York*. Albany, NY: J.B. Lyon, p. 26.

[146] *New York Times*, April 20, 1918.

[147] Board of Trustees, 1918. *Annual Report of the Lenox Hill Hospital*. New York, NY: The Hospital and Dispensary.

[148] Board of Trustees, 1916. *Annual Report of the Board of Trustees of the German Hospital and Dispensary in the City of New York*. New York, NY: The Hospital and Dispensary.

name was chosen to bear the institution's close connections to the neighbourhood it served in the Upper East Side.

Spectacles of Patriotism

The removal of references to the cultural or ethnic origins of businesses, which were once a prominent part of the city's economy and society, emphasised how deeply embedded the reaction towards 'hyphenated Americans' was in the metropolis. As part of a public demonstration of loyalty, groups now began regulating themselves to ensure their commitment to the nation could be in no doubt. This monitoring of expression was in evidence from the higher reaches of authority to the individual citizen. Displays of patriotism from the city's migrant groups became a means to emphasise attachment and place. This was particularly evident in the parades of the city's drafted men in February 1918. Returning from training and ready to be transported across to the war in Europe, the men from Camp Upton were organised to march through the streets of Manhattan through the work of the Mayor's Committee on National Defense.[149] The spectacle was designed to coincide with the anniversary of George Washington's birth on 22 February, and nearly 10,000 soldiers participated in what was reported as a grand statement of loyalty and 'Americanism'.[150]

The assembled crowds along Fifth Avenue witnessed the cavalcade, which was accompanied by a significant display of flags and patriotic emblems.[151] Emma Goldman, being transported from her cell in New York to a penitentiary in Missouri, witnessed the crowds on Fifth Avenue and hoped that such scenes would ferment a Bolshevik uprising.[152] However, such was the fervour of the crowds that the police and National Guard were called upon to clear onlookers from the path of the troops.[153] This show of the nation's mobilisation enabled both the authorities to provide a powerful statement of unity but also offered the city's immigrant population to proclaim their loyalty. The association between citizenship and martial service was also extended to the city's African American soldiers, as commentators remarked upon the demonstration of service shown during the draft.[154] However, this assessment did not allow for a deviation from the principle of 'separate but equal'.[155] Such views were represented in the response of the poet Allan Tucker (1866–1939) to

---

[149]   *New York Times*, February 5, 1918; *New York Tribune*, February 3, 1918.

[150]   *New York Times*, February 22, 1918; *New York Tribune*, February 22, 1918.

[151]   *New York Times*, February 23, 1918.

[152]   E. Goldman, 1919. On the Way to Golgotha. *Mother Earth Bulletin*, 1(5): 1.

[153]   *New York Tribune*, February 23, 1918.

[154]   Union League Club, 1918. *The Presentation of Colors to the 367th Regiment of Infantry, Colonel James A. Moss Commanding*. New York, NY: S.L. Parsons and Company.

[155]   *New York Age*, February 23, 1918.

the parades in a piece entitled *The 367th Infantry* which whilst hailing the admission as citizenry still regarded these men as fighting 'for us' and 'with us':

> From Africa to Manhattan,
> From slavery to freedom,
> Men – Citizens – at last![156]

With the parades of soldiers through the city and their departure for the battlefields, the metropolis took upon a distinctly military air. Indeed, with Mayor Hylan assuming office on 1 January 1918, a call was made to put the city on a 'war basis', emphasising economies in spending and investment whilst calling for a renewal of purpose for the fight ahead.[157] However, such financial demands inevitably inflicted far greater problems upon the city's workforce, as high prices and increasing demands to provision the United States and its allies ensured decreasing living standards and stagnant wages.[158] At the outset of the New Year, the disputes between the city and national authorities and the unions had begun to assume the same issues as the battles over identity that had marked the city over the last three years of war.[159] Socialism was, once again, equated with an 'alien' ideology, whilst the actions of, especially, Jewish and Irish labour unions, in supporting members' rights, was frequently cast as evidence of dual loyalty or even treachery.[160] These concerns were only exacerbated by the excellent results of the Socialist Party during the November mayoral elections and the news later that month that revolution in Russia had brought Vladimir Lenin's Bolsheviks to power.[161]

Indeed, concerns had been expressed as the United States entered the war in April 1917 that New York's unions, some dominated by Jewish workers, would prove to be a hindrance to the war effort through their pacifism, socialism and 'un-American' attitudes.[162] As if to confirm these suspicions, the unions within the city had been prominent in the organisation of the 'Conference for Democracy and Terms of Peace' at Madison Square Garden in May 1917, which was attended by thousands of workers, and had called for the end of the

---

[156] *New York Times*, June 12, 1918.

[157] *New York Herald*, January 2, 1918; *New York Times*, January 2, 1918.

[158] M. Dubofsky, 1961. Organised Labor in New York City and the First World War, 1914–1918. *New York History*, 42(4): 380–400.

[159] J.A. McCartin, 1998. *Labor's Great War: The Struggle for Industrial Democracy and the Origins of Modern American Labor Relations, 1912–1921*. Chapel Hill, NC: University of North Carolina Press, p. 38; F. Grubbs, 1968. *The Struggle for Labor Loyalty: Gompers, the A.F. of L., and the Pacifists, 1917–1920*. Durham, NC: Duke University Press, p. 43.

[160] *New York Times*, January 31, 1918.

[161] *New York Times*, November 13. 1917; *New York Times*, November 30, 1917.

[162] *New York Evening Post*, April 10, 1917; *New York Tribune*, April 10, 1917.

'capitalist war'.[163] Prominent New York unions such as the ILGWU and the United Garment Workers had proclaimed their unwillingness to follow the call of pledging not to strike during the war, issued by the body coordinating industrial action, the American Federation of Labor (AFL).[164] To combat the problem of perceived disloyalty amongst labour unions in the city, the Wilson administration sponsored the development in New York of the American Alliance for Labor and Democracy in July 1917.[165] This organisation was coordinated by the AFL, with the head of this governing body, New York immigrant Samuel Gompers (1850–1924), leading its development.[166] Essentially, the Alliance for Labor and Democracy was a patriotic, pro-war group which disseminated information and literature to foster nationalist sentiment amongst the city's immigrant-led unions and thereby 'Americanise' the metropolitan's workforce.[167] By the beginning of 1918, the drive for this commitment from organised labour in the city was accelerated in the face of apparently increasing support for socialism in New York. American values, liberties and democracies in opposition to foreign tyranny and revolution were stressed in this appeal to the fellow citizens of the United States.[168]

The importance of ensuring the commitment of the city's workforce to the nation was reinforced with the trial of Franz von Rintelen (1877–1949) in February 1918.[169] Although arrested in Britain in August 1915, on completion of his detainment, von Rintelen was deported to the United States in April 1917 to confess and testify regarding his role in Germany's campaign of espionage in the United States and specifically in New York.[170] The case against von Rintelen was alarming; after arriving in the city under a false name, he had operated under orders from the

---

[163] People's Council of America for Democracy and Peace, 1917. *Report of the First American Conference for Democracy and Terms of Peace Held at Madison Square Garden, New York City, May 30 and 31st, 1917*. New York, NY: Organizing Committee, People's Council of America for Democracy and Peace.

[164] American Federation of Labor, 1917. *American Labor's Position in Peace or in War*. Washington, DC: Executive Council of the American Federation of Labor.

[165] S. Gompers, 1917a. Labor and Democracy. *American Federationist*, 24(10): 837–42.

[166] S. Gompers, 1917b. *America's Fight for the Preservation of Democracy*. New York, NY: American Alliance for Labor and Democracy.

[167] J. Luff, 2012. *Commonsense Anticommunism: Labor and Civil Liberties Between the World Wars*. Chapel Hill, NC: University of North Carolina Press, p. 49.

[168] American Federation of Labor, 1918. *To the Workers of Free America: An Appeal by the Executive Council of the American Federation of Labor, February 17, 1918*. New York, NY: American Alliance for Labor and Democracy; J. Commons, 1918a. *German Socialists and the War*. New York, NY: American Alliance for Labor and Democracy; J. Commons, 1918b. *Why Workingmen Support the War*. New York, NY: American Alliance for Labor and Democracy.

[169] *New York Times*, February 6, 1918; *New York Herald*, February 6, 1918.

[170] *New York Evening World*, May 9, 1917.

German Foreign Office in New York from April 1915 and had sought to disrupt the trade of war materials by sabotage and market speculation.[171] However, the most disturbing of his activities had been to ferment unrest and foster activism within the immigrant-led trade unions within the city as a means to ensure that strikes, walkouts and industrial unrest prevented commerce between the Allies and the United States. Indeed, von Rintelen was indicted by a Federal Court in Brooklyn at the end of 1917 for using the city's workers to arrange for explosive devices to be planted on the British ship, *Kirk Oswald*, in May 1915, and organising the anti-war union, Labor's National Peace Council, in June 1915, for disruptive purposes.[172] Such a sensational trial served to heighten the fear that the city's workers were either disloyal or easily swayed by the influence of 'alien' agents. In such a climate of suspicion, the work of the Alliance for Labor and Democracy was able to win support from workers, unions and socialist politicians alike through the promotion of literature that connected anti-war sentiment with 'un-American' attitudes.[173]

This critical coverage of anti-war labour unions within the city was coordinated by the Alliance for Labor and Democracy through the work of the Committee on Public Information (CPI), a national body initiated in April 1917 by President Wilson, but which placed many of its offices and operations in New York.[174] Its location in the city enabled the mobilisation of the city's financial and commercial resources as well as its advertising acumen, as a variety of patriotic literature and visual materials regarding the war effort were distributed from New York across the nation.[175] The effect of this implicit programme of Americanisation was substantial, with the CPI ensuring that the city's union members and its leaders were acutely aware of the dangers posed by 'alien' subversives.[176] The negative associations of the anti-war stance, which were promoted through these materials, and the effects of the von Rintelen trial formed an atmosphere of fear and distrust within the city which was used to 'Americanise' the labour force.[177] The CPI's recruitment and deployment of 'Four Minute Men' in 1917 to the city's theatres before the major productions, which was shown to mobilise the crowd with brief patriotic speeches, also served

---

[171]   F. von Rintelen, 1933. *The Dark Invader: Wartime Reminiscences of a German Naval Intelligence Officer*. New York, NY: Macmillan Co., p. 166.

[172]   *New York Times*, December 22, 1917; *New York Herald*, December 22, 1917.

[173]   American Alliance for Labor and Democracy, 1918. *Red, White and Blue Book of the American Labor Movement: Organized Labor's Record in Relation to the War as Shown in the Official Documents*. New York, NY: American Alliance for Labor and Democracy.

[174]   Committee on Public Information, 1918a. *The Activities of the Committee on Public Information*. Washington, DC: Government Printing Office.

[175]   A. Axelrod, 2009. *Selling the Great War: The Making of American Propaganda*. New York, NY: Palgrave Macmillan, p. 94.

[176]   G. Creel, 1920. *How We Advertised America: The First Telling of the Amazing Story of the Committee on Public Information that Carried the Gospel of Americanism to Every Corner of the Globe*. New York, NY: Harper and Brothers, p. 174.

[177]   Committee on Public Information, 1918b. *The German-Bolshevik Conspiracy*. Washington, DC: Government Printing Office.

to encourage support for 'one hundred per cent Americanism' in both metropolitan society and politics.[178] Whilst the 'Four Minute Men' operated on a national basis, with the dense population in New York, the volunteer unit was able to focus attention on what was regarded as the connected evils of 'hyphenated Americans' and 'socialism'.[179] Speeches in Yiddish, Russian and Italian were, therefore, prepared for this purpose to encourage citizenship and loyalty.[180] Socialism was, therefore, framed not only as 'foreign' but specifically as 'German'. Such perceptions were used to deter workers from socialist politics within the city:

> As a political party that section was first organized in this country by German exiles. They have always been led by German sympathisers. It has been a rule among them that a man is not a socialist unless he pays dues to the party leaders, accepts all the party nominees of those leaders without question, subscribes to every plank of the party platform, and votes only a straight ticket under the party emblem ... That is a Prussian idea of organized servility and unquestioning obedience.[181]

To emphasise this distinction, in early February 1918, the Alliance for Labor and Democracy had organised the national 'Labor Loyalty Week', which saw parades, speeches and rallies in New York as a spectacle of patriotic fervour from within the city's labouring classes. The week of activities was selected to coincide with the birthday of Abraham Lincoln on 12 February and the anniversary was used to attest labour's 'commitment to democracy'.[182] The week was opened by a large gathering in Century Theatre, where the leaders of the city's unions stood alongside members of the AFL to announce that the fight for liberty across the world was a cause for the American working man.[183] This event proved a useful platform to promote a programme of 'Americanisation'. Indeed, in the aftermath of the meeting Samuel Gompers had urged the workers of the city to stand by the flag in the spirit of national unity and reject the overtures of foreign elements.[184] By the spring of 1918, some of the larger unions within the city had begun to openly declare their loyalty to the nation and their rejection of any association with

---

[178] *Four Minute Men Bulletin*, May 22, 1917.

[179] *Four Minute Men Bulletin*, January 28, 1918; *Four Minute Men Bulletin*, April 6, 1918.

[180] A.E. Cornebise, 1984. *War as Advertised: The Four-Minute Men and America's Crusade, 1917–1918*. Philadelphia: American Philosophical Society, p. 20.

[181] Committee on Public Information, 1918c. *The Kaiserite in America: One Hundred and One German Lies*. Washington, DC: Government Printing Office, pp. 7–8.

[182] *New York Herald*, February 10, 1918; *New York Times*, February 10, 1918; *New York Tribune*, February 10, 1918.

[183] S. Gompers, 2007. *The Samuel Gompers Papers, Vol 10: The American Federation of Labor and the Great War, 1917–18*. Edited by S.B. Kaufman, P.J. Albert and G. Palladino. Urbana, IL: University of Illinois Press, p. 312.

[184] *New York Times*, February 23, 1918.

'Teutonic politics'. Indeed, during a meeting of the New York Central Federated Union the notion of a German association with 'loyal American' labour was rejected outright.[185] The pressure of patriotic conformity as opposed to what was increasingly framed as sedition formed a divide within socialist politics in the city. Such was the bitterness of this divide that *The Class Struggle*, the socialist magazine published in New York, repeatedly lambasted Gompers for his apparent betrayal of working class interests to capitalist power.[186] However, the degree to which labour in the city had been 'Americanised' and turned away from an 'alien' influence was demonstrated in the preparation and campaign for the Third Liberty Loan in New York. Socialist politicians in the city were forced to assent to the necessity of the programme of raising capital or appear to be pandering to foreign elements. Whilst Hillquit and his allies within the party had previously been vigorous opponents of previous drives for the Liberty Loan, even gaining political capital out of this stance, at the outset of this new initiative in April 1918, they pledged their full and unwavering support.[187]

Therefore, before even six months had passed since their election to the city's Board of Aldermen, New York's socialist voice, which had professed pacifism and campaigned on an anti-war platform, now proclaimed the need for national unity to the ire of their socialist comrades.[188] Though the issue was divisive for the socialist party members in New York, the support pledged by the prominent unions within the city to the cause of the Third Liberty Loan attested to a wider commitment from labour in the metropolis to the 'Americanisation' programme of the CPI. For example, the ILGWU had urged its members both to advertise the war bonds and to purchase them 'despite the present abnormal cost of living'.[189] Even before the launch of the Liberty Loan campaign in the city, the United Hebrew Trades released a statement which detailed their support for the national scheme.[190] Through such protestations of loyalty from the unions and the socialist Aldermen of the city, the issue of labour in the city and its reliability for ensuring the furtherance of the cause of the United States was resolved. This shift was mirrored on a wider level with the creation in April 1918 of a National War Labor Board that supervised and coordinated the deployment of workers for wartime needs.[191] The process of Americanisation that had been present since the outbreak of the war in August 1914 had served to redefine the cause of labour

---

185 *New York Herald*, March 18, 1918; *New York Times*, March 18, 1918.

186 A. Germer, 1918. Samuel Gompers. *The Class Struggle*, 2(1): 9–15.

187 *New York Herald*, April 9, 1918; *New York Tribune*, April 9, 1918.

188 *New York Call*, April 10, 1918.

189 Anon., 1918. The Greatest Convention in the Annals of our International Union. *The Ladies' Garment Worker*, 9(6): 3.

190 *New York Times*, March 13, 1918.

191 Bureau of Labor, 1922. *National War Labor Board: A History of its Formation and Activities, Together with its Awards and the Documents of Importance in the Record of its Development*. Washington, DC: Government Printing Office, pp. 9–10.

in the city, which now sought victory on the battlefield and the extension of American democracy to their German counterparts.

One City, One Nation, One Loyalty

The changes in the city and its representation as 'one hundred per cent American' were aptly demonstrated in the extravaganza held for the Third Liberty Loan. This effort not only served to galvanise support from the city's labour representatives, it also offered a platform on which the city's and its citizens' allegiance could be proclaimed.[192] The advertisement of war bonds ran from April to May with the New York district expected to provide $900,000,000, far in excess of any other area of the country, and drawn particularly from the businesses, communities and individuals of New York City.[193] Nearly 300,000 workers were prepared for the Second Federal Reserve District to serve as promoters and salesmen for the loan.[194] The campaign in the city was planned with a sense of military precision and it was through this emphasis that groups aligned themselves to the cause. Prominent Jewish groups in the city held public meetings to urge their communities to demonstrate their patriotism to their country and the belief in the cause.[195] Jewish trade union activists in the city, such as Joseph Barondess (1867–1928), worked in the Lower East side to promote the support for the loan from the immigrant Jewish enclave.[196] This work was monitored within the city by the National Security League, who had worked with Rabbis and theologians to send letters to synagogues in the city and further afield to request full participation in the programme.[197] Such focus on the city's Jewish communities, both orthodox and reform, ensured that by the end of the liberty loan campaign, New York's synagogues had been a substantial contributor to the scheme:

- Temple Emanu-El – $500,000 worth of bonds bought;
- Free Synagogue – $100,000 worth of bonds bought;
- Congregation Ohab Zedek – $97,000 worth of bonds bought;
- Temple Beth-El – $50,000 worth of bonds bought.[198]

The Third Liberty Loan emphasised the changes that had occurred within the metropolis, which could now avowedly state its loyalty and its status as a city of

---

[192]   Liberty Loan Committee, Second Federal Reserve District, 1918a. *Selling the Third Liberty Loan: Suggestions for the Use of Liberty Loan Committees*. Washington, DC: Government Printing Office.

[193]   *New York Herald*, March 29, 1918; *New York Times*, March 29, 1918.

[194]   *New York Times*, March 31, 1918.

[195]   S.M. Melamed, 1918. Editorial. *American Jewish Chronicle*, 4(26): 721.

[196]   *New York Times*, April 1, 1918.

[197]   *New York Times*, March 31, 1918.

[198]   Anon., 1918. Our New York Letter. *The Advocate*, 55: 321.

'one hundred per cent Americans'. It was these sentiments that were promoted at the outset of the drive for the purchase of war bonds as patriotism became a commodity that once bought could proclaim the identity of the city and its citizens.[199] Such purchases were facilitated by the provision once again of booths in major department stores, and shoppers were guided by prominent signage to the places where they could demonstrate their loyal support.[200] Once again, aerial bombardments of advertising literature were targeted upon the city; there was also a city-wide operation which involved large numbers of recruits from the city's schools and the Home Defense League ringing the doorbells of households and leaving a small paper Liberty Bell, adorned with the slogan, 'Ring it Again' upon each doorknob.[201]

Through these measures, the Publicity Department of the Liberty Loan Committee of the Second Federal Reserve District were able not only to sell a sense of national identity to the city's residents, they were able to sell the war.[202] The same approach by the committee was utilised to ensure the support of the city's churches, with a detail from the publicity department coordinating a united churches approach to uphold the moral purpose of both the war and of the nation.[203] The mobilisation of patriotism within New York was emphasised in the prominence given to the national flag in the city; shops, businesses and private residences were encouraged to unfurl the 'stars and stripes' for the drive and to mark the first anniversary of the nation's declaration of war against Germany.[204] Such public demonstrations served to reinforce the singular concept of 'Americanisation' that had transformed the metropolis. This was also evident in the promotional literature for the Third Liberty Loan which was prominently displayed across the city. One poster, decorated with flags, an eagle and heavy artillery motifs, asked the pertinent question:

Are you 100% American? Prove it! Buy U.S. government bonds.[205]

---

[199] *New York Tribune*, April 3, 1917; *New York Sun*, April 3, 1917.

[200] *New York Times*, April 2, 1918.

[201] *New York Times*, April 5, 1918.

[202] J.P. Jones, 1918. *Report of John Price Jones, Assistant Director and Manager, Press Bureau, to Guy Emerson, Director, Publicity Department, Liberty Loan Committee, Second Federal Reserve District. Third Liberty Loan Campaign*. New York, NY: Liberty Loan Committee, Second Federal Reserve District, pp. 5–6; Liberty Loan Committee, Second Federal Reserve District, 1918b. *Handbook for Speakers: Third Liberty Loan*. Washington, DC: Government Printing Office.

[203] W. Laidlaw, (Ed.) 1918. *The Moral Aims of the War: Comprising a Series of Addresses Given at an All Day Interchurch Clerical Conference in the City of New York, April 4th, 1918*. New York, NY: Fleming H. Revell Company.

[204] *New York Herald*, April 6, 1918; *New York Times*, April 6, 1918.

[205] Stern, 1917. *Are you 100% American? Prove it! Buy U.S. Government Bonds. Third Liberty Loan*. New York, NY: Sackett and Wilhelms Corp.

Similarly, another poster depicted a family of immigrants, standing in front of the flag with the reminder for those foreign-born citizens of their duty:

Remember! The Flag of Liberty! Support it! Buy U.S. Government Bonds.[206]

By advertising the war bonds as a national duty for those at home a direct connection could be made between the service in the armed forces and financial contributions. Both served to attach yourself to the nation and demonstrate your allegiance. Such concepts were also reiterated through a variety of cultural forms, as the city's entertainment industry was mobilised to ensure the success of the Third Liberty Loan. Stars such as Enrico Caruso (1873–1921), Charlie Chaplin (1889–1977) and Douglas Fairbanks (1883–1939) made appearances in the city, with the latter two attracting crowds of thousands for a patriotic rally on the corner of Wall Street.[207] Caruso also pleased a large crowd in the city with his rendition of the popular song *Over There*.[208] The song, which was written in 1917 and published through the city's Tin Pan Alley music industry, conveniently reflected the impetus towards patriotic affirmation; extolling 'every son of Liberty' to fight for the 'old red, white and blue'.[209] Similar sentiments were also expressed in the 'official song' of the Liberty Loan Committee, *Liberty Bell*, which reminded citizens of their obligations.[210]

Liberty Loan, it's time to buy again,
Liberty Loan, it's time to try again,
We need your dollars, each one
To fight the Kaiser and Hun,
It's all for you that it's done,
So rally round us like you did before.
Oh, Liberty Loan, your help is needed now,
American hearts will heed the call, one and all,
For the drive they're making over there,
Ev'ry one back here must do their share,
Don't cheat Uncle Sam – go out and buy a bond.[211]

---

[206] Anon., 1917. *Remember! The Flag of Liberty! Support it! Buy U.S. Government Bonds*. New York, NY: Heywood, Strasser and Voigt Lithograph Company.

[207] *New York Tribune*, April 9, 1918; *New York Times*, April 9, 1918.

[208] *New York Tribune*, April 14, 1918.

[209] G.M. Cohan, 1917. *Over There*. New York, NY: William Jerome Publishing Corporation.

[210] *New York Morning Telegraph*, April 7, 1918.

[211] J. Goodwin and H.K. Mohr, 1917. *Liberty Bell (It's Time to Ring Again)*. New York, NY: Shapiro, Bernstein and Company.

Popular patriotism was expected from the city's diverse citizens but it was also policed and controlled in its expression by members of the metropolitan social and cultural elite. This division was emphasised with the outcry organised through the mainstream press over plans by the Liberty Loan Committee to construct a series of trench systems in Central Park to raise support for the cause.[212] The plans, which would have seen front line and communication trenches dug out on either the Great Lawn or Sheep Meadow, affronted the tastes of some New Yorkers who argued that such despoliation of the park's aesthetics in the name of the war bonds was akin to 'Teutonic autocracy'.[213] Whilst the park had previously hosted war trophies and the trenches were regarded as an exciting addition to the Liberty Loan campaign, the designs were quickly removed after the scale of displeasure was made known.[214] The incident demonstrated for whom the programme of patriotic avowals were for; it was for the city's diverse, first or second-generation immigrant communities to declare their loyalty, not for the 'old New Yorkers'.[215] In this manner, the control over identity in the city was an object to be monitored to ensure the commitment of the populace. The National Security League within New York promoted this surveillance, particularly during the Liberty Loan campaign, as speeches, dinners, leaflets and educational programmes were used to promote 'one hundred per cent Americanism'.[216] As the drive for war bonds focused on this issue of identity, the League took a prominent role in combating expressions of disloyalty or of 'hyphen identities', including stating its determination to see the sale of German-language newspapers banned in the city.[217]

Whilst rigidly controlled in the expression of national sentiment, the Liberty Loan was, nevertheless, a highly useful tool through which minority communities, ethnic, religious or political, that were perhaps regarded as 'suspect', could willingly demonstrate their allegiance. Rather than a acquiescing under a wider programme of identity formation, groups within the city willingly redefined themselves through their patriotic work for the Liberty Loan. Jewish émigré and prominent Republican politician in the city, Samuel S. Koenig (1872–1955), spoke about war bonds and national service to the congregation at the Orthodox synagogue Ohab Zedek on the Upper West Side on 25 April, and declared them to be 'loyal Jews' who were '100% American' through their efforts.[218] Similar declarations of belonging were made within

---

212   *New York Evening Post*, March 19, 1918; *New York Times*, March 21, 1918.

213   *New York Times*, March 23, 1918; *New York Tribune*, March 28, 1918.

214   *New York Times*, March 29, 1918.

215   *New York Sun*, March 19, 1918.

216   E. Sperry, 1918. *The Tentacles of the German Octopus in America*. New York, NY: National Security League; National Security League, 1918a. *Money, Munitions and Ships Luncheon under Auspices of the National Security League, Hotel Astor, New York City, April 13, 1918*. New York, NY: National Security League.

217   *New York Times*, April 26, 1918; *New York Tribune*, April 17, 1918.

218   Engelman, *Four Years of Relief and War Work by the Jews of America*, p. 57.

the Italian and Polish communities in the city.[219] Socialist activists on the Lower East Side held rallies and collections for war bonds and were urged by organisers to show how they were '101 per cent American'.[220] However, the patriotic appeal of the war bonds for this group may also have been aided by the sense of solidarity brought about by the reporting of the seemingly exacting terms of the Treaty of Brest-Litovsk, between Germany and the newly formed Russian Soviet Federated Socialist Republic.[221]

The desire to be seen as 'American' was promoted through the appeals to the founding promise of the nation: liberty. Speaking to an assembled crowd of Wall Street financiers, Republican Party member and lawyer James M. Beck (1861–1936) spoke in April 1918 of the city's and the nation's role of preserving the 'heritage of liberty'.[222] Such ideas were echoed across the pageants held in the city during the Third Liberty Loan campaign. 'Liberty', whether expressed as a figure of the nation itself or as an immutable value of its people, was a prominent feature of the Liberty Loans Committee.[223] The value of such an appeal was in its ability to secure commitment from all sections of the metropolis; 'liberty' functioned as a means by which the conflict could be sold and identity could be formed around with parades to celebrate this 'self-evident' and wholly 'American' right.[224] As such, citizens could marvel at 'Liberty Land', held at the 69th Regiment Armory on Lexington Avenue and 25th Street, which featured displays of the battlefields, trophies of war as well as American and French veterans of the conflict who spoke of their experiences.[225] A 'Liberty Theatre' was also erected on the steps of the Public Library on 42nd Street where patriotic orations and songs entertained large crowds throughout the campaign.[226] Such was the popularity of this temporary venue, the rendition of the 'Star Spangled Banner' at this site by the soprano Geraldine Farrar (1882–1967) caused a significant disruption to traffic along Fifth Avenue.[227]

In keeping with this focus on 'liberty', the inauguration by President Wilson of 26 April as a national 'Liberty Day' provided another means to express national identity through this cohesive quality.[228] This was exemplified in the 'Win-the-War Parade', held on Liberty Day, which featured prominent members

---

[219]   J.H. Mariano, 1922. *The Italian Contribution to American Democracy*. Boston, MA: Christopher Publishing House, p. 253.

[220]   *New York Times*, April 14, 1918; *New York Tribune*, April 15, 1918.

[221]   *New York Call*, March 21, 1918.

[222]   *New York Times*, April 16, 1918.

[223]   D.H. Fischer, 2004. *Liberty and Freedom: A Visual History of America's Founding Ideals*. Oxford: Oxford University Press, p. 431.

[224]   *New York Herald*, April 21, 1918; *New York Times*, April 21, 1918.

[225]   *Brooklyn Daily Eagle*, April 26, 1918; *New York Sun*, April 15, 1918; *New York Evening Post*, April 29, 1918.

[226]   *New York Tribune*, April 22, 1918.

[227]   *New York Evening World*, April 15, 1918.

[228]   *New York Tribune*, April 19, 1918.

of the city's political and financial sectors, volunteers from patriotic and
charitable organisations, union members as well as the families of servicemen.[229]
Numbering over 30,000, the parade through Broadway to Washington Square
was garlanded with national flags as loyalty to the state, through military service
or financial contribution, was heralded as a civic virtue.[230] Indeed, participation
provided the public affirmation of the devotion to the American principles of
liberty that were being fought for on the battlefields of Europe. The United
Garment Workers took a prominent part in the parade for these purposes:

> It was an inspiring occasion, and every one who witnessed the display must
> have been impressed with the fact that American labor can be counted on to do
> its duty in workshop, in factory and in the Army to win the war for freedom and
> democracy ... The members of the organisation are 100 percent loyal ...[231]

By the closing of the Liberty Loan campaign in the city in early May, the political
figures within the metropolis could once again use the success of the drive for war
bonds as a declaration of its citizens' steadfast dedication to the United States.[232]
Once again, all areas of the city had exceeded their quotas by a significant margin.
Indeed, the scale at which New Yorkers had subscribed to the war bonds as a
testament to their loyalty was staggering (Table 6.1).[233]

Table 6.1   Quotas and Amounts Raised for the Third Liberty Loan in
             New York

Borough	Quota	Amount of Subscription
Manhattan	$618,794,000	$701,167,700
Brooklyn	$39,616,900	$53,001,950
Queens	$4,354,400	$10,825,300
Bronx	$3,317,100	$5,381,150
Staten Island	$1,032,900	$3,386,800

Source: Federal Reserve Bank of New York, 1918. *Fourth Annual Report*. Washington, DC:
Government Printing Office, p. 81.

The effect of the Liberty Loan campaigns and the introduction of the draft into the
city had altered the physical appearance as well as the identity of the metropolis.
New York had even become a symbol of the wider nation in its extolling of liberty
and loyalty. In this regard and in its position as the major transportation hub for both

---

229   *New York Herald*, April 26, 1918; *New York Tribune*, April 26, 1918.

230   *New York Times*, April 27, 1918.

231   Anon., 1918. Labor Day Celebration. *The Garment Worker*, 17(47): 6.

232   *New York Times*, May 4, 1918; *New York Tribune*, May 5, 1918.

233   Federal Reserve Bank of New York, 1918. *Fourth Annual Report*. Washington,
DC: Government Printing Office, p. 81.

men and materials to the battlefields of Europe, New York presented a particular challenge for policing and governance.[234] However, with the transformation of the city onto a 'war footing', the alteration in its 'American' character enabled a far greater sense of social and political cohesion. This is perhaps reflected in the announcement of July 1918 by Du Bois that the African American cause for equality and representation should be postponed to enable the victorious pursuance of the war 'shoulder to shoulder' with 'fellow citizens'.[235] To fight for the country, therefore, demonstrates allegiance and requires democratic representation as 'Americans':

> America is the American Negro's country. He has been here three hundred years; that is, two hundred years longer than most of the white people.[236]

The process of 'Americanisation' was, therefore, not a hegemonic display of power and control, but one which communities in the city committed themselves to as a means of identification with their nation. Collective events, such as parades, afforded a means by which a public display could be made. For example, 'Loyalty Week', celebrated during June 1918, was affirmed by Mayor Hylan as an occasion when all peoples in the city could state their allegiance to 'one flag, one people, one country'.[237] In the same spirit, the celebrations of 4 July in New York were extensive. Proclaimed by President Wilson as 'Loyalty Day' and marked across the United States, the highlight of the festivities in New York was a grand procession through Manhattan, organised by the Mayor's Committee on National Defense, with over 40 sizeable floats depicting glorious scenes from the history of allied nations but carrying banners proclaiming the loyalty of these 'hyphenated Americans'.[238] Preparations had been marred by a public dispute between the Hungarian and Italian contingents, with the latter decrying any Hungarian cultural display as an incongruous addition considering the war that was being waged.[239] Rather than reflecting the tensions between ethnic groups who stood on opposing sides of the war in Europe, the issue was fuelled by a debate as to which group was more loyal and more 'American'.[240] In this manner, New York citizens were encouraged, accepted and welcomed their status as 'undifferentiated Americans'.[241]

This was also the framework through which the city initiated a period of mourning upon the death of John Purroy Mitchel. The former mayor was killed during a flying operation in Louisiana on 6 July and his body was brought back to

---

[234] New York Police Department, 1918. *Annual Report*. New York, NY: Bureau of Printing, City of New York, p. 5.

[235] W.E.B. Du Bois, 1918. Close Ranks. *The Crisis*, 16(3): 111.

[236] *New York Age*, June 29, 1918.

[237] *New York Times*, June 7, 1918; *New York Tribune*, June 7, 1918.

[238] *New York Herald*, June 29, 1918; *New York Times*, June 4, 1918.

[239] *New York Times*, June 26, 1918.

[240] *New York Times*, June 28, 1918.

[241] *New York Times*, June 7, 1918.

New York for burial.[242] The funeral procession on 11 July was lined by mourners from across city along Fifth Avenue to St Patrick's Cathedral, whilst a squadron of 'Liberty Birdmen' flew overhead showering attendants with rose petals as they stood by the burial plot on Woodlawn Cemetery, Bronx.[243] A collective outpouring of grief for one of the leading proponents of 'one hundred per cent Americanism' served to galvanise the cause of 'Americanisation'. It was these qualities that were promoted and policed during September 1918 as the wartime demands for both money and manpower required a greater degree of sacrifice from the citizens of the metropolis. This was demonstrated in the announcement of another phase of draft registration in the city which was scheduled to take place on 12 September.[244] All men aged between 18 and 45 in the city were required to sign up with their local draft board for assessment. The surveillance of potential 'slackers' began before the registration day, with those not carrying their registration cards regarded as potential 'draft dodgers' and, therefore, liable for arrest.[245] Such a monitoring of the populace had been present since the draft was initiated, but its intensity had increased throughout the spring of 1918.[246] Both the police and private patriotic organisations were involved in this process in September 1918, as identity and allegiance within the city were vigilantly overseen whilst 900,000 New Yorkers registered for the draft.[247]

The National Security League, the American Defense Society and groups such as the American Protective League participated with the New York police and the War Department in Washington, but also worked on their own initiative to conduct 'slacker raids' in the city during early September 1918.[248] Such operations were extensive; swoops on theatres, bars and hotels in the city were conducted with a demand that registration cards be presented from men of eligible age. In one raid, conducted with the city's police as well as conscripted soldiers, nearly 20,000 men were taken and detained in the city's armouries.[249] Such activities were justified in the newspaper publication of individual cases of avoidance, such as that of Abraham Ituro, a 26-year-old Russian immigrant living in Harlem, who had been in the country 14 years, and had not signed up because 'he did not want to'.[250] However, the extrajudicial powers assumed by these groups did bring censure within the city and from Senators in Washington, as the rights of private organisations to arrest and detain were challenged.[251] Despite these criticisms, such

---

242 *New York Herald*, July 7, 1918; *New York Tribune*, July 7, 1918.

243 *New York Times*, July 12, 1918; *New York Tribune*, July 12, 1918.

244 *New York Times*, August 31, 1918; *New York Tribune*, August 31, 1918.

245 *New York Times*, September 2, 1918.

246 *New York Times*, March 22, 1918.

247 *New York Tribune*, September 1, 1918; *New York Times*, September 8, 1918.

248 *New York Herald*, September 1, 1918; *New York Times*, September 1, 1918.

249 *New York Tribune*, September 5, 1918; *New York Times*, September 5, 1918.

250 *New York Times*, September 4, 1918.

251 *New York Times*, September 13, 1918.

intrusive and illegal operations in New York were not marked by a widespread protest in the metropolis. Indeed, most citizens complied with the measures, even if it meant their arrest and detention, in order to reinforce their status as 'good Americans'.[252]

The End of the War

As the sense of 'one hundred per cent Americanism' appeared so pervasive by the autumn of 1918, public arms of the state and private groups began using the power of patriotic proselytisation to further entrench notions of loyalty within the city. Frequently, this operated under the term of 'Americanisation', as a means of reforming the character of the 'foreign-born'.[253] The National Security League initiated their programme in 1918 which focused on the service that 'loyal' citizens could do to 'Americanise' their fellow citizens.[254] Similarly, Frances Kellor also promoted her concept of 'Neighbourhood Americanisation', which behoved upon 'American women', newly enfranchised after the elections in 1918, to engage with 'foreigners' as a process of encouraging assimilation through their good example.[255] In this understanding, the 'alien' is weak-minded and in need of the moral and patriotic fibre of the 'one hundred per cent American':

> The foreign-born resident of this city who is cut off from you by language limitations; who lives under crowded unsanitary conditions; who works long hours to the point of exhaustion; who is hungry and cold and neglected and forgotten and ignored by you turns a more willing ear to the enemy propagandist, finds it harder to bear the burdens of war, and breaks into mobs and strikes more easily.[256]

This drive for public displays of patriotic endeavour was also mobilised for the campaign for the Fourth Liberty Loan from late September to October 1918.[257] This drive for wartime bonds was the most extensive yet held within the metropolis,

---

[252]   *New York Tribune*, September 14, 1918.

[253]   Bureau of Education, 1919. *Americanization Work in New York State: As Outlined by the Bureau of Immigrant Education.* Washington, DC: Government Printing Office.

[254]   National Security League, 1918b. *Americanization Service: What You Can Do for America Through Americanization of the Foreign-born.* New York, NY: National Security League.

[255]   F. Kellor. 1918a. *Americanization of Women: A Discussion of an Emergency Created by Granting the Vote to Women in New York State.* New York, NY: s.n.

[256]   F. Kellor, 1918b. *Neighborhood Americanization.* New York, NY: Information Service of the National Americanization Committee.

[257]   Guaranty Trust Company of New York, 1918. *The Victory Drive: Fourth Liberty Loan.* New York, NY: Guaranty Trust Company of New York.

with $6,000,000,000 sought nationally and a quota of $1,800,000,000 assigned to New York's Second Federal Reserve.[258] To emphasise the significance of the metropolis, the national campaign was opened in the city by President Wilson on 27 September, who spoke at City Hall of the great national mission for unity that the war had brought.[259] To emphasise this unity, Fifth Avenue was adorned with a grand procession of national flags as the publicity launched by the Liberty Loan Committee sought to mobilise the nationalist sentiment of the city.[260] Blocks from 23rd Street to 59th Street along Fifth Avenue were transformed into a ceremonial passage, with advertising for war bonds intermingled between flags of the United States and its allies. Indeed, the section of the city was renamed 'Avenue of the Allies' by the committee for the promotion of the Fourth Liberty Loan.[261] The Mayor's Committee on National Defense also assisted in the proceedings with their Committee on Arts and Decoration, headed by the artist Francis E. Gallatin (1881–1952), which commissioned and organised the prominent display of patriotic art and sculpture along Fifth Avenue.[262] In keeping with the theme of 'liberty', these installations were intended to arouse the national sentiment of the crowds. A classically-inspired 'Altar of Liberty', designed by the architect Thomas Hastings (1860–1929), was erected on the west side of Madison Square Park, which served to focus parades and as a meeting point for rallies.[263] It was at this site that the proceedings were initiated for each of the allied nations to raise money on specified days during the loan drive.[264]

The altar was inscribed the quotations from President Wilson and allied statesmen, while opposite to the altar before the Flatiron Building, a sculptural group of soldiers was placed, behind which the figure of Liberty was placed driving on the efforts of the men.[265] Outside the Public Library on Fifth Avenue, a platform was erected upon which a portrait of the 'spirit' of one of the allied nations was prominently displayed.[266] Along Fifth Avenue, patriotic plays, songs and orations were provided to the crowds to encourage public participation in the Liberty Loan.[267] Through these displays, the cause of the war as a patriotic

---

[258]   *New York Times*, September 25, 1918.

[259]   W. Wilson, 1918. *Opening Campaign for Fourth Liberty Loan: Address of President Wilson Delivered in New York City, Sept. 27, 1918*. Washington, DC: Government Printing Office.

[260]   J.P. Jones, 1919. *Report of John Price Jones, Assistant Director, in Charge of Feature Bureau, Press Bureau, and Transportation Service to Guy Emerson, Director, Publicity Department, Liberty Loan Committee, Second Federal Reserve District. Fourth Liberty Loan Campaign*. New York, NY: s.n.

[261]   *New York Times*, September 29, 1918; *New York Tribune*, September 28, 1918.

[262]   A.E. Gallatin, 1918. *Committee on Arts and Decoration*. New York, NY: Hall of Records.

[263]   *New York Times*, October, 3, 1918; *Wall Street Journal*, October 3, 1918.

[264]   *New York Tribune*, October 4, 1918.

[265]   Anon., 1918. *Notes*. American Magazine of Arts, 20(1): 29.

[266]   *New York Times*, October 4, 1918.

[267]   *New York Times*, October 5, 1918.

endeavour was reinforced for the citizens of New York.[268] This sentiment was also confirmed through some of the promotional material for the Fourth Liberty Loan.[269] The artist Joseph Pennell's (1857–1926) contribution to this effort was to depict the Statue of Liberty in flames, its head destroyed and a squadron of German planes flying overhead with the title, a quote from Abraham Lincoln, 'that liberty shall not perish from the earth'.[270] Liberty as a figure and as a symbol upon which the citizens of New York could associate themselves with became a central feature of the sale of the war bonds in the city. 'Liberty Day', sanctioned by President Wilson as a national event, was also held in the city on 12 October to coincide with the anniversary of Columbus Day, marking the discovery of the New World, which afforded an opportunity for reflecting on the significance of 'American' democracy being provided to Europe.[271] With the conclusion of the drive came the news that New York had once more fulfilled its quota for the war bonds, thereby demonstrating its citizens' sacrifices and dedication for the purpose of liberty.[272]

Conclusions

The campaign for Liberty Loans in the city had confirmed how the metropolis, once seemingly composed of a multitude of 'foreign villages', now had assumed the air of a patriotic, 'one hundred per cent' American city. The ability of individuals and communities to proclaim loyalty to the nation in the metropolis had provided both a means of control for the authorities as well as a platform for groups to take a greater role within the city. The preparation for the war and its pursuance had ensured that the 'hyphenated identities' that had marked New York as 'different' and set apart from the wider United States had been ameliorated. The process of 'Yanking out' the differences within communities, however, had not been accomplished by an enforced dedication to the nation, rather by a subtle means of engagement and reciprocation. New York's diverse communities, who had regarded themselves as American before the war, were now able to state their allegiance through a far more tangible effect than cultural habits or political ideals. Through the military service to the nation of their fathers and sons, the war work of their mothers and daughters, the city was now home to those who were American

---

[268] Department of the Treasury, 1918. *Advertisements, Fourth Liberty Loan*. New York, NY: Liberty Loan Committee, Second Federal Reserve District.

[269] E. Van Schaack, 2005. The Coming of the Hun! American Fears of a German Invasion, 1918. *The Journal of American Culture*, 28(3): 284–92.

[270] J. Pennell, 1918. *That Liberty Shall Not Perish From The Earth*. New York, NY: Heywood Strasser and Voigt Lithograph Company.

[271] *New York Tribune*, October 12, 1918.

[272] *New York Times*, October 19, 1918.

by action and deed. It is this sentiment that brought New Yorkers onto the streets in celebration of the announcement of the Armistice in November 1918.[273]

Whilst false reports of an earlier peace in November had also generated huge crowds, the publication of news of the cessation of hostilities served to inspire an impromptu parade of thousands through Manhattan.[274] These celebrations also saw mob violence enacted upon effigies of the Kaiser throughout the city; this included throwing effigies from skyscrapers, hosing effigies with water, burning effigies in the streets, placing hanged effigies over roads, and attempting to persuade law courts to prosecute effigies.[275] The fervour in which many New Yorkers responded to the news of peace in Europe and the treatment of effigies was a product of the 'Americanisation' that had reshaped the ideas and identities of the city since the outbreak of war in 1914. The relief of citizens upon hearing the news of the end of the war brought to a close a conflict which had once appeared to demonstrate the impossibility of a city populated by first and second generation immigrants. Religious, ethnic and national loyalties in the metropolis were regarded as a potential tinderbox. However, as a singular concept of 'American' identity was promoted ahead of former ties and associations, a diverse city utilised these same concepts to demonstrate a sense of belonging and loyalty. As such, the war provided a solution to the problem of assimilation that had seemingly beset the city at the beginning of the twentieth century. Therefore, because of the city's involvement in the European conflict from its outset, the war had made Americans out of New Yorkers.

---

[273] *New York Times*, November 11, 1918; *New York Herald*, November 11, 1918.

[274] *New York Evening Post*, November 11, 1918; *New York Sun*, November 11, 1918.

[275] *New York Times*, November 12, 1918.

Chapter 7
Conclusions

The close of the war brought a realisation of the scale of the efforts made within New York to pursue victory. The privations, price rises and philanthropy exhibited by all sections of the city were notable.[1] However, it was the service on the battlefields which was remarked upon in the aftermath of the war as affirming New York's status as an 'American city'; the martial effort and sacrifices of members of the city's diverse communities were heralded as emblematic of the spirit of 'one hundred per cent Americanism'.[2] Following the denouement of this global conflagration, it was the memory of these actions that provided a further means of shaping the identity of the city and its citizens. As the troops returned from the battlefields of Europe, the desire to mark their achievements and the deaths of their comrades was expressed by both communities and the authorities within the metropolis. The nature of this remembrance continued the process of 'Americanisation' as the war was remembered as a national effort which saw the mobilisation of citizens for the cause of their country. In the years following the Armistice, the city was adorned with over a hundred monuments and memorials to those who lost their lives in the conflict.[3] However, as no central memorial to the dead in the city was constructed, it would appear that the 'European War' had been selectively forgotten or blithely disregarded in the fullness of time. Such notions misconceive the nature of remembering within society as an active process of engagement, alteration and development.[4] The war was not forgotten within the different areas of the city. Rather it was remembered successfully as evidence of those communities' place within the United States and their status as Americans.

The Homecoming

Whilst the end of the war had resulted in celebrations in New York, the troops themselves would not be able to return home for several months after November 1918. Before their arrival, the city had been seriously compromised by the

---

[1] *New York Times*, November 13, 1918.

[2] J. Leonard, 1920. *The Story of New York in the World War*. New York, NY: National Service Magazine: New York.

[3] C. Snyder, 2010. *Out of Fire and Valor: The War Memorials of New York City from the Revolution to 9/11*. Piermont: Bunkerhill Publishing, p. 78.

[4] J. Wertsch, 2002. *Voices of Collective Remembering*. Cambridge: Cambridge University Press.

emergence of Spanish Influenza, which had spread across the metropolis from August 1918 onwards.[5] As the major global hub of the era and the main embarkation point for United States soldiers, the city was more at risk than most from this resilient strain of the virus.[6] Compromised by poor quality housing, cramped environs and malnutrition, the infection rates were particularly high in sections of the Lower East Side and poorer areas of the Bronx, Brooklyn and Queens.[7] The City Health Commissioner, Royal Copeland (1868–1938), had responded slowly initially but, after the fatality rates had started to rise substantially during September and October, restrictions on public movement and behaviour were enacted.[8] An estimated 20,000 individuals died in the city, with a peak in fatalities during October 1918.[9] Perhaps unsurprisingly, therefore, there were concerns that the residents of the city, fatigued by the effects of both war and disease, would not respond positively to the homecoming of both New York's own citizen soldiers and those of the rest of the United States.[10] Nevertheless, the response to the return of troops was well-supported as it provided a further opportunity to demonstrate those civic qualities that had been reiterated throughout wartime New York's economy, society, culture and politics.

The organisation of homecoming events was undertaken in the same manner as the conflict itself, with Mayor Hylan appointing a commission in November 1918 specifically detailed to prepare for the parades and to assess how the war should be marked in the city.[11] Named the Mayor's Committee on a Permanent War Memorial, the group was chaired by the politician Rodman Wanamaker (1863–1928), who appointed the architects Thomas Hastings (1860–1929) and Paul Wayland Bartlett (1865–1925) to design the ceremonial processional route along Fifth Avenue.[12] Funds were raised through public subscription, with the city police aiding the collection campaign within the five boroughs.[13] The resulting plans reflected the wartime concern for 'Liberty' whilst emphasising the collected

---

[5] F. Aimone, 2010. The 1918 Influenza Epidemic in New York City: A Review of the Public Health Response. *Public Health Reports*, 125(3): 71–9.

[6] *New York Evening Post*, September 19, 1918.

[7] A. Keeling, 2009. 'When the City is a Great Field Hospital': The Influenza Pandemic of 1918 and the New York City Nursing Response. *Journal of Clinical Nursing*, 18(19): 2732–8.

[8] *New York Tribune*, September 29, 1918; *New York Times*, September 19, 1918.

[9] Department of Health of the City of New York, 1919. *Annual Report for the Calendar Year 1918*. New York, NY: William Bratter, Inc., p. 210.

[10] S. Jobs, 2013. *Welcome Home, Boys! Military Victory Parades in New York City 1899–1946*. Frankfurt am Main: Campus Verlag, p. 217.

[11] M. Bogart, 1989. *Public Sculpture and the Civic Ideal in New York City*. Chicago, IL: University of Chicago Press, p. 276.

[12] Mayor's Committee on a Permanent War Memorial, 1919. *Report of the Mayor's Committee*. New York, NY: s.n.

[13] *New York Tribune*, November 24, 1918; *New York Times*, November 24, 1918.

purpose of the nation that the war had seemingly generated. The three elements of the memorial avenue were; the 'Arch of Victory' located on 24th Street on Fifth Avenue, measuring over 30 metres high, depicting allegorical figures of Democracy and Justice and exhibiting panels commemorating the efforts at home and on the battlefield; the 'Arch of Jewels' on 60th Street, a columned gateway decorated with over 20,000 pieces of crystal, lit up by searchlights at night, and an American flag draped along its centre; and the 'Court of the Dead', outside the New York Public Library, where the passing parade could honour the fallen. The 'Court of the Dead' was comprised of two pylons, bearing the emblems of United States divisions and depicting shields, spears and palm leaves, connected by a purple sheath, upon which the names of battles fought by American troops were etched in gold. For the return of the New York regiments, 189 wreaths, one from each of the city's draft boards, were placed at the foot of the monument.

The completion of these structures was not reached by the time some of the troops had begun to return. Regardless, it was this redesigned Fifth Avenue that heralded the return of some of New York's servicemen. The 15th New York National Guard Regiment, rechristened as 369th Infantry Regiment for the war, were the first of the city's own recruits to come back from the now peaceful European theatre of operations.[14] The 369th had garnered a fine reputation for their exploits serving within the French Army, acquiring the nickname the 'Harlem Rattlers' and later the 'Harlem Hellfighters'. Though forbidden from engaging in combat under the segregation policies of the United States Army, the 369th were posted to front line positions as part of the French military effort upon their arrival in the warzone. Their return to New York on 17 February 1919 illustrated how communities used concepts of 'Americanisation' to demonstrate their place within the nation.[15] Indeed, Du Bois proclaimed the returning troops in 1919 as 'soldiers of democracy' who should 'return fighting' for that right in their own country.[16] This procession, attended by hundreds of thousands from the city, was used as a means of emphasising the role of African Americans within wider society:

> Here is a regiment of black men, who won more distinction as individuals and as a regiment than any other unit in the New York Guard, and perhaps more than any other single unit in the whole American army ... We wonder how many people who are opposed to giving the Negro his full citizenship rights could watch the Fifteenth on its march up the Avenue and not feel either shame or alarm?[17]

---

[14] A. Little, 1936. *From Harlem to the Rhine: The Story of New York's Colored Volunteers*. New York, NY: Covici Friede, p. 357.

[15] *New York Call*, February 17, 1919.

[16] W.E.B. Du Bois, 1919. Returning Soldiers. *The Crisis*, 18(1): 13.

[17] *New York Call*, February 22, 1919.

Sections of the mainstream city press also regarded this return of the 369th as representing the wider cause of equality within the United States.[18] A similar process could be witnessed in the homecoming parades of New York's 77th Infantry Division, known initially as the 'Liberty Division'; on its return it was lauded as the 'Melting Pot' Division, for its apparent demonstration of unity amongst a diverse populace.[19] The parade of the 77th Division on 7 May 1919 served to reaffirm these specific ideas of citizenship. The 77th Division were thereby extolled as an example of valour and patriotism for all of New York's residents:

> Better, more thoughtful, more loyal citizens they are for their warring – the men of the 77th. And whereas New York City sent forth a heterogeneous mass, she has welcomed back a unified class, annealed like tested steel in the fires that burn out impurities – the fires that leave the American wholly American.[20]

To welcome home these wholly 'American' New Yorkers, Fifth Avenue, decorated with its classically inspired architectural pieces, provided a suitable locale where citizens could demonstrate their own allegiance through spectatorship and support. The spectacle was one that all sections of the metropolis could contribute to. Indeed, for the return of the 27th Infantry Division in March 1919, stores along Fifth Avenue were all draped in the national flag whilst one store used its shop frontage to display the 'stars and stripes' which measured five stories high.[21] The homecoming parades provided a highly structured means of identification for the citizens of the city but enabled communities to associate themselves with the service and sacrifice for the nation.

The grand architecture for the returning troops was removed by the summer of 1919. Nevertheless, after the homecoming events this reciprocal form of remembrance was demonstrated in the construction of the monuments and memorials in the city. Despite a centralised programme of remembrance issued by the Mayor's Office, New York residents formed themselves into particular 'communities of mourning' which echoed official ideas of national identity but utilised these to state their place within the nation.[22] Indeed, as the plans for a grand memorial floundered it was within these individual locales that the memory of the war was maintained. The failure to secure a central commemorative site for

---

[18]   *New York Times*, February 18, 1919; *New York Tribune*, February 18, 1919.

[19]   *New York Times*, May 4, 1919.

[20]   A. McKeogh, 1919. *The Victorious 77th Division (New York's Wwn) in the Argonne Fight*. New York, NY: John H. Eggers, Co., p. 30.

[21]   New York Mayor's Committee of Welcome, 1919. *Review and Parade of the 27th Division*. New York, NY: s.n.

[22]   J.M. Winter, 1995. Communities of Mourning. In F. Coetzee and M. Shevin-Coetzee (eds), *Authority, Identity and the Social History of the Great War*. Providence, RI: Berghahn Books, pp. 325–51.

the war demonstrated the problems of governing within a democratic city ridden with financial and political self-interests. By the spring of 1919 the Mayor's Committee had declared a period of consultation and had opened out the design of a city monument to the war dead to competition.[23] By December 1919, the process had resulted in three separate designs offered for approval:

- The construction of a 'Liberty Bridge' over the Hudson River between the Lower West Side of Manhattan and Jersey City.
- The construction of a 'Liberty Hall' in Midtown Manhattan which would operate as a veterans centre and as a convention site.
- The construction of a 'Liberty Arch' which would be erected in downtown Manhattan and serve as a reminder of the war dead.

Immediately on announcement, the flaws of many of these schemes were highlighted. Principal in all three proposals was the cost. The purchasing of real estate in Manhattan would ensure the outlay for any project located there would be exorbitant.[24] Later proposals that involved disruption to existing hotels and restaurants in Manhattan and a large-scale memorial in Central Park were also rejected on the basis of cost, access and aesthetics.[25] By 1921, the plans for a memorial for the city were in disarray, with no firm plan of action and an absence of support. However, by April 1922 a final effort to construct a large memorial in Central Park, designed by Thomas Hastings, was forwarded and a public fundraising campaign was initiated.[26] Despite donations of nearly $300,000, due to the cost of the project, which was estimated at over $700,000, as well as persistent criticism of both the design and the disruption to the city's park, the plan was postponed indefinitely by 1924.

Remembering America

One of the prominent criticisms of the permanent war memorial scheme was that it did not reflect the way in which the war had forged a new 'Americanized' city. Such an insistence on a commitment to the principles of the nation was particularly pertinent in the post-war fears of Bolshevik and anarchist subterfuge (the 'Red Scare', 1919–1921). The drive for 'Americanisation' during the war manifested itself into a programme of surveillance of suspect groups after 1918. In New York, political radicals were targeted by the Lusk Committee, which was formed through the New York State Senate in March 1919 and headed by Clayton Lusk (1872–

---

23 *New York Tribune*, December 10, 1919.

24 *American Art News*, April 24, 1920, p. 6.

25 *New York Times*, February 28, 1920.

26 Mayor's Committee on a Permanent War Memorial, 1923. *Submitting the Memorial Project and New Playground Area to Be Added to the Central Park*. New York, NY: Brown.

1959) and former head of the Committee on Aliens for the Mayor's Committee on National Defense, Archibald E. Stevenson. The Lusk Committee carried out raids on schools and institutions suspected of socialist sympathies, held public hearings and distributed membership lists of socialist parties to the authorities.[27] The fear of subversives was exacerbated in June 1919 after the discovery of an anarchist plot to send explosives to businessmen and politicians across the nation.[28] In New York, two suspected bombers were killed in their attempt to detonate a device outside the home of Judge Charles C. Nott Jr (1869–1957).[29] The attacks led Attorney General Alexander Palmer (1872–1936) to initiate further raids and arrests on radical political groups within the United States. In turn, the 'Palmer Raids' led to growing discontentment regarding political repression which culminated in the detonation of a large bomb, killing 38 people and damaging financial institutions on Wall Street on 16 September 1920.[30] This political violence occurred simultaneously with racial attacks on African Americans across the United States, particularly in the summer of 1919, as the post-war settlement seemingly failed to address the underlying tensions within the state.

In such circumstances, 'Americanisation' became the goal of public and private enterprises in New York seeking to ensure absolute loyalty to the nation. In this assessment, the 'melting pot' model of the metropolis had failed and the drive for 'one hundred per cent Americanism' was required. This assessment was also associated with veterans groups in New York, which after the end of the war became increasingly vocal within the metropolis and across the wider nation on what it meant to be a citizen. The ending of the war had brought a greater degree of scrutiny towards the private patriotic associations that had formed to demand preparedness and police the draft. Indeed, the National Security League and the American Protective League were subject to investigation in the early 1920s regarding financial affairs and their political involvement. The mantle of protecting America was taken by veterans groups who directed their ire against the perceived weakness of a diverse nation and the fear of Bolshevik activism within a disloyal immigrant community. Groups such as the American Legion (founded in 1919 by returning soldiers), the Gold Star Mothers (founded in 1919 to honour the women whose sons died in the service of their country), and the Veterans of Foreign Wars (founded in 1914 as a lobby group for former soldiers), all campaigned for the continuance of the 'spirit' of the war. These issues were reflected in the construction of memorials within the city, as veterans groups took an interest as to how the war should be remembered.

---

[27]   Joint Legislative Committee of the State of New York Investigating Seditious Activities, 1919. *Testimony of Ludwig C.A.K. Martens*. New York, NY: s.n.

[28]   *New York Times*, June 4, 1919.

[29]   *New York Tribune*, June 3, 1919.

[30]   B. Gage, 2009. *The Day Wall Street Exploded: A Story of America in Its First Age of Terror*. Oxford: Oxford University Press, p. 5.

The most extensive veterans' memorial structure proposed for the city was the Victory Hall, a grand edifice that was designed to occupy an entire block between Lexington and Park Avenues and 41st and 42nd Streets. The building was designed as an imposing monument for the men and women who served in the United States Army during the conflict. It would comprise of an arena which would seat 20,000, numerous meeting rooms, a swimming pool and a rifle range. It would be replete with bronze plaques naming the dead and house a record of the service of United States citizens in the war.[31] The organisation behind the project was comprised of politicians and veterans with business and political connections in the city and they succeeded in gathering support for the project in its initial planning. However, they soon floundered under both the cost and the accusations of elitism, as an institution in the centre of Manhattan was criticised for not providing the universal idea of service that the conflict had promoted.[32] To deflect such accusations, the group behind the Victory Hall petitioned to have their own burial of an 'Unknown Soldier', as a symbol of democratic representation, replicating the internment at the National Cemetery in Arlington, Virginia.[33] Such a proposal was swiftly dismissed by government officials as it was regarded as potentially challenging or confusing the national commemoration.[34]

It was on a local level that the veterans concerns found their greatest expression as local communities across the city began seeking to commemorate the service of local men in the United States Army. In those sections of New York that had shown themselves to be 'one hundred per cent American', a desire to mark their patriotism and loyalty was expressed. This drive emanated from the members of the local draft board, local businessmen and the families of those whose relatives had been killed. However, the body controlling the erection of public or private monuments in New York on public property was the Art Commission, which was established in 1898 to curtail the profusion of individual monuments and establish aesthetic principles for the construction of artwork in the metropolis.[35] The Art Commission's board was composed of the President of the Metropolitan Museum of Art, the President of the New York Public Library, the President of the Brooklyn Institute of Arts and Sciences, three artists and three 'lay' members unattached to the arts profession. The commission possessed the power to accept, veto and request alterations on any proposed structure in the city. Directly after 1918 and lasting throughout the 1920s, the Commission's main source of work was concerned with the erection of war memorials in communities across the city. Groups and

---

[31] *Victory Hall Association Records, 1920–1921.* New York Public Library, MSS Col 3165.

[32] *Brooklyn Daily Eagle*, November 28, 1920; *New York Times*, February 28, 1920.

[33] M. Snell, (ed.) 2008. *Unknown Soldiers: The American Expeditionary Forces in Memory and Remembrance.* Kent, OH: Kent State University Press.

[34] *New York Times*, November 20, 1920.

[35] M. Bogart, 2006. *The Politics of Urban Beauty: New York and its Art Commission.* Chicago: University of Chicago Press, p. 25.

organisations desiring to build a monument on public land were required to obtain permission from the Commission on issues of design and location. Each proposal for a memorial required a map, plans and designs to be submitted alongside a written description of the costs and details of the memorial.[36]

Being American in the City

The careful control over the appearance of the city's memorials enabled the promotion of a singular vision of what the war meant for New York and its residents. Whilst social groups and some émigré organisations called for the construction of community halls and community facilities, a dominant movement within the Art Commission dismissed these proposals as potentially divisive and against 'the spirit of remembrance'. The American Legion, the Gold Star Mothers and the Veterans of Foreign Wars were sympathetic to this principle and offered financial support and guidance to districts planning their own 'suitable' memorials.[37] These projects were, thereby, restricted to a number of forms which were thought most suited to communicate these concepts. Designs such as flagpoles, tablets, allegorical statues and soldier statues of 'artistic' merit were considered appropriate and consistently found favour in developing a scheme of commemoration that reflected the correct 'spirit'. For example, permission was granted to erect a memorial in Staten Island Borough Hall which consisted of a small bronze tablet costing $1000, listing the names of the dead and engravings which were 'emblematic of the glory of the flag'.[38] Similarly, the substantial project in Highland Park, Brooklyn, which saw the artist Pietro Montana (1890–1978) create a bronze sculpture entitled 'Dawn of Glory', an allegorical figure representing the spirit of service, at a cost of over $15,000, was regarded as suitable by the Art Commission.[39]

In this manner, plans for meeting places, libraries and public amenities were rejected as they were considered to encourage and perpetuate ethnic, cultural or religious enclaves within society. The remembrance of the war was considered to require a dedication to unity, the principles of liberty and an assertion of 'one hundred per cent Americanism'. The ability of the Art Commission to control these local memorials was an inevitable by-product of the inability of communities to obtain private land for construction. As the price of real-estate was at a premium, and the future progress of areas still unknown, there was a

---

[36] Art Commission of the City of New York, 1904. *The Art Commission of the City of New York: Its Powers, Organization and Methods*. New York, NY: Martin Brown.

[37] E. Root, 1919. The Memorial Spirit and the Future of America. *American Magazine of Art*, 10(11): 407–410.

[38] Borough Hall Tablet, Richmond – 1028 A, Design Commission of New York. Archives and Photographs Collection.

[39] Highland Park War Memorial, Brooklyn – 1188 A, Design Commission of New York. Archives and Photographs Collection.

marked hesitancy in building memorials which would subsequently become obstacles to housing, traffic or development. As such, the only recourse groups had to ensure the building of their memorial was to request permission from the Parks Commission to build structures in the city's parks, squares and gardens. As memorials on public property, the final decision on their form would lie entirely with the Art Commission. Such an arrangement was also favoured by the new Park Commissioner for the city, Francis Gallatin, who was appointed to the post in 1919. Gallatin argued that the memorials and monuments in the city's public spaces could do more to 'Americanize' the city's foreign-born residents than 'all the sermons on Americanisation'.[40]

Local memorials were rapidly constructed within all five boroughs. By 1921, the total number of these local war memorials numbered nearly 50. By the 1930s, there were approximately 100 memorials. Communities were desirous of connecting themselves with the war effort and quickly raised funds to support the work of the various local 'War Monument Committees' and 'Victory Associations' which were initiated to oversee developments. The residents of Long Island raised the majority of the $20,000 required to build a memorial in their area through a circus held for the community in 1920.[41] To acquire the funds for the memorial in Highland Park, Brooklyn, the local memorial committee organised block parties for local businesses and political groups as well as the Polish and Italian communities in the area.[42] This process reveals the reasons for the enthusiasm in which local areas responded to the construction of memorials; just as participation in the conflict, either on the home front or on the battlefields, confirmed a status as 'American', so too did the commemoration of the war dead through memorialisation. In this manner, neighbourhood interests fused with official ideas as it had during the war as communities in the city utilised the call for 'Americanisation' to their own advantage.

This is most aptly demonstrated in the profusion of 'Doughboy' statues in the city; stone or bronze renditions of the archetypal American soldier that reflected a common cause and purpose whilst providing a homogenous image of national identity.[43] The statue was popular within New York, with ten areas selecting a version of the statue as their contribution to the act of commemoration. The community around Greenwich Village funded the $10,000 required for the construction of a bronze 'Doughboy' in Abingdon Square, whilst memorial associations organised the construction of the Chelsea Park and De Witt Clinton

---

[40] *New York Times*, February 18, 1923; *New York Times*, March 4, 1923.

[41] *Long Island City Memorial League*, Queens Library and Archives, 295H.

[42] H. Rockefeller, 1924. *History of the Memorial Monument in Highland Park and Memoir of the Soldiers who Served in the World War from the Twenty-Second Assembly District of Brooklyn.* New York, NY: s.n.

[43] Keene, *Doughboys*, p. 12; J. Wingate, 2005. Over the Top: The Doughboy in World War I Memorials and Visual Culture. *American Art*, 19(2): 29–32.

Park 'Doughboys'.[44] The 'Doughboy' statue was also erected across the other boroughs of the city, with the Woodside Doughboy in Queens paid for by the local chapter of the Gold Star Mothers. This memorial was unveiled in November 1921 and contains a dedication to the 'Unknown Soldier', 'to those unknown heroes of the community who died in the service'.[45] In this manner, the Doughboy statue cemented the image of 'one hundred per cent American' for communities in the city. For the veterans groups, the figure reflected the martial spirit which brought the nation together as one; for the city authorities, such sculptures were both aesthetically suitable and politically expedient. However, for the areas where these figurines were constructed, they offered tangible evidence of their community's place within the United States. In a post-war era where loyalty and allegiance were still the object of state surveillance, New York's diverse populace could demonstrate their identity through the memorials to the Great War.

Such symbols of inclusivity did not manifest themselves for all sections of the metropolis's population. The efforts of the American Legion and the Gold Star Mothers, whose posts throughout the city sponsored a third of the memorials on public property, were not extended to the city's African American servicemen.[46] The Gold Star Mothers did not allow African American members and the American Legion and Veterans of Foreign Wars opted for segregated posts, mirroring the racial division of the army. Neither did these organisations sponsor memorials for African American troops as they had elsewhere within New York. Despite this absence of support, African American areas of Harlem and Brooklyn participated in fundraising drives and campaigns to construct memorials to their dead.[47] These commemorative structures of tablets and plaques mirrored the aesthetics of the pieces favoured by the Art Commission but lacked the same ideological investment. Where there was a degree of similarity was in the meanings attached to these constructions by those communities. Commemorative architecture was invested with the capacity to anchor a group within the city and the wider nation; as a declaration of citizenship and nationality. Inevitably, it was the 369th that attracted the majority of focus. Sites in Harlem were renamed after members of the 'Hellfighters'. Indeed, in 1925, the Dorrance Brooks Square was dedicated to the last member of the unit to die in France in November 1918.[48] The Proctor-Hopson Memorial Circle was dedicated in the early 1930s to honour John Proctor and Arthur Hobson, the first members to die during the war.[49]

---

[44]   *New York Times*, September 22, 1919; *New York Times*, June 23, 1921.

[45]   *New York Times*, September 21, 1921.

[46]   J.D. Keene, 2008. The Memory of the Great War in the African American Community. In M. Snell (ed.) *Unknown Soldiers: The American Expeditionary Force in Memory and Remembrance*. Kent, OH: Kent State University Press, pp. 60–79.

[47]   *New York Age*, January 3, 1920; *New York Amsterdam News*, April 11, 1925.

[48]   *New York Age*, June 13, 1925.

[49]   *New York Amsterdam News*, October 19, 1932; *New York Amsterdam News*, October 26, 1932.

The activities of the 369th did receive official acknowledgement with the incorporation of members of the regiment into the National Guard and the initial construction of a new armoury in the centre of Harlem at the intersection of 142nd Street and Fifth Avenue in 1924.[50] After successive additions, the dedication of the regimental headquarters in 1933 was greeted with enthusiasm by attendees who regarded the institution as a demonstration of the role of African Americans within national life.[51] However, continued segregation, the absence of official recognition and the failure to incorporate African American achievement into the wider commemoration within the city ensured that by the 1930s the use of the war to promote identity no longer held the same symbolic significance. The African American sections within the metropolis were able to exalt particular individuals as exemplars, but these figures remained purely within that community. For example, Colonel Charles Young (1863–1922), the first African American to achieve that rank, who was stationed on the Mexican border during the Great War, was honoured in the city with the dedication of an American Legion Post in Harlem as the Colonel Charles Young Post, No. 398.[52] Whilst the venue served to remind residents of their contribution in the 'great war for democracy' it was not a civics lesson which was shared by the entirety of the city or the nation.[53]

Whilst streets and squares in areas of the city were renamed in a process which was specifically for those areas, other sections of New York were renamed for the benefit of the majority. Across the metropolis, areas commemorating the heroes of the war were used to inculcate a sense of national pride within the European immigrant population of the city. Immediately after the end of the war, the city moved to rename the plaza facing Grand Central Station to Pershing Square, after the leader of the American Expeditionary Force General John Pershing (1860–1948).[54] This was followed in June 1919 by name changes to the city honouring the service of the ordinary 'Doughboys'. In the Dyckman area of the city, three small thoroughfares, all beginning on the south side of Dyckman Street between Broadway and the ferry landing at the bottom of Dyckman Street, were named Henshaw Street, Staff Street and Daniels Street, after soldiers from that area of the city. The Manhattan approach to Washington Bridge was renamed McNally Square, after a soldier and son of a policeman of the city who had died in France. Similarly, in West Harlem, a single block from 126th Street from old Manhattan Street to Claremont Avenue was named Moylan Place after William Moylan, a soldier who died in the war and who had resided in the block before the draft. In 1926, Latkin Square in the Bronx, which was bounded by 196th Street, Intervale Avenue, Home Street and Tiffany Street was re-titled after Private David Latkin,

---

[50] *New York Age*, November 15, 1924; *New York Amsterdam News*, November 15, 1924.

[51] *New York Age*, November 4, 1933.

[52] *New York Age*, May 6, 1922.

[53] *New York Age*, May 28, 1922; *New York New Amsterdam News*, May 30, 1923.

[54] *New York Times*, December 8, 1918.

one of the first Jewish soldiers from the city to die in the war.[55] Such a process of renaming, combined with the construction of memorials, ensured that the city was shrouded in mourning for the dead of the conflict. Indeed, the money raised for the central war memorial in the 1920s was invested in the construction of nine playgrounds across the city in the early 1930s, each bearing the name of a soldier who had died in the war.[56]

The renaming of the city to mark the sacrifice of servicemen materially embedded the concept of 'one hundred per cent American' within New York. In the decade following the cessation of hostilities, the metropolis was transformed as a centre of patriotic intent. Such a concept was emphasised as early as April 1919, during the campaign for the Victory Loan, which saw a further sale of war bonds to assist in the post-war recovery and reconstruction. In this drive of commercial patriotism, Bruce Barton (1886–1967), advertising executive and Republican politician, penned an uplifting, epic narrative of the city entitled *I am New York and This Is My Creed*.[57] In this account, readers are presented with the image of a soaring city whose bedrock is liberty, honour and loyalty; qualities that no matter the origin of the individual can be accessed to ensure their status as 'Americans'. Throughout the succeeding years, through commemoration and memorialisation, these ideas were demonstrated by authorities, organisations and communities themselves as a demonstration of their place within the nation. Such concepts were also reiterated with the unveiling of the statue to Father Francis Duffy (1871–1932) in Times Square in May 1937 (Figure 7.1).[58] Chaplain to the 69th, the 'Fighting Irish', Duffy had been involved in the conflict and risked his own life to retrieve the dead from the battlefield. Born in Canada and a Roman Catholic, Duffy was an immigrant to the United States but the statue masks such potential discordant identities. Whilst the statue features an ornate Celtic cross in the background, it is the figure of Duffy, decorated in the uniform of the United States Army that marks the piece as a dedication to the service and sacrifice for the nation.[59]

Conclusions

The physical and ideological transformation of New York was completed through the war and the post-war period. The alteration in both the perception and representation of the city provided a marked difference to the pre-war associations of alien subversives and un-American ideas. In this manner, the Great War had, therefore, made the city into a truly American metropolis. The politics of the post-

---

[55]   *New York Times*, December 6, 1926.

[56]   *New York Times*, July 15, 1934.

[57]   B. Barton, 1919. *I Am New York and This Is My Creed*. New York, NY: Bankers Trust Company.

[58]   *New York Tribune*, May 3, 1937.

[59]   *New York Times*, May 3, 1937.

Figure 7.1   Father Duffy Statue, Times Square, 1937.
Source: Library of Congress (LC-USZ62-123762).

war era that saw the restriction of immigration and the surveillance of suspect political groups continued the process of 'Americanisation' set in place during the conflict. Whereas the city at the turn of the century had appeared to offer little as evidence of commitment to the nation from a diverse citizenry, New York after 1918 possessed monuments and memorials to its sacrifices for the state. In this respect, the process of reforming an immigrant city into an American city, which had been advocated since the nineteenth century, was encouraged and accomplished by the changes initiated because of the global conflict after August 1914. This was not just a process of reshaping the city to suit the ideals of the authorities and private groups seeking homogenisation. Rather, immigrant groups themselves, even before the war, had regarded themselves as 'American', declaring principles of democracy and liberty to define their allegiance. During the conflict, whilst a singular idea of American identity had emerged which was promoted and insisted upon, communities in the city drew upon this ideal to restate their place and purpose in the nation. In the post-war era, this strengthened the value of once 'alien' groups, removed entirely the presence of German Americans and failed to include African Americans as part of the character and identity of the city and the nation. New York had become an American city, replete with the contradictions and celebrations of the country, through the trials and privations of warfare.

The significance of the war for the city would appear to be forgotten today. Despite the presence of over a hundred post-war memorials to the war dead of New York across the five boroughs, the conflict of 1914–1918 can be perceived to be ephemeral to the metropolis. The commemoration of the war has seemingly slipped from public consciousness and the once significant memorial architecture is perhaps now only to be glimpsed by the tourist or passed by the preoccupied office worker. The memorial to the wartime mayor, John Purroy Mitchel, located in Central Park on the eastern section of the reservoir, would reflect just these sentiments. Initiated in 1918, after the death of Mitchel and dedicated in 1928, the stele, bust and ornamental wall commemorates the life of the 'boy mayor' who served and died for his nation.[60] Now, the memorial is another Central Park curio, listed in guide books and itineraries, apparently divorced from its meaning and context. This is not evidence of the absence of the war within the modern city. Indeed, such a response is a testament to the success of the post-war remembrance of the conflict. The war served to integrate communities within the metropolis whilst providing those communities with their own statements of belonging. The absence of conflicting memories in the aftermath of the war would indicate the utility of such commemoration for the city as a whole. Forgetting the war was not a conscious act of avoiding a history where identity was policed, but evidence of the successful incorporation of that identity within the city. New York today is the metropolis that was reshaped by the war of 1914–1918, a conflict that the city was drawn into right from its outset, a war that made the city, its citizens and its place within the nation 'one hundred per cent American'.

---

[60] Mitchel Memorial Committee, 1918. *Mitchel Memorial Committee, Organized for the Erection of a Memorial to the Late Major John Purroy Mitchel. Minutes of the Organization. Meeting Held in the City hall, New York City, on Monday, July 29th, 1918.* New York, NY: s.n.

Bibliography

Newspapers, Magazines and Periodicals

America
American Art News
Brooklyn Daily Eagle
Daily Standard Union
Die Varheit
Deutsch-Amerika
Baltimore Sun
Cornell Daily Sun
Forverts
Four Minute Men Bulletin
Fraye Arbeter Shtime
Gaelic American
Harper's Weekly
Il Proletario
Internationale Arbeiter Chronik
Irish American
Irish World
Journal of Commerce
Life Magazine
Literary Digest
Morgen Zhurnal
Narodni List
New York Age
New York American
New York Amsterdam News
New York Call
New York Evening Journal
New York Evening Mail
New York Evening Post
New York Evening Telegram
New York Evening Telegraph
New York Herald
New York Morning Telegraph
New York Sun
New York Times
New York Tribune

New York World
New Yorker Herold
New Yorker Staats-Zeitung
New Yorker Volkszeitung
Novyi Mir
Outlook
St. Louis Globe-Democrat
The Evening World
The Survey
The Nation
The Voice
Wall Street Journal
Washington Post

Archives

Borough Hall Tablet, Richmond – 1028 A, Design Commission of New York. Archives and Photographs Collection.
Duryea War Relief. European War Scrapbooks, 1914–1918. New York Public Library, MSS Col 952.
Highland Park War Memorial, Brooklyn – 1188 A, Design Commission of New York. Archives and Photographs Collection.
Letter from Theodore Roosevelt to Charles Evans Hughes. August 9, 1916. Theodore Roosevelt Collection. MS Am 1540 (381). Houghton Library, Harvard University.
Long Island City Memorial League, Queens Library and Archives, 295H.
Real Estate – Citizen Preparedness Parade, May 13, 1916. Museum of the City of New York, 96.79.13.
The Mayor's Committee on National Defense. 1917a. *The Mayor's Committee on National Defense: Committee on Aliens wants Good American Volunteers for American Service among New Americans.* Princeton University Poster Collection, Map Case 1, Drawer 8, Folder 5.
The Mayor's Committee on National Defense. 1917b. *To All Aliens.* Library of Congress, POS-WWI-US, no. 435.
Victory Hall Association Records, 1920–1921. New York Public Library, MSS Col 3165.

Secondary Sources

Abbott, G. 1917. *The Immigrant and the Community.* New York, NY: Century Company.

Adler, C. 1921. *Jacob Henry Schiff: A Biographical Sketch*. New York, NY: American Jewish Committee.

Adler, J.O. 1919. *History of the Seventy Seventh Division: August 25th, 1917 to November 11th, 1918*. New York, NY: W.H. Crawford Company.

Agstner, R. 2006. *Austria (-Hungary) and its Consulates in the United States of America since 1820*. Zurich: Lit Verlag GmbH and Co. KG Wien.

Aimone, F. 2010. The 1918 Influenza Epidemic in New York City: A Review of the Public Health Response. *Public Health Reports*, 125(3): 71–9.

Albert, B. 2002. *South America and the First World War: The Impact of the War on Brazil, Argentina, Peru and Chile*. Cambridge: Cambridge University Press.

Aleandri, E. 2002. *Little Italy*. Charleston, SC: Arcadia Publishing.

Alexander, C. 1962. Prophet of American Racism: Madison Grant and the Nordic Myth. *Phylon*, 23(1): 73–90.

Alexander, J. 2004. *Ethnic Pride, American Patriotism: Slovaks and Other New Immigrants in the Interwar Era*. Philadelphia, PA: Temple University Press.

Alexander, S.L. 2012. *An Army of Lions: The Civil Rights Struggle Before the NAACP*. Philadelphia, PA: University of Pennsylvania Press.

Alphaud, G. 1914. *L'action allemande aux États-Unis de la mission Dernburg à l'incident Dumba*. Paris: Payot et Cie.

American Alliance for Labor and Democracy. 1918. *Red, White and Blue Book of the American Labor Movement: Organized Labor's Record in Relation to the War as Shown in the Official Documents*. New York, NY: American Alliance for Labor and Democracy.

American Artists' Committee of One Hundred. 1916. *Exhibition of Contemporary French Art: For the Relief Fund for the Families of French Soldier Artists. Ritz-Carlton Ballroom, New York, January, 1916*. New York, NY: Knickerbocker Press.

American Federation of Labor. 1917. *American Labor's Position in Peace or in War*. Washington, DC: Executive Council of the American Federation of Labor.

American Federation of Labor. 1918. *To the Workers of Free America: An Appeal by the Executive Council of the American Federation of Labor, February 17, 1918*. New York, NY: American Alliance for Labor and Democracy.

American Truth Society. 1914. *Plan and Scope of American Truth Society*. New York, NY: American Truth Society.

American Truth Society. 1916a. *The Telegram to Woodrow Wilson, President of the United States, and the Answer to Jeremiah A. O'Leary, President of the American Truth Society*. New York, NY: American Truth Society.

American Truth Society. 1916b. *A Statement Issued by the American Truth Society in Defense of its President against an Unjust Attack Made upon Him by the President of the United States*. New York, NY: American Truth Society.

American Union Against Militarism. 1917. *Conscription and the 'Conscientious Objector' to War: Facts Regarding Exemptions from Military Service under the Conscription Act*. New York, NY: American Union Against Militarism.

Anon. 1914. *Truth About Germany: Facts about the War*. New York, NY: Trow Press.

Anon. 1914. Our Baby Pictures. *The Crisis*, 8(6): 298–303.

Anon. 1914. Out of Africa I have Called my Son! *The Crisis*, 9(1): 26–7.

Anon. 1914. Men of the Month. *The Crisis*, 9(2): 68.

Anon. 1915. Russian Revolutionists and the War. *The Melting Pot*, 3(3): 20.

Anon. 1915. *Germany's War Mania: The Teutonic Point of View as Officially Stated by Her Leaders*. New York, NY: Dodd, Mead and Company.

Anon. 1916. New York's Parade for Preparedness. *The Survey*, 36: 196–7.

Anon. 1916. How the 'Hyphen' Voted. *The Literary Digest*, 53(22): 1394.

Anon. 1917. From Coast to Coast. *American Jewish Chronicle*, 3(20): 536.

Anon. 1917. The Riot in East St. Louis. *The Crisis*, 14(4): 172–6.

Anon. 1917. Peace. *The Messenger*, 1: 7.

Anon. 1917. The Negro Silent Parade. *The Crisis*, 14(5): 241–4.

Anon. 1917. Hillquit and the Lower East Side. *The Nation*, 105(2731): 475–6.

Anon. 1917. National Aspects of the Mayoralty Contest in New York City. *Current Opinion*, 63: 292–4.

Anon. 1917. Current Affairs: The New York Mayoralty Campaign. *The Class Struggle*, 1(4): 100–101.

Anon. 1917. *Remember! The Flag of Liberty! Support it! Buy U.S. Government Bonds*. New York, NY: Heywood, Strasser and Voigt Lithograph Company.

Anon. 1918. The Greatest Convention in the Annals of our International Union. *The Ladies' Garment Worker*, 9(6): 3.

Anon. 1918. Our New York Letter. *The Advocate*, 55: 321.

Anon. 1918. Labor Day Celebration. *The Ladies' Garment Worker*, 17(47): 6.

Anon. 1918. Notes. *American Magazine of Arts*, 20(1): 29.

Aquilano, B. 1925. *L'Ordine Figli d'Italia in America*. New York, NY: Societa Tipografica Italiana.

Army and Navy Field Comfort Committee. 1917. *U.S. Army and Navy Bazaar, Grand Central Palace*. New York, NY: Carey Print Lith.

Art Commission of the City of New York. 1904. *The Art Commission of the City of New York: Its Powers, Organization and Methods*. New York, NY: Martin Brown.

Ash, M. 1897. *The Greater New York Charter as Enacted in 1897*. Albany, NY: Weed-Parsons.

Austro-Hungarian Consulate-General. 1916. *Austria-Hungary and the War*. New York, NY: Austro-Hungarian Consulate-General.

Axelrod, A. 2009. *Selling the Great War: The Making of American Propaganda*. New York, NY: Palgrave Macmillan.

Barbeau, A.E. and Henri, F. 1996. *The Unknown Soldiers: African-American Troops in World War I*. New York, NY: Da Capo Press.

Barton, B. 1919. *I Am New York and This Is My Creed*. New York, NY: Bankers Trust Company.

Batchelder, R. 1918. *Camp Upton*. Boston, MA: Small, Maynard and Company.

Bauer, Y. 1974. *My Brother's Keeper: A History of the American Jewish Joint Distribution Committee, 1929–1939*. Philadelphia, PA: Jewish Publication Society of America.

Beard, C.A. 1913. *Municipal Year Book of the City of New York*. New York, NY: J.W. Pratt Co.

Becker, M. 1914. Hearst: 'My, What Inhuman Brutes these Europeans Are!'. *The Masses*, 5(12): 14.

Bencivenni, M. 2011. *Italian Immigrant Radical Culture: The Idealism of the Sovversivi in the United States, 1890–1940*. New York, NY: New York University Press.

Bénézet, L.P. 1918. *The World War and What Was Behind It*. New York, NY: Scott, Foresman and Company.

Berkman, A. 1917. America and the Russian Revolution. *Mother Earth*, 12(3): 75–7.

Berkman, A. and Goldman, E. 1917. *Anarchism on Trial: Speeches of Alexander Berkman and Emma Goldman Before the United States District Court in the City of New York, July, 1917*. New York, NY: Mother Earth Publishing Association.

Berlin, I., Leslie, E. and Meyer, G. 1917. *Let's All Be Americans Now*. New York, NY: Waterson, Berlin and Snyder.

Birmingham, G. 1915. *Crowns for the Valiant*. New York, NY: Commission for Relief in Belgium.

Blake, A.M. 1999. *How New York Became American, 1890–1924*. Baltimore, MD: Johns Hopkins University Press.

Board of Education, New York. 1916. *School Library Bulletin*, 9(5).

Board of Elections. 1916. *Maps Showing the Assembly Districts of the City of New York*. New York, NY: Board of Elections.

Board of Elections. 1917. *Annual Report of the Board of Elections of the City of New York, for the Year Ending 1917*. New York, NY: Board of Elections.

Board of Trustees. 1916. *Annual Report of the Board of Trustees of the German Hospital and Dispensary in the City of New York*. New York, NY: The Hospital and Dispensary.

Board of Trustees. 1918. *Annual Report of the Lenox Hill Hospital*. New York, NY: The Hospital and Dispensary.

Bodnar, J. 1992. *Remaking America: Public Memory, Commemoration, and Patriotism in the Twentieth Century*. Princeton, NJ: Princeton University Press.

Bodnar, J. 1994. Public Memory in an American City: Commemoration in Cleveland. In J.R Gillis (ed.), *Commemorations: The Politics of National Identity*. Princeton, NJ: Princeton University Press, pp. 74–89.

Bogart, M. 1989. *Public Sculpture and the Civic Ideal in New York City, 1890–1930*. Chicago, IL: University of Chicago Press.

Bogart, M. 2006. *The Politics of Urban Beauty: New York and its Art Commission*. Chicago, IL: University of Chicago Press.

Bogen, E. 1987. *Immigration in New York*. New York, NY: Praeger.

Bohemian National Alliance of America. 1915. *The Position of the Bohemians (Czechs) in the European War*. Chicago, IL: Bohemian National Alliance of America.

Bohn, F. 1917. The Re-election of Wilson. *The Masses*, 9(3): 15–16.

Booth, C. 1903. *Life and Labour of the People in London: Summary*. London: Macmillan.

Booth, M.B. 1891. *New York's Inferno Explored: Scenes Full of Pathos Powerfully Portrayed*. New York, NY: Salvation Army.

Bouvier, V. 2001. *Whose America? The War of 1898 and the Battles to Define the Nation*. Westport, CT: Praeger.

Breckenridge, C.A. 1914. Down with Militarism! Up with the Rights of Man. *Mother Earth*, 9(6): 185–7.

Breckinridge, H. 1916. Universal Service as the Basis of National Unity and National Defense. *Proceedings of the Academy of Political Science in the City of New York*, 6(4): 436–41.

British War Relief Association. 1917. *How to Make Surgical Dressings*. New York, NY: British War Relief Association.

Browne, J.H. 1869. *The Great Metropolis: A Mirror of New York*. Hartford, CT: American Publishing Company.

Bruére, H. 1916. *New York City's Administrative Progress, 1914–1916: A Survey of Various Departments under the Jurisdiction of the Mayor*. New York, NY: M.B. Brown.

Buckley, J.P. 1976. *The New York Irish: Their View of American Foreign Policy, 1914–1921*. New York, NY: Arno Press.

Budreau, L. 2010. *Bodies of War: World War I and the Politics of Commemoration in America, 1919–1933*. New York, NY: New York University Press, 2010.

Bureau of Applied Economics. 1920. *Changes in Cost of Living and Prices, 1914 to 1920*. Washington, DC: Government Printing Office.

Bureau of Education. 1919. *Americanization Work in New York State: As Outlined by the Bureau of Immigrant Education*. Washington, DC: Government Printing Office.

Bureau of Labor. 1922. *National War Labor Board: A History of its Formation and Activities, Together with its Awards and the Documents of Importance in the Record of its Development*. Washington, DC: Government Printing Office.

Bureau of Labor Statistics. 1915. *Wholesale Prices, 1890 to 1914*. Washington, DC: Government Printing Office.

Bureau of the Census. 1894. *Vital Statistics of New York City and Brooklyn: Covering a Period of Six Years Ending May 31, 1890*. Washington, DC: Government Printing Office.

Bureau of the Census. 1902. *Abstract of the Twelfth Census of the United States, 1900*. Washington, DC: Government Printing Office.

Bureau of the Census. 1913. *Thirteenth Census of the United States Taken in the Year 1910*. Washington, DC: Government Printing Office.

Burgess, J.W., Schrader, F.F. and Sloane, W.M. 1914. *Germany's Just Cause, as Viewed by Eminent Native American Writers & Thinkers*. New York, NY: The Fatherland.

Burk, K. 1979. The Diplomacy of Finance: British Financial Missions to the United States 1914–1918. *The Historical Journal*, 22(2): 351–72.

Burnstein, D.E. 2006. *Next to Godliness: Confronting Dirt and Despair in Progressive Era New York City*. Urbana, IL: University of Illinois Press.

Burrows, E.G. and Wallace, M. 1999. *Gotham: A History of New York City to 1898*. Oxford: Oxford University Press.

Cahalane, C. 1914. *Police Practice and Procedure*. New York, NY: E.P. Dutton.

Cahan, A. 1896. *Yekl: A Tale of the New York Ghetto*. New York, NY: D. Appleton and Company.

Capek, T. 1915. The Slovaks of Hungary. In T. Capek (ed.), *Bohemia under Hapsburg Misrule: A Study of the Ideals and Aspirations of the Bohemian and Slovak Peoples, as they Relate to and are Affected by the Great European War*. New York, NY: Fleming H. Revell, pp. 113–22.

Capek, T. 1921. *The Čech (Bohemian) Community of New York*. New York, NY: The Czechoslovak Section of America's Making, Inc.

Capozzola, C. 2002. The Only Badge Needed Is Your Patriotic Fervor: Vigilance, Coercion, and the Law in World War I America. *The Journal of American History*, 88(4): 1354–82.

Capozzola, C. 2008. *Uncle Sam Wants You: World War I and the Making of the Modern American Citizen*. Oxford: Oxford University Press.

Carlson, O. and Bates, E.S. 1936. *Hearst: Lord of San Simeon*. New York, NY: The Viking Press.

Carter, W. 1916. *The Necessity of Preparedness: An Address on National Preparedness by Rev. Wm. Carter in a Debate with Rev. Washington Gladden at the Broadway Tabernacle, New York City, February 8th, 1916*. New York, NY: National Security League.

Case, H.J. 1916. How Organization Helps. *The American Red Cross Magazine*, 11: 396–401.

Casement, R. 1914. *The Crime Against Ireland and How the War May Right It*. New York, NY: s.n.

Casement, R. 1915. *The Crime Against Europe: A Possible Outcome of the War of 1914*. Philadelphia: Celtic Press.

Chamberlain, M. 1914. The Clutch of Militarism: Some Reactions of the War upon Our Immigrant Population. *The Survey*, 33: 44–72.

Chickering, R. 2007. *The Great War and Urban Life in Germany: Freiburg, 1914–1918*. Cambridge: Cambridge University Press.

Chickering, R. and Förster, S. (eds). 2000. *Great War, Total War: Combat and Mobilization on the Western Front, 1914–1918*. Cambridge: Cambridge University Press.

Cianfarra, C. 1904. *Il diario di un emigrato*. New York, NY: Tipografia dell'Araldo Italiano.

Citizens' Protective League of New York. 1900. *Story of the Riot*. New York, NY: Arno Press.

Čizmić, I. 1970. Dobrovoljacki pokret Jugoslovenskih iseljenika u sad u Prvom svjetskom ratu. *Historijski Zbornik*, 23–24: 21–43.

Clarke, I. 1918. *American Women and the World War*. New York, NY: D. Appleton and Company.

Coffman, E. 1968. *The War to End All Wars: The American Military Experience in World War I*. Oxford: Oxford University Press.

Cohan, G.M. 1917. *Over There*. New York, NY: William Jerome Publishing Corporation.

Cohen, A.J. 2006. Bild und Spiegelbild: Deutschland in der russischen 'Russkoe slovo' (1907–1917). In D. Hermann (ed.), *Deutsche und Deutschland aus russischer Sicht 19./20. Jahrhundert: Von den Reformen Alexanders II bis zum Ersten Weltkrieg*. Munich: W. Fink, pp. 258–79.

Collman, C. 1915a. The Scandal of the Navy League. *The Fatherland*, 3(16): 271–3.

Collman, C. 1915b. *The War Plotters of Wall Street*. New York, NY: The Fatherland Corporation.

Collman, C. 1916a. Who Betrayed the Irish People? *The Fatherland*, 4(14): 211–12.

Collman, C. 1916b. Morgan's Great War Parade, May 13, 1916. *The Fatherland*, 4(15): 227–9.

Commission for Relief in Belgium. 1915a. *General Instructions*. New York, NY: Commission for Relief in Belgium.

Commission for Relief in Belgium. 1915b. *General Instructions for Making Contributions of Food, Clothing and Money*. New York, NY: Commission for Relief in Belgium.

Commission for Relief in Belgium. 1915c. *Clothe Belgium and Northern France*. New York, NY: Commission for Relief in Belgium.

Commission for Relief in Belgium. 1915d. *The Need of Belgium*. New York, NY: Commission for Relief in Belgium.

Commission for Relief in Belgium. 1915e. *Financial Statement*. New York, NY: Commission for Relief in Belgium.

Commission for Relief in Belgium: Woman's Section. 1915. *History of the Woman's Section of the Commission for Relief in Belgium*. New York, NY: Commission for Relief in Belgium.

Commissioners of Accounts. 1917. *The Pushcart Problem in New York City: Progress Toward its Solution and Need for Prohibition of Pushcart Peddling in the Vicinity of the Williamsburg and Manhattan Bridge Markets*. New York, NY: Brown.

Committee for Immigrants in America. 1915. *Professional Course for Service Among Immigrants: Prepared for the Use of Colleges and Universities, Schools of Civics and Philanthropy, to Fit Men and Women for Service Among Immigrants*. New York, NY: The Committee for Immigrants in America.

Committee for Immigrants in America. 1916. *Citizenship Syllabus: A Course of Study and Syllabus.* New York, NY: Committee for Immigrants in America.

Committee on Public Information. 1918a. *The Activities of the Committee on Public Information.* Washington, DC: Government Printing Office.

Committee on Public Information. 1918b. *The German-Bolshevik Conspiracy.* Washington, DC: Government Printing Office.

Committee on Public Information. 1918c. *The Kaiserite in America: One Hundred and One German Lies.* Washington, DC: Government Printing Office.

Committee on Regimental Affairs. 1915. *Bulletin of the First Training Regiment: The Business and Professional Men's Military Training Camps, Plattsburg, N.Y.* New York, NY: New York, NY: Wynkoop Hallenbeck Crawford.

Committee of the Political Federation of Slovaks. 1914. *An Open Letter Addressed to Count Michael Károlyi, Member of Hungarian Parliament on the Occasion of His American Voyage.* New York, NY: s.n.

Commons, J. 1918a. *German Socialists and the War.* New York, NY: American Alliance for Labor and Democracy.

Commons, J. 1918b. *Why Workingmen Support the War.* New York, NY: American Alliance for Labor and Democracy.

Congressional Record, House, 65th Congress, April 6, 1917.

Connelly, M. 2006. *Steady the Buffs: A Regiment, a Region and the Great War.* Oxford: Oxford University Press.

Conolly-Smith, 2008. P. Casting Teutonic Types from the Nineteenth Century to World War I: German Ethnic Stereotypes in Print, on Stage, and Screen. *Columbia Journal of American Studies*, 9: 48–73.

Conolly-Smith, P. 2009. Transforming an Ethnic Readership Through 'Word and Image': William Randolph Hearst's *Deutsches Journal* and New York's German-Language Press, 1895–1918. *American Periodicals: A Journal of History, Criticism and Bibliography*, 19(1): 66–84.

Coogan, J. 1981. *The End of Neutrality: The United States, Britain, and Maritime Rights, 1899–1915.* Ithaca, NY: Cornell University Press.

Cooper, J. 2003. The Great War and American Memory. *Virginia Quarterly Review*, 79(1): 70–84.

Cornebise, A.E. 1984. *War as Advertised: The Four-Minute Men and America's Crusade, 1917–1918.* Philadelphia: American Philosophical Society.

Crapsey, E. 1872. *The Nether Side of New York; or, The Vice, Crime and Poverty of the Great Metropolis.* New York, NY: Sheldon and Company.

Creel, G. 1920. *How We Advertised America: The First Telling of the Amazing Story of the Committee on Public Information that Carried the Gospel of Americanism to Every Corner of the Globe.* New York, NY: Harper and Brothers.

Croly, H. 1916. The Effect on American Institutions of a Powerful Military and Naval Establishment. *Annals of the American Academy of Political and Social Science*, 66(1): 157–72.

Crowder, E.H. 1920. *The Spirit of Selective Service*. New York, NY: The Century Co.

Cuddy, J.E. 1967. Irish-American Propagandists and Neutrality, 1914–1917. *Mid-America*, 49: 252–75.

Cuddy, J.E. 1969. Irish-Americans and the 1916 Election: An Episode in Immigrant Adjustment. *American Quarterly*, 21(2): 228–43.

Cuddy, J.E. 1976. *Irish America and National Isolationism, 1914–1920*. New York, NY: Arno Press.

Das, S. 2011. Introduction. In S. Das (ed.), *Race, Empire and First World War Writing*. Cambridge: Cambridge University Press, pp. 1–32.

Dawkins, W. 1918. *Police Reserve and Home Defense Guard Manual*. New York, NY: E.P. Dutton and Co.

DeForest, R.W. and Veiller, L. 1903. *The Tenement House Problem: Including the Report of the New York State Tenement House Commission of 1900*. Cambridge, MA: Harvard University Press.

Democratic National Committee. 1916. *The Democratic Text Book*. New York, NY: Democratic National Committee.

Department of Health of the City of New York. 1919. *Annual Report for the Calendar Year 1918*. New York, NY: William Bratter, Inc.

Department of Justice. 1918. *Interpretation of War Statutes, Bulletin No. 19*. Washington, DC: Government Printing Office.

Department of the Treasury. 1918. *Advertisements, Fourth Liberty Loan*. New York, NY: Liberty Loan Committee, Second Federal Reserve District.

Dernburg, B. (ed.). 1914. *The Case of Belgium in the Light of Official Reports Found in the Secret Archives of the Belgian Government After the Occupation of Brussels*. New York, NY: International Monthly, Inc.

Dernburg, B. 1915a. *Germany and the War: Not a Defense but an Explanation*. New York, NY: The Fatherland.

Dernburg, B. 1915b. *Search-lights on the War*. New York, NY: The Fatherland.

Devlin, P. 1975. *Too Proud to Fight: Woodrow Wilson's Neutrality*. Oxford: Oxford University Press.

De Witt, B.P. 1915. *The Progressive Movement: A Non-Partisan, Comprehensive Discussion of Current Tendencies in American Politics*. New York, NY: The Macmillan Company.

De Witt Talmage, T. 1878. *The Night Side of New York*. Chicago, IL: J. Fairbanks Co.

Dixon, R. 1916. *Americanization*. New York, NY: Macmillan.

Dixon, T. 1915. *The Clansman*. New York, NY: Doubleday.

Dixon, T. 1916. *The Fall of a Nation*. New York, NY: D. Appleton and Company.

Dobbert, G.A. 1967. German-Americans between New and Old Fatherland, 1870–1914. *American Quarterly*, 19(4): 663–80.

Dubofsky, M. 1961. Organised Labor in New York City and the First World War, 1914–1918. *New York History*, 42(4): 380–400.

Du Bois, W.E.B. 1914a. World War and the Color Line. *The Crisis*, 9(1): 28–30.

Du Bois, W.E.B. 1914b. Of the Children of Peace. *The Crisis*, 8(6): 289–91.

Du Bois, W.E.B. 1917a. Editorial. *The Crisis*, 13(6): 267–71.

Du Bois, W.E.B. 1917b. Editorial. *The Crisis*, 14(1): 7–10.

Du Bois, W.E.B. 1917c. Editorial. *The Crisis*, 14(2): 59.

Du Bois, W.E.B. 1918. Close Ranks. *The Crisis*, 16(3): 111.

Du Bois, W.E.B. 1919. Returning Soldiers. *The Crisis*, 18(1): 13.

Du Bois, W.E.B. and Gruening, M. 1917. The Massacre of East St. Louis. *The Crisis*, 14(5): 219–38.

Dumba, C.T. 1914. Ambassador of Austria-Hungary to the United States. *The Outlook*, August 29: 1028–1029.

Eastman, M. 1917a. In Case of War. *The Masses*, 9(6): 7–8.

Eastman, M. 1917b. The Religion of Patriotism. *The Masses*, 9(9): 8–12.

Edwards, J. 1976. Playing the Patriot Game: The Story of the American Defense Society, 1915–1932. *Studies in History and Society*, 1(1): 54–72.

Edwards, J. 1982. *Patriots in Pinstripe: Men of the National Security League*. Washington, DC: University Press of America.

Eisenhower, J. 2001. *Yanks: The Epic Story of the American Army in World War I*. New York, NY: The Free Press.

Eksteins, M. 1989. *Rites of Spring: The Great War and the Birth of the Modern Age*. Boston, MA: Houghton Mifflin.

Elbert, G. 1916. *Report of the Mayor's Committee on Unemployment*. New York, NY: C.S. Nathan, Inc.

Eliot, T.S. 1924. *The Wasteland*. London: Hogarth Press.

Ellis, M. 1992. 'Closing Ranks' and 'Seeking Honors': W.E.B. Du Bois in World War I. *Journal of American History*, 79(1): 96–124.

Ellis, M. 1993. Federal Surveillance of Black Americans during the First World War. *Immigrants and Minorities*, 12(1): 1–20.

Ellis, M. 2001. *Race, War, and Surveillance: African Americans and the United States during World War I*. Bloomington, IN: Indiana University Press.

Emergency Peace Federation. 1917. *Alternatives to War: Findings of the Unofficial Commission which Met at the Holland House, New York City, March 19–24, 1917 'to Devise Ways and Means of a Peaceful Solution of Our International Crisis'*. New York, NY: Emergency Peace Federation.

Engelman, M. 1918. *Four Years of Relief and War Work by the Jews of America, 1914–1918*. New York, NY: Schoen.

Ernst, R. 1994. *Immigrant Life in New York City: 1825–1863*. Syracuse, NY: Syracuse University Press.

Esslinger, D.R. 1967. American German and Irish Attitudes toward Neutrality, 1914–1917: A Study of Catholic Minorities. *The Catholic Historical Review*, 53(2): 194–216.

Ewers, H.H. 1914. We and the World. *The Fatherland*, 1(7): 9.

Executive Committee of the Citizens Preparedness Parade. 1916. *Official Program: Citizens Preparedness Parade, New York City, May 13, 1916*. New York, NY: Citizens Preparedness Parade.

Fainstein, S.S. and Campbell, S. (eds). 2011. *Readings in Urban Theory*. Oxford: Wiley-Blackwell.

Falcke, H. 1928. *Vor dem eintritt Amerikas in den weltkrieg deutsche propaganda in den Vereinigten Staaten von Amerika 1914/1915*. Dresden: C. Reissner.

Farwell, B. 1999. *Over There: The United States in the Great War, 1917–1918*. New York, NY: Norton.

Fatherless Children of France. 1915. *The Fatherless Children of France*. New York, NY: National Executive Office.

Federal Reserve Bank of New York. 1917. *Third Annual Report*. Washington, DC: Government Printing Office.

Federal Reserve Bank of New York. 1918. *Fourth Annual Report*. Washington, DC: Government Printing Office.

Ferdinand, F., Archduke of Austria-Hungary. 1896. *Tagebuch meiner Reise um die Erde, 1892–1893, Volume II*. Vienna: A. Hölder.

Ference, G.C. 1995. *Sixteen Months of Indecision: Slovak American Viewpoints toward Compatriots and the Homeland from 1914 to 1915 as Viewed by the Slovak Language Press in Pennsylvania*. Selinsgrove, PA: Susquehanna University Press.

Ferrell, R. 2007. *America's Deadliest Battle: Meuse-Argonne, 1918*. Lawrence, KS: University Press of Kansas.

Fire Department of the City of New York. 1916. *Annual Report*. New York, NY: Fire Department.

Fischer, D.H. 2004. *Liberty and Freedom: A Visual History of America's Founding Ideals*. Oxford: Oxford University Press.

Foner, N. 2000. *From Ellis Island to JFK: New York's Two Great Waves of Immigration*. New Haven, CT: Yale University Press.

Forbes-Robertson Hale, B. 1914. *What Women Want: An Interpretation of the Feminist Movement*. New York, NY: Frederick A. Stokes.

Forbes-Robertson Hale, B. 1916. *The Nest-Builder*. New York, NY: Frederick A. Stokes.

Ford, N.G. 1997. 'Mindful of the Traditions of His Race': Dual Identity and Foreign-born Soldiers in the First World War American Army. *Journal of American Ethnic History*, 16(2): 35–57.

Ford, N.G. 2001 *Americans All: Foreign-born Soldiers in World War I*. College Station, TX: Texas A&M University Press.

Foster, G. 1849. *New York in Slices: By an Experienced Carver*. New York, NY: W.F. Burgess.

Foster, G. 1850. *New York by Gas-Light and Other Urban Sketches*. New York, NY: DeWitt and Davenport.

France-America Society. 1916. *Lafayette Day Dinner of the France-America Society, in Honor of His Excellency, the Ambassador of France, on the Evening of September 16th, 1916, at the Waldorf-Astoria Hotel, New York*. New York, NY: McGuire.

France-America Society. 1918. *Lafayette Day*. New York, NY: McGuire.

Francke, K. 1915. *A German-American's Confession of Faith*. New York, NY: B.W. Huebsch.

Frank, D. 1985. Housewives, Socialists, and the Politics of Food: The 1917 New York Cost-of-Living Protests. *Feminist Studies*, 11(2): 355–85.

Frieburger, W. 1984. War Prosperity and Hunger: The New York Food Riots of 1917. *Labor History*, 25(2): 217–39.

Friends of Irish Freedom. 1920. *Constitution and State, Local and Branch By-laws of the Friends of Irish Freedom*. New York, NY: Friends of Irish Freedom.

Frobenius, H. 1914. *Germany's Hour of Destiny*. New York. NY: International Monthly, Inc.

Fronc, J. 2009. *New York Undercover: Private Surveillance in the Progressive Era*. Chicago, IL: University of Chicago Press.

Funck, M. and Chickering, R. (eds). 2004. *Endangered Cities: Military Power and Urban Societies in the Era of the World Wars*. Leiden and Boston, MA: Brill.

Fusion Committee. 1917. *Record of Fusion under Mayor Mitchel*. New York, NY: Fusion Committee.

Fussell, P. 1975. *The Great War and Modern Memory*. Oxford: Oxford University Press.

Gage, B. 2009. *The Day Wall Street Exploded: A Story of America in its First Age of Terror*. Oxford: Oxford University Press.

Gaiduk, M. 1918. *Utiug: materialy i fakty o zagotovitelnoi dieiatelnosti russkikh vooennykh kommissii v Amerikie*. New York, NY: M. Gaiduk.

Gallatin, A.E. 1918. *Committee on Arts and Decoration*. New York, NY: Hall of Records.

Ganz, M. 1920. *Rebels: Into Anarchy and Out Again*. New York, NY: Dodd, Mead and Company.

Gardner, A.P. 1915. *Gardner or Daniels?* New York, NY: American Defense Society.

Garvey, M. 1923. *The Philosophy and Opinions of Marcus Garvey*. New York, NY: Universal Publishing House.

Garvey, M. 1983. *The Marcus Garvey and Universal Negro Improvement Association Papers, Vol. I: 1826–August 1919*. Edited by R.A. Hill. Berkeley, CA: University of California Press.

Gay, G.I. and Fisher, H.H. 1929. *Public Relations of the Commission for Relief in Belgium*. Stanford, CA: Stanford University Press.

German, Austrian, Hungarian and Their Allies War Relief Fund, Inc. 1914. *Charity Bazaar for the Benefit of the Widows and Orphans of German, Austrian and Hungarian Soldiers Under the Auspices of the German, Austrian and Hungarian War Relief Fund, Inc: 71st Regiment Armory, New York City, December 5th to 20th, 1914*. New York, NY: J.F. Geis.

German, Austrian, Hungarian and Their Allies War Relief Fund, Inc. 1916. *Charity Bazaar: For the Benefit of the Widows and Orphans of German, Austrian, Hungarian and Their Allied Soldiers under the Auspices of the German,*

Austrian, Hungarian and Their Allies War Relief Fund, Inc. Madison Square Garden, New York City, March 11th to 23rd. New York, NY: J.F. Geis.

Germer, A. 1918. Samuel Gompers. *The Class Struggle*, 2(1): 9–15.

Getting, M. 1933. *Americkí Slováci a vývin československej myšlienky v rokoch 1914–1918*. Masaryktown, FL: Slovenská telocvičná jednota Sokol v Amerike.

Giant, T. 1993. The War for Wilson's Ear: Austria-Hungary in Wartime American Propaganda. *Hungarian Studies Review*, 20(1–2): 25–51.

Gibbs, W. 1917. *The Minimum Cost of Living: A Study of Families of Limited Income in New York City*. New York, NY: Macmillan.

Gier, C. 2013. War, Anxiety, and Hope in American Sheet Music, 1914–1917. *Music and Politics*, 7(1). http://dx.doi.org/10.3998/mp.9460447.0007.102 (accessed 21 April 2013).

Giftin, F.C. 1999. Morris Hillquit and the War Issue in the New York Mayoralty Campaign of 1917. *International Social Science Review*, 74(3/4): 115–28.

Giovannitti, A. 1917. Militant Pacifism. *The Masses*, 9(7): 31–2.

Glassberg, D. and Moore, J.M. 1996. Patriotism in Orange: The Memory of World War I in a Massachusetts Town. In J. Bodnar (ed.), *Bonds of Affection: Americans Define their Patriotism*. Princeton, NJ: Princeton University Press, pp. 160–90.

Goebel, J. 1914. The German-American and the President's Neutrality Proclamation. *The Fatherland*, 1(7): 10.

Goebel, S. and Keene, D. (eds). 2011. *Cities into Battlefields: Metropolitan Scenarios, Experiences and Commemorations of Total War*. Farnham: Ashgate.

Goldman, E. 1915. *Preparedness: The Road to Universal Slaughter*. New York, NY: Mother Earth Publishing.

Goldman, E. 1916. Observations and Comments. *Mother Earth*, 11(4): 497–503.

Goldman, E. 1917a. The Promoters of the War Mania. *Mother Earth*, 12(1): 5.

Goldman, E. 1917b. Hunger Demonstrations: The Outcome of National Prosperity. *Mother Earth*, 12(1): 17–19.

Goldman, E. 1917c. The No Conscription League. *Mother Earth*, 12(4): 112–14.

Goldman, E. 1919. On the Way to Golgotha. *Mother Earth Bulletin*, 1(5): 1.

Goldman, E. 1931. *Living my Life*. New York, NY: A.A. Knopf.

Goldstein, H.S. 1928. *Forty Years of Struggle for a Principle: The Biography of Harry Fischel*. New York, NY: Bloch Publishing Company.

Gompers, S. 1917a. Labor and Democracy. *American Federationist*, 24(10): 837–42.

Gompers, S. 1917b. *America's Fight for the Preservation of Democracy*. New York, NY: American Alliance for Labor and Democracy.

Gompers, S. 2007. *The Samuel Gompers Papers, Vol 10: The American Federation of Labor and the Great War, 1917–18*. Edited by S.B. Kaufman, P.J. Albert and G. Palladino. Urbana, IL: University of Illinois Press.

Goodwin, J. and Mohr, H.K. 1917. *Liberty Bell (It's Time to Ring Again)*. New York, NY: Shapiro, Bernstein and Company.

Goričar, J. 1915. *Political Intrigues of Austria and Germany against Balkan States*. New York, NY: New Yorské Listy.

Gover, W.C. 1875. *The Tammany Hall Democracy of the City of New York: And the General Committee for 1875, Being a Brief History of the Tammany Hall Democracy from 1834 to the Present Time*. New York, NY: M.B. Brown.

Goyens, T. 2007. *Beer and Revolution: The German Anarchist Movement in New York City, 1880–1914*. Urbana, IL: University of Illinois Press.

Graff, G. Jr and Glogau, J. 1916. *Wake Up, America!* New York, NY: Leo Feist.

Grant, M. 1916. *The Passing of the Great Race; or, The Racial Basis of European History*. New York, NY: Charles Scribner's Sons.

Graves, E. 1894. *Greater New York, Reasons Why*. New York, NY: H.A. Rost.

Grose, H.B. 1906. *Aliens or Americans*. New York, NY: Young People's Missionary Movement.

Grotelueschen, M. 2006. *The AEF Way of War: The American Army and Combat in World War I*. Cambridge: Cambridge University Press.

Grubbs, F. 1968. *The Struggle for Labor Loyalty: Gompers, the A.F. of L., and the Pacifists, 1917–1920*. Durham, NC: Duke University Press.

Guaranty Trust Company of New York. 1917. *The Liberty Loan*. New York, NY: Guaranty Trust Company of New York.

Guaranty Trust Company of New York. 1918. *The Victory Drive: Fourth Liberty Loan*. New York, NY: Guaranty Trust Company of New York.

Guglielmo, J. 2010. *Living the Revolution: Italian Women's Resistance and Radicalism in New York City, 1880–1945*. Chapel Hill, NC: University of North Carolina Press.

Guthrie, W. 1916. *America's Debt to France: The Most Unalterable Gratitude*. New York, NY: American Society for the Relief of French War Orphans.

Haberstroh, R. 2014. Kleindeutschland: Little Germany in the Lower East Side. http://www.lespi-nyc.org/history/kleindeutschland-little-germany-in-the-lower-east-side.html (accessed 15 April 2013).

Haenni, S. 2008. *The Immigrant Scene: Ethnic Amusements in New York, 1880–1920*. Minneapolis, MN: University of Minnesota Press.

Harkavy, A. 1902. *Harkavy's Amerikanisher Briefenshteler*. New York, NY: Hebrew Publishing Co.

Harris, B. 2002. *The Hellfighters of Harlem: African-American Soldiers Who Fought for the Right to Fight for Their Country*. New York, NY: Carroll & Graf.

Harris, M. 2011. Full Faith and Credit: The United States' Response to the Panic of 1914. *Tempus*, 12(2): 1–22.

Harrison, H. 1917. *The Negro and the Nation*. New York, NY: Cosmo-Advocate Publishing, Co.

Harrison, H. 1920. *When Africa Awakes*. New York, NY: Porro Press.

Hart, A.B. 1917. *Handbook of the War for Public Speakers*. New York, NY: National Security League.

Hartmann, E.G. 1948. *The Movement to Americanize the Immigrant*. New York, NY: Columbia University Press.

Hassam, F.C. 1916. *The Fourth of July, 1916*. Frederick Hassam Private Collection.

Healy, M. 2004. *Vienna and the Fall of the Habsburg Empire: Total War and Everyday Life in World War I*. Cambridge: Cambridge University Press.

Hearings before the Special Committee Investigating the Munitions Industry, United States Senate, Seventy-third (Seventy-fourth) Congress, Pursuant to S. Res. Washington, DC: Government Printing Office.

Hemingway, E. 1929. *A Farewell to Arms*. New York, NY: Charles Scribner's Sons.

Herve, G. 1914. Insurrection Rather Than War. *Mother Earth*, 9(6): 188–90.

Hill, D.J. 1916. *Americanism: What Is It?* New York, NY: D. Appleton and Company.

Hillquit, M. 1914a. Murderous War in Europe is the Inevitable Culmination of Murderous European Capitalism. *The American Socialist*, 1(8): 1–3.

Hillquit, M. 1914b. Socialism and War, I. *Metropolitan*, 28: 56–7.

Hillquit, M. 1915a. Socialism and War, II. *Metropolitan*, 36: 51–2.

Hillquit, M. 1915b. Socialism and War, III. *Metropolitan*, 37: 39–41.

Hofmann, A. 2004. Reweaving the Urban Fabric: Multiethnicity and Occupation in Lódz, 1914–1918. In M. Funck and R. Chickering (eds), *Endangered Cities: Military Power and Urban Societies in the Era of the World Wars*. Leiden and Boston, MA: Brill, pp. 81–94.

Hogan, M.J. 2007. *The Shamrock Battalion in the Great War*. Columbia, MI: University of Missouri Press.

Holmes, J.H. 1917. *The Messiah Pulpit: A Statement to My People on the Eve of War*. New York, NY: The Church of the Messiah.

Holmes, J.H. and Eaton, C.A. 1916. War, Religion and Preparedness. *The Advocate of Peace*, 78(6): 174–5.

Hoover, H.C. 1951. *The Memoirs of Herbert Hoover: Years of Adventure, 1874–1920*. New York, NY: Macmillan Co.

Horčička, V. 2006. The United States of America and Austria-Hungary on the Eve of the First World War. *Prague Papers on the History of International Relations*, 2006: 163–80.

Horn, M. 2000. A Private Bank at War: J.P. Morgan and Co. and France, 1914–1918. *Business History Review*, 74(1): 85–112.

Horn, M. 2002. *Britain, France, and the Financing of the First World War*. Montreal: McGill-Queen's University Press.

Hourwich, I.H. 1914. Socialism and the War. *The New Review*, 2(10): 561–78.

Howard, E. 1898. *To-Morrow: A Peaceful Path to Real Reform*. London: Swan Sonnenschein.

Hudson-Fulton Celebration Commission. 1905. *Official Minutes of the Hudson-Fulton Celebration Commission, Together with the Minutes of its Predecessor, the Hudson Tercentenary Joint Committee*. Albany, NY: J.B. Lyon.

Hudson-Fulton Celebration Commission. 1909. *Historical Pageant: Hudson-Fulton Celebration, September 25 to October 9, 1909.* New York, NY: Redfield.

Hudson-Fulton Celebration Commission. 1910a. *The Fourth Annual Report of the Hudson-Fulton Celebration Commission to the Legislature of the State of New York.* Albany, NY: J.B. Lyon.

Hudson-Fulton Celebration Commission. 1910b. *Testimonials of Appreciation to Herman Ridder, Acting President and Henry W. Sackett, Secretary of the Hudson-Fulton Celebration Commission, March, 1910.* New York, NY: The De Vinne Press.

Hughes, C. 1916. *Speech of Acceptance at Carnegie Hall, New York, July 31, 1916. Republican Campaign Text-book.* Washington, DC: Republican Party, National Committee.

Irwin, J.F. 2013. *Making the World Safe: The American Red Cross and a Nation's Humanitarian Awakening.* Oxford: Oxford University Press.

Jacobs, J. 1916. The Federation Movement in American Jewish Philanthropy. *American Jewish Year Book*, 17: 159–98.

Jaffe, S. 2013. *New York at War: Four Centuries of Combat, Fear, and Intrigue in Gotham.* New York, NY: Doubleday.

Jamison, J.C. 1917. Negro Soldiers. *The Crisis*, 14(5): 249.

Jaworowski, K. 1915. Polish American Opinion. In *New York Times Current History: The European War from the Beginning to March 1915. Vol. 1, No. 2: Who Began the War, and Why?* New York, NY: New York Times.

Jobs, S. 2013. *Welcome Home, Boys! Military Victory Parades in New York City 1899–1946.* Frankfurt am Main: Campus Verlag.

Johnson, C.T. 1999. *Culture at Twilight: The National German–American Alliance, 1901–1918.* Frankfurt: Peter Lang.

Johnston, R.M. 1915. *The Ounce of Prevention: Switzerland Versus Belgium, with a Lesson for the United States.* New York, NY: American Defense Society.

Joint Legislative Committee of the State of New York Investigating Seditious Activities. 1919. *Testimony of Ludwig C.A.K. Martens.* New York, NY: s.n.

Jones, J.P. 1918. *Report of John Price Jones, Assistant Director and Manager, Press Bureau, to Guy Emerson, Director, Publicity Department, Liberty Loan Committee, Second Federal Reserve District. Third Liberty Loan Campaign.* New York, NY: Liberty Loan Committee, Second Federal Reserve District.

Jones, J.P. 1919. *Report of John Price Jones, Assistant Director, in charge of Feature Bureau, Press Bureau, and Transportation Service to Guy Emerson, Director, Publicity Department, Liberty Loan Committee, Second Federal Reserve District. Fourth Liberty Loan Campaign.* New York, NY: s.n.

Jones, J.P. and Hollister, M. 1918. *The German Secret Service in America.* Boston, MA: Small, Maynard and Company.

Jones, M.A. 1992. *American Immigration.* Second Edition. Chicago, IL: University of Chicago Press.

Jones, T.J. 1904. *The Sociology of a New York City Block.* New York, NY: Columbia University Press.

Jordan, W.G. 2001. *Black Newspapers and America's War for Democracy, 1914–1920*. Chapel Hill, NC: University of North Carolina Press.

Joyce, J. 1922. *Ulysses*. Paris: Shakespeare and Company.

Kaganoff, N. 1966. Organized Jewish Welfare Activity in New York City, 1848–1860. *American Jewish Historical Quarterly* 5, 27–61.

Kaganoff, N. 1986. The Jewish Landsmanshaftn in New York before World War I. *American Jewish History* 76, 56–67.

Kahn, O.H. 1917. *Americans of German Origin and the War: Extracts from an Address Delivered before the Merchants Association of New York, at its Liberty Loan Meeting, Held on June 1, 1917*. Washington, DC: Government Printing Office.

Kallen, H.M. 1915a. Nationality and the Hyphenated American. *The Menorah Journal*, 1: 79–85.

Kallen, H.M. 1915b. Democracy Versus the Melting Pot: A Study of American Nationality. *The Nation*, February 25, pp. 217–19.

Karlowich, R. 1991. *We Fall and Rise: Russian-Language Newspapers in New York City, 1889–1914*. Metuchen, NJ: Scarecrow Press.

Kates, A. 1916. New York's Home Defense League. *The Review: Prison Association of New York*, 6: 4–6.

Katz, D. 1988. *Yiddish English Hebrew Dictionary*. New York, NY: Schocken Books, pp. vi–xxiii.

Katz, D. 2011. *All Together Different: Yiddish Socialists, Garment Workers, and the Labor Roots of Multiculturalism*. New York, NY: New York University Press.

Keeling, A. 2009. 'When the City is a Great Field Hospital': The Influenza Pandemic of 1918 and the New York City Nursing Response. *Journal of Clinical Nursing*, 18(19): 2732–8.

Keene, J.D. 2000. *The United States and the First World War*. Harlow: Longman.

Keene, J.D. 2001. *Doughboys: The Great War and the Remaking of America*. Baltimore, MD: Johns Hopkins University Press.

Keene, J.D. 2008. The Memory of the Great War in the African American Community. In M. Snell (ed.), *Unknown Soldiers: The American Expeditionary Force in Memory and Remembrance*. Kent, OH: Kent State University Press, pp. 60–79.

Keller, P. 1979. *States of Belonging: German-American Intellectuals and the First World War*. Cambridge, MA: Harvard University Press.

Kellor, F. 1915a. The Trenches of Peace. *The Immigrants in America Review*, 1(1): 5.

Kellor, F. 1915b. Immigrants in America: A Domestic Policy. *The Immigrants in America Review*, 1(1): 9–15.

Kellor, F. 1915c. National Americanization Day: July 4th. *The Immigrants in America Review*, 1(3): 18–29.

Kellor, F. 1916a. *Straight America: A Call to National Service*. New York, NY: Macmillan.

Kellor, F. 1916b. Americanization: A Conservation Policy for Industry. *Annals of the American Academy of Political and Social Science*, 65(1): 240–44.

Kellor, F. 1918a. *Americanization of Women: A Discussion of an Emergency Created by Granting the Vote to Women in New York State*. New York, NY: s.n.

Kellor, F. 1918b. *Neighborhood Americanization*. New York, NY: Information Service of the National Americanization Committee.

Kennedy, D. 1980. *Over Here: The First World War and American Society*. Oxford: Oxford University Press.

Kittredge, T.B. 1918. *The History of the Commission for Relief in Belgium, 1914–1917*. New York, NY: Commission for Relief in Belgium.

Knock, T. 1992. *To End All Wars: Woodrow Wilson and the Quest for a New World Order*. Princeton, NJ: Princeton University Press.

Koegel, J. 2009. *Music in German Immigrant Theater: New York City, 1840–1940*. Rochester, NY: University of Rochester Press.

Koester, F. 1916. America's Perilous Position. *The Fatherland*, 4(23): 357–9.

Kosak, H. 2009. *Cultures of Opposition: Jewish Immigrant Workers, New York City, 1881–1905*. Albany, NY: State University of New York Press.

Lafayette Day Citizens' Committee of New York. 1916. *Lafayette Day, 1916*. New York, NY: Law.

Lafayette Day National Committee. 1917. *Lafayette Day Exercises in Commemoration of the Double Anniversary of the Birth of Lafayette and the Battle of the Marne: September 6th, 1917*. New York, NY: Law.

Laidlaw, W. (ed.). 1918. *The Moral Aims of the War: Comprising a Series of Addresses Given at an All Day Interchurch Clerical Conference in the City of New York, April 4th, 1918*. New York, NY: Fleming H. Revell Company.

Lamont, T.W. 1915. *Discussion of Financial Administration Budget and Tax Rate: The Government of the City of New York*. New York, NY: The New York State Constitutional Convention Commission.

Landau, H. 1937. *The Enemy Within: The Inside Story of German Sabotage in America*. New York, NY: G.P. Putnam's Sons.

Leary, W. 1967. Woodrow Wilson, Irish-Americans, and the Election of 1916. *Journal of American History*, 54(1): 57–72.

Lees, A. 1985. *Cities Perceived: Urban Society in European and American Thought, 1820–1940*. Manchester: Manchester University Press.

Leonard, J. 1920. *The Story of New York in the World War*. New York, NY: National Service Magazine: New York.

Levine, L. 1924. *The Women's Garment Workers: A History of the International Garment Workers' Union*. New York, NY: Huebsch.

Lewinson, E.R. 1965. *John Purroy Mitchel: The Boy Mayor of New York*. New York, NY: Astra Books.

Liberty Loan Committee, New York. 1917. *Allotments, Second Liberty Loan, Second Federal Reserve District*. New York, NY: Liberty Loan Committee.

Liberty Loan Committee, Second Federal Reserve District. 1917. *Report of the Publicity Committee on Work Done in Connection with the Flotation* of the First United States Government Liberty Loan of 1917, Amounting to $2,000,000,000. Washington, DC: Government Printing Office.

Liberty Loan Committee, Second Federal Reserve District. 1918a. *Selling the Third Liberty Loan: Suggestions for the Use of Liberty Loan Committees.* Washington, DC: Government Printing Office.

Liberty Loan Committee, Second Federal Reserve District. 1918b. *Handbook for Speakers: Third Liberty Loan.* Washington, DC: Government Printing Office.

Library of Congress, 2004. *From Haven to Home: 350 Years of Jewish Life in America: A Century of Immigration, 1820–1924.* http://www.loc.gov./exhibits/ haventohome/havencentury/html (accessed 14 March 2014).

Link, A. 1960. *The Struggle for Neutrality, 1914–1915.* Princeton, NJ: Princeton University Press.

Little, A. 1936. *From Harlem to the Rhine: The Story of New York's Colored Volunteers.* New York, NY: Covici Friede.

London, M. 1915. There Must Be an End. *The Masses*, 6(8): 18.

London, M. 1917. *Speeches of Congressman Meyer London.* New York, NY: s.n.

Lord, E. 1905. *The Italian in America.* New York, NY: B.F. Buck.

Lorini, A. 1999. *Rituals of Race: American Public Culture and the Search for Racial Democracy.* Charlottesville, VA: University Press of Virginia.

Love, H.K. 1916. *'National Security': As It Involves the Preparation and Use of the Citizenry.* New York, NY: National Security League.

Luebke, F. 1974. *Bonds of Loyalty: German-Americans and World War I.* DeKalb, IL: Northern Illinois University Press.

Luff, J. 2012. *Commonsense Anticommunism: Labor and Civil Liberties Between the World Wars.* Chapel Hill, NC: University of North Carolina Press.

Lusk, C.R. 1920. *Revolutionary Radicalism: Its History, Purpose and Tactics with an Exposition and Discussion of the Steps Being Taken and Required to Curb it, Being the Report of the Joint Legislative Committee Investigating Seditious Activities, Filed April 24, 1920, in the Senate of the State of New York, Part 2(4).* Albany, NY: J.B. Lyon.

Lyddon, W. 1938. *British War Missions to the United States, 1914–1918.* Oxford: Oxford University Press.

MacColl, R. 1956. *Roger Casement: A New Judgment.* London: Hamish Hamilton.

Majerus, B. 2004. Controlling Urban Society during World War I: Cooperation between Belgian Authorities and the Forces of Military Occupation. In M. Funck and R. Chickering (eds), *Endangered Cities: Military Power and Urban Societies in the Era of the World Wars.* Leiden and Boston, MA: Brill, pp. 65–80.

Mamatey, A. 1915. The Situation in Austria-Hungary. *The Journal of Race Development*, 6(2): 203–217.

Manor, E. 2009. *Forward: The Jewish Daily Forward (Forverts) Newspaper: Immigrants, Socialism and Jewish Politics in New York, 1890–1917.* Brighton: Sussex Academic Press.

Manning, W.T. 1914. A Form of Supplication and Intercession for the Restoration of the World's Peace and for Divine Guidance for All Men. *Year Book and Register of the Parish of Trinity Church in the City of New York, 1914*. New York, NY: Trinity Church.

Manning, W.T. 1917a. *The Easter Call to America: A Sermon Preached in Trinity Church, New York*. New York, NY: Trinity Church.

Manning, W.T. 1917b. *America's Part in the World-War: A Sermon Preached April 22, 1917, in the Church of the Incarnation*. New York, NY: The American Rights League.

Mariano, J.H. 1922. *The Italian Contribution to American Democracy*. Boston, MA: Christopher Publishing House.

Marks, M. 1915. *Report on Market System for New York City and on Open Markets Established in Manhattan*. New York, NY: M.B. Brown.

May, R.R. 1959. *The World War and American Isolation, 1914–1917*. Cambridge, MA: Harvard University Press.

Mayhew, H. 1851. *Life and Labour and the London Poor, Vol. 1*. London: George Woodfall and Son.

Mayor's Committee on Food Supply. 1914a. *Reports of the Executive Committee of Mayor Mitchel's Committee on Food Supply*. New York, NY: C.S. Nathan, Inc.

Mayor's Committee on Food Supply. 1914b. *Substitutes for Meat*. New York, NY: Brooklyn Eagle Press.

Mayor's Committee on Food Supply. 1914c. *Preparation of Vegetables for the Table*. New York, NY: Brooklyn Eagle Press.

Mayor's Committee on Food Supply. 1914d. *Information about Fish and How to Use Them, Issued by Mayor's Committee on Food Supply*. New York, NY: G.W. Pratt.

Mayor's Committee on Food Supply. 1915. *How to Use Left-overs, Issued by Mayor Mitchel's Committee on Food Supply*. New York, NY: G.W. Pratt.

Mayor's Committee on Food Supply. 1917. *Hints to Housewives on How to Buy, How to Care for Food, Meats, Drippings and Butter Substitutes, Substitutes for Meat, Fish, Vegetables, Cereals, Bread, How to Use Left-overs, How to Make Soap, Fireless Cooker, Canning Fruits and Vegetables, How to Preserve Eggs*. New York, NY: I. Goldmann.

Mayor's Committee on a Permanent War Memorial. 1919. *Report of the Mayor's Committee*. New York, NY: s.n.

Mayor's Committee on a Permanent War Memorial. 1923. *Submitting the Memorial Project and New Playground Area to Be Added to the Central Park*. New York, NY: Brown.

Maxim, H. 1915. *Defenseless America*. New York, NY: Hearst International.

McCabe, J. 1882. *New York by Sunlight and Gaslight: A Work Descriptive of the Great American Metropolis*. Philadelphia, PA: Douglass Brothers.

McCartin, J.A. 1998. *Labor's Great War: The Struggle for Industrial Democracy and the Origins of Modern American Labor Relations, 1912–1921*. Chapel Hill, NC: University of North Carolina Press.

McCartney, H. 2005. *The Liverpool Territorials in the First World War*. Cambridge: Cambridge University Press.

McCartney, P.T. 2006. *Power and Progress: American National Identity, the War of 1898, and the Rise of American Imperialism*. Baton Rouge, LA: Louisiana State University Press.

McGuire, K. 1915. *The King, the Kaiser and Irish Freedom*. New York, NY: Devin-Adair.

McGuire, K. 1916. *What Could Germany Do for Ireland?* New York, NY: Wolfe Tone Company.

McKeogh, A. 1919. *The Victorious 77th Division (New York's Own) in the Argonne Fight*. New York, NY: John H. Eggers, Co.

Mead, G.W. 1915. *The Conquest of the United States: A Book of Facts – The Remedy*. New York, NY: American Truth Society.

Mead, G.W. 1917. *The Conscientious Objector*. New York, NY: National Security League.

Melamed, S.M. 1918. Editorial. *American Jewish Chronicle*, 4(26): 721.

Mennell, J. 1999. African-Americans and the Selective Service Act of 1917. *The Journal of Negro History*, 84(3): 275–87.

Merchants' Association of New York. 1918. *Report of the Food Problem Committee. March, 1918*. New York, NY: Food Problem Committee.

Merwood-Salisbury, J. 2009. Patriotism and Protest: Union Square as Public Space, 1832–1932. *Journal of the Society of Architectural Historians*, 68(4): 540–59.

Michels, T. 2002. *A Fire in Their Hearts: Yiddish Socialists in New York*. Cambridge, MA: Harvard University Press.

Miller, A. 2010. Rupert Brooke and the Growth of Commercial Patriotism in Great Britain, 1914–1918. *Twentieth Century British History*, 21(2): 141–62.

Miller, K. 1922. *The Czecho-Slovaks in America*. New York, NY: George H. Doran.

Mitchell, W. 1919. *International Price Comparisons*. Washington, DC: Government Printing Office.

Mitchel Memorial Committee. 1918. *Mitchel Memorial Committee, Organized for the Erection of a Memorial to the Late Major John Purroy Mitchel. Minutes of the Organization. Meeting Held in the City Hall, New York City, on Monday, July 29th, 1918*. New York, NY: s.n.

Mitrović, A. 2007. *Serbia's Great War, 1914–1918*. West Lafayette, IN: Purdue University Press.

Morgan, D.T. 1973. The Revivalist as Patriot: Billy Sunday and World War I. *Journal of Presbyterian History*, 51(2): 199–215.

Morrow, J. 2005. *The Great War: An Imperial History*. London: Routledge.

Mott, F.L. 1938. *A History of American Magazines, Vol. III: 1865–1885*. Oxford: Oxford University Press.

Mueller, J.C. 1917. *Hero Land: The Greatest Spectacle the World has Ever Seen for the Greatest Need the World has Ever Known*. New York, NY: The Hegeman Print.

Mumford, L. 1963. *The City in History*. London: Martin Secker and Warburg.

Münsterberg, H. 1914. *The War and America*, New York, NY: D. Appleton and Company.

Münsterberg, H. 1915. Hugo Münsterberg Defines Theo. Roosevelt as a Presidential Possibility. *The Fatherland*, 3(20): 346–8.

Nadel, S. 1990. *Little Germany: Ethnicity, Religion, and Class in New York City, 1845–1880*. Urbana, IL: University of Illinois Press.

National Allied Relief Committee. 1915. *Some of America's Contributions to European War Relief*. New York, NY: Herald Square Press.

National Allied Relief Committee. 1916. *The Allied Bazaar Under the Auspices of National Allied Relief Committee, War Relief Clearing House for France and Her Allies, and the Commission for Relief in Belgium, Grand Central Palace, June 3 to June 14, 1916*. New York, NY: Herald Square Press.

National Allied Relief Committee. 1917. *Some of America's Contributions to European War Relief: A Brief Account of the Personnel and Aims*. New York, NY: Herald Square Press.

National Americanization Committee. 1915. *Americanizing a City*. New York, NY: National Americanization Committee.

National Americanization Committee. 1917. *A Partial Record of Alien Enemy Activities, 1915–1917: A Compelling Appeal for a War Policy for Aliens to Be Adopted by the Government and Citizens of the United States*. New York, NY: National Americanization Committee.

National Association for the Advancement of Colored People. 1919. *Thirty Years of Lynching in the United States, 1889–1913*. New York, NY: Negro Universities Press.

National Municipal League. 1915. *Report of a Committee of the National Municipal League, November 19, 1914*. Philadelphia, PA: National Municipal League.

National Security League. 1915. *Report of the Committee on Militia*. New York, NY: National Security League.

National Security League. 1916. *Officers, Committees and Branches*. New York, NY: National Security League.

National Security League. 1917a. *What It Is and Why, What It Has Done and Is Doing: A National Defense Catechism for the Busy Man or Woman*. New York, NY: National Security League.

National Security League. 1917b. *Why We Are at War. Why You Must Help. What You Can Do*. New York, NY: National Security League.

National Security League. 1917c. *Proceedings of the Congress of Constructive Patriotism: Held under the Auspices of the National Security League, Washington, D.C., January 25–27*. New York, NY: National Security League.

National Security League. 1918a. *Money, Munitions and Ships Luncheon under Auspices of the National Security League, Hotel Astor, New York City, April 13, 1918*. New York, NY: National Security League.

National Security League. 1918b. *Americanization Service: What You Can Do for America Through Americanization of the Foreign-born*. New York, NY: National Security League.

Nelson, P. 2009. *A More Unbending Battle: The Harlem Hellfighters' Struggle for Freedom in WWI and Equality at Home*. New York, NY: Basic Civitas.

New York Board of Estimate and Apportionment, Bureau of Personal Service. 1917. *Report on the Increased Cost of Living for an Unskilled Labourer's Family in New York City*. New York, NY: M.B. Brown.

New York Chamber of Commerce. 1918. *Sixtieth Annual Report of the Corporation of the Chamber of Commerce of the State of New York*. New York. New York, NY: Press of the Chamber of Commerce.

New York Mayor's Committee of Welcome. 1919. *Review and Parade of the 27th Division*. New York, NY: s.n.

New York Police Department. 1915. *Annual Report*. New York, NY: Bureau of Printing, City of New York.

New York Police Department. 1916. *Annual Report*. New York, NY: Bureau of Printing, City of New York.

New York Police Department. 1918. *Annual Report*. New York, NY: Bureau of Printing, City of New York.

New York Senate. 1918. *Documents of the Senate of the State of New York, Volume 5*. Albany, NY: J.B Lyon.

New York State. 1917a. *Joint Report on Foods and Markets of Governor Whitman's Market Commission, Mayor Mitchel's Food Supply Committee and the Wicks Legislative Committee. Transmitted to the Legislature January 3, 1917*. Albany, NY: J.B. Lyon.

New York State. 1917b. *The New York Red Book*. Albany, NY: J.B. Lyon.

New York State Legislative. 1917. *Preliminary Report of the Joint Legislative Committee on Dairy Products, Live Stock and Poultry. Transmitted to the Legislature February 15, 1917*. Albany, NY: J.B. Lyon.

New Yorker Staatszeitung. 1997. History of a New York City Institution. http://www.germancorner.com/NYStaatsZ/history.html (accessed 12 February 2012).

Noble, H.G.S. 1915. *The New York Stock Exchange in the Crisis of 1914*. Garden City, NY: Country Life Press.

North, W. (Dir.) 1915. *The Battle Cry of Peace*. Vitagraph Company of America.

O'Brien, W. and Ryan, D. (eds). 1953. *Devoy's Post Bag, 1871–1928, Vol. II*. Dublin: C.J. Fallon.

O'Keefe, K. 1972. *A Thousand Deadlines: The New York Press and American Neutrality, 1914–17*. The Hague: Martinus Nijhoff.

O'Leary, J. 1916a. *The Slave-mind in the United States*. New York, NY: American Truth Society.

O'Leary, J. 1916b. *The Fable of John Bull and Uncle Sam: A History in Prose and Picture of the Real Relations of John Bull and Uncle Sam*. New York, NY: American Truth Society.

O'Leary, J. 1917. *An Open Letter to George W. Perkins Criticising His Report on the Food Question*. New York, NY: American Truth Society.

O'Leary, J. 1919. *My Political Trial and Experiences*. New York, NY: Jefferson Publishing.

O'Neil, J. and Savage, J. 1868. *To the State Centres, Centres of Circle and Members of the Fenian Brotherhood*. New York, NY: s.n.

O'Sheel, S. 1915. *The Catechism of Balaam*. New York, NY: H.H. Masterson.

Office of the Provost Marshal General. 1917. *Selective Service Regulations Prescribed by the President: Under the Authority Vested in Him by the Terms of the Selective Service Law (Act of Congress Approved May 18, 1917)*. Washington, DC: Government Printing Office.

Ogborn, M. 1998. *Spaces of Modernity: London's Geographies, 1680–1780*. London and New York: Guilford Press.

Olneck, M.R. 1989. Americanization and the Education of Immigrants, 1900–1925: An Analysis of Symbolic Action. *American Journal of Education*, 97(4): 398–423.

Omissi, D. 1999. *Indian Voices of the Great War: Soldiers' Letters, 1914–18*. Basingstoke: Palgrave Macmillan.

Orleck, A. 1995. *Common Sense and a Little Fire: Women and Working-Class Politics in the United States, 1900–1965*. Chapel Hill, NC: University of North Carolina Press.

Øverland, O. 2000. *Immigrant Minds, American Identities: Making the United States Home, 1870–1930*. Champaign, IL: University of Illinois Press.

Ovington, M.W. 1911. *Half a Man: The Status of the Negro in New York*. New York, NY: Longmans, Green and Co.

Pankhurst, C. 1914. *America and the War: A Speech Delivered at Carnegie Hall, New York*. London: Women's Social and Political Union.

Park, R.E. 1922. *The Immigrant Press and Its Control*. New York, NY: Harper and Brothers.

Pauco, J. 1969. Slovak Pioneers in America. *Slovakia*, 19(42): 108–24.

Pauco, J. 1973. Slovaks Abroad and Their Relationship with Slovakia. In J. Kirschbaum (ed.), *Slovakia in the 19th and 20th Centuries*. Toronto: Slovak World Congress, pp. 333–42.

Pennell, J. 1918. *That Liberty Shall Not Perish From The Earth*. New York, NY: Heywood Strasser and Voigt Lithograph Company.

People's Council of America for Democracy and Peace. 1917. *Report of the First American Conference for Democracy and Terms of Peace Held at Madison*

Square Garden, New York City, May 30 and 31st, 1917. New York, NY: Organizing Committee, People's Council of America for Democracy and Peace.

Peoples Relief Committee for the Jewish War Sufferers. 1916. *The Book of the Exile: Souvenir of the Bazaar and Fair Held under the Auspices of the Peoples Relief Committee for the Jewish War Sufferers, March, 1916*. New York, NY: Peoples Relief Committee for the Jewish War Sufferers.

Pergler, C. 1916a. *Bohemian (Czech) Hopes and Aspirations*. Chicago, IL: Bohemian National Alliance in America.

Pergler, C. 1916b. *Bohemia's Claim to Independence*. Chicago, IL: Bohemian National Alliance in America.

Peterson, H. 1935. *Propaganda for War: The Campaign Against American Neutrality, 1914–1917*. Norman, OK: Oklahoma University Press.

Philadelphia War History Committee. 1922. *Philadelphia in the World War, 1914–1919*. New York, NY: Wynkoop Hallenbeck Crawford.

Philip Randolph, A. 1917. *Terms of Peace and the Darker Races*. New York, NY: Poole Press Association.

Piantadosi, A. and Bryan, A. 1915. *I Didn't Raise My Boy to Be a Soldier*. New York, NY: Leo Feist.

Piehler, G.K. 1994. The War Dead and the Gold Star: American Commemoration of the First World War. In J.R Gillis (ed.), *Commemorations: The Politics of National Identity*. Princeton, NJ: Princeton University Press, pp. 168–218.

Piehler, G.K. 1995. *Remembering War: The American Way*. Washington, DC: Smithsonian Institution Press.

Plattsburg Military Training Camp. 1917. *The Plattsburger*. New York, NY: Plattsburger, Inc.

Pratt, N.F. 1979. *Morris Hillquit: A Political History of an American Jewish Socialist*. New York, NY: Greenwood Press.

Price, J.M. 1918. Fusion Mistakes and a Way Out. *National Municipal Review*, 7(2): 183–6.

Pulsifer, H. 1915. The Security League Conference. *Outlook*, 111: 853–4.

Purseigle, P. 2005. Introduction. Warfare and Belligerence: Approaches to the First World War. In P. Purseigle (ed.), *Warfare and Belligerence: Perspectives in First World War Studies*. Leiden and Boston, MA: Brill, pp. 1–37.

Purseigle, P. and Macleod, J. 2004. Introduction: Perspectives in First World War Studies. In J. Macleod and P. Purseigle (eds), *Uncovered Fields: Perspectives in First World War Studies*. Leiden and Boston, MA: Brill, pp. 1–23.

Putnam, G.H. 1915. *Memories of a Publisher, 1865–1915*. New York, NY: G.P. Putnam's Sons.

Rappaport, J. 1957. The American Yiddish Press and the European Conflict in 1914. *Jewish Social Studies*, 19(3): 113–28.

Rappaport, J. 2005. *Hands Across the Sea: Jewish Immigrants and World War I*. New York, NY: Hamilton.

Rawls, W. 1988. *Wake up America! World War I and the American Poster*. New York, NY: Abbeville Press.

Read, J.M. 1941. *Atrocity Propaganda: 1914–1919*. New Haven, CT: Yale University Press.

Recchiuti, J.L. 2007. *Civic Engagement: Social Science and Progressive Era Reform in New York*. Philadelphia, PA: University of Pennsylvania Press.

Reed, J. 1917. Whose War? *The Masses*, 9(6): 11–12.

Reiling, J. 1997. *Deutschland, Safe for Democracy? Deutsch-amerikanische Beziehungen aus dem Tatigkeitsbereich*. Stuttgart: Franz Steiner Verlag.

Rhodes, A. 1916. Women's Organizations and Americanization. *The Journal of the New York State Teachers' Association*, 4(3): 103–4.

Ribak, G. 2012a. *Gentile New York: The Images of Non-Jews among Jewish Immigrants*. Piscataway, NJ: Rutgers University Press.

Ribak, G. 2012b. "A Victory of the Slavs Means a Deathblow to Democracy": The Onset of World War I and the Images of the Warring Sides among Jewish Immigrants in New York, 1914–1916. In Y. Levin and A. Shapira (eds), *War and Peace in Jewish Tradition: From the Biblical World to the Present*. London: Routledge, pp. 203–18.

Ridder, H. 1915. *Hyphenations*. New York, NY: Max Schmetterling.

Riis, J. 1890. *How the Other Half Lives*. New York, NY: Charles Scribner's Sons.

Ringrose, H. 1914. *Why is America Neutral?* New York, NY: The Marlow Press, Inc.

Robert, J.-L. and Winter, J.M. 1997. *Capital Cities at War: Paris, London, Berlin 1914–1919. Volume 1*. Cambridge: Cambridge University Press.

Robert, J.-L. and Winter, J.M. 2007. *Capital Cities at War: Paris, London, Berlin 1914–1919. Volume 2*. Cambridge: Cambridge University Press.

Rockefeller Foundation, 1915. *The Relief of Suffering Non-combatants in Europe: Belgian Refugees in Holland*. New York, NY: Rockefeller Foundation War Relief Commission.

Rockefeller, H. 1924. *History of the Memorial Monument in Highland Park and Memoir of the Soldiers who Served in the World War from the Twenty-Second Assembly District of Brooklyn*. New York, NY: s.n.

Roosevelt, T. 1915a. Americanization Day. *Metropolitan Magazine*, 42(3): 3–4.

Roosevelt, T. 1915b. *Americanism. Address before the Knights of Columbus, Carnegie Hall, New York, October 12, 1915*. New York, NY: s.n.

Roosevelt, T. 1916. *Fear God and Take Your Own Part*. New York, NY: George H. Doran.

Roosevelt, T. 1917. *Americanism and Preparedness*. New York, NY: Mail and Express.

Root, E. 1919. The Memorial Spirit and the Future of America. *American Magazine of Art*, 10(11): 407–10.

Rosenberg, L. and Rubinstein, M. 1909. *Leben Zol Amerika*. New York, NY: A. Tores.

Rosenblaut, C.J. 1917. *Mitchel's Election a National Triumph*. New York, NY: Public Welfare Committee.

Rosenwaike, I. 1972. *Population History of New York City*. Syracuse, NY: Syracuse University Press.

Ross, E.A. 1914. *The Old World in the New*. New York, NY: The Century Co.

Roster of Company 'F', 1st Training Regiment. 1915. *A Military Training Camp for Business and Professional Men Held Near the U.S. Army Post, Plattsburg Barracks, N.Y., August 10 to September 6, 1915*. New York, NY: s.n.

Rowntree, B.S. 1902. *Poverty: A Study of Town Life*. London: Macmillan.

Rubenstein, J. 2011. *Leon Trotsky: A Revolutionary's Life*. New Haven, CT: Yale University Press.

Sandos, J. 1992. *Rebellion in the Borderlands: Anarchism and the Plan of San Diego, 1904–23*. Norman, OK: University of Oklahoma Press.

Sassoon, S. 1932. *Memoirs of a Fox-Hunting Man*. London: Faber and Faber.

Saul, N.E. 2001. *War and Revolution: The United States and Russia, 1914–1921*. Lawrence, KS: University Press of Kansas.

Schaffer, R. 1978. *The United States in World War I: A Selected Bibliography*. Santa Barbara, CA: ABC-CLIO.

Schaffer, R. 1991. *America in the Great War: The Rise of the War Welfare State*. Oxford: Oxford University Press.

Schiff, J. 1915. The Jewish Problem Today. *Menorah Journal*, 1: 75–8.

Schnapp, A. 1998. Une archéologie de la Grande Guerre estelle possible? In A. Schnapp (ed.), *14–18: Aujourd'hui, Today, Heute. No. 2, l'archéologie et al Grande Guerre*. Péronne: Historial de la Grande Guerre, pp. 19–27.

Schrader, F.F. 1914a. A Question for German-Americans. *The Fatherland*, 1(3): 7–10.

Schrader, F.F. 1914b. German-Americans. *The Fatherland*, 1(16): 7–10.

Schrader, F.F. 1915a. German Sympathizers, Roosevelt and Others. *The Fatherland*, 3(5): 84–6.

Schrader, F.F. 1915b. Warring on Women and Children. *The Fatherland*, 3(17): 291–3.

Schrader, F.F. 1916a. *Handbook: Political, Statistical and Sociological, for German Americans and All Other Americans who have Not Forgotten the History and Traditions of their Country, and who Believe in the Principles of Washington, Jefferson and Lincoln*. New York, NY: The Fatherland Corporation.

Schrader, F.F. 1916b. N.Y. Congressional Candidates Worthy of Support. *The Fatherland*, 5(14): 2–3.

Schrader, F.F. 1916c. The Presidential Election Reviewed. *The Fatherland*, 5(16): 243–4, 255.

Schulman, S. 1916a. War, Religion and Preparedness. *The Advocate of Peace*, 78(6): 136–8.

Schulman, S. 1916b. *Gratitude with Apology: A Thanksgiving Sermon, Sunday, November 26th, 1916*. New York, NY: Chambers.

Scott, E.J. 1919. *Scott's Official History of the American Negro in the World War*. Chicago, IL: Homewood Press.

Seibel, G. 1916. *The Hyphen in American History*. New York, NY: New Yorker Staats-Zeitung.

Seipp, A.R. 2009. *The Ordeal of Peace: Demobilization and the Urban Experience in Britain and Germany, 1917–1921*. Farnham: Ashgate.

Senate Foreign Relations Committee. 1920. *Investigation of Mexican Affairs: Report of Senator Albert B. Fall to the Subcommittee of the Committee on Foreign Relations, Examining into Mexican Affairs, Reports and Hearings*. Washington, DC: Government Printing Office.

Serbian National Defense League of America. 1918. *For Freedom: A Manifestation of Oppressed Slavic Nationalities of Austria-Hungary in Honor of the Serbian War Mission to the United States*. New York, NY: Serbian National Defense League of America.

Shenk, G. 2006. *Work or Fight: Race, Gender, and the Draft in World War I*. New York, NY: Palgrave Macmillan.

Sherry, V. 2003. *The Great War and the Language of Modernism*. Oxford: Oxford University Press.

Shiels, A. (ed.). 1916. *The School and the Immigrant: A Series of Articles*. New York, NY: Department of Education, the City of New York.

Silber, W.L. 2006. *When Washington Shut Down Wall Street: The Great Financial Crisis of 1914 and the Origins of American Monetary Superiority*. Princeton, NJ: Princeton University Press.

Sloan, J. 1978. *New York Etchings*. Edited by Helen Farr Sloan. New York, NY: Dover.

Slobodin, H.L. 1917. The State of the Socialist Party. *International Socialist Review*, 17: 539–41.

Slotkin, R. 2005. *Lost Battalions: The Great War and the Crisis of American Nationality*. New York, NY: Henry Holt.

Smith, M.H. 1868. *Sunshine and Shadow in New York*. Hartford, CT: J.B. Burr and Co.

Smith, R. 2004. *Jamaican Volunteers in the First World War: Race, Masculinity and the Development of National Consciousness*. Manchester: Manchester University Press.

Smulewitz, S. and Rumshisky, J.M. 1911. *Zei gebensht Du Freie Land*. New York, NY: Hebrew Publishing Company.

Snell, M. (ed.). 2008. *Unknown Soldiers: The American Expeditionary Forces in Memory and Remembrance*. Kent, OH: Kent State University Press.

Snyder, C. 2010. *Out of Fire and Valor: The War Memorials of New York City from the Revolution to 9/11*. Piermont: Bunkerhill Publishing.

Soyer, D. 1997. *Jewish Immigrant Associations and American Identity in New York, 1880–1939*. Detroit, MI: Wayne State University Press.

Spaulding, E.W. 1968. *The Quiet Invaders: The Story of the Austrian Impact upon America*. Vienna: Österreichischer Bundesverlag.

Sperry, E. 1918. *The Tentacles of the German Octopus in America*. New York, NY: National Security League.

Sperry, E. and West, W. 1918. *German Plots and Intrigues in the United States During the Period of our Neutrality*. Washington, DC: The Committee on Public Information.

Squires, J.D. 1935. *British Propaganda at Home and in the United States from 1914 to 1917*. Cambridge, MA: Harvard University Press.

Stanwood Menken, S. 1917. *Knowledge by the People True Basis of National Security*. New York, NY: National Security League, Inc.

State of New York. 1919. *Annual Report of the Superintendent of Banks of the State of New York*. Albany, NY: J.B. Lyon.

St. Clair, L. 1919. *The Story of the Liberty Loans: Being a Record of the Volunteer Liberty Loan Army, its Personnel, Mobilization and Methods. How America at Home Backed her Armies and Allies in the World War*. Washington, DC: James William Bryan Press.

Steiner, E.A. 1906. *On the Trail of the Immigrant*. New York, NY: Fleming H. Revell Company.

Sterba, C.M. 2003. *Good Americans: Italian and Jewish Immigrants During the First World War*. Oxford: Oxford University Press.

Stern. 1917. *Are you 100% American? Prove it! Buy U.S. Government Bonds. Third Liberty Loan*. New York, NY: Sackett and Wilhelms Corp.

Stimson, H. 1915. *The Duty of Preparedness Today: Address of Henry L. Stimson before the National Security League at Carnegie Hall, June 14, 1915*. New York, NY: National Security League.

Stolarik, M. 1968. The Role of American Slovaks in the Creation of Czecho-Slovakia, 1914–1918. *Slovak Studies*, 7: 7–82.

Straight, W.D. 1917. *The Mobilization of the National Guard, 1916: Its Economic and Military Aspects*. New York, NY: Mayor's Committee on National Defense.

Straus, O. 1916. *Address of Oscar S. Straus at the National Security League Mass Meeting at the Century Theatre, February 29th, 1916*. New York, NY: National Security League.

Street, J. 1915. *Our Next War*. New York, NY: American Defense Society.

Strother, F. 1918. *Fighting Germany's Spies*. New York, NY: Doubleday.

Strunsky, S. 1916. Armaments and Caste. *Annals of the American Academy of Political and Social Science*, 66(1): 237–46.

Stürenburg, C. 1886. *Klein-Deutschland: Bilder aus dem New Yorker Alltagsleben*. New York, NY: E. Steiger Company.

Sunday, B. 1917. *Billy Sunday, the Man and his Message: With his Own Words which have Won Thousands for Christ*. Philadelphia: J.C. Winston.

Supreme Court of the United States. 1917. *Emma Goldman and Alexander Berkman, Plaintiffs-in-Error vs The United States*. New York, NY: s.n.

Swann, E. 1919. *War Charities Frauds in the City of New York*. New York, NY: M.B. Brown.

Szajkowski, Z. 1970. The Jews and New York City's Mayoralty Election of 1917. *Jewish Social Studies*, 32(4): 286–306.

Szajkowski, Z. 1972. *Jews, Wars, and Communism, Vol. 1*. New York, NY: KTAV Publishing.

Szarski, A. and De Walsh, F. 1914. *The Great Conspiracy*. New York, NY: German-American Literary Defense Committee.

Szold, H. 1904. Elements of the Jewish Population in the United States. In C.S. Bernheimer (ed.), *The Russian Jew in the United States*. Philadelphia, PA: J.C. Winston Co., pp. 9–17.

Tansill, C.C. 1957. *America and the Fight for Irish Freedom, 1866–1922: An Old Story Based upon New Data*. New York, NY: Devin-Adair.

Tate, T. 1998. *Modernism, History and the First World War*. Manchester: Manchester University Press.

Thomas, N. 1917. *War's Heretics: A Plea for the Conscientious Objector*. New York, NY: Civil Liberties Bureau of the American Union Against Militarism.

Thomson, A. 1994. *Anzac Memories: Living With the Legend*. Oxford: Oxford University Press.

Tippman, H.K. 1942. *Amerikanische balladen und andere gedichte*. New York, NY: Arrowhead Press.

Tolzmann, D.H. 1995. *German-Americans in the World Wars, Vol. 1: The Anti-German Hysteria of World War One*. Munich: K.G. Saur.

Tousley, B.E. 1917a. Bombing New York City on Behalf of the Liberty Loan. *Flying*, 6(7): 484–5, 500.

Tousley, B.E. 1917b. Aeronautics Again Plays an Important Part in Arousing Interest in Liberty Loan. *Flying*, 6(10): 856–9.

Trachtenberg, A. 1917. *The American Socialists and the War: A Documentary History of the Attitude of the Socialist Party toward War and Militarism since the Outbreak of the Great War*. New York, NY: The Rand School of Social Science.

Treasury Department. 1917. *The Second Liberty Loan of 1917: A Source Book*. Washington, DC: Government Printing Office.

Trout, S. 2010. *On the Battlefield of Memory: The First World War and American Remembrance, 1919 to 1941*. Tuscaloosa, AL: University of Alabama Press.

Tunney, T. 1919. *Throttled! The Detection of the German and Anarchist Bomb Plotters*. Boston, MA: Small, Maynard and Company.

Union League Club. 1918. *The Presentation of Colors to the 367th Regiment of Infantry, Colonel James A. Moss Commanding*. New York, NY: S.L. Parsons and Company.

United States Congress, Committee on Foreign Affairs. 1917. *Emergency Peace Federation: Hearings before the Committee on Foreign Affairs, House of Representatives, Sixty-fourth Congress, Second Session: Statements of Cedric Long and Others. February 22, 1917*. Washington, DC: Government Printing Office.

United States Congress, Committee on Military Affairs. 1917. *Increase of Military Establishment: Hearings Before the Committee on Military Affairs, House of Representatives, Sixty-fifth Congress, First Session, on the Bill Authorizing the President to Increase Temporarily the Military Establishment of the United States. April 17.* Washington, DC: Government Printing Office.

United States Congress, Committee on the Judiciary. 1917. *Espionage and Interference with Neutrality: Hearings before the Committee on the Judiciary, House of Representatives, Sixty-fifth Congress, First Session on H.R. 291, April 9 and 12, 1917.* Washington, DC: Government Printing Office.

United States Congress, Special Committee to Investigate the National Security League. 1918. *Hearings Before a Special Committee of the House of Representatives, Sixty-fifth Congress, Third Session on H. Res. 469 and H. Res. 476, to Investigate and Make Report as to the Officers, Membership, Financial Support, Expenditures, General Character, Activities and Purposes of the National Security League, a Corporation of New York, and of Any Associated Organizations, Parts 1–13.* Washington, DC: Government Printing Office.

United States Department of Labor, Bureau of Labor Statistics. 1915. *Unemployment in New York City, New York.* Bulletin of the United States Bureau of Labor Statistics, 172(10).

United States Mortgage and Trust Company. 1916. *Preparedness Parade New York City, May 13, 1916: Views Along the Line and Other Preparedness Pictures.* New York, NY: Mortgage and Trust, Co.

United States Postal Service. 1918. *Annual Report of the Postmaster General.* Washington, DC: Government Printing Office.

United States Postal Service. 1919. *Annual Report of the Postmaster General.* Washington, DC: Government Printing Office.

United States Senate, Committee on Military Affairs. 1919. *Regulating Collection of Money: Hearings Before the Committee on Military Affairs, United States Senate, Sixty-fifth Congress, 3rd Session on S.4972.* Washington, DC: Government Printing Office.

United States Senate, Committee on the Judiciary. 1919. *Brewing and Liquor Interests and German Propaganda: Hearings Before a Subcommittee of the Committee on the Judiciary, United States Senate, Sixty-fifth Congress, Second and Third sessions, Pursuant to S. Res. 307, Vol.1.* Washington, DC: Government Printing Office.

Vance, J.F. 1997. *Death So Noble: Memory, Meaning, and the First World War.* Vancouver, BC: University of British Columbia Press.

Van Schaack, E. 2005. The Coming of the Hun! American Fears of a German Invasion, 1918. *The Journal of American Culture*, 28(3): 284–92.

Vasilijevic, Z. 1976. *The American South Slav Attitude to the Creation of Yugoslavia, 1914–1918.* Madison, WI: University of Wisconsin.

Veiller, L. 1900. *Tenement House Reform in New York, 1834–1900.* New York, NY: Evening Post Job Printing House.

Vezzosi, E. 1985. Class, Ethnicity, and Acculturation in *Il Proletario*: The World War One Years. In C. Harzig and D. Hoerder (eds), *The Press of Labor Migrants in Europe and North America, 1880s to 1930s*. Bremen: Labor Migration Project, Labor Newspaper Preservation Project, Universität Bremen, pp. 443–55.

Viereck, G.S. 1914. For Widows and Orphans. *The Fatherland*, 1(20): 12.

Viereck, G.S. 1915. From G.S. Viereck, Editor, The Fatherland. In H. Maxim (ed.), *Leading Opinions Both For and Against National Defense*. New York, NY: Hearst International, pp. 20–21.

Viereck, G.S. 1916a. The Significance of the War Bazaars. *The Fatherland*, 4(7): 105.

Viereck, G.S. 1916b. The Jewish Bazaar. *The Fatherland*, 4(10): 158.

Viereck, G.S. 1916c. War's Great Irish Hero. *The Fatherland*, 4(13): 122.

Viereck, G.S. 1916d. Editorial. *The Fatherland*, 4(16): 250–52.

Viereck, G.S. 1916e. The Allied Bazaar. *The Fatherland*, 4(22): 347.

Viereck, G.S. 1916f. Casement and Liebknecht. *The Fatherland*, 4(23): 232.

Viereck, G.S. 1916g. Editorial. *The Fatherland*, 5(1): 10.

Viereck, G.S. 1916h. Editorial. *The Fatherland*, 5(13): 202.

Viereck, G.S. 1917. America First. *The Fatherland*, 6(2): 1.

Viereck, G.S. 1931. *Spreading Germs of Hate*. London: Duckworth.

Viereck, G.S. and Schrader, F.F. 1914. Editorial. *The Fatherland*, 1(10): 2.

Viereck, G.S., Schrader, F.F. and Sherwin, L. 1914. Preamble. *The Fatherland*, 1(1): 3.

von Bernstorff, J.H. 1920. *My Three Years in America*. New York, NY: Charles Scribner's Sons.

von Mach, E. 1914. *What Germany Wants*. Boston, MA: Little Brown.

von Rintelen, F. 1933. *The Dark Invader: Wartime Reminiscences of a German Naval Intelligence Officer*. New York, NY: Macmillan Co.

von Wiegand, K. 1915. *Current Misconceptions about the War*. New York, NY: The Fatherland.

Walker, J.B. 1917. *The Great Emergency*. New York, NY: National Security League.

Walkowitz, J. 1992. *City of Dreadful Delight: Narratives of Sexual Danger in Late Victorian London*. Chicago, IL: University of Chicago Press.

Wallace, D. 1916. *The Revelations of an American Citizen in the British Army*. New York, NY: American Truth Society.

Walter, F. and Hudemann, R. (eds). 1997. *Villes et guerres mondiales au XXe siècle*. Paris and Montréal: L'Harmattan.

Warburg, F. 1916. *Reports Received by the Joint Distribution Committee of Funds for Jewish War Sufferers*. New York, NY: C.S. Nathan.

Warburg, F. 1918. *A Message from Felix M. Warburg, Chairman: Jewish War Relief 1918 Campaign, New York City*. New York, NY: Jewish War Relief.

Ward, D. 1989. *Poverty, Ethnicity and the American City, 1840–1925: Changing Conceptions of the Slum and Ghetto*. Cambridge: Cambridge University Press.

Ward, R.D. 1960. The Origin and Activities of the National Security League, 1914–1919. *The Mississippi Valley Historical Review*, 47(1): 51–65.

Warne, F.J. 1916. *The Tide of Immigration*. New York, NY: D. Appleton and Company.

Watterson, H. 1915. *History of the Manhattan Club: A Narrative of the Activities of Half a Century*. New York, NY: De Vinne Press.

Weinstein, J. 1959. Anti-War Sentiment and the Socialist Party, 1917–1918. *Political Science Quarterly*, 74(2): 215–39.

Wertsch, J. 2002. *Voices of Collective Remembering*. Cambridge: Cambridge University Press.

Wetzsteon, R. 2002. *Republic of Dreams: Greenwich Village, the American Bohemia, 1910–1960*. New York, NY: Simon and Schuster.

Wheeler, H.D. 1915. Plattsburg: How it Works. *Harper's Weekly*, 61: 248–50.

Whiteclay Chambers, J. 1987. *To Raise an Army: The Draft Comes to Modern America*. New York, NY: Free Press.

Whiteclay Chambers, J. 1992. *The Tyranny of Change: America in the Progressive Era, 1890–1920*. New York, NY: St. Martin's.

Whitridge, F.W. 1914. *One American's Opinion of the European War: An Answer to Germany's Appeals*. New York, NY: E.P. Dutton.

Wiedemann-Citera, B. 1993. *Die Auswirkungen des Ersten Weltkrieges auf die Deutsch-Amerikaner im Spiegel der New Yorker Volkszeitung und der New York Times 1914–1926*. Frankfurt am Main: Peter Lang.

Williams, C. 2010. *Torchbearers of Democracy: African American Soldiers in the World War I Era*. Chapel Hill, NC: University of North Carolina Press.

Williams, J. 1918. *The Voluntary Aid of America*. New York, NY: Williams.

Wilson, R. 2011. *Landscapes of the Western Front: Materiality during the Great War*. London: Routledge.

Wilson, W. 1915. *Address of President Wilson at the Fiftieth Anniversary Dinner of the Manhattan Club (Biltmore Hotel), New York City, November 4, 1915*. Washington, DC: Government Printing Office.

Wilson, W. 1916. *Address of President Wilson before the Press Club in New York City, June 30, 1916*. Washington, DC: Government Printing Office.

Wilson, W. 1917. *Why We are At War*. New York, NY: Harper Brothers.

Wilson, W. 1918. *Opening Campaign for Fourth Liberty Loan: Address of President Wilson Delivered in New York City, Sept. 27, 1918*. Washington, DC: Government Printing Office.

Wilson, W. and J.P. Mitchel. 1917. *President Woodrow Wilson's Address to Congress April 2, 1917. Proclamation of the President April 6, 1917. Proclamation of the Mayor of the City of New York, April 6, 1917. Address of the President to His Fellow Countrymen, April 16, 1917*. New York, NY: American Exchange National Bank.

Wingate, J. 2005. Over the Top: The Doughboy in World War I Memorials and Visual Culture. *American Art*, 19(2): 29–32.

Winter, J.M. 1992. *Sites of Memory, Sites of Mourning: The Great War in European Cultural History*. Cambridge: Cambridge University Press.

Winter, J.M. 1995. Communities of Mourning. In F. Coetzee and M. Shevin-Coetzee (eds), *Authority, Identity and the Social History of the Great War*. Providence, RI: Berghahn Books, pp. 325–56.

Winter, J.M., Parker, G. and Harbeck, M. 2000. Introduction. In J.M Winter, G. Parker and M. Harbeck (eds), *The Great War and the Twentieth Century*. New Haven, CT: Yale University Press, pp. 1–12.

Woman's Liberty Loan Committee. 1917. *Report of the Woman's Liberty Loan Committee of the Second Federal Reserve District, Second Liberty Loan, October, 1917*. New York, NY: Woman's Liberty Loan Committee.

Wood, H.A.W. 1917. *American, Look Into Your Heart!* New York, NY: National Security League.

Woods, A.H. 1915. Police Administration. *Proceedings of the Academy of Political Science in the City of New York*, 5(3): 54–61.

Woods, A.H. 1919. *Policeman and Public*. New Haven, CT: Yale University Press.

Woodward, D.R. 1985. *America and World War I: A Selected Annotated Bibliography of English-language Sources*. New York, NY: Garland.

Xu, G. 2011. *Strangers on the Western Front: Chinese Workers in the Great War*. Cambridge: Cambridge University Press.

Yeates, P. 2012. *A City in Wartime: Dublin 1914–1918*. Dublin: Gill and Macmillan.

Young, C.C. 1915. *Abused Russia*. New York, NY: Devin-Adair.

Zangwill, I. 1909. *The Melting Pot*. New York, NY: The Jewish American Book Company.

Zieger, R. 2001. *America's Great War: World War I and the American Experience*. Oxford: Rowman and Littlefield.

Index

For Product Safety Concerns and Information please contact our EU
representative GPSR@taylorandfrancis.com Taylor & Francis Verlag GmbH,
Kaufingerstraße 24, 80331 München, Germany

Printed and bound by CPI Group (UK) Ltd, Croydon, CR0 4YY
01/05/2025
01858420-0002